REPORTING
PUBLIC AFFAIRS

REPORTING
PUBLIC AFFAIRS
Problems & Solutions

Second Edition

RONALD P. LOVELL

Oregon State University

WAVELAND
PRESS, INC.
Prospect Heights, Illinois

On the Cover

President Franklin D. Roosevelt meets the press at Warm Springs, Georgia on April 4, 1939. Courtesy of the Franklin D. Roosevelt Library.

Acknowledgements

Chapter 1 Selection on pp. 11-13 is reprinted with permission of the *Medical World news.*

Chapter 2 Lou Cannon interview material is used with his permission. Selection on pp. 42-45 is reprinted with permission of *The Washington Post.* © 1988, *The Washington Post.*

Chapter 3 Brad Cain interview material is used with his permission. Selections on pp. 74-76, 76-78 are reprinted with permission of the Associated Press.

Chapter 4 Bill Boyarsky interview material is used with his permission. Selection on pp. 100-105 is reprinted with permission of the *Los Angeles Times.* © 1990, the *Los Angeles Times.*

Chapter 5 Donna Schmidt and Steve Clark interview material is used with their permission. Selections on pp. 124-27, 127-30 are reprinted with permission of *The Tigard Times.*

Chapter 6 Les Zaitz interview material is used with his permission. Selection on pp. 156-62 is reprinted with permission of *The Oregonian.* © 1984 Oregonian Publishing Co.

Chapter 7 Neal Hirschfeld interview material is used with his permission. Selections on pp. 201-3, 204-10 are reprinted with permission of the *New York Daily News.*

Chapter 8 Don Van Natta, Jr. interview material used with his permission. Selections on pp. 257-60, 261-64 are reprinted with permission of the *The Miami Herald.*

Chapter 9 John Noble Wilford interview material is used with his permission. Selections on pp. 297-302, 302-7 are reprinted with permission of *The New York Times.* © 1979/83 by The New York Times Company.

Chapter 10 Casey Bukro interview material is used with his permission. Selections on pp. 338-42, 342-46, 346-48 are reprinted with permission of the *Chicago Tribune.*

Chapter 11 William Ingram interview material is used with his permission. Selections on pp. 376-79, 379-81 are reprinted with permission of *Medical Tribune.*

Chapter 12 Paul B. Carroll interview material is used with his permission. Selections on pp. 427-31, 431-34 are reprinted with permission of *The Wall Street Journal.* © 1991 Dow Jones & Company, Inc. All Rights Reserved Worldwide.

Appendix B Code of Ethics reprinted with permission of the Society of Professional Journalists.

Appendix C "The Paper Trail" reprinted with permission of Les Zaitz and the Willamette Valley Chapter of the Society of Professional Journalists.

For information about this book, write or call:

Waveland Press, Inc.
P.O. Box 400
Prospect Heights, Illinois 60070
(708) 634-0081

Contents

Preface to the Second Edition

Never before in history has public affairs so dominated the lives of the citizens of the United States. Whether a local tax increase or zoning change, the Senate confirmation hearings of a Supreme Court nominee, or information about a new treatment for AIDS, people need to be kept informed.

That task is the job of the public affairs reporter, an area of reporting that has grown steadily in journalism over the past twenty years. The purpose of this book is to help prospective public affairs reporters understand the distinct nature of these specialty beats and to deal with the problems they will encounter.

Public affairs reporting contains elements that are no different from other kinds of reporting. A reporter gets an assignment, interviews sources and observes events, then returns to the office and writes a story with a lead, a body, and an ending. The copy is edited and then printed in a newspaper or magazine and read by thousands or, in some cases, millions of readers.

But public affairs reporting has other elements that are vastly different from general reporting. The subject matter is complicated and includes special problems of coverage not found on the usual beats. For example, people working in various public affairs areas — mayors, governors, politicians, educators, lawyers, judges, business leaders, doctors, and scientists — often are intentionally ambiguous and difficult to understand. They use big words and the jargon of their trades frequently, sometimes because they assume others understand such terminology, but often because it gives them a dominance over those who are not as knowledgeable. Sometimes the problems are more of tradition or process than outright obfuscation.

Whatever the cause, readers can be left groping for the meaning of it all. Leading them out of the confusion and chaos inherent in many specialized fields is the job of the public affairs reporter, who can surmount most of these problems with time, experience, and constant carefulness.

I have written this book to anticipate common problems in the various public affairs subject areas and suggest ways to solve them. The book will accomplish its purpose in several ways: 1) by introducing real public affairs reporters from large and small newspapers (and a wire service) who discuss the excitements and frustrations of doing their jobs, 2) by outlining the background of a particular field, 3) by presenting current problems of coverage and typical kinds of stories, and 4) by analyzing the writing of reporters.

Each chapter ends with a review of likely problems found on a particular beat and suggestions on how to solve them. To help prepare future public affairs reporters, the book also contains a number of boxes that explain how an important element of a beat works: city government procedures, the Federal Reserve system, the research cycle of a new drug, and the like. Key Terms and Additional Reading lists appear at the end of each chapter or part, depending on the subject matter.

A secondary aim of the book is to give readers the "feel" for public affairs reporting. What was it like to arrive in Prince William Sound, Alaska several days after the *Exxon Valdez* went aground; or to cover a cult that was threatening a whole region of a state, or to be given a memo that revealed the inner workings of a major corporation? This book will describe such events to readers in a way that will make them feel they were there alongside the reporter.

Part I gives a background to public affairs reporting. Part II (Politics and Government) contains chapters on politics and elections, state government, local government, education, and investigative reporting. Part III (Law) covers police and courts in separate chapters. Part IV (Science and Medicine) has chapters on science, environment, and medicine and health. Part V (Business) includes a chapter on business and the economy. Appendices on legal problems, ethical problems, and methods of searching public records end the book.

A number of topics do not rate their own chapter in the book primarily because fewer publications employ people to write about them full-time. Energy is sometimes part of the business beat or is done part-time by a science or environment reporter. I have dropped two subject areas I covered in the first edition of this book — consumer reporting and urban affairs reporting — because neither is found as a separate beat as frequently as it was ten years ago.

Although I have not worked as a reporter in every area included in the book, I have been a business reporter (for *Business Week*), a medical writer (for *Medical World News*), a science correspondent (for *McGraw-Hill World News*), and a small-town government reporter (as editor of my own weekly newspaper). My comments, then, are not based on academic experience alone. I have faced some of the same problems that the reporters included in these pages have encountered.

I have two hopes for the readers of this book — the public affairs reporters of tomorrow: that they discover enough about such reporting to make them want to enter its ranks and that they gain sufficient information to do well once they are on the job. If they do so, I can promise them an interesting, challenging, and stimulating career — one that *can* make a difference.

I could not have completed this Second Edition of *Reporting Public Affairs: Problems and Solutions* without the help of a great many people. First, I want to thank the reporters and editors who told me what they do and why: Bill Boyarsky, Casey Bukro, Brad Cain, Lou Cannon, Paul Carroll, Steve Clark, Neal Hirschfeld, Bill Ingram, Donna Schmidt, Don Van Natta, Jr., John Noble Wilford, and Les Zaitz. I appreciate the help of Hugh Van Swearinger of the *Associated Press* and Pete Weitzel of the *Miami Herald* for their help in arranging two interviews.

The Second Edition of this book would not have been possible without the help and support of Neil Rowe, publisher of Waveland Press, and Laurie Prossnitz, my editor.

I am grateful for useful suggestions from several instructors: Maurice Odine, Frank McCahill, Shelton Guneratne, June Nicholson, William Miller, George Flynn, and William Cote. I am also beholden to the small band of loyal adopters whose interest in the book and desire to see it revised led to the new edition.

I leave a final graf for two people whose help has been crucial: my typist Treena Martin for her knowledge of the arcane (my handwriting) and the modern (WordPerfect 5.1) and my mother, Verna Lovell, to whom I dedicate this book, for her many years of support of me and my writing.

— Ron Lovell

A Note About the Photographs in this Book

Massive press coverage of the presidency and the federal government in a manner resembling modern times began in 1933 when Franklin D. Roosevelt launched his program to save the country, the New Deal. The cover photograph shows Roosevelt doing something he enjoyed immensely: sparring with the press to gain favorable coverage of himself and his programs.

In 1935, Roosevelt established the Resettlement Administration as part of the New Deal to provide low interest loans to poor farmers, carry out land renewal projects like reforestation, relocate some families from big cities to farms or small towns, and sponsor camps for migrant farm workers. In 1937, the Department of Agriculture absorbed the Resettlement Administration and changed its name to the Farm Security Administration (FSA).

From 1935 to 1943, a group of photographers hired by the Historical Section of the FSA took 270,000 photos to document both the government's work and conditions in the United States at that time. The efforts of such dedicated men and women as Walker Evans, Dorothea Lange, Carl Mydans, Arthur Rothstein, Ben Shahn, and others recorded all aspects of American life.

To me, the diversity of subject matter and the excellence of the images make them ideal photos to introduce the varied kinds of reporting covered in this book. Even though the photos were taken fifty to sixty years ago, they record a time when serious public affairs reporting began.

"We had a sense that we were in on the beginning of something," wrote Roy Emerson Stryker, director of the FSA photography project, in a later collection of some of the photos. "In 1936 photography, which theretofore had been mostly a matter of landscapes and snapshots and family portraits, was fast being discovered as a serious tool of communications, a new way for a thoughtful, creative person to make a statement. . . ."

part

I Background

Our jobs are tough enough, even if we are not diverted by pressures or subverted by our own status and success. What journalism can produce for a society always falls short of the society's needs, and even further short of historical or philosophical truth.

The way we cover the news is to dig for facts, in hopes they will yield an approximation of truth. They rarely do. . . .

—David S. Broder
Behind the Front Page

Lancaster, Pennsylvania, 1942 by Marjory Collins. [*Courtesy U.S. Farm Security Administration Collection, Prints and Photographs Division, Library of Congress*]

1

Background to Public Affairs Reporting

The press is no substitute for institutions. It is like the beam of a searchlight that moves restlessly about, bringing one episode and then another out of darkness into vision. Men cannot do the work of the world by this light alone. They cannot govern society by episodes, incidents, and eruptions. It is only when they work by a steady light of their own, that the press, when it is turned upon them, reveals a situation intelligible enough for a popular decision.

—Walter Lippmann
Public Opinion

Some definitions
Meager beginnings
Basic requirements
Writing public affairs stories
Key terms
Additional Reading

Some Definitions

On the surface at least, public affairs reporting sounds like the coverage of governmental organizations. It is that, of course, as the chapters on state and local governments, education, police, courts, federal government politics and elections, and investigating budgets and records will prove. But public affairs reporting encompasses other areas as well. People today are faced with concerns and dilemmas that go beyond the governmental entities already noted. Events in science, the environment, medicine and health, and business — involving both the public and private sector — affect the average person now more than at any time in history. For that reason, these areas have been included under the broad category of public affairs. To avoid repetition in wording, this text sometimes substitutes "specialized," "specialty," or "beat" for "public affairs reporting."

Meager Beginnings

Newspapers and magazines began to cover some of the subjects now grouped under the category of "public affairs" when readers became more sophisticated and demanded such coverage. In the early days of American journalism editors were lucky to get their modest product out at all. The first newspapers were little more than printed versions of what they had replaced: the discussion of news around the stove in the general store where people stopped to pass the time of day. Early newspapers even left a blank page for readers to write down their own items before passing along copies to friends.These publications gradually thrived, as did the magazines that joined them a number of years later, as a means for readers to keep up with events of the day.

A shrewd editor, James Gordon Bennett of the *New York Herald*, was the first to see the possibilities in specialized coverage. If people could read stories about specialized subjects of interest to them, he reasoned, they would buy more papers.

Bennett saw the sense of his idea after he started to cover the Ellen Jewett murder case in 1836. Circulation figures for the newspaper increased dramatically. Thereafter he began to cover police news on a more systematic basis. He later applied the same technique — without the sensationalism — to news of Wall Street, the federal government, and international affairs.

By the middle of the nineteenth century, newspapers in a number of cities were including coverage of specialized subjects on a regular basis. Sometimes the coverage was just a ploy to increase circulation, as in the yellow journalism war fought by William Randolph Hearst and his *New York Journal* and Joseph Pulitzer and his *New York World* in the 1890s and early 1900s.

At other times public affairs reporting performed a real service to readers as citizens. The long series of exposés written by a group of writers known as the "muckrakers" for *McClure's* and other magazines early in the twentieth century revealed an evil underside to business, government, and other parts of national life and sparked corrective legislation.

The trend toward public affairs reporting has grown in the succeeding years because of the increasing complexity of American life and the need to explain that life to people experiencing it. Although the earlier newspapers and magazines told readers *what* had happened in the flamboyant manner of a Bennett or a Hearst, modern papers—joined by radio and television—explain the *why* and *how*.

This need to inform and educate readers and viewers constitutes the foundation of good public affairs reporting. Public affairs reporters and editors provide coverage of subjects that affect large numbers of people. The information gained by the readers and viewers is vital to them as citizens of their communities and of the world.

Basic Requirements

Although public affairs reporting encompasses distinctly different subjects, these subjects have striking similarities as well. From these similarities we can distill a list of basic requirements for anyone making a career in the field:

1. **Perfecting interviewing and note-taking skills.** No matter what the subject, a public affairs reporter must ask good questions and take careful notes of the answers. This requirement also holds true for general reporting, except for one important consideration: The subjects included in public affairs reporting are often technical and involve words that are hard to spell and techniques that are difficult to grasp. A reporter must ask questions that bring forth answers that make sense and can be translated into words the general reader can understand. If a reporter does not understand the initial answer, he or she must keep asking follow-up questions until the subject becomes clear.

Note taking isn't much different from the same process in general reporting, except for the unfamiliar expressions or technical terms that can confound a reporter. It is a good idea to stop the interviewee immediately and ask for the correct spelling or to make a note or a large X in the margin of the notepad page, indicating that the word needs to be spelled correctly before the reporter leaves the room at the end of the interview.

It is also a good idea to use X's to mark subjects that come up in the interview that the reporter either does not understand or encounters for the first time. The interview will proceed more smoothly if it is not interrupted the first time such a subject comes up. Instead, it is a good idea to pause at the end of an interview to look over the X's, and ask follow-up questions.

When in doubt on a technical subject of any kind—especially in science and medicine—it is possible to get the basic facts for a story by asking three rudimentary questions: 1) describe your discovery (or project or findings); 2) what is the background to getting involved with it?; 3) what is its significance?

2. **Gathering general knowledge.** As soon as a reporter is assigned to a specialized beat, he or she should read several basic books on that subject to become familiar in a general way with how the beat works. If a governmental area is involved—for example, a state legislature or a court system—a reporter should not go on a first assignment without knowing how that particular unit operates. Libraries contain such books, although it is better for reporters to buy their own copies for future reference. No medical reporter can work successfully without a good medical dictionary, for example. Nor should a business reporter be without a basic economics text. City directories and telephone books from all cities in a reporter's area of coverage are valuable tools, as are internal directories of the organizations he or she will encounter on the beat. Having such numbers—which are often impossible to obtain officially—will enable a reporter to bypass impediments and reach potential sources quickly.

Other indispensable tools are the materials government organizations publish explaining basic operations; for example, a court often gives such a booklet to people selected for jury duty. Companies and nonprofit organizations often prepare explanatory materials that can be very useful. For example, a public utility might publish a booklet on how a nuclear reactor works. Another way to gain background knowledge is to interview a few experts on a subject, not in order to do a story, but to find out as much as possible to aid in future coverage. These experts should be used whenever questions of a general nature arise. They will usually be flattered at the attention and will enjoy playing "teacher" about a subject on which they are knowledgeable.

3. **Building reference files.** After a reporter has been grounded in the basics of the public affairs beat, he or she should set up permanent files on the subject to be covered. The process is a simple one. The reporter organizes and files articles from magazines, technical journals, local and national newspapers, public relations news releases, and such items as company annual reports. These

files can be categorized based on organizations (Superior Court), people (Brown, Judge Martha), and social concerns/problems (juvenile offenders). Everything that goes into the file should be dated and, if the item is so small that it will get crumpled, mounted on an 8½ x 11 sheet of paper. Items should be placed in the folder in chronological order with the most recent entry in the front. Material should be filed daily, if possible, because it will often accumulate at such a rapid rate that the process of filing becomes too burdensome and time consuming to do easily. Storage of such files can become a problem in a crowded newsroom. A reporter can usually get the space for one filing cabinet. When it is full, it is a good idea to regularly clean out the folders or set up files at home to hold the overflow. A "pack rat" mentality can be helpful to a public affairs reporter, as long as it doesn't get out of control. In time, specialty reporters should develop a kind of built-in alert system so that every time they read materials on certain subjects they save them for future use.

4. **Keeping up with the technical aspects.** Most all public affairs subject areas have their own technical journals and trade magazines. Because these publications cover one field in depth, they usually report information before the general press knows about it. By regularly reading such periodicals and filing appropriate articles in the reference files noted earlier, a reporter can keep up with events and get leads on stories. It would be impossible for anyone covering space or aviation to do without *Aviation Week*, for example, or for a medical writer to get by without the *New England Journal of Medicine.*

5. **Going to technical meetings.** The annual meetings that people in almost all specialized fields in this country attend also provide an excellent means to keep abreast in that field. Usually a specialized reporter would cover such a meeting anyway because of the technical papers presented there and because so many key sources will attend. Even without a specific assignment, however, it is important for reporters to go, at least during the first few years on the beat. The general knowledge gained and sources established for future use offset the expense of such attendance.

6. **Learning the special problems and rules of a beat.** Each subject area in public affairs reporting has its own set of problems and rules. What applies to one field will not work with another. In the rough and tumble arena of police reporting, for example, a reporter can shout questions to detectives at a murder scene. If a court reporter did the same thing to a judge when court was in session, however, that reporter would likely be held in contempt and

wind up in a jail cell. Some states allow reporters to peruse police records; others do not. Some states have open meeting laws that enable the press to cover every gathering of a governmental body. In other states some agencies meet in secret regularly. A reporter must know such rules so that he or she will be able to cover the beat completely.

7. **Knowing how to "mine" a beat with good sources.** It is equally important to develop sources in the field to be covered. Sometimes a reporter can establish a relationship with someone in an official capacity who becomes a good source. Often, however, the best sources on a beat are unofficial—the clerks, secretaries, and functional workers who often know what is going on throughout the organization. Reporters should contact them regularly—over coffee or lunch, when possible—for information. Often such sources can tip off reporters about an upcoming event. Their names should never get into print; if the information they provide is sensitive and if its revelation is tied to them, they might lose their jobs. If the source is overly dissatisfied and negative about the agency involved, however, a reporter needs to determine the source's motives so that the reporter and the publication are not misused. (How to turn the material gathered in reporting into a well-written story is explained in Box 1.1)

These requirements apply to each of the public affairs subjects covered in this book, despite the great differences in substance among the various subjects. The reporter who has mastered these skills can cover any of the public affairs subjects almost interchangeably allowing, of course, time to cultivate sources, learn the terminology, and become familiar with the audience.

After investing time and money to train a reporter for a specific beat, most news organizations are reluctant to make changes unnecessarily. It is rare to transfer a science writer to the police beat or to turn a business writer into a court reporter. It is more common to change assignments from within similar areas. For example, a city hall reporter might logically be asked to cover the state capital or a police reporter switched to the court beat.

People do get bored with their beats, however, so sometimes drastic switches do occur. Most of the time, however, reporters who enjoy writing about specific subjects and are good at it can remain where they are.

In theory, however, because of the similarity of the basic requirements, one specialized reporter could do the job of one of the others. Indeed, on smaller newspapers and magazines, public affairs reporters may have to jump from one subject to another because

Box 1.1

A Few Rules of Writing

Most readers of this book will already have read basic journalism texts and taken basic journalism courses. They may also have developed their own style of writing. Nevertheless, with the view that repetition enhances learning because it reinforces the known, a few rules of writing are presented here. In the same spirit a list of common journalism terms is included at the end of this chapter.

1. Use simple, straightforward sentences, each with a subject and a verb and uncluttered with unnecessary adjectives, adverbs, or subordinate clauses.

2. When possible, keep one idea, or at the most two ideas, to a sentence.

3. Use present tense, unless it violates the rules of a news organization, because it makes sentences flow more smoothly.

4. Group like subjects into the same paragraph, unless that arrangement makes the paragraph too long. In that case the paragraph can be divided to diminish the possibility of a dull-looking story on the printed page.

5. Use the active voice whenever possible; avoid the passive because of the sluggish quality it gives a sentence.
   Active: The governor told the legislature yesterday . . .
   Passive: The legislature was told by the governor yesterday . . .

6. Let the story tell itself; that is, let sources speak to readers through their quotes and your paraphrases of quotes. Do not use quotes to impart routine information.

7. Smooth the way with several simple devices:
   a. A colon to introduce a topic in a dramatic way—The governor has one topic on his mind: new taxes.
   b. A "bullet" (# or •) to organize a longer story with many topics and thus avoid frequent transition sentences.
      The governor also discussed:
   • Farm policy—"Let me say this about that, blah, blah."
   • Energy shortages—"I am told there has been an energy crisis, blah, blah."
   c. A dash is a perfectly acceptable substitute for either the colon or the bullet unless its use conflicts with the style of the publication.
   d. A space—four on a computer or a typewriter, double in final printed form—can serve to avoid subheads or difficult transitions, in the same way various scene changes move the events in acts of a play.

8. Use precise and uncomplicated words to tell the story. If a technical subject is being explained, do it in a brief clause or parenthetical phrase in a way that does not send readers running to their dictionaries.

9. Consult a good dictionary for spelling and meaning, a thesaurus for synonyms and antonyms, and a stylebook for form. Relying on the spell-check feature of a computer can result in serious errors.

10. Leave the completed story for a day or an hour, deadline permitting, and then take a fresh look at writing, spelling, and organization.

11. Use a word from the lead as the first word of the second paragraph to achieve a good transition. Good transitions must be made from sentence to sentence as well as from paragraph to paragraph to achieve the unity necessary for a readable article.

12. Select a theme and keep it running through the story; if possible, tie the end to the beginning in a circular fashion.

13. Know when to let a story go. Some writers worry and revise too long; there is a point when things start getting worse, not better.

14. Keep out of the story, except in rare instances when there is no other way to tell it.

of budgetary limits on staff size. There is a significant difference between working for a large metropolitan newspaper or national magazine and a small daily or weekly publication. A metropolitan newspaper or national magazine has specific beats, and assigned reporters seldom stray from their beats. On a smaller newspaper, however, the public affairs reporter may end up covering everything from politics to education to the court system. This possibility means that reporters must have a general knowledge of all public affairs fields as well as of the communities in which they are working.

The ability to make the transition from one kind of coverage to another will make the reporter more valuable as an employee and a journalist. Only large newspapers and magazines can afford separate reporters for each of the public affairs subject areas. A position on one of them is a good goal but usually out of the reach of a beginner.

Whether they work for a large news organization or a small one, wear one hat or four, public affairs reporters should be ready at all times to turn the beam of their searchlight to bring the public affairs of the day "out of darkness into vision."

Writing Public Affairs Stories

This article, which I wrote for *Medical World News*, is an illustration of my style of writing as outlined in the rules of writing in Box 1.1. Although I wrote it for a medical magazine, the story does not deal with a technical subject. The approach would work in any kind of writing. I use simple, straightforward language (Rule 1) and keep one idea to a sentence (Rule 2). I also use the present tense to give it movement (Rule 3).

Quote leads are sometimes frowned upon by journalism teachers and editors. They can be overdone, of course, but they can also entice a reader into a story. It all depends on how good the quote is. This one is just right as a point upon which I construct my theme. My source characterizes her patients as she looks around the room in her poetry therapy class.

I use my source's name, "Tobie Harris," to make the transition. By using it first, I am saying that she is the one speaking in paragraph 1. I cheat a bit in making the transition to the second paragraph. I wasn't allowed to observe the class or to see my source "glancing around." But she told me how she did it, so I put it in to make readers feel they were there. I go on to tell the what and where of the story and reveal for the first time that the students are psychiatric patients. I deliberately save this latter fact until the last sentence of the paragraph.

IN THE "PSYCH" WING, THE SOUND OF POETRY

1 "Linda is depressed today, so I won't ask her to speak in class. John, who is always outspoken, is continuing his habit of interrupting everybody else. The older lady seems more withdrawn than usual, and I've got to draw her out."

2 Tobie Harris is glancing around the room in the class she has taught weekly for the past year at Passavant Memorial Hospital in Chicago, making mental notes about her students. They are all patients in the hospital's psychiatric wing; she is a published poet who gives them an hour a week of poetry therapy.

I expand on this idea in Paragraph 3, then let the chairman of the psychiatry department talk about it in Paragraph 4.

3 Although the technique is not new, Passavant's formal commitment to it is unusual. Mrs. Harris, who is called associate for poetry therapy, is a member of the hospital staff and runs two separate hour courses a week — one for open ward patients, another for those in the locked ward.

4 "Our underlying philosophy is based on the fact that people who are distressed are sometimes inarticulate," says Dr. Harold Visotsky, chairman of the department of psychiatry at Northwestern which administers the program. "Medical professionals are also inarticulate, using shorthand descriptive terms, an 'in' code. We feel there are poets and authors who have particular insights in describing people's pain and distress."

I go back to the class in Paragraphs 5 and 6 and tell how she conducts sessions. In so doing, I am returning readers to the room with the patients and making them feel a part of things ("She then begins to read the poem aloud, line by line.") I was lucky here in that the source was so articulate, telling me how she did what she did. This is a good example of letting a story tell itself (Rule 6).

5 Mrs. Harris begins each class by passing out copies of the poem to be discussed that day. She waits while the class reads it, and she then talks about poetry in general and gives them information on the life of the poet concerned.

6 She then begins to read the poem aloud, line by line. "I wring out the sound and meaning, then relate it to their lives," she says. "I find out how they feel about it." Later, they will write up what they think of the poem to enable them to articulate their own feelings. (She visits them in the ward before or after class to offer comments and suggestions about any of their own poetry they submit to her.)

I give patient reactions in Paragraph 7 and go on in Paragraph 8 to tell which poets are used.

7 At first, only a few respond. Because Passavant's psychiatric ward is for short-term patients only, she gets few seriously ill patients. "They are mainly depressed — no psychotics or schizophrenics," she says.

8 In her selections, she tries to deal with what she calls "large topics — love, marriage, children, parents." She relies on selections from Kahlil Gibran's *The Prophet*, Emily Dickinson, Samuel Taylor Coleridge, and William Wordsworth.

Paragraphs 9, 10 and 11 add more detail on the structure of the class and bring the department head back in again.

9 During sessions, she allows participants to express themselves but must sometimes eventually steer the discussions back to poetry. "I try not to get into group therapy," she says. "I'm not a therapist."

10 Some staff members sit in as participants, however, and sometimes use patients' reactions to the poems as clues to their psychiatric problems. Says Dr. Visotsky: "If they see silent weeping or laughing at inappropriate times, the staff tries to incorporate these observations into the treatment plan." But the session has never carried anyone to the extreme. "Patients are not quite that fragile," he says. "If they perceive that a person likes them, they give them no problems."

I switch the action back to my original source by having her "agree" with her boss, the head of psychiatry.

11 Mrs. Harris agrees. "I've had people say, 'I don't like this; I don't like you.' You have to take whatever guff they give you and get in touch with their feelings."

In Paragraph 12 I tell who the students are and use her good quote about their relationship to poets (like the poets, the patients "have not found a practical niche in life").

12 Who are her students? "Teen-agers through those age 50, tender people who are not fighters and have not found a practical niche in life," say Mrs. Harris, who thinks the same can be said for poets. "Poetry is written by people not fitting into regular channels, not finding their own way into the mainstream."

In Paragraph 13 I am ready to end the story. I bring readers once again into the session ("Tobie Harris is trying to bring them together, poet and patient"). She had told me that the Eliot poem was a favorite, so I use an excerpt here that I looked up in *Bartlett's Quotations*.

13 Tobie Harris is trying to bring them together, poet and patient. One of her favorite mechanisms for this is T.S. Eliot's "The Love Song of J. Alfred Prufrock":

Let us go then you and I,
When the evening is spread out
  against the sky
Like a patient etherized
  upon a table . . .

In the last paragraph I use one of my favorite devices (Rule 12): I bring readers full circle back to the beginning of the story ("She finishes her reading") and use the same names I used in the lead ("Linda, John, the old lady"). She has almed them with her reading. I use her good quote about what she tells them to end the story.

14 She finishes her reading, and Linda, John, the old lady, and the others seem more relaxed. "Close your eyes," she tells them. "Try to visualize what kind of a night it is."

Key Journalistic Terms

Anecdotal lead   A lead that uses an anecdote (short narrative of an interesting or amusing incident) to interest readers.

Article   A factual piece of writing on a specific subject; usually used in connection with magazines.

Assignment   Instructions to a reporter on what story to cover.

Attribution   Identification of the source of a story, in or near the lead paragraph.

Background   Information that helps a reporter write a story but does not necessarily appear in the story.

Beat   The part of the city or the subject area assigned to a reporter.

Body   The main part of the story; the text that follows the lead paragraph.

Byline   The name of the reporter writing the story; usually this appears at the beginning.

Civil libel   Printed and published defamation of a person, written in a malicious and false manner, which subjects those responsible to damage payments.

Code of Ethics   The accepted practice in journalism as set down in documents prepared by organizations like the Society of Professional Journalists.

Copy desk   The place in a newsroom where copy editors edit reporters' copy and write headlines for their stories.

Coverage   The gathering of material for, and writing of, stories.

Deadline   The time when a final version of the story is due.

Delayed-identification lead   A lead that delays or slightly obscures the meaning of the story until the second or third paragraph to heighten reader interest.

Editor   A person who edits the stories of reporters and prepares them for publication.

Editorializing   Expressing opinion in a news or feature story, as opposed to doing so on the editorial page or in an article labeled ''opinion'' or ''analysis.''

Exclusive   A story that only one reporter knows about and writes for publication.

Features   Stories oriented less to recording the news than to evoking reader interest in special persons, places, or things.

Five W's and an H   Who, what, when, where, why, and how; one or more of these elements should be used in every summary lead.

Focus structure   Using the dramatic account of an individual or event in the lead to exemplify the issues of the larger story.

Follow-up   A story that appears the day after a news event to tell readers what has happened since it was first reported.

General assignment   The status of a reporter not assigned to a specific beat.

Graf   Accepted journalistic term for ''paragraph.''

Handout   A news release or other form of information submitted to reporters and editors for direct use in the publication or as background.

Hard news   News that is topical, timely, perishable, and included in the newspaper as soon as it happens.

Headline   Large, bold words appearing over a news or feature story to attract the attention of readers by presenting a few key facts of the story.

Interview   The two-way exchange between reporter and source that is used to gain information for stories; ideally reporters ask the questions, sources give the answers.

Inverted-pyramid style   The most common way to write a news story; most important facts come first, followed by all the other facts in the descending order of their importance.

Investigative reporting   A careful and complete investigation of a subject by a reporter or team of reporters that often exposes facts not known before.

Layout   The arrangement of headlines, stories, photos and illustrations, and advertising on the page before printing.

Lead   First paragraph of story; it is important because it is the reporter's first opportunity to capture a reader's attention.

Morgue   Files of past stories and issues of the publication used for reference by reporters and editors.

News peg   The reason a reporter's story is being published or the element in the story that makes it newsworthy.

News release   A story written by an organization to give its point of view of an event; releases are sent to reporters and editors in the hope they will use them in print; most releases are not used verbatim because they are considered to be self-serving, but they often provide good ideas and background for stories; also called a press release.

News source   Person or persons who give reporters the information from which they write stories.

Not for attribution   Information, gained in interviews, whose sources are not to be revealed by the reporter; the information itself, however, can be used.

Off the record   Material, gained in an interview, that serves only as background for the reporter and cannot be used in print.

Personal lead   A lead that uses "you" or an "implied you" approach to gain reader interest.

Piece   An article or story in journalistic jargon.

Press conference   A planned event during which a potential news source answers the questions of reporters; also called a news conference.

Publication   Any newspaper, magazine, or booklet in printed form.

Public relations   The art and technique of promoting good will toward a company or other organization by printed or other means; also called PR.

Question lead   A lead that gains the interest of readers by asking a question.

Quotation lead A lead that begins with a quote from a source to gain reader interest.

Quotes The actual words of an interviewee set off with quotation marks in the story; they are used to heighten reader interest and to give readers a good "feel" for the person.

Reporter A person who gathers material and writes news and feature stories.

Rewriting Editing and changing stories to improve them.

Secondary sources Printed material, or any source other than a person, that is used by a reporter to gather facts for a story; examples include documents, transcripts, and reports.

Sidebar A short story that explores one aspect of a larger story to make it more understandable.

Soft news Stories that are interesting and informative but not necessarily timely; features are soft news because they can appear at any time, whereas hard news must be in the publication as soon as possible.

Story A written or spoken account of something that has happened; usually used in connection to newspapers.

Style Rules by which a publication wants its stories to be written in terms of abbreviation, spelling, and capitalization.

Stylebook The details of the publication's style in printed form.

Summary lead A lead that summarizes the important facts of a story, usually through use of the five W's and an H.

Takeout A longer than average story.

Transition The sentence that guides readers from the lead to the body of a story.

Wire service A journalistic organization like the Associated Press which gathers news for a number of other print and broadcast clients.

Additional Reading on Public Affairs Reporting and on Writing

Brady, John. *The Craft of Interviewing*. Cincinnati, OH: Writers Digest Books, 1976.

Brooks, Brian S., George Kennedy, Daryl Moen, and Don Ranly. *News Reporting and Writing*. New York: St. Martin's, 1988.

Fowler, Henry. *Dictionary of Modern English Usage*. 2nd ed. New York: Oxford University Press, 1965.

Franklin, Jon. *Writing for Story*. New York: New American Library, 1987.

Guth, Hans P. *Concise English Handbook*. 4th ed. Belmont, CA: Wadsworth, 1977.

Kessler, Lauren and Duncan McDonald. *When Words Collide*. Belmont, CA: Wadsworth, 1984.

MacDougall, Curtis D. *Interpretative Reporting*. 8th ed. New York: Macmillan, 1982.

McCombs, Maxwell, David Lewis Shaw, and David Grey. *Handbook of Reporting Methods.* Boston: Houghton Mifflin, 1976.

Mencher, Melvin. *News Reporting and Writing.* 5th ed. Dubuque, IA: Wm. C. Brown, 1991.

Metzler, Ken. *Creative Interviewing.* Englewood Cliffs, NJ: Prentice-Hall, 1977.

Rivers, William L. *Finding Facts: Interviewing, Observing, Using Reference Sources.* Englewood Cliffs, NJ: Prentice-Hall, 1975.

_____. *Writing: Craft and Art.* Englewood Cliffs, NJ: Prentice Hall, 1975.

Schulte, Henry H. *Reporting Public Affairs.* New York: Macmillan, 1981.

Strunk, William, Jr., and E. B. White. *The Elements of Style.* 3rd ed. New York: Macmillan, 1979.

Zinsser, William. *On Writing Well.* 3rd ed. New York: Harper & Row, 1985.

Additional General References for Public Affairs Reporters

Dictionaries

Mencken, H. L. *The American Language.* 4th ed. New York: Alfred A. Knopf, 1936.

The Random House Dictionary of the English Language. 2nd ed. unabridged. New York: Random House, 1987.

Webster's New Collegiate Dictionary. 9th ed. Springfield, MA: G. & C. Merriam Co., 1988.

Biographies

American Men and Women of Science. New York: Jacques Cattell Press/ Bowker, 1971 to present.

Current Biography. New York: Wilson, 1940 to date

Dictionary of American Biography. New York: Scribner's, 1928 to present.

Atlases

Hammond Medallion World Atlas. New York: C.S. Hammond, 1977.

National Geographic Atlas of the World. 5th ed. Washington, DC: National Geographic Society, 1981.

Rand McNally New Cosmopolitan World Atlas. Skokie, IL: Rand McNally, 1977.

Stylebooks

Associated Press Stylebook and Libel Manual. New York: Addison-Wesley, 1987.

Chicago Manual of Style. 13th ed. Chicago: University of Chicago Press, 1982.

The Washington Post Deskbook on Style. 2nd ed. New York: McGraw Hill, 1989.

Miscellaneous

Bartlett, John. *Bartlett's Familiar Quotations.* 15th ed. Boston: Little, Brown, 1980.

Information Please Almanac. Boston: Houghton Mifflin, published annually.

Jane's Series on Fighting Ships, All the World's Aircraft, Infantry Weapons, Weapon Systems, Armor and Artillery. London: Jane's Information Group, published annually.

National Zip Code and Post Office Directory.

The People Shall Judge. 4th ed. 2 vols. Chicago: University of Chicago Press, 1957.

Roget's International Thesaurus. 4th ed. New York: Thomas Y. Crowell, 1977

Roget's Thesaurus in Dictionary Form. Garden City, NY: Doubleday, 1977.

The World Almanac and Book of Facts. New York: Newspaper Enterprise Association, published annually.

Journalism Publications

Columbia Journalism Review

Editor & Publisher

Editor & Publisher Yearbook

Gale Directory of Publications (formerly *Ayer's Directory of Newspapers & Periodicals*)

IRE Journal

Journalism Quarterly

The Quill

Washington Journalism Review

part

II Politics and Government

*I am the people—the mob—the crowd—the mass.
Do you know that all the great work of the world is
done through me?*

—Carl Sandburg

County courthouse just before primary election, Waco, Texas, 1938 by Dorothea Lange. [*Courtesy U.S. Farm Security Administration Collection, Prints and Photographs Division, Library of Congress*]

Politics, Elections, and the Federal Government

Politics has got so expensive that it takes lots of money to even get beat with.

— Will Rogers

One Political Reporter

"The problem of covering the White House is the news tends to get compressed through a small funnel. On any given White House story you can get reaction from only a small number of people who know what is happening. If you can't get them, you have to depend on the official line. This is one of the reasons you have got to make as many contacts as you can."

For Lou Cannon, who covered the White House for the *Washington Post* for all eight years of the Reagan presidency and parts of the Nixon and Ford administrations, that "funnel" was the daily briefing for reporters by the president's press secretary. Although details about the president's programs and daily activities were revealed at the briefing, so was the administration's infamous "line of the day" — the topic and carefully honed reaction to the topic that would emerge from the lips of all top officials. Reporters wanting to avoid writing the same story with the same quotes from the same people would somehow have to slip beyond the line.

"The best stories did not come from the briefing room," continues Cannon, now Western correspondent for the *Post* in Los Angeles. "The worst part was trying to find out what was really going on."

To do so, Cannon and the other reporters working with him on the White House beat (at least three rotated into that slot to assist Cannon, who was senior correspondent), did not let attendance at the briefing get in the way of setting up an interview with a source in the executive branch who could give them a better story.

"Often, one of us would go to the daily briefing while the other one would have an appointment or be calling sources," he says. "Both of us had a rule: the White House briefing was for their benefit, not ours. But it was not often that neither of us would be there. If not, it was easy to catch up by reading the transcript or talking to other reporters."

Cannon had an advantage in setting up his interviews. "I knew the players." Indeed, many high administration officials had held posts in the Ford and Nixon regimes.

That acquaintanceship was, for Cannon, "a double-sided thing. The advantage for me as a reporter was I knew it was a coalition government," he says, that is, one containing self-styled "conservatives" and "pragmatists." "The problem comes in not wanting to be the champion of one side or the other. If I did, one side would think well of me, the other not. I didn't want to be perceived as being in the pocket of one against the other, of being the conduit of one faction. The advantage is that sometimes I'd be working all sides and come out with something closer to the truth. This kind of thing wears you down. You try to cover the beat as much as possible with critical detachment. After you do that for a long period of time, people become wary of you."

Two tenets govern the *Washington Post*'s White House coverage, according to Cannon. "White House reporters, no matter what, will be influenced by what the president does," he says. "You can go at a story in different ways but still have to concentrate on what the president does, whether he's holding a meeting with a foreign leader or giving a political speech." The other rule is that the newspaper always assigns two reporters to the White House beat so one can back up the other.

Cannon says that no two days on the White House beat are ever alike. "There wasn't a particular day to label as typical," he explains. "One of the problems and frustrations of covering the White House is that every day is different and every day the same."

Cannon and his colleague decided the night before what they would be doing the next day. Because Cannon lived twenty miles away, the other reporter often covered early morning events. On Mondays, Cannon did a regular commentary on National Public Radio's "Morning Edition" before going to the White House. Much of Thursday was devoted to reporting and writing his syndicated column. He would arrive at the White House at 9:30 A.M. to see what was going on and possibly attend the 11 A.M. press briefing.

Neither reporter spent much time in the tiny and cramped cubicle assigned to the *Post* amid all the other newspapers, magazines, and networks in an area just off the briefing room. "A lot of people write their stories from here," he says. "Early in the Reagan administration I used it for presidential news conferences and evening events. But I didn't like to write there because it's so jammed and everyone can see what you're doing. We were so close to the *Post* — about six blocks — that, except in unusual circumstances, it was easier to walk over there."

If Cannon was working on a story involving a number of telephone interviews, he would go to the newspaper and spend much of the day at his desk in the newsroom making phone calls and waiting for sources to call him back. "You'd have to call by 10 A.M. to get a call back by deadline," he says. "With some people, I'd have to try three or four times and they might not call back until 3 P.M. or 4 P.M. or later. I didn't want to miss the calls so I stayed in the office." The regular copy deadline for the Post is 7 P.M., 8 P.M. for page one stories.

Cannon was aided in his work by another tradition at the *Washington Post*, the cooperatively reported and cooperatively written story. "I'm an advocate of that," he continues. "The more reporting there is, the better your story is going to be."

For example, for stories about then-Attorney General Edwin Meese, Cannon worked with the *Post*'s Justice Department reporter. For stories on the long struggle to secure aid for the contra forces in Nicaragua, Cannon worked with *Post* reporters covering Congress.

"Who did what wasn't that clear cut," he says. "We would do our stories together, pool our resources, and discuss our approach with editors. Often, we would not know who would be writing the story until the middle of the afternoon. There would be a lot of informal talking in the *Post* newsroom and the editors would decide."

Cannon thinks he and other *Post* reporters have an advantage over their beat counterparts from Washington bureaus of publications headquartered elsewhere: "We are the hometown paper. Other *Post* reporters would tell me things. The White House was the narrow end of the funnel, Congress the broad end. It all spills out [at the White House]. The beat rule: the White House is too important to cover from just the White House, from one end of Pennsylvania Avenue."

The longtime correspondent had an advantage because of his long years of covering Ronald Reagan, beginning in Sacramento when Reagan was governor of California. "I had an entree to Reagan — he knew my name," laughs Cannon. "Some access to Reagan and his people derived from covering him a long time. They knew me and I knew them. Any single story was a small piece of the whole. I had written about him for so many years. I had no ideological ax to grind. I wasn't impressed with the line of the day, but the line of the day is a given. It's true of the White House and any other news beat — the Pentagon, the State Department, state government, or city hall.

Cannon has used what he calls the "small pieces of the whole" of Ronald Reagan to write three biographies of the president: *Ronnie and Jesse: A Political Odyssey*, *Reagan*, and *President Reagan: The Role of a Lifetime*, all of them fair and honest accounts of the life and presidency of a highly successful — and strangely complicated — man.

Rules for covering the White House or any other beat in Washington? Lou Cannon has two of them:

- "Don't be afraid to ask [what may seem] a strange question. Often times, people won't ask a question that ought to be asked, it's so obvious; I remember during the 1976 campaign, Fred Barnes asked President Ford, 'You always refer to Richard Nixon as your predecessor. Is this a deliberate attempt to avoid using his name?' Ford thought for a moment and answered, 'Yes!'"

- "There is no such thing as an over-reported story. That phone call you don't make is usually the phone call that provides you with something you really need to know. The single source story is the bane of Washington journalism. No matter how important the person — including the president himself — you shouldn't go with a sole source. With Reagan, what he was saying was not necessarily coming from him anyway, but was a concoction of someone else."

Now away from the Washington scene, Cannon remembers his times on the White House beat with fondness, but does not miss being there: "The White House beat was once exalted beyond any kind of rational emphasis, during the years when news was official news. [*New York Times* Washington bureau chief] Arthur Krock once won a Pulitzer Prize for an *interview* with the president. After Watergate, reporters didn't want to be kicked around and a certain kind of cynicism emerged. It's a terrific, important beat and a wonderful thing to do. The thing is, you've got to keep a balance on that beat and not let the beat go to your head because of the aura of power radiating from the White House. It's not the power I'm afraid of. It's there. But people become very self-important. They've got to remember, they still put their pants on one leg at a time. It's important for a reporter covering the White House to know who he or she is and not get distorted."

Background to Political Reporting

Political reporting consists of gathering information and writing about politicians when they run for office and, once elected, their efforts to stay there. (It should not be confused with state government reporting and local government reporting—to be covered in Chapter 3 and 4—which follow the functioning of institutions more than people.) Political reporting is as old as politics itself.

In the United States such reporting dates to the colonial period. James Franklin published a letter, which was supposed to be from a Rhode Island correspondent, in the *New England Courant* in June 1722: "We are advised from Boston that the Government of Massachusetts are fitting out a ship to go after the pirates, to be commanded by Captain Peter Papillon, and 'tis thought that he will sail sometime this month, wind and weather permitting."

Government officials took this sentence as an accusation of undue delay in going after the pirates. James Franklin was imprisoned for weeks when he admitted writing the letter. While he was in jail, Franklin's brother, Benjamin, took over the paper.

Political criticism was the basis for the first milestone in American press freedom, the John Peter Zenger case in 1735. Zenger had started the *New York Weekly Journal* in November 1733 with backing from a group of men opposed to the autocratic British governor, William Cosby. After Zenger printed stories critical of the governor for his handling of various issues, the editor-printer was arrested in November 1734 for "raising sedition."

Zenger did not come to trial until August 1735, when he was defended by famed attorney Andrew Hamilton. The lawyer admitted that Zenger had written and published the material he was accused of writing and publishing. Hamilton's argument was that everything included in the stories was true. The jury agreed with his reasoning, and truth was established as a defense in libel cases from that day forward.

Political coverage was important to the success of the American Revolution and the formation of the government afterward. Following the convention of 1787, which drafted the Constitution, arguments raged over the adoption of the document. Newspapers helped assure ratification by printing the Federalist papers, a series of eighty-five essays written in 1787 and 1788 by Alexander Hamilton, James Madison, and John Jay in support of the Constitution.

In a pattern that was to be repeated in other kinds of public affairs reporting, political writing grew to prominence after editors and publishers realized that people would buy newspapers to read it.

Journalism historian Edwin Emery credits Nathaniel Carter with beginning the permanent Washington press corps in 1822 when Carter established a news bureau there for his newspaper, the *New York Statesman and Evening Advertiser*. Carter was first to use "Washington Correspondence" to describe his activities. Eliab Kingman perfected the system a few years later when he became a permanent correspondent in Washington for a number of out-of-town newspapers.

James Gordon Bennett was a Washington correspondent before establishing the *New York Herald* in 1835. As an editor, he saw the value of this coverage and assigned several reporters to write regularly about Congress and the White House.

From this point, the story becomes more complicated and lengthy than the space in this chapter allows. Since the Civil War, newspapers and magazines — and later, radio and television — have covered politics and elections as subjects crucial to the well-being of readers and viewers.

Since the inauguration of Franklin D. Roosevelt in 1933, coverage of national politics and the Federal government has increased dramatically. The handful of reporters who used to crowd around the president's desk for press conferences has grown into a small army. That same sixty-year period has seen a steady increase in reporters and has made Washington, D.C. the nation's major news center. Election campaigns and the performance of people after they are in office have become the subject of standard journalistic beats on local and state levels too. Such coverage should not be confused with that of the government, where reporters are observing permanent institutions and programs and how they function. Politics deals with the people in government and their methods, maneuvers, and intrigues to obtain the power and control necessary to get what they want.

The predominance of government, especially the federal government, in everyday life in recent years has made its political aspects that much more newsworthy. A large percentage of stories in national news magazines, big-city newspapers, and television network news programs deals with political news of one kind or another — the maneuvers of a president to get a program passed by Congress; the fighting among senators and representatives as they consider important cabinet appointments or various bills before them; the long election campaigns and the issues discussed in them; gossip and rumor about what important government officials are, or are not, going to do.

This dominance results from the endless fascination readers seem to have with politics almost as a kind of spectator sport. The subject is undoubtedly interesting and stimulating; according to some critics, however, it is more interesting to reporters and editors who participate than to readers and viewers who get tired of the subject.

Since the 1980s, national politics has changed dramatically and so has its coverage. Beginning with the 1980 election, television has come to dominate election campaigns on the national level. As a result, issues have become secondary to staged, spectacular events (discussing an urban policy using the bombed out-looking South Bronx as a backdrop, explaining an environmental policy in a national park, etc.) and "sound bites" (short, pithy, and preferably, controversial statements by candidates that do not last more than thirty seconds and are made in the morning before the deadlines of network news programs). This trend has turned presidential campaigns into superficial entertainment shows where serious discussion usually winds up on the floor of TV editing booths.

While deplorable, this situation has at least enhanced the value of print political reporters, making them less the purveyors of "news" in its truest sense — that is, providing information to readers for the first time — than analysts of why something was done and what it means.

How to Cover National Politics and Elections

Although only a small number of reporters will ever cover a presidential campaign, an understanding of the mechanics of doing so helps in the reporting of politics and elections on state and local levels.

Primary and Caucus Period

The presidential campaign year begins with a series of primaries and caucuses in many states. (Box 2.1 explains the mechanics of the system.)

The press is both the victim and the cause of so many primary and caucus events. The candidates travel to the states to get their convention delegates elected, but they also go there for the press attention — especially on the evening television news. The reporters, editors, and camera and sound people expend much time and money to cover an event that would not exist without their presence. The victimization comes in having to sit through the same basic speech day after day and coming up with a fresh lead. The only solace comes in the fact that candidates are gradually eliminated as the primary season continues.

Reporters who cover the primary and caucus period, whether on the presidential, state, or local level, need to prepare themselves for the assignment:

1. **Plan early and carefully.** Political reporters should become familiar with the laws of the state and the plans of both parties to nominate convention delegates. When will the caucuses, convention, or primary take place? What local officials will be running? What major candidates will be visiting the state? How much coverage does the publication plan to devote to it? If the coverage is to be extensive, political reporters and editors should draw up a plan of action indicating the dates and times of major campaign events leading up to the caucus, convention, or primary; the activities of the local, state, and national candidates; possible news stories with dates when they would appear in print; features and background stories with dates when they would appear in print; the number of reporters required for coverage; and the approximate cost.

2. **Get to know important people.** Reporters assigned to cover this period should get acquainted with knowledgeable sources in both major political parties, any important third party movements, state and local elections departments, the major candidates' "advance men" who come into states early to plan appearances, and

Box 2.1

How a Primary or Caucus Operates

In the past only a few states held primaries, and these were covered as news events if they were important enough to attract candidates. For example, New Hampshire's primary was covered because it is the earliest primary in an election year. Beginning in 1976 and continuing to a greater extent in 1980, 1984, 1988, and 1992, the number of primaries has grown, and the combination of caucus and convention has merged as an equally important mechanism in presidential politics. The two methods differ greatly, although the purpose of both is to select delegates to the nominating conventions.

In caucus states, convention delegates are selected in a complicated system which involves holding caucuses, or open meetings, in each voting precinct in the state. Any eligible voter is permitted to attend. The people who go to caucuses elect delegates to the county convention; the number of delegates varies according to the votes cast in that precinct for the party's last candidate for governor. In some states, like Iowa, the process is different for the two political parties. The Democrats divide their caucuses by the presidential preferences of delegates, creating the "horse race" aspect political reporters love. The Republicans elect their delegates as individuals without necessarily considering their presidential preference.

Other states hold presidential primary elections. These contests give voters the chance to nominate candidates for all offices either directly or through selection of delegates to the party nominating convention.

Presidential primaries began early in this century as part of a Progressive movement push to get control of nominations from party bosses. Wisconsin held the first statewide primary in 1903, and it included presidential candidates for the first time in 1905. By 1917 most states had established the direct primary for party nominees, and today the device serves to choose at least some nominations in all fifty states.

States hold either open or closed primaries. Any eligible voter, regardless of party affiliation, can participate in an open primary. In the closed version two separate primary slates of candidates are put up and can only be voted upon by registered voters from each party who declare their affiliation at the polls; independents cannot participate.

Although voter turnout for primaries is usually low, they get a lot of attention because presidential candidates and the press consider them important in the presidential "horse race."

campaign officials for candidates at all levels. If there is time, a series of "get acquainted" luncheons, dinners, or even chats over coffee are ideal. In this way a political reporter establishes a friendship early, when things are calm, that can pay off in much needed information when things are hectic during a campaign.

3. **Determine campaign issues.** Early background interviews with candidates, managers, and political party officials will enable reporters to find out what the issues of the campaign will be. Reporters should also cultivate one or two disinterested observers, such as political science professors from local universities, who can advise them on issues and strategy in an unbiased way. From this background work should emerge a list of issues likely to dominate the campaign at all levels. These subjects can then form the basis of an article or series of articles that, in effect, sets the agenda for candidates in the campaign itself.

Convention Period

The conventions of the two major parties are the next events in an election year. The mechanics of a convention are explained in Box 2.2. Despite of the decline in power of conventions, they are legitimate news events that need to be covered. Whether the convention is at the national or state level, reporters must prepare themselves for the assignment:

1. **Plan early and carefully.** Know the party rules for conventions and the dates, times, and location. How important will the work of the local delegation be? Will it merit coverage? If so, how many reporters will it take beyond the regular political reporter?

The political reporter should draw up a list of story possibilities: personality profiles on key members of the delegation, stories on the impact of the delegation, articles on the logistics of putting a convention together.

2. **Get to know important people.** Well in advance of a convention, a political reporter should make friends with leading members of the local delegation, local party officials, and officials at the convention itself, especially those in charge of press arrangements. National parties make extensive arrangements for the press at their conventions, so coverage is only a matter of getting the proper credentials and badge that allows free passage on and off the convention floor. Convention press rooms are usually well equipped with typewriters, laptop computers, copying machines, and telephones. Because state conventions may not be so well organized, a political reporter assigned to cover such a meeting

should know in advance what he or she will be facing in terms of access, the need for credentials, and the facilities to write and file copy.

3. **Determine important issues.** By talking to these carefully cultivated sources, a political reporter can find out what issues will likely dominate the convention and where controversy might occur. The issues will provide advance story ideas, and the controversies will make good news stories if and when they occur.

Campaign Period

The campaign for office, whether it be for the presidency, a state legislative seat, or the local county board, represents the high point of any political year and the most exciting and newsworthy event or series of events a political reporter covers. At least on paper, the process is rather simple: The candidate moves around a geographic area, whether it be the entire nation or a single state or district, and talks to gatherings in an effort to influence citizens to vote for him or her. But time, distance, the large number of voters, and the availability of television have all changed the modern campaign on the presidential level.

Candidates still do for television cameras some of the things they used to do by necessity because it was the only way to contact voters, i.e., such old-fashioned activities as "whistle-stop" trips by train or standing at factory gates in the predawn hours to shake the hands of workers. But they also now spend a great deal of time and money on television advertising. This enables them to reach a maximum number of voters in a short amount of time and eliminates some travel. A presidential candidate no longer pledges, as Richard Nixon did in 1960, to visit all fifty states.

The train rides and handshaking survive as media events designed to secure a one- to two-minute spot on the evening news. Indeed, Ronald Reagan's 1980 and 1984 campaigns were carefully constructed to avoid exposure to hard questioning by print and broadcast reporters. When the day's footage of a "colorful" appearance had been shot, the candidate was whisked away out of reach of the carefully managed press corps. A *Wall Street Journal* reporter called it a policy of "containment."

Reporters from the print media resent the orientation toward television, but there is little they can do about it. They must try to find a new lead for a speech they hear ten times a day. But still they board the airplanes and buses and fight with the candidate's press secretary for more access and worry that their luggage will be lost.

Box 2.2

How a Political Convention Operates

The political conventions of the two major parties used to be exciting, unpredictable events. Now, says political columnist David Broder, they are "places where nothing happens for four consecutive days" and events that "clutter up the television schedule." In 1992, conventions didn't even do that because the television networks cut back their coverage of both conventions drastically lest they lose advertising revenues because of low ratings.

Presidential elections are no longer decided at conventions. Because of the tortuous caucus, convention, and primary selection of delegates, one candidate has usually gathered enough votes for nomination in June at the time of the last primary. The delegates arrive in the convention city pledged to vote for a certain candidate and seldom change. The only important thing that emerges is whether all factions of the party will coalesce around the nominee.

Various reforms enacted by the two parties since 1972 have altered forever the structure of both the parties and their conventions to insure broader participation by all groups and a more open delegate selection process.

The effect of the reforms and all the caucuses, state conventions, and primaries has been to lessen the importance of both the national party conventions, as noted earlier, and the national party itself. By the time a presidential candidate has beaten the opponents in all of these earlier contests, the influence of party officials with that candidate is diminished.

The party structure has remained the same, despite the decline in importance. The precinct is the basic unit of the party organization; each is headed by committeemen or committeewomen or precinct captains chosen in caucuses, direct primary elections, the general election, or by party officials. This person is the only contact point between voters in the precinct and the professionals in the party structure. Thus, he or she can influence and encourage people to vote, and, at times, may tell them how to vote. The county committee is the next level and consists of precinct captains. This unit can be quite powerful; for example, it may select congressional district delegates to the national convention. Precinct people are also important in getting voters registered.

The state committee, made up of state committeemen and committeewomen, conducts campaigns, helps govern the party, and either influences the choice of delegates to the national convention or actually selects them.

The national committee is the most important entity of the party organization. It consists of representatives—at least one man and one woman—from each state and helps choose presidential candidates. The committee's role here, however, is less predominant now than in the past days of "smoke-filled rooms" and big-city political bosses. The national chairman, usually selected by the party's presidential candidate, is the chief executive of the party. His or her job is directing the party between elections, raising funds, helping to hold the "party line" in votes on Congress, and if the party is out of power, developing a strategy to regain the presidency and majorities in both houses of Congress. The chairman presides at meetings of the national committee and the national convention.

The two national parties hold their conventions in the summer of every presidential year. Although conventions have no legal standing, they do perform four major roles: 1) nominating the presidential and vice-presidential candidates; 2) adopting a national party platform of goals and plans for the coming four years in various phases of national life; 3) governing the party by approving members of the national committee and policies and procedures for the next convention; and 4) stimulating morale for the upcoming campaign by attacking the opposition and healing the wounds of the party.

After all, the candidate might make a major misstatement — or say something new.

The 1980 presidential campaign saw the rise of a charge and countercharge mentality between the two candidates and the press; there was no substance to the campaign because issues were rarely discussed. The candidates said the press concentrated on their mistakes and inflammatory rhetoric and did not explore the issues facing the country; the members of the press said they did not make the news but were only reporting what the candidates did. If candidates would talk about issues, the reporters said, they would report them. The "issueless" nature of campaigns continued in 1984 and 1988.

In the 1992 campaign, candidates tried harder to discuss major issues than in recent years, but their words were often drowned out by a flurry of stories about their private lives and alleged past improprieties. Once again, true coverage of issues for the harried voters was often overlooked. The emergence of Texas billionaire Ross Perot as a possible presidential candidate upset the carefully laid plans of both major political parties and raised the possibility for the first time in American history that a third party candidate could be a serious contender.

Meanwhile, President George Bush's handling of the economy and a check-kiting scandal involving 302 members of the U.S. House of Representatives created a public cynicism and distrust of government not seen in this country since the nineteenth century.

State and local races are not as difficult to cover. The geographic area is smaller, and the whole campaign is carried out on a smaller scale. It is easier to get interviews with candidates who need the coverage. But there are also fewer events — a speech here, a debate there. Generally, political reporters have to work at covering state and local campaigns by asking all candidates the same set of questions on issues or by getting their news organizations to sponsor debates.

Political reporters must prepare for campaign coverage at whatever level they are working:

1. **Plan early and carefully.** As in the other aspects of political coverage already discussed, campaign reporting requires early planning. The travel schedules and news events that will form the structure of the campaign cannot be anticipated precisely, but the decision to cover can be made early. Reporting a presidential campaign is a major undertaking if it is done right. It requires that at least one person accompany each of the major candidates on all their travels. This means a substantial investment of a reporter's time as well as paying a prorated share of the chartered press plane and lodging and food costs. To reduce the problem of bias for or against a candidate, reporters should be switched every two or three weeks.

2. **Get to know important people.** On a campaign the people to know are the important aides, not only the first-level ones who advise and see the candidate regularly, but the second-level ones who are knowledgeable because they do a lot of substantive work that gets less attention but is equally important. These aides are usually young, fun to be around, and what longtime *Los Angeles Times* political reporter Bill Boyarsky calls "real junkies about politics." They can be the source for background information and tips of upcoming, but not yet announced, campaign events.

3. **Determine important issues.** In recent issueless campaigns this requirement is often difficult to achieve. A reporter's political scientist consultants, the platform of the two parties, and the position papers issued by the candidates during the campaign will all help.

4. **Be prepared for the appearance of sameness.** In recent presidential campaigns the candidates made their "basic speech" every day, occasionally throwing in a new stand on an issue or a local reference. Reporters quickly become bored and desperate in this situation, especially if they are kept from talking to the candidate except on the run through shouted questions and answers over the hood of a limousine. The result are stories that accentuate the negative — mistakes, the lack of issues, and the name-calling between candidates. Reporters who are prepared with knowledge and information about the problems facing the country can sometimes set the agenda for the campaign by forcing candidates

away from their basic speech and into a discussion of the issues. Stories on the logistics of the campaign, the content of campaign advertising—especially negative advertising, important advisers, financial aspects, use of language in speeches, audience reaction, and many other aspects of the campaign are good alternatives to the basic speech.

The coverage of state campaigns is somewhat different. The biggest change is the reduced geographic area. This means fewer campaign trips lasting more than a day or two. Usually candidates for United States Senator or governor will give only a limited number of speeches and occasionally debate their opponents, relying instead on paid television advertisements. The atmosphere is informal enough, however, for reporters to get frequent chances for personal interviews. Candidates for local races are very accessible and often so eager for coverage that political reporters will have to beat them off with a stick.

Election Day

The entire political period culminates in an event that is largely anticlimactic—election day. All over the country, state, district, or city, voters go to the polling places, enter the voting booths, and make their choices. At this point the candidates or reporters can do little but wait until the returns begin to come in later in the day and throughout the night.

Large news organizations employ polling organizations and extra staff members to find out voting results as quickly as possible. In 1980 NBC News used interviews with voters leaving polling places— so-called exit interviews—to predict a presidential winner at 8:15 P.M. (EST), many hours before the polls had closed on the West Coast.

Critics charged that the early projection of a winner at the head of the ticket caused people to stay home and, thus, affected the outcome of local races. Despite the criticism, the networks used the same technique in 1984. A report by the Committee for the Study of the American Electorate found that in twenty-five states where network projections were broadcast before the polls closed in 1984, nineteen states had lower turnouts than in 1980 and only six showed increases. By contrast, in the twenty-four states and the District of Columbia where polls were closed by the time of the first projected winner, fourteen states and the District reported increased turnouts, while ten showed a decrease. Congress later held hearings on the problem and asked the networks to refrain from making early predictions. They held back until a little later in the evening in 1988, but still used exit interviewing data to predict a winner.

Smaller news organizations can set up a similar information-gathering process around the state, district, or city by hiring extra people to gather totals at the various polling places or county courthouses.

The rest of the election night coverage is fairly straightforward: an analysis of what the wins and losses mean and why they happened, interviews with the winning and losing candidates in all important contests, stories on related subjects like new voting machines, the breakdown of voting machines, and rural versus urban voting.

The atmosphere of election night is exciting. Returns bring elation in the headquarters of the winning candidates, gloom in the offices of the losers, and a sense of relief and anticipation by voters who wonder what changes will occur.

How to Cover Local Politics and Elections

Much of what has been detailed in this chapter so far has dealt with the national and state levels of politics. A beginning reporter, however, will be working in city and county political campaigns and elections. This emphasis has not been by accident. Reporters on a local level can learn a lot from national political reporters. By knowing how campaigns and elections are supposed to be conducted, they can judge how local counterpart events are being carried out.

A small town election is a microcosm of a national election. The only difference is that everything is smaller — the ability of the candidates, the scope of the issues, the number of voters, the geographic area, the cost of campaigning, and the impact of the results.

The process is exactly the same locally as nationally, except that a reporter has to do more digging. The work is more of an individual effort. There is little of the "pack journalism" approach that characterizes national and even some state races. Local political and election coverage consists of a number of important steps (see also Figure 2.1):

1. **Find out who has filed.** A candidate must obtain a predetermined number of voter signatures on a nominating petition by a certain date and must file the petition with the office that holds jurisdiction (city clerk for a city, county clerk for county, and

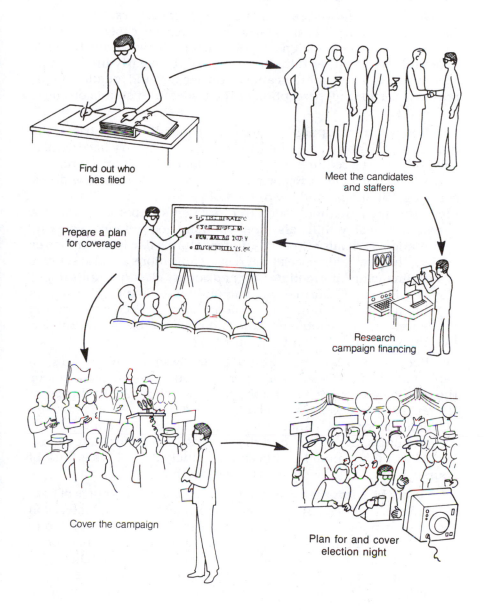

Figure 2.1 **How to cover an election**

secretary of state for the state). Such information is public and easily obtained by reporters after the deadline.

2. **Meet the candidates and their staff members.** This task is the easiest because all candidates want coverage, especially in the early days of their campaigns. A political reporter will probably have to fend them off rather than ferret them out. In early interviews a reporter should find out the candidate's background, qualifications, reasons for running, perception of the issues, and stands on those issues.

3. **Research campaign finances.** Federal law restricts the financing of national campaigns, and many states now have similar rules or at least a requirement that candidates file financial reports and lists of contributors. Reporters need to know the state laws about campaign financing and keep track of periodic reports if they are filed. In states without such requirements reporters can ask candidates. Party officials are another good source of this information. Officials of special-interest groups like labor unions or some of the New Right special-interest organizations are also sources of such financing information. City and county elections units might also provide such information. The main aim of such research is to find out who is funding a candidate in order to determine the influences on that candidate now and after the election. (Box 2.3 examines Political Action Committees.)

4. **Prepare a plan for campaign coverage.** After talking to candidates and their staffs, a reporter should have a good feel for the candidates, the issues, and the sequence of events. At this point the reporter can develop a rough plan of campaign coverage through election day for each candidate; the plan should list major stories on candidates, the issues, and the travel schedule (for state races). In this way the planned events can be anticipated. News events, of course, will have to be dealt with as they happen.

5. **Cover the campaign.** Reporters should balance coverage of both sides in every contest. Some newspapers, magazines, and television news departments seem to measure the space and time devoted to presidential candidates. To avoid charges of bias and unfairness, local reporters might consider a similar approach. During a campaign reporters should watch out for trends beyond the day-to-day grind, such as a change in tone or the introduction of an unexpected issue.

6. **Plan carefully for election night.** Local election returns come into a central place either by electronic means or manual means. A political reporter should make arrangements to go to this office

Box 2.3

How PAC's Work

Political Action Committees (PAC's) are organizations that raise and distribute campaign contributions to congressional candidates. During the 1970s and 1980s, the wealth and power of these committees grew at a remarkable rate. Accompanying this growth was an equal amount of controversy from those who felt that PAC's corrupt the campaigns of the senators and representatives they help pay for by the money given to them and the favors asked in return after the election.

PAC's are set up in two ways. Some are connected with specific parts of society, like labor or business or even teachers. These groups give money to elect candidates who will encourage fair treatment for their members. The other kind of PAC's are independent and set up to promote the political beliefs of members. These groups might even supply and fund candidates who support their point of view, for example, on abortion or arms control.

Under federal law, a PAC cannot give more than $5,000 per election. But PAC's are not limited in the total amount they can contribute to all candidates. They can also spend as much as they desire to help individual candidates with campaign costs — like television advertising, for example — as long as they operate in a way that is totally separate from the campaign staff of the candidate.

PAC's started to grow after the enactment of the 1971 and 1974 campaign financing reform laws. In 1974, 608 PAC's were registered with the federal elections commission and donated $12.5 million to House and Senate candidates. In 1986, there were over 4,000 PAC's and they spent $132 million on the candidates of their choice. House candidates now get more than half their campaign funds from PAC's, Senate candidates 20 percent.

Incumbents have the advantage in attracting PAC funding because people are reluctant to anger an office-holder and take a chance on an unknown. Critics contend that PAC's enable organized, well-funded special interest groups to amass too much power over the candidates they help to elect. They say that a person, once elected with help from a PAC, is afraid to vote against its interests. Defenders of this system say that PAC's encourage people to enter politics and get the funding needed to get elected.

PAC's play a role in presidential campaigns only in the primary/caucus stage before nomination. They are not allowed to operate during the election campaign itself which is now publicly financed.

for at least part of the evening to get raw figures as they come in. But the reporter will need some help to fulfill such additional responsibilities as covering the statements of winners and losers and getting the opinions of experts on why the election turned out as it did. Other reporters in the newsroom can help share this load. Reporters should also prepare background information in advance for use in the final story: Who won last time, how long has the city voted, what issues dominated in the past? The atmosphere of election night is exciting and fun. It is, after all, the culmination of a lot of work by many people. Reporters must be careful, however, not to get too carried away in the euphoria of the evening. The clock is still ticking toward their deadline no matter who wins or loses.

More suggestions of political coverage can be found in "Likely Problems and How to Solve Them" later in this chapter.

Kinds of Political Stories

Political stories vary depending on the year and the time of year. Although some kind of election is usually held every year, even-numbered years generally see the more important races. On smaller newspapers a political reporter might be assigned to other subjects in the odd-numbered years.

Election Years

1. **News of candidates.** Who are they, what do they stand for, who is backing them, and how qualified are they? How well organized are they, and what is the organization of their staff? How closely tied are they to party organization and special-interest groups? How are they being financed? Is there anything newsworthy in their past background?

2. **Background on the issues.** What problems will dominate the campaign? How will the candidates solve them if elected? How practical are the solutions?

3. **News of the campaign.** How are the candidates doing on a week-by-week basis? What are they saying in their speeches? How are crowds reacting? What do the polls say? What unplanned events have taken place—an unpleasant incident in a crowd or the endorsement by a prominent person or group.

4. **Election night.** Who won, who lost, and why? Were there any polling place incidents worthy of reporting? Were there breakdowns in counting ballots? What do the winners and losers think, and how do party officials and objective experts such as political science professors view results?

5. **Election machinery.** Will the votes be counted by hand or with a new computer? What have been the trends in the city and county in recent years and a hundred years ago?

6. **Campaign financing.** Who are the major contributors to a candidate's campaign and what, if any, connection have they had to the candidate in the past? How powerful and prevalent are PAC's to the candidate? Is there even a hint of scandal or corruption in the way the campaign is being financed?

Non-election Years

1. **Party activities.** Efforts by political party organizations to regroup (if they lost heavily in the last election) or expand (if they won) are newsworthy.

2. **Voter registration drives.** How are they going? How are they backed?

3. **Personality profiles.** Losing candidates on the comeback trail and visiting politicians make interesting reading in off-years.

4. **Analysis of issues and trends.** Why did the last election turn out as it did? What changes have taken place? What will happen next time?

Writing Political Stories

"You are writing for your editors in one sense," says Lou Cannon, former senior correspondent at the White House for the *Washington Post*. "In a larger sense you are writing for the guy who picks up the paper. He's probably not going to read the whole story. You must convey a sense of what it is you're telling high in the story. You need to write as directly as you can. I don't think you need an elaborate construction. Keep it simple."

"Leads: You don't need to be Ernest Hemingway but should write with directness, using simple, action verbs. It's no different in the White House; you should pontificate as little as possible. Be sure to explain when you have to, for example, 'throw weight, the lifting power of missiles.'"

Cannon also believes in the importance of writing constantly. "I have a hard time writing," he says, "but I always write a lot. You should do it every day. I think you've got to put something down regularly."

The former White House reporter calls the story reproduced here "a modest story, serving a purpose. Essentially, it is a contextual story explaining Reagan's role in the campaign even though its St. Louis dateline ostensibly serves a dual purpose as a day story. The story relates little of the content of Reagan's speech that day, which was much the same as the content of most of his other partisan speeches."

Cannon says the *Post* tries, when possible, to point out the political as well as the policy consequences of a story. In going through his clips of the 1988 campaign, however, he says he was surprised to find how few of them actually concerned the campaign itself, even if Reagan was out making speeches. "That was a reflection of Reagan's role as 'super surrogate' and of mine as White House correspondent. The focus of the Republican campaign, of course, was on George Bush, not Reagan."

PRESIDENT STUMPS AS SUPER-SURROGATE
By Lou Cannon
Washington Post Staff Writer

Lou Cannon's lead is a mixture of fact and analysis that often characterizes *Washington Post* stories ("the president campaigned and played a supporting role that has transformed the White House into a willing extension of the Bush campaign").

1 ST. LOUIS, Sept. 14 — President Reagan campaigned today in Missouri as a super-surrogate for Republican presidential nominee George Bush, playing a supporting role that has transformed the White House into a willing extension of the Bush campaign.

The transition is made with the words "Reagan's speeches," followed by a brief characterization of them.

2 Reagan's speeches featured a warning that peace and prosperity would be endangered by the election of Michael S. Dukakis and included the usual comparison of the Democratic presidential nominee to former president Jimmy Carter.

Graf 3 expanded upon the previous graf by giving more details.

3 It is a campaign message carefully tailored for Americans who have prospered during the Reagan years and are considered susceptible to a contention that Bush's election would mean more of the same. Today Reagan likened the Carter administration to the horror film "Nightmare on Elm Street" and suggested darkly that economic and foreign policy nightmares are in store for America if "the liberals" prevail.

By graf 4, Cannon turns to the main focus of his story: how the Reagan White House is aiding the Bush campaign.

He continues this line of thought with details in graf 5 of the close connection ("control the agenda") and . . .

. . . in graf 6, the scheduling of speeches by cabinet members.

In graf 7, Cannon gets even more specific by starting a rundown on how the plan has been in evidence throughout the week. From Monday (8, 9) . . . to Tuesday (10).

4 Reagan's speeches today were his only avowed campaign appearances of the week. But as White House officials readily acknowledge, almost all presidential actions and ceremonies are now taken with a view to their impact on the Bush campaign.

5 White House chief of staff Kenneth M. Duberstein and Bush chief of staff Craig Fuller talk with each other almost every day. Duberstein also works closely with Bush campaign manager James A. Baker III. Soon after Duberstein succeeded Howard H. Baker, Jr. in July, senior White House officials adopted a four-point game plan. It called for the president to "control the agenda" with actions favorable to Bush, appeals to non-Republican demographic groups and campaign speeches in key states.

6 The other element of the plan directed Reagan Cabinet officials, except for the attorney general and secretaries of state and defense, to campaign for Bush. This surrogate operation is scheduled directly by Bush headquarters, but White House officials and Reagan have personally urged Cabinet members to campaign for Bush.

7 Every element of the White House plan has been in evidence this week.

8 On Monday, the White House held a Rose Garden ceremony where Reagan signed the fair-housing bill and extolled the "enormous courage" demonstrated by Bush in voting for the original federal housing anti-bias bill as a Texas congressman 20 years ago.

9 Later in the day, the president courted Hispanic-Americans, a demographic group among which he has usually run ahead of the GOP ticket, and put in a plug for Bush's child-care proposal and attacked Dukakis' child-care program.

10 Today the sites, timing and content of the speeches were carefully designed to assist Bush. Southeastern Missouri is a conservative area that gave Carter his margin of

victory when he carried the state against President Ford in 1976. But it has been Reagan country since 1980.

In graf 11, Cannon gives readers the overall plan of targeting various states for Reagan appearances.

11 Reagan is targeting swing states with a significant number of electoral votes where his approval rating remains high. Missouri meets this test, as does Texas, where Reagan will campaign next Thursday.

12 Polls taken for Bush and the White House show a high correlation between the president's approval rating, particularly on economic issues, and Bush's standing versus Dukakis.

In graf 13, he quotes the White House spokesman for the President's popularity and expands on the use of a theme ("We are the change") in graf 14.

13 "It's hard to say if the president's popularity translates directly but it does translate into the idea that the economy is sound and the administration is a success," said White House spokesman Marlin Fitzwater today. "This bolsters the basic tenet of the Bush campaign that we are the change."

14 This phrase — "we are the change" — was introduced by Reagan in his speech to the Republican National Convention. Reagan concluded a speech in Cape Girardeau with these words, to tumultuous applause from the predominantly youthful audience.

In graf 15, Cannon indicates that Reagan is also raising large amounts of money.

15 Reagan is also raising significant amounts of money for the Republican campaign, an estimated $1.5 million in speeches that punctuated his California vacation, and $500,000 in his speech tonight to a $250-a-plate fund-raiser.

In graf 16, he begins to sum up by indicating how Reagan and his aides are using the presidency and its trappings to help Bush.

16 Overall, Reagan and his aides are using the prestige, political advantages and "photo opportunities" provided by White House incumbency much as they did four years ago when he was seeking reelection.

In graf 17, he explains that an incumbent has only occupied the White House three times in sixteen elections and backs up that assertion with direct quotes (18) and paraphrases (19) from the White House political director to end the story. With this story, readers

17 Only three times in the past 16 presidential elections has the White House been occupied by an incumbent who was compaigning for a nominee of his party other than himself.

18 "In 1952 and 1968 the nominees [Democrats Adlai Stevenson and Hubert Humphrey] were running away from the

have been provided a great deal of context beyond the daily "sound bite" approach they get from television coverage.

president," said White House political director Frank Donatelli. "In 1960, the president was running away from the nominee [Richard Nixon]. It's only this time that the nominee and the president are working closely together."

19 Donatelli believes that this working together could make the difference in a close election. He is mindful that the common denominator in the campaigns of Stevenson, Humphrey and Nixon was that all of them lost.

Political and Election Reporting: Likely Problems and How to Solve Them

Problem	Solution
1. Not knowing the candidates.	1a. Interview candidates and their staff members early.
	1b. Probe their backgrounds carefully.
2. Not knowing the issues.	2a. Ask candidates and objective experts what the issues are.
	2b. Do background interviews with experts and the general public.
	2c. Do background reading to discover historical comparisons.
3. Complicated financing laws and party procedures.	3a. Interview local and state election officials.
	3b. Interview political party officials.
	3c. Do background reading.
4. Too many events going on simultaneously.	4a. Organize campaign coverage carefully and systematically.
	4b. Get help from other reporters if necessary.

5. Appearing to favor one candidate over another.	5a. Be fair and objective. 5b. Cover both sides equally; measure space devoted to each candidate if necessary.

How to Cover the Federal Government

Because whole books have been written on covering the federal government, a chapter—or part of one—in this volume can only scratch the surface of what has become a behemoth. Reporters who aspire to ply their trade in Washington, D.C. will soon discover, however, that techniques they have learned in covering state and local government work at the federal level as well. The old saying, "All politics is local," applies equally to United States government coverage.

The difficulty in covering the federal government comes mainly from its size. Not only are there three equal branches of government—executive, legislative, and judicial—but subdivisions within these branches, like regulatory agencies (executive) or congressional committees (legislative), that all yield news (see Box 2.4). No single reporter can cover the entire federal government. Large news organizations divide it into beats, sometimes by the three branches, sometimes by broad subject matter, for example, health or justice or national security which may combine activities in a number of specific departments and agencies. Smaller news organizations with only one reporter in Washington will concentrate on activities affecting readers in the geographic area covered by the news organization. Such a reporter will not be able to cover any agency regularly, but only when news warrants. The news organization of such a reporter will get broader federal coverage from wire services and other news agencies.

The emergence of C-SPAN—a nonprofit channel paid for by TV cable companies to cover sessions of Congress, congressional hearings, and other public affairs and events—has greatly helped overworked reporters. If they can't attend key news events in person, they can watch them live or view a tape at a more convenient time. As with all reporting, coverage at the federal level involves cultivating sources; receiving a steady flow of news releases and other official materials; attending official events like press conferences, briefings, and ceremonies, and keeping track of laws and regulations both proposed and enacted.

Box 2.4

How the Federal Government is Organized

As established by the United States Constitution in 1787, the federal government consists of three equal branches: executive, legislative, and judicial.

- The executive branch includes the president, the cabinet departments, and regulatory agencies. Members of this branch execute laws and also formulate and carry out government policies. The president directs foreign relations, commands the armed forces, approves or disproves legislative acts, recommends legislation, appoints or dismisses executive officials, and pardons criminals wrongly convicted of crimes. The executive may also issue ordinances and interpret statutes for the guidance of other officials. In these powers, the executive may perform some legislative and judicial acts, not originally intended by those who wrote the Constitution with its firm provision for separation of powers.

- The legislative branch consists of the United States Congress: 435 members of the House of Representatives elected every two years from districts apportioned by population figures from the last census; and 100 senators, two from each state elected for six-year terms. Both houses do their work in sessions lasting two years. Members take care of constituent needs with the help of large staffs. Members propose legislation on a variety of subjects which, after hearings and votes, may become law. Members also serve on committees which hear testimony on appointments, budgets, and laws proposed by the executive and vote, first in committee, then on the floor as one body.

- The judicial branch, consisting on the federal level of the United States Supreme Court, and a number of Courts of Appeals and District Courts located geographically, passes judgment on the constitutionality of executive action and legislative laws. The nine-person Supreme Court meets from October to July to hear, first, arguments that the Court accept a case, and next, arguments for and against the validity of the law in question. Its members hand down their decision before adjournment. They also function as the court of last resort in cases that are first decided on other levels of the federal court system. A decision of the Supreme Court is considered the law of the land—until a new law enacted by Congress replaces it.

Cultivating Sources

Washington has two kinds of sources: official and unofficial. The first are the easiest to access for general news of an agency or department, but they tend to give a one-sided, self-serving, and optimistic view. Unofficial sources, often not named in stories for fear of losing their jobs, can provide a more truthful picture. Such relationships take time to develop, however, and a new reporter cannot expect to have their trust instantly.

All agencies, from the White House to individual executive departments and regulatory bodies to members of Congress, have their own press offices and public relations operations. Such entities have at least one press secretary working full-time to handle the routine inquiries of reporters. These press officers hold regular press conferences and briefings, arrange official interviews, and provide a steady flow of news releases and other printed materials. A reporter responsible for covering a department must get on the mailing lists of the press office and get to know the press officer, key staff members, and executives on an official basis. In addition to departments and individual representatives and senators, reporters on the federal level should not overlook the staffs of congressional committees. They delve into problems faced by the government and the funds needed to solve them and have access to a great deal of information. They will share it officially in briefings and unofficially after a reporter gets to know them.

While it is very important to keep up on official activities in the ways just described, true news often comes from unofficial sources. Such people work in many parts of the vast federal establishment. They might be appointed officials who are disgruntled with policies and want to enlist the reporter's help in bringing about change. They might be members of the permanent bureaucracy who talk to reporters for the same reason. They might be former officials with axes to grind. They might be one of the thousands of lobbyists who work full-time to influence votes in Congress and actions by federal agencies to the benefit of the interest group they represent.

There is no magical way to cultivate either official or unofficial sources at the federal level. It takes time and patience and reputation—all built up over a considerable period. Such sources will want to see how individual reporters handle material in general before they will entrust them with the delicate task of revealing their secrets.

Receiving Official Information

It is not difficult to get on official mailing lists provided a reporter is accredited, a process that involves application, a security check, and issuing of appropriate I.D. badges. Indeed, after a time, a reporter may feel buried in material, some of it useful, much of it not. It is better to get everything that comes out of a public affairs office, however, than restrict what comes in. If a reporter keeps on top of the daily mail, he or she need not be buried. It is a good idea to file useful material regularly and throw the rest away before it builds up to a useless mound. (Such files should be augmented with general background materials from other publications, along with reference books about how the particular agency being covered works.)

Beyond the seeming avalanche of news releases and sometimes self-serving documents from congressional committees and individual members are verbatim transcripts of hearings. Although they are not available immediately after the hearings end, they provide useful background on the subject under investigation and reporters should save them for future reference. When a congressional committee holds hearings on a subject, it can usually enlist the testimony of the foremost experts in the country. The transcript of this testimony and other information entered into the official record is compiled into book-length documents that can be invaluable. And, they are usually free for the asking.

The same kind of permanent record is published in the *Congressional Record*—a daily compilation of what is said on the floor of the Senate and House of Representatives when both bodies are in session. Much of what takes place is pure rhetoric, however, designed to influence voters at home. The real work of Congress takes place in congressional hearings and committees.

Attending Official Events

The White House and most major executive departments conduct official briefings for the press at a set time each day. Reporters covering these departments are notified in advance of the briefings and will need to be present to get official news releases, statements, or other printed materials and to hear any official statement read by the press officer, usually followed up by a question and answer period. On occasion, the president or cabinet secretary may appear at the regular briefing. These official events rarely elicit much news but a reporter responsible for covering an agency must be there in case something important occurs. Then, too, the official announcements do present details of official plans and policies and should not be ignored.

Full-blown press conferences by the president and other agency heads are less frequent but are important sources of news, less for what is said in the inevitable official statement than in the question and answer period which follows. Another advantage to a press conference is the possibility of talking to the official—except, of course, the president—on an informal basis. In such a brief exchange a reporter can at least let the official know who he or she is.

Ceremonies, of which there are many in Washington, help reporters get a feel for the traditions the capital exemplifies, beyond whatever news value the event holds. These events include wreath layings, medal presentations, the opening of buildings, and the arrival of foreign heads of state at the White House.

Keeping Track of Laws and Regulations

Several government publications can assist reporters on that beat—or any reporter anywhere wanting to gain information about that level of government in their daily work.

The *United States Government Manual*, published annually by the federal government, lists major government agencies and their missions in brief form, along with appropriate telephone numbers. This will help keep track of all the parts of the huge federal bureaucracy.

The *Federal Register*, which comes out five days a week, gives detailed descriptions and sometimes the complete text of many government documents. The information is organized by agency name and information type, for example, agency regulation, legal document, proposed rules, notices. All of these kinds of information are required by law to be published. The *Register* may be the only place reporters can find out quickly the specific wording of new laws and regulations.

The *Code of Federal Regulations*, published annually, compiles the general and permanent rules already published in the *Federal Register*. This information is divided into fifty areas that are regulated by the federal government, for example, food and drug or securities. This helps reporters check on new laws and other regulations enacted over a whole year.

Problems and Solutions

The problems of covering any government beat—keeping up with the flow of news, meeting sources and getting them to deal openly with reporters, dealing with jargon, being used by sources with their own agendas—are compounded in Washington by the sheer number of reporters trying to uncover the same stories from the same sources. In 1945, twenty-five reporters were present when President Truman announced the dropping of the atomic bomb on Japan, according to longtime journalist Hedrick Smith. In 1987, 1,708 people had regular White House press credentials. In 1961, 1,532 reporters were accredited to cover Congress. By 1987, this number had increased to 5,250.

Everywhere a reporter goes in Washington, he or she will be surrounded by a multitude of other journalists, both print and broadcast, many from foreign media. This means that reporters from major news organizations—the *New York Times*, *Washington Post*, *Los Angeles Times*, *Time*, *Newsweek*, CBS, ABC, NBC, CNN—will easily crowd out their colleagues from less prominent media. This is because news sources always want to get the most prominent coverage possible for themselves, their ideas, and their programs. A reporter for a good, but second tier publication may have to do with the proverbial crumbs from the table. In many ways, a single reporter content to cover local politicians and agency stories affecting local interests could have an easier time. Local representatives and even United States senators with a perpetual eye on the next election cannot ignore a local reporter.

A Washington reporter can shape the coverage agenda by following the usual sources of official news as explained in the last section, cultivating enough sources, and reading enough of documents to generate background and feature stories. What will readers want to know about this event or agency or law? How will this law or policy affect their readers? Who are the officials whose actions most affect readers in their daily lives?

A good strategy for agency coverage is to follow broad subjects, then report the work of all the agencies concerned. For example, health coverage would include several divisions of the Department of Health and Human Services, the Medicare part of the Social Security Administration, and appropriate committees of Congress, along with lobbyists. Drug control might entail gathering material from the Justice Department, including the Drug Enforcement Administration, the FBI, and the Department of Treasury, Commerce, and State, along with the President's "Drug Czar." Covering the environment would include reporting on the Departments of Agriculture, Interior, and Justice and the Environmental Protection Agency, plus appropriate members and committees of Congress, and private environmental groups. Moreover, any reporting on the federal government must include actions of the Office of Management and Budget which prepares the federal budget and often decides how money is spent. (Box 2.5 explains how the federal budget deficit is financed.)

Box 2.5

How the Federal Budget Deficit is Financed

The gap between what the federal government takes in in revenues and what it spends to operate its programs is called a deficit. Although it did not seem to harm the economy during the 1980s, the deficit is considered by many to be one of the nation's biggest problems in the 1990s. The deficit increased greatly during the presidency of Ronald Reagan when the national debt tripled from $908.5 billion in 1980 to $2,684.4 trillion in 1989. By contrast, most state governments are prevented by state law from having any deficit.

Even though it theoretically does not have enough money to pay its bills, the federal government nonetheless presses on, continuing to spend money at home and abroad in a manner that suggests it didn't have a financial care in the world. How do federal officials accomplish this cynical sleight of hand? They sell U.S. Treasury securities.

The government borrows the money to pay its bills, finance the deficit, and refinance existing debt as it comes due by selling periodically three types of fixed income securities to investors: Treasury bills with due dates of three months, six months or one year; notes due in periods of two years to ten years; and bonds due in more than ten years. Investors buy the securities either at special auctions or through their brokers.

The government then uses the funds gained from such sales—a great deal of it from foreign investors—to pay its bills. The money involved in government securities is staggering: about $2.3 trillion in the Treasury bill, note, and bond market in 1991, according to the *Wall Street Journal*.

In many ways, covering the United States Supreme Court is the easiest beat in Washington. It is such a closed society—no press conferences or interviews with justices, for example. Reporters basically attend open court sessions and read the written decisions when they are handed down. Period. The most crucial part of the beat is understanding court procedure, legal terminology, and being able to interpret the ramifications of a decision.

Federal Government Reporting:
Likely Problems and How to Solve Them

Problem	**Solution**
1. Too many agencies to cover (for a single Washington reporter).	1a. Concentrate on agencies and actions in Congress affecting local readers.

	1b. Focus on people and interesting subjects.
	1c. Make a list of all agencies with potential stories and try to cover them systematically as time permits.
2. Too much material, too many events (beat reporter for larger news organization).	2a. Keep track of all activities.
	2b. Study issues in order to decide what merits coverage.
3. Complicated material, hard to understand and convey to readers.	3a. Explain how the agency operates, stress effect on local readers.
	3b. Give adequate background to readers, don't assume a pre-knowledge.
	3c. Build up a group of experts to consult on issues.
	3d. Build up files of background material from government agencies, congressional committees, and private groups like the American Civil Liberties Union, Amnesty International USA, Brookings Institution, Common Cause, Consumer Federation of America, Leadership Conference in Civil Rights, National Association for the Advancement of Colored People; read the material to keep up.
4. Writing in jargon, adopting language of bureaucrat or legislator being interviewed.	4a. Be clear and concise.
	4b. Avoid adopting jargon of the beat; always explain unfamiliar terms.

5. Becoming too close to sources, tending to help them publicize their favorite issues.

5a. Keep a distance.

5b. Select stories to do, don't let sources pick them.

5c. Don't accept gifts or favors from sources.

5d. Be objective, letting the news value of a story dictate coverage of it.

5e. Use a variety of sources for balance and avoid using the same sources for every story, however accessible they are.

Summary

Political reporting is as old as politics itself. It consists of gathering information and writing about politicians when they run for office and, once elected, their efforts to stay in office. It should not be confused with government reporting, which follows the functioning of institutions more than people. Political reporting reaches its pinnacle every four years, when a new president and state, district, and local officials are elected. Because of staggered terms, other officials are elected every two years; however, an election meriting coverage takes place every year. A presidential campaign year includes the caucus, convention, and primary period; the national convention period; the campaign period; and election day. Between election years political reporters write about how political battles are fought in Congress and state legislatures, whether winning candidates and parties live up to their promises, and what the losers are doing to regain power. Whatever the subject, the political reporter plays a central role as a chronicler and watchdog.

Covering the federal government is not all that different from covering government at any level. The biggest difference comes mainly from its size and the competition from other reporters. Reporters on various federal government beats will do best if they: cultivate knowledgeable sources; get on the mailing lists to receive a steady flow of news releases and other official materials; attend official events like press conferences, briefings and ceremonies; and keep track of new laws and regulations.

Exercises: Politics and Elections

In an Election Year:

1. Spend a day covering the campaign of a state senator, state congressional candidate, or U.S. senator. Your story can follow "a day in the campaign" approach or be more news oriented and report what the candidate said in speeches.

2. Spend a day covering the opponent of the candidate you wrote about in Exercise 1. Look for similarities and differences, and write about them.

3. Spend election night at a candidate's headquarters or the county courthouse where results are tabulated and announced. Write a story that encompasses information on important winners, their reactions, the comments of losers, and the long-term effect of the outcome in the opinion of outside experts.

In a Non-election Year:

1. Interview the local director of elections, and write a story about new voting machines, election trends, or voter registration.

2. Interview the state chairman of both political parties, and find out their views about the candidates and issues in the next election. Write a story about what you find out, comparing and contrasting the two opposing points of view.

3. Conduct research and write an article on the role of Political Action Committees in election campaigns in your state. Interview campaign officials and state elections staff members.

Exercises: Federal Government

1. Watch a presidential press conference on television or C-SPAN coverage of a congressional hearing and take notes of what goes one. Make a list of subjects covered and work out how you would structure a story (or stories) gained from your reporting.

2. Write a story using material gained in Exercise 1.

3. Visit the local office of a federal agency (check the telephone book under "U.S. Government" for a list) and obtain recent releases and background material given to reporters. Work out a list of stories to do based on your scrutiny of this material.

4. Conduct the necessary interviews and write a story based on one idea developed from your reporting in Exercise 3.

Key Terms for Political/Federal Government Reporting

Abortion Expulsion of a human fetus before it is viable; a big political issue in the United States.

Advance A person who makes arrangements in advance for the appearance of a political candidate in a city or state.

Ballot A sheet of paper used for voting.

Basic speech The same speech given day after day, typically by presidential candidates, in all parts of the nation or state.

Blue-collar vote Factory workers who tend to vote for one candidate.

Bossism Domination of a political party by a small group of political leaders, especially those from big cities.

Budget deficit The difference between what the federal government takes in in revenue and what it spends.

Campaign finance reform law A law passed in 1974 to limit the amount of money spent on presidential campaigns and provide for federal financing for candidates who qualify.

Campaign manager A person who manages the campaign of a political candidate.

Candidate A person who seeks a political office.

Catholic vote Members of the Catholic Church who tend to vote for the same candidate.

Caucus The meeting of local members of a political party to nominate candidates and determine policy.

Checks and balances The process built into the United States Constitution whereby one branch of government can amend or void laws or actions of the other two branches.

Closed primary A primary in which only registered voters of a particular party can vote.

Commercials Television and radio advertisements paid for by political candidates to extol their attributes.

Conservative One who tends to want to preserve existing institutions and conditions.

Convention The periodic gathering of national or state political party members to select candidates for office and adopt a platform of programs.

Debates Public discussions between opposing candidates on issues and on reasons people should vote for them.

Defense spending Amount of money spent on national defense; usually an issue in presidential campaigns.

Delegate A person designated to act for and represent others at a meeting.

Dirty tricks Deliberate sabotage by the workers of one candidate against the campaign of another.

Economy The organized system of managing money and resources to create employment and well-being; whether good or bad, the state of the economy is always an important campaign issue.

Election   The selection of people to fill public offices at a series of polling places on the same day.

Endorsement   Recommendation of a person (or group representative) to vote for a candidate; depending on the person or group, the endorsement might be influential.

Equal Rights Amendment   A proposed amendment to the United States Constitution granting equal rights to women.

Equal-time rule   The Federal Communications Commission rule that all political candidates must have equal access to radio and television.

Farm vote   The way farmers vote in elections.

Favorite son   A person whose candidacy for president is advocated only by his or her friends in the state; sometimes used to hide support for a well-known candidate until later.

Federal Elections Commission   Organization that supervises the government funding of presidential election campaigns.

GOP   Acronym for "Grand Old Party"; another name for the Republican party.

Grass-roots politics   Political organization and campaigning on a state and local level rather than on a national level.

Gun control   The question of whether the sale of handguns should be regulated; always a controversial issue in state and national campaigns.

Handler   An aide to a politician or public official whose job it is to suggest strategies for influencing public opinion.

Infrastructure   The basic structure of a country, including roads, highways, bridges, and communications systems.

Jewish vote   Voters of Jewish origin who tend to cast their vote for the same candidate.

Labor vote   Members of organized labor who tend to vote for one candidate.

Leak   The deliberate disclosure of information to the media by a government official or candidate for political reasons.

Liberal   One who favors change and reform.

Lobbyists   People paid by special interest groups to influence the votes of legislators.

Media events   Campaign events designed to attract the attention of the media, primarily television.

National Committee   Main organizational body of political parties, Democratic and Republican, headed by a chairperson.

Nomination   The act or process by which a political party chooses a candidate to run for office.

Open primary   A primary in which all registered voters can vote.

Opinion polls   The periodic sampling of the opinions of a carefully selected group of participants about various candidates and issues.

Oversight   The responsibility of committees of Congress to keep track of executive branch agencies in terms of commenting upon handling of affairs and approving budgets.

PAC   Political Action Committee, a fund-raising technique used by candidates in elections.

Pack journalism   The tendency of national reporters, especially in an election campaign, to do the same stories, ask the same questions, almost seeming to "gang up" on candidates.

Photo opportunity   A photo session with the president or any public official during which no questions are allowed.

Platform   A set of principles on which a political party takes a stand.

Poll watcher   A person who observes polling places on election day to make sure no irregularities take place.

Precinct   A subdivision of a city or town marked off for voting purposes.

Primary   A preliminary election in which voters of each party nominate candidates for office and party officials.

Right-to-life movement   A political group opposed to abortion.

Separation of powers   The system of vesting in separate branches the executive, legislative, and judicial powers of a government.

Smoke-filled room   The old way of selecting a candidate for president in which political leaders sat in a room and made the choice.

Sound bite   The few words—often provocative—that are uttered by a candidate or public official that wind up being used in a television news report.

Spin   Putting a certain political slant on events or perceptions of events to influence reporters and the public.

Trial balloon   A tentative statement or action designed to test public reaction to it.

Vote   A formal expression of opinion or choice on a candidate or an issue as expressed through the casting of a ballot.

Voter   One who votes; the prize of all politicians.

Voter registration   The registration of voters so they will be eligible to vote in the next election; registration drives are sometimes conducted by the two political parties to get more voters for their candidates.

Write-in campaign   An organized campaign to encourage voters to write on the ballot the name of a candidate who is not already listed on the ballot.

Gilded pediment eagle, Charleston, South Carolina, March 1936 by Walker
Evans. [*Courtesy U.S. Farm Security Administration Collection, Prints
and Photographs Division, Library of Congress*]

3

State Government

Government is a trust, and the officers of the government are trustees; and both the trust and the trustees are created for the benefit of the people.

—Henry Clay

One State Government Reporter

Brad Cain's life as a reporter has two distinct parts.

Once every two years for six or seven months, he spends most of his waking hours covering the Oregon Legislature in that state's capital, Salem. After the legislature adjourns in late June or early July, he switches his attention to the other branches of government and politics.

"You have to be flexible," says Cain, who is the Associated Press correspondent in Salem. That is an understatement for any wire service reporter who, by the nature of his or her job, meets one constant deadline from morning until night. With so many news-papers and broadcast clients to serve, the work is constant and hectic and, in Cain's case, very rewarding. "I'm a citizen too and pay taxes and raise my family," he says. "I get a kick out of doing my civic duty in bringing news to people about how their state government operates."

During a legislature year, Cain's day begins about 8 A.M. when he arrives at the dingy press room in the basement of the Capitol Building. He and his partner, news reporter Charles Beggs, share cramped quarters in a large, windowless room with reporters from *The Oregonian*, the *Salem Statesman-Journal*, the *Eugene Register-Guard*, and United Press International. Cain and Beggs sit at two facing desks in the open room. The AP also has a small closet-sized cubicle a few feet away where the two send their stories to the main bureau in Portland via two computer terminals.

The small space means that no reporters have any privacy as they write at their desks and conduct telephone interviews. "Obviously, you do hear things from other reporters," says Cain. "But there is honor among thieves and people don't take advantage of the situation. But I have to tell you, if I overheard someone saying, 'What exactly did the governor die of?' I wouldn't ignore it. There are some stories I don't care how I hear. A story's a story. Sometimes we confer in the small cubicle. I conduct some interviews in the capitol coffee shop down the hall."

On his way to the press room, Cain has stopped at the Bill Room to pick up a printed schedule of all committee hearings and the floor sessions of the house and senate. He and Beggs confer on what to cover and spend the rest of the day doing just that.

At first, it is hard to determine the importance of a bill or a committee meeting, based on the cryptic one-line entry on the schedule. "It will say, 'House Bill 800 relating to dogcatchers,'" he says. "You wonder what that is and get the bill and read it. Three months later, when you come across HB 800, you know what it is."

Cain also bases his decisions about coverage on what he thinks the eighteen daily newspapers in the state who are AP clients are covering themselves or might want him to look into. He also is responsible for sending a broadcast version of his stories to the AP's sixty radio and television stations in Oregon.

These preliminary activities out of the way, Cain turns his attention to writing the "menu," a list of all the stories he and Beggs will be working on the rest of the day and filing. The AP adds this to a longer menu dealing with its coverage from the entire state and sends it to clients for use in laying out pages and determining news priorities. If a story does not work out, Cain will send a "late news advisory," telling the Portland bureau to disregard some earlier items, and will usually add several new stories.

"There's no real science to dividing up the stories to cover," continues Cain. "We have no real line of demarcation between who covers what; we rotate things around. There are obviously issues one becomes familiar with. For example, this last session I became the expert on the video poker issue. My partner covered school finance. But there was no plan in the beginning to do it that way."

As Cain makes the rounds of legislative hearings, he sits down and listens to what is being said and leaves if it isn't newsworthy. As an accredited state government reporter he is allowed to occupy one of the small desks at the sides of each chamber when the house or senate is in session and take notes quietly, no laptop computers allowed. If he wants to talk to a representative or senator personally, however, he must ask a page to ask the legislator and then the two will walk to the rear of the chamber to confer. He also gets good background information from committee staff members and aides to legislators.

"If I go to the chamber, it's because of a bill I am covering," he says. "I catch the debate and record the vote. Often, I'll pull people aside and ask them to clarify what they've said. These people [the legislators] are not always real clear. Once I have all the information in hand, I'll scamper back to the office and write the story. This is not a large building so it is easy to gather material for stories and then go to the office and write and send in the story. During the session we file continuously, probably five to ten stories a day."

Except in the last few frantic weeks of the session, when legislators are trying to adjourn by July 1, the day ends by 7 P.M. "There is not much night work here," says Cain. "Even when it gets hectic, it is not really hard to keep up. There is a rhythm to it. You get a sense of where they are."

After the legislature adjourns, the correspondent turns his attention to covering everything else in Oregon's government—the supreme court, court of appeals, state agencies, and politics. He keeps what he calls a tickler file—a series of folders labeled one to thirty-one in which he puts cryptic notes to remind himself of things that will be taking place on certain days.

Here he is helped by a group of sources in various state agencies who he can call for updates on activities. The courts issue dockets listing their upcoming hearings. In an election year, many stories revolve around election campaigns. Even if they don't wind up with a Salem dateline, Cain covers them from his office by telephone.

"The value of these agency sources is that they can turn gibberish into something," he says. These experts were even more important to Cain in his last AP post, as second reporter in the AP bureau in Jefferson City, the capital of Missouri. "It was very difficult," he continues, "and I wasn't a green pea either. This is my fifth AP bureau—after Chicago, St. Louis, Kansas City, and Jefferson City. But it was really tough, not only knowing the technical issues at hand but how the legislature itself works. State government is really one of the toughest beats. I felt dazed. You just have to muddle through. Some colleagues are helpful, glad to take a rookie in tow. That legislature had a chart—how a bill becomes law—which helped. But I mainly learned by hitting and missing."

Some of what he learned in Missouri was easily transferred to his assignment in Oregon, some not. "In Oregon, there was a whole new set of issues," he says. "In my mind, Missouri and Oregon are blended together."

Cain encounters only one major problem as he carries out his job. "During sessions, there is not time to really develop stories," he says. "For example, if there is a bill on unifying school districts, I'm not able to take it outside this building. If a hearing goes into the need to control drug houses in Northeast Portland, I have to rely on the police detective who testifies. It would be nice to go to that area myself, but there's no time. Many times, I wish I could get more deeply into a subject."

He offers several suggestions to people planning careers as state government reporters: "You have to enjoy politics, but without taking sides. Beware of people who try to put their spin on the story by giving you only their point of view. We have no friends or enemies. We just tell it all, without getting caught up in the story. This means you try for a certain amount of detachment. If I would get involved in an issue, then someone else should cover it. People read my stories and my mission will be accomplished if they get both sides and make their own judgments."

Background to State Government Reporting

Newspapers began to cover the activities of state government when their editors and publishers decided it was in their best interest financially to do so. Editors like James Gordon Bennett of the *New York Herald* and Horace Greeley of the *New York Tribune* saw the value of presenting news of government as a way to sell papers as early as 1835.

Bennett, especially, made good use of information gained from reporters assigned to the president and Congress. Other newspapers followed this lead when their editors saw that such government stories were well received. As still happens today, newspapers around the country were influenced greatly by New York publications. These newspapers started covering the activities of state legislatures. This early coverage, until well into the twentieth century, was of an exposé nature much of the time.

The corruption that will be noted in the chapter on local government existed in state governments as well, although it was not as widespread. In Missouri late in the nineteenth century, for example, the lobbyists representing the railroads and business interests of the state virtually controlled party caucuses in the legislature. In New Jersey, leaders of the dominant Republican party were also in control of the business and financial community. They bought and sold judges and state officials. The press was slow to report this story. In fact, it was not until the early twentieth century that the muckrakers exposed the corruption in the state governments (see Chapter 6).

Problems and Solutions

Editors and reporters too often report only what Thomas B. Littlewood, a former Springfield, Illinois, state capital reporter, calls "the clowns and crooks and trivia that are a part of every legislative scene." They never treat the relevant issues with much clarity and depth. Vital questions go unanswered. Do cities get an adequate share of the state budget? How do regional interests align (rural versus urban, farmers versus business leaders)? What is the quality of state government officials? How influential are lobbyists and other representatives of special-interest groups?

Littlewood says that the image of the legislature as a "den of intrigue" stands in the way of a better exploration of these larger issues. So do the limits on time and resources of the too few government beat reporters. Other problems are the complicated nature of laws, regulations, and issues in state government and the fact that much of it makes boring reading. Reporters, who often use their state experience as a stepping-stone to Washington assignments, may not bother to acquire the depth of knowledge they need to do the job adequately. This is less of a problem on the local level where there are fewer agencies and less complicated issues and where expectations are lower because the beat is often assigned to beginners.

Reporters on the state government beat have three basic problems: 1) Although the subjects they cover are of vital interest to readers as citizens, these readers often ignore the stories because they become bored and/or lack the basic knowledge to understand what they are reading; 2) Reporters are required to cover too many government entities—the governor, the legislature, the courts, and numerous agencies—to do a thorough job on any; 3) They must work closely with the people they write about, and many of these sources have a vested interest in favorable publicity.

The average citizen's knowledge of state government is frighteningly low. Most pay their taxes but give the matter scant attention after that. They have little idea how legislators and government agency bureaucrats spend their tax money.

Reporters dutifully record what goes on in the official hearings and other meetings in terms of who, what, when, and even how. What they often fail to reveal is *why*. It is easy for government reporters to get caught up, like "groupies," in the details of the legislative process. The challenge is for them to explain the process to those not as informed—the citizens who pay the taxes that keep the government functioning.

Reporters who cover government have one shot at a person's attention. They will lose their readers if they waste that opportunity with too many words, vague concepts, and mysterious acronyms. They will be more successful if they act as the eyes and ears of their readers and as their chroniclers.

The plethora of government agencies to keep track of is staggering in most state capitals. News organizations rarely staff statehouse bureaus adequately to do the job well. The result is a concentration on dramatic and one-time stories—the scandalous, the inefficient, the ridiculous.

The governor and the legislature get most of the attention, in a kind of "squeaky-wheel-gets-the-grease" way. Both entities by their very nature do things publicly that affect people either in general (by raising or lowering taxes) or in specific groups (by requiring motorcycle riders to wear helmets or beauty operators to take examinations).

Broader questions concerning the quality of air citizens breathe, the water they drink, and the use of the land they live on often have to be ignored. Such issues are normally dealt with in the permanent agencies that get less press attention.

A state capital is like a small town, even if its geographic boundaries are large. A relatively small group of people form the basic pool of sources. Reporters find themselves going back again and again to the same officials for stories. All of the people interviewed have an interest in the subject the reporter wants to find out about. The governor is pushing a specific program, a legislator is publicizing a favorite bill, a lobbyist is protecting the subject area he or she is paid to protect, and a bureaucrat is trying to save his or her job.

It is only natural for such advocates to put their projects in the best possible light and be selective in providing facts. It is common for these sources to talk in the jargon of their specialized areas. Reporters owe it to their readers to remain outside the snare of these vested interests and the quicksand of the often indecipherable verbiage.

Because of the large number of reporters covering certain parts of state government — the governor and the legislature — a certain "pack" mentality exists. Unless they are careful, statehouse reporters tend to go to the same events and write stories about the same subjects, subsisting on a diet of news releases and other handouts. They owe it to their readers to go beyond the predictable and play the role of the skeptic at times.

In the 1990s there have been a lot of high-visibility stories coming out of state capitals, most of them dealing with budget shortages and state government attempts to do something about them without raising taxes. In the 1970s, states and cities got used to federal support, which increased to as high as 29 percent of their total budgets. During the 1980s, however, the Reagan Administration cut funding for states to 16.8 percent.

These cuts came at the same time that responsibility for programs like welfare were shifted to the states. Congress also enacted laws requiring cleaner water, but Reagan cut funds for sewage plants. Medical coverage for the poor expanded at the same time a requirement was added for the states to pay half. This resulted in a growth in Medicaid costs from 9 percent of state spending in 1980 to 14 percent in 1991.

Federal court mandates to ease prison overcrowding by limiting the number of inmates per cell has also increased state costs by requiring them to build more prisons. In some states judges have ordered legislatures to impose tax increases to equalize spending for schools between rich and poor areas.

Added to these problems are substandard housing in nearly every state, a decaying system of roads and bridges with no funds for repairs, and large increases in salaries for state workers — which drives up budgets — because politicians are afraid the workers might go on strike.

All of these stories make state capital reporting less the backwater it once was.

More suggestions on dealing with the state government beat can be found in "Likely Problems and How to Solve Them" later in this chapter.

How to Cover State Government

Reporting government at the local, state, or federal level has its similarities as well as its differences. The institutions affect the citizens they control in contrasting ways. For example, a person feels the immediate effect of a local law regulating seat belt use compared to a federal law dealing with foreign trade. The three levels also have a vastly different financial base and varying amounts of funds.

All state government reporters can do well by following a few basic rules.

1. **Learn your way around.**   Statehouse reporters should find out where to get copies of bills and the location of the offices of key legislators and agency heads. They should learn where hearing rooms are located.

2. **Learn the system of government.** How does a piece of legislation originate, and what happens to it as it proceeds to defeat or passage into law? What are the factors that cause some bills to proceed through the process fairly quickly and others to be derailed permanently? It helps to read a good basic government text and to attend orientation sessions for freshman legislators. Some legislators publish booklets on how a bill becomes law. Figure 3.1 and Box 3.1 help explain the operation of state government.

3. **Establish good sources.** A reporter new to the state government beat needs to identify key legislators and staff members as well as agency heads and then make a concerted effort to meet and get to know them. It is not a bad idea to memorize the faces of all members. Beyond the official sources, it is important to develop a rapport with committee clerks, secretaries, and non-government people like lobbyists, consultants, and political scientists at local colleges. Out of all these acquaintances will emerge the handful of people who are useful and trustworthy.

4. **Don't get too close to sources.** Even though it is crucial to the success of a government reporter to establish good official and unofficial sources, it is equally vital not to get too close to them. In a small state legislature there develops a kind of close-knit, "we're all in this together" atmosphere. The legislature is like an exclusive club to which reporters are admitted for a purpose. The atmosphere can get very claustrophobic and the unwary reporter can wind up compromised by a legislator or a lobbyist pushing one bill or point of view or the other. A good reporter will do business with anyone but at the same time, keep his or her eyes and ears open to attempts to trick them into writing a one-sided story.

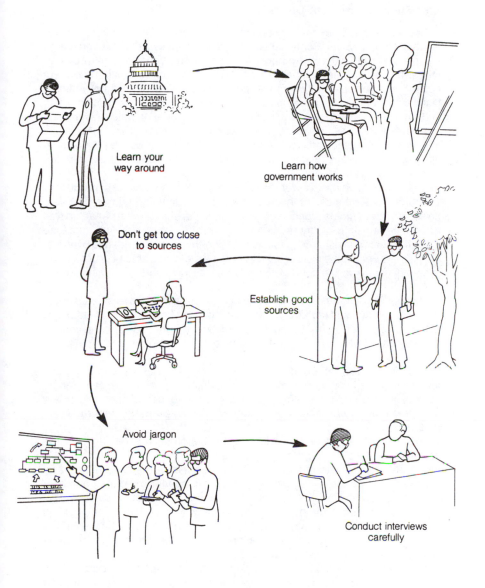

Figure 3.1   **How to cover state government**

Box 3.1

How State Government Operates

The typical state government is headed by a *governor*, who is elected to office every four years. Some states elect other officials; lieutenant governor, secretary of state, attorney general, treasurer, comptroller, agriculture commissioner, land commissioner, railroad commissioner, and superintendent of public instruction. The governor appoints a number of other agency heads: highway commissioner, banking commissioner, insurance commissioner, fish and game commissioner, and the trustees or regents of state universities.

A governor acts as the chief of state, the highest elected official in the state, and the appointer of officials. Although a governor proposes an annual budget, the legislature modifies the amounts in it and oversees the governor's expenditure of the money.

Governors have the power of *clemency*; that is, they can pardon or commute the sentences of those convicted of committing crimes. The veto power of a governor is significant. This refusal to sign the bills enacted into law by the legislature often makes the governor's word absolute, because it is difficult for a legislature to muster the two-thirds vote needed to override.

The members of the *judiciary*, including the state supreme court, the court of criminal appeals, the court of civil appeals, district courts, and minor courts are also elected.

The *legislature* is elected. It consists of a senate and a house of representatives in all states but Nebraska, which has only one house. Some states have full-time legislators, who are paid a salary and meet in session every year. Others consist of "citizen" legislators, who hold other jobs and meet every other year.

The single most important responsibility of a legislature is to make the laws that govern the state. It also has the financial power to raise revenue, provide for expenditures, and administer the finances of the state. State revenues usually come from three kinds of taxes: property, general sales, and income.

The legislative process by which a bill becomes law begins with the introduction of a bill by a member, a group of members, or a committee. Bills are drafted by the attorney general at the request of the governor and by state agency heads, lobbyists, attorneys for special-interest groups, or legislators themselves. A member introduces a bill either by discussing it in a speech on the floor of the legislature or by filing it in the "hopper" (a collection point for bills under consideration, usually an "in" basket on the desk of the clerk). Either way, the clerk assigns the bill to the committee with jurisdiction over that subject area.

The committee holds public hearings on the bill during the course of the legislative session. Interested people are invited to participate by arguing in support or opposition. A legislature includes a number of standing committees on various subject areas; these standing committees may be special or select (to look at temporary problems), interim (to do work between sessions of the legislature), and joint (to make changes in the wording of bills so as to avoid differences between the two houses).

After a bill has been heard in the appropriate committee, it will be considered by each house of the legislature. A bill is usually introduced into both houses at the same time; any differences on provisions are ironed out later in the joint committee. A bill normally gets three readings: 1) before all members, at its introduction, when only the title is read aloud; 2) during floor debate, when amendments might be offered by other members; and 3) just before the final vote, when amendments have already been added to it. A quorum of members must be present to enact a bill into law.

After the vote, a bill is ready for consideration by the other house. After passage it goes to the governor's desk for signature or veto.

The size of legislatures varies among the different states. The names of the houses also vary. The house of representatives in one state may be the house of delegates or general assembly in another.

The basis for representation differs as well. The upper house usually has the longer term. In three-fourths of the states it is four years; in the others it is two. Most lower house members have two-year terms. In some states terms are staggered so part of the membership comes up for election every two years.

Sessions historically began after the corn had been picked and the Christmas holidays observed. The tradition has remained, and most legislatures begin in January of odd-numbered years and continue for sixty or ninety days. Because sessions are too short to get everything finished, they are often held every year.

A speaker presides over the lower house. This person is elected by the entire membership; the choice of candidates are made in caucus by members of the majority party. In states with a lieutenant governor, that official presides over the senate; if there is no lieutenant governor, senate members choose their own president.

Members of a legislature come from the two major political parties with an occasional third-party or independent member. The legislators run for office and are elected for a specific term.

While in office they look after the interests of their *constituents*, the people in their districts. They serve on various committees and meet with the house or senate as a whole. They keep in touch with constituents by visiting the district, by mail, and by seeing them in their offices in the state capitol building.

Legislators are also influenced by *lobbyists*, people representing organized groups with the same interests and viewpoints, who are hired to influence policy. Lobbyists, who must register with the government they are trying to influence, represent a wide variety of special interest groups.

The legislators vote after receiving often conflicting information from all of these groups and from citizens in their districts.

Soon after a national census, legislatures also have the power of redistricting (sometimes called *gerrymandering* — that is, to redraw the boundary lines of congressional districts based on changes in population numbers).

5. **Avoid jargon.** Legislators and bureaucrats use so many unfamiliar terms and mysterious acronyms in written documents and even casual conversations that a reporter must be careful to keep them out of stories. This can best be done by getting sources to explain what they are talking about right in the interview or by consulting outside experts. Reporters need to keep in mind that they write for citizens, not legislators or bureaucrats.

6. **Conduct interviews carefully and prepare for them thoroughly.** A reporter who interviews a government agency official or legislator should be familiar with the subject beforehand through background reading and the cumulative knowledge gained on the beat. It helps to think that there are no embarrassing or dumb questions. When the query is answered both reporters and their readers learn.

7. **Remain interested no matter what.**   Amid the boredom that comes with the government beat are important stories on subjects that will affect readers. Reporters cannot get so bored they tune out, thinking they have heard it all before. That would be unfair to readers and government sources.

Kinds of State Government Stories

Stories from the state government beat fall into a number of common categories:

1. **News of government agencies.** How these agencies enforce laws and regulations and the effect on citizens. The organization of new departments and the inefficiency and/or corruption in old ones.

2. **News of the legislature.** The content of bills, the leadership, the slowness or swiftness in the way it works, committee hearings, and scandal and corruption.

3. **News of the state supreme court and court of appeals.** Non-criminal matters come before these courts and some may affect the government and citizens directly.

4. **News of the governor.** What the governor does from day-to-day or proposes in the way of programs. Who he or she sees, appoints, or fires. How the governor works or plays and how he or she runs the state political machinery.

5. **People features.** Who are the dominant people in the state capital? Who are the so-called little people who make things work?

Who are the people behind the news? Who is the most influential legislator or staff member or lobbyist?

6. **Background articles.** How the system works. Problems of the state and how they are or are not being solved.

7. **Tie-ins with national issues.** How the state is coping with a problem felt elsewhere (for example, effects of inflation on revenues, redistricting for legislative and congressional seats, or televising legislative sessions).

Writing State Government Stories

"In my writing, I strive for the conversational approach," says Associated Press Correspondent Brad Cain. "This means you keep it simple and imagine when you are writing that you are just talking over the back fence with a neighbor. Beginning reporters use ponderous prose filled with dazzling words they somehow think add weight to the story. They seldom do. The AP tells us to write short, simple, declarative sentences using the active voice."

News stories are typically 400 words, most using the inverted pyramid style. The AP really invented that approach to writing news during the Civil War for the very reason it works well now. If a reporter puts the essence of the story — the who, what, when, where, why, and how — into the lead, readers will understand it even if the story is interrupted, then by enemy troops cutting telegraph lines, now by AP member newspapers who regularly lop off stories for lack of space to run them.

Cain is encouraged to use other styles as well, in his words, "pieces so seamless no one would dare to cut out grafs." He does follow such non-inverted pyramid styles whenever he can, especially on longer stories which rarely go beyond 800 words without special permission.

He has the responsibility to write broadcast versions of every story and finds it useful to do them before his print pieces. "I have to distill the essence of the story into three or four sentences and this helps me do my stories for newspapers."

One of the biggest aids in his writing is the file of clips which he uses for background information beyond what he has picked up in interviews and attendance at the legislative sessions and committee hearings. He has one filing cabinet filled with folders filed by category into which he puts newspaper clippings of his and other reporters' work, most recent first. "You have to have a good, up-to-date clip file because there is no time to call someone up to get background on something. You ask yourself, 'What did the legislature do on this subject last session' and get into the file to find out.''

#1

PAY HIKES SOUGHT
FOR STATE OFFICIALS
By Brad Cain
The Associated Press

This good summary lead details a pay raise proposal and who is making it, followed by a few words giving another side.

1 SALEM (AP)—A state commission has proposed pay raises for Oregon's top elected officials and judges, but at least two of those officials said Friday they don't want an increase.

Grafs 2, 3, 4, 5, and 6 augment the lead by directly quoting one of the "officials."

2 Secretary of State Phil Keisling and State Treasurer Tony Meeker said that with budget problems looming in the wake of Measure 5, this isn't the time to give pay hikes to high-ranking officials.

3 "I don't think the Legislature will pass it," Keisling said of the proposed pay boosts. "I wouldn't take it if they did."

4 "These are tough times for all of us," Keisling said.

5 The secretary of state said, however, that he believes pay hikes for rank-and-file state workers would be justified.

6 "There are many people in government who do deserve pay increases to let them keep up with the cost of living and health care," Keisling said.

Grafs 7 and 8 quote a spokesman for the other official.

7 A spokesman for Meeker, Mike Ryan, said the state treasurer agrees that proposed pay hikes for top officials are ill-timed.

8 "In light of Measure 5, Tony feels it would be inappropriate to talk about increasing officials' salaries," Ryan said.

In graf 9, Cain tells the reader the amount of salary increase both of these officials would get.

9 Both Keisling's and Meeker's salaries would increase from the current level of $61,500 to $64,000 under a recommendation from the state Public Officials Compensation Commission.

He goes on in grafs 10 and 11 to give the salaries and increases of the governor and attorney general. Following this, a spokeswoman for the attorney general gives his reaction.

10 Governor Barbara Roberts' annual $80,000 salary would remain the same under the commission's proposals.

11 The annual salary of Attorney General Dave Frohnmayer would increase from $66,000 to $72,000.

12 Asked whether the attorney general thinks salary hikes should be given at this point, Frohnmayer spokeswomen Marla Rae said, "Candidly, he hasn't given it any thought."

13 "He assumes that the salaries of all public employees, not just elected ones, will be the subject of a healthy debate in the Legislature," Rae said.

Graf 14 gives readers some background to put the salary issue into the context of the whole budget shortage.

14 The state is facing a budget squeeze mainly because Measure 5, the property tax limit enacted by voters, forces the state to replace $633 million that local schools will lose because of the tax cut.

Graf 15 indicates what salary increases were included in the budget.

15 Even so, the governor's proposed 1991-93 state budget includes $66 million for salary and benefit increases, subject to negotiations with employee unions.

Graf 16 tells the status of the measure, while grafs 17 and 18 quote a member of the commission with reasons for the recommendation.

16 The compensation commission's pay raise recommendations for top officials are contained in a measure, SB 448, that was introduced in the Legislature this week.

17 Robert Ingalls of Corvallis, a member of the compensation commission, said the citizen panel came up with what it considers reasonable salary recommendations.

18 "The Legislature can make its own decision (on the pay hikes) in view of Measure 5," Ingalls said Friday. "That should be their decision, not ours."

The story ends with more salaries and proposed increases. In the classic AP style, the story could be cut anywhere after graf 16 without losing any meat or meaning.

19 Under the commission's proposal, the $61,500 salaries of state School Superintendent Norma Paulus and Labor Commissioner Mary Wendy Roberts would rise by only $100 a year each.

20 However, the commission proposes hefty increases for members of the Oregon Supreme Court and Oregon Court of Appeals.

21 The annual salaries of Supreme Court judges would go from $76,400 to $96,000 while Appeals Court judges' pay would rise from $74,600 to $93,695.

Total interviews: 4, all but one in the Capitol Building.

22 And the pay of circuit court judges and district court judges would go from $69,600 to $81,600.

#2

NUMBER OF LOBBYISTS AT OREGON CAPITOL INCREASES
By Brad Cain
The Associated Press

This is a typical news feature reported and written during the legislative session when Brad Cain was chasing news stories. He leads with a general summary of what lobbyists do, followed by facts on who they represent (2), and how many there are (3) and (4).

1 SALEM (AP)—Each working day, several hundred lobbyists descend on the Capitol in hopes of influencing a legislative session dominated by Measure 5 budget problems.

2 Representing interests such as business, labor, education and local government, the lobbyists are part of an army whose ranks appear to be growing.

3 As of last month, 1,147 people had registered to lobby the Legislature, compared with 967 people at the same point during the 1989 legislative session, according to the state Ethics Commission.

4 The current session appears well on its way toward drawing more lobbyists than the record 1,400 who had registered by the end of the Legislature's 1989 session, said Pat Hearn, executive director of the commission.

Graf 5 gives reasons for the increase, followed by a quote from one (6 and 7) and a summary of what others said (8).

5 Lawmakers, lobbyists and others said the increase can be attributed partly to better compliance with a law requiring anyone who spends much time trying to influence legislation to register as a lobbyist.

6 Salem lobbyist Mark Nelson, for instance, said he hasn't noticed a big increase in the number of what he considered hard-core, full-time, paid lobbyists.

7 "You have a lot more people who are registering because they don't want to run afoul of the lobby registration laws," Nelson said.

8 Others who were interviewed, however, said they have observed more lobbyists and more lobbying going on at the Capitol these days.

In graf 9 he states once more, as he does in nearly every story, the fact that the new property tax limit is dominating everything. He quotes another lobbyist to that effect (10 and 11).

9 And they said the budget squeeze brought on by Measure 5, the property tax limit passed by voters, accounts for some of that as various special interests fight for their piece of the state budget pie.

10 "You go outside of hearing rooms and look down the hallways and it's a traffic jam of lobbyists," said Ted Hughes, one of Salem's most successful contract lobbyists.

11 "If your pet programs are subject to cuts, are you going to accept it and say, 'Too bad,' or come here and try to change things?" Hughes asked.

In grafs 12, 13, and 14, he quotes a member of the legislature.

12 Rep. Bruce Hugo, D-Scappoose, noted that for the first time the Eugene, Beaverton and Oregon City school districts have hired their own lobbyists to keep an eye on things in Salem.

13 Those districts don't want to have to depend solely on education associations to protect their interests when it comes to fighting for state school aid dollars in the wake of Measure 5 budget problems, Hugo said.

14 "Those people are going to be down here to make sure they are taken care of," Hugo said. "It's enlightened self-interest."

Having quoted a representative, he switches to a senator on the same subject (15, 16, 17).

15 Sen. Lenn Hannon, R-Ashland, said he's noticed a steady increase in the number of lobbyists in his 17 years as a lawmaker.

16 "Each session there are more and more people," Hannon said. "Measure 5 has certainly added to that."

17 "I told my staff, 'There aren't enough hours in the day to meet with all of the special interests that want to meet with me,'" Hannon said.

In graf 18, he changes from Measure 5 to another reason for the increase in lobbyists.

18 Measure 5 aside, Hughes said, more lobbyists are roaming the halls of the Capitol because special interests know the federal government has shifted more and more regulatory power to the states.

In graf 21, he notes what lobbyists spent in the last session and what they spent it on.

He amplifies one item (wining and dining), given Oregon's "super clean" and ethical reputation. He quotes a Common Cause spokes-man (22) and tells readers what the law says legislators can accept (23).

He ends the story by letting the Common Cause source raise a mild alarm about what all of this is doing to the Legislature.

Total interviews: 6, all in the Capitol Building. Unlike the news story, this feature would be harder for editors to cut. It was also accom-panied by a photo of lobbyists at work in Salem.

19   That means it often is the Legislature that can most directly help or hurt businesses or other special interests, he said.

20   "Businesses are becoming aware that they had better start getting involved" in the legislative process, Hughes said.

21   To help get their point of view across to lawmakers, special interests spent a record $8.4 million lobbying the 1989 legislative session. That included the cost of wining and dining lawmakers; printing, postage and telephone bills; advertising, public relations and research.

22   David Buchanan, executive director of Oregon Common Cause, said he's not as bothered by the wining and dining and other perks lobbyists offer to lawmakers as he is by the issue of campaign contributions.

23   State law prohibits campaign money from flowing when the Legislature is in session. That means lobbyists can't offer campaign contributions and lawmakers can't solicit or receive such money.

24   Still, Buchanan said lawmakers can't help but be influenced to some degree by campaign money they receive before the session or the money they hope to get from special interests after the session adjourns.

25   "Being taken out to dinner is nothing when what you really need from a special interest is a $5,000 or $10,000 campaign contribution," Buchanan said.

26   For that reason, Common Cause favors placing limits on campaign contributions as a way to cut down on special interests' influence over the Legislature, he said.

State Government Reporting:
Likely Problems and How to Solve Them

Problem	**Solution**
1. Dull subject matter, boring to readers.	1a. Humanize stories.
	1b. Explain significance to average reader.
2. Complicated subjects; readers lack basic understanding of government processes.	2a. Explain how government operates.
	2b. Give adequate background to readers; don't assume they have any preknowledge.
	2c. Build up group of experts, such as political science professors, to consult.
	2d. Do background reading in state and national reference books; get on the mailing list for material from organizations interested in state government issues like Common Cause, the Brookings Institution, the National Governors' Association, the Council of State Governments, and local and state good government associations.
3. Becoming too close to sources, tending to help them publicize their "pet" causes.	3a. Keep a distance.
	3b. Select what stories to do, don't let sources pick them.
	3c. Be objective; never advocate causes or promote special interests.
	3d. Use a variety of sources for balance.

4. Writing in jargon, adopting language of the bureaucrat or legislator.

   4a. Be clear and concise.

   4b. Avoid adopting the language of the beat.

   4c. Explain unfamiliar terms carefully.

5. Too many agencies to cover and not enough space and time to do job adequately.

   5a. Cover breaking news as necessary.

   5b. Make a list of all agencies with potential stories, and do something on them systematically as time permits.

6. Learn the nuances of society in your state; that is, the forces at work behind the scenes.

   6a. Become familiar with sources and issues at the state branch of the National Association of Colored People; pro- and anti-abortion groups; lobbyists for banking, transportation, agriculture, education, timber, fishing, or other interests vital to your state's economy.

   6b. Once in a while, as time permits, step back and do a story on where the state is going, how it will deal with future problems.

Summary

People need to know about the men and women and institutions that govern them on local, regional, state, and federal levels. Information about these executive, legislative, and judicial agencies is gathered by government reporters. Although less exciting than political coverage, government reporting provides the facts the public uses to vote, pay taxes, and act as good citizens. Government reporters work best by learning how their beat operates administratively, analyzing the way it works practically, establishing good sources but not getting too close to them, avoiding government jargon, conducting interviews carefully, and remaining impartial no matter how outraged they become over the actions of a government agency. Government stories should be written clearly and concisely. Since such subjects tend to be dull, stories should be humanized so readers can identify the bill or the agency with a person.

Exercises

1. Select a state problem and find out how various parts of state government are handling it. Write about what you discover in a news feature.

2. Trace a bill through the legislature, talking to opponents and proponents of it to find out why they are for or against it. What pressures are being exerted on them and how are they staving them off? Write a story about what you find out, after the bill has been voted upon.

3. Write a feature on the state capitol building, its history and present condition.

4. Accompany a state senator and state legislator as he or she visits the district and handles constituent problems. Write a story on what you find.

5. Figure out the most influential state agency and the one with the least impact on citizens. Write a story that compares and contrasts the two.

Main Street, Macon, Georgia, March 1936 by Walker Evans. [*Courtesy U.S. Farm Security Administration, Prints and Photographs Division, Library of Congress*]

4

Local Government

Today, the eyes of all people are truly upon us, and our governments, in every branch, at every level, national, state, and local, must be as a city upon a hill, constructed and inhabited by men aware of their grave trust and their great responsibilities.

—John F. Kennedy

One City Reporter

"There is a civic reason to cover local government because it determines everything around us—schools, police, traffic. All the things that are important to people. The newspaper has to report how the city services are performed, well or not."

Bill Boyarsky is talking about the beat he has covered for over twelve years in one capacity or another for the *Los Angeles Times*. Now as a city affairs columnist, and earlier as city/county bureau chief, Boyarsky has devoted a lot of his career to making news of city government interesting and understandable to readers of his newspaper.

"People will be interested if such news is presented in an interesting way," he says. "Garbage collection and sewage disposal and planning and traffic flow and infrastructure are all real important—and real boring. But that doesn't have to be the case. Garbage disposal is exciting and so are a number of other things if they are made exciting. What you do is find out the political conflict involved. It's not a story about a sewer line but what Councilman A is doing to Councilman B relating to the sewer line. That will determine how interesting your story is."

To Boyarsky, the secret of success on the local government beat is not all that much of a secret. "You write about people," he says. "You convey insights into why things happen, the little dramas around city hall. This requires a lot of reporting, observing, knowing sources. Any reporter can do that if they learn how to describe people, what they look like, what clothes they wear, their personal mannerisms. The reader doesn't know these people but you can lure them into the story with these techniques. I admit it. I never read these [city beat] stories before I got into this coverage."

Boyarsky can write a successful city column because of the long years he spent reporting the city beat himself or directing other reporters to do so. The daily grind of sitting in on meetings of the city council and county board of supervisors, of covering the mayor and all city departments, has paid off because he knows who and what makes the city tick.

"The idea for my column is to explain why things happen in L.A.," he says. "Something happens, let's say in the police department, and people hear that the police chief can't be fired. There is political opposition to him and political support for him. This takes a lot of explaining. Immediacy is everything. Writing a column is like putting on a show because it has to be entertaining. It can't be dull. Making it entertaining is quite an education in journalism."

His goal has never been punditry. "Mine is heavily news based," he says. "Much of what I do is to go to things to get my material. I can't write about something if I haven't seen it. Basically, it is politics made entertaining. The way to do it is to write about people, to describe people and events. You have to be there to see it. I can't write if I have not seen someone, how they talk and look."

To this end, he attends meetings of both the city council and board of supervisors—less to gather material for a specific column than to soak up the atmosphere. If he attends a news event it will be for another reason than to cover the event as an event. When the Gulf War broke out, he went to the demonstrations downtown to see how the police handled the demonstrators. After Rodney King, a black man, was beaten up by police and the incident captured on videotape, he went to black churches to find out the reaction of ministers and congregations.

When the report of the Christopher Commission set up to investigate the incident came out, he approached it a bit differently than most reporters. "I draw upon my experience and my memory," he says. "I looked at it in a 'great commission reports I have known' way. These commission reports are usually filed and forgotten. I compared it to the McCone Commission report on the Watts riot of 1965. I went to the press conference where the report findings were announced and described the scene."

Boyarsky's editor encourages him to relate his column content to what he had done in the past. Before the city/county assignment, he was a political writer for the newspaper in Washington and a general assignment reporter in Los Angeles. Before joining the *Times*, he covered Sacramento, California's state capital, for the Associated Press.

Boyarsky's biggest problem since making the switch from city reporter to city columnist in 1989 is writing to a relatively tight word limit — 800, or twenty-one inches. Most reporters write their stories to tell what happened and length sorts itself out depending on the importance of the subject.

The column appears twice a week on Wednesday and Friday on page 2 of the Metro section, alternating with two other columnists. Boyarsky structures his week around his two columns. He begins his day by bringing up the City News Service list of upcoming events on his home computer. "I see if there is anything I should be going to," he says. "If so, I change whatever plans I have."

Most weeks, he uses Mondays and Wednesdays — and sometimes weekends — to gather material by attending events or meetings or calling sources. "I might phone around to see what is going on," he continues. "I spend a lot of time talking to people."

On the days he writes he often gets up at 4 A.M. because "my body works better then." Several hours and about 200 words later, he will pause and send the first part of the column to his office computer by modem.

On his way downtown to the *Times*, he may drop in on yet another meeting. He arrives at the newsroom by late morning to begin the final push to deadline.

Boyarsky likes to work in the chaos of the newsroom. Although he could probably get a private office with real walls, he prefers to work in a newsroom work station he shares with two other reporters. "If you are sitting in some office, you don't really know what is going on," he says. "If I'm with the reporters who are covering stories I find out things. I also talk to the city desk all the time."

Boyarsky's inspiration as a news-oriented columnist is Mike Royko, a longtime Chicago newspaper columnist: "I'd seen him and admired his desk in the city room."

Boyarsky's actual deadline is 7 P.M., but the columnist usually finishes by 5 P.M., depending on how things go.

"Writing is so hard, I often don't know if it will work out," he explains. "At 4:30, I sometimes have a panic attack. Suddenly, it all comes together. I turn it in and sometimes my editor suggests changes, sometimes not. Then I go home."

Boyarsky says that covering a city government is more difficult than covering state or national government because there are fewer people to talk to and less written documentation to consult: "With Congress, you can always talk to people on the staff. At city hall, there aren't that many staff members. And they don't do reports. You've got to be aware of how information flows, and cultivate a lot of sources, clerks and secretaries. You've got to know where to find things out."

For the *Times*, city coverage has evolved over the years into a greater concentration on the central city—which as in many cities, is where most of the biggest problems exist—rather than on outlying and more affluent areas. In the past, the newspaper was often criticized for spending much of its resources on national and international news and not enough on the city itself. "There is much more concentration on social services, and in L.A., social services mean ethnic minorities," he says. "There is a concern by the paper about how these services are delivered. This reflects changes in journalism and newspapers as a whole. How to make them relevant and get people to read them."

In Boyarsky's view, Los Angeles—and many other cities—have gotten much worse as places to live and to work and to cover: "The middle class has abandoned cities as a residential place and, as a result, abandoned their institutions—schools, parks, libraries. They have been given over to the poor. The electorate won't support or send their kids to them. The city, with so many industrial jobs gone, has become a place of poor people without any hope. This creates a lot of tension, especially racial tension."

Background to Local Government Reporting

Reporting the activities of local government grew along with the governments themselves. Villages, towns, and cities needed some kind of organized structure to govern the affairs of their citizens, to collect taxes, and to use those funds to provide services. A council of elected officials was the most commonly accepted solution to this problem. Members were usually chosen from the ranks of citizens to preside over the affairs of the city on a day-to-day basis.

Editors learned quickly that meetings of these councils were a good source of news. They were held at a set time and place, and the subjects that were discussed and the people who attended were often newsworthy. Reporters first covered this beat in as unsystematic a manner as the operation of the council. Business was conducted somewhat haphazardly, and reporters wrote about it in a chatty way — much as if they were sitting around the pot belly stove or the cracker barrel at the general store trading stories with friends.

During much of the nineteenth century in the United States the power of local newspapers existed not in the depth or expertise of their coverage of local government but rather in the opinions expressed in their editorials. As a result of the ability to comment on civic affairs, editors became influential citizens in the villages, towns, and cities covered by their newspapers.

By the end of the nineteenth century the story of the city governments had gone beyond simple chronicling of daily and weekly events. A new element had appeared in the way medium and large cities were governed: widespread corruption. Although reporters and editors may have been attending official government meetings for some years, they had missed events going on behind the scenes.

City charters had been granted during the period of Jacksonian democracy in the 1830s. At that time power was distributed among a number of agencies — the mayor, a council, even independent boards and commissions — so that no one of them became overly powerful. The result, according to historian Arthur S. Link, was that struggles between these various factions rendered representative government nonexistent. The tight system of checks and balances and rigid division of authority created a power vacuum that was filled by political machines.

Most American cities were ruled by machines, which had replaced the system of representatives chosen impartially by voters. These organizations began on the precinct level and kept everyone in line by dispensing small favors. Above this level was the ward leader, called the "heeler," who followed the orders of the central leader, called the "boss," and helped organize and manage campaigns and make important decisions. The ward heeler often held official office, such as alderman or water commissioner. The ward heelers joined the boss and his immediate assistants to make up the ruling body of the organization, called the "ring."

Given his rather unsavory reputation the boss usually did not hold an office. But he exercised tight control over his lieutenants, and they, in turn, gave orders to the precinct captains. In this way he could control elected officials, who feared his widespread influence and ability to affect re-election campaigns.

The machines stayed in power for years largely because they did things for people. In return for such favors people remained loyal to the boss and did what he wanted them to do. Bribes, the principal instrument of these favors, were paid to politicians and policemen. The amounts seem staggering even by today's somewhat jaded standards. The Chicago Vice Commission, for example, reported in 1911 that the annual profit from vice in the city was $15 million, one-fifth of that amount paid to the police as graft.

Nowhere was this graft more prevalent than in the awarding of municipal contracts. The boss simply used his control of city council members to give contracts for railway lines and sewerage, gas, electrical, and water lines to companies he owned or to companies that paid a kickback.

The press was the first institution to reveal the corruption, and the revelations began the process of change. Cases included the *New York Times* and *Harper's Weekly* disclosures in 1871 that political boss William M. Tweed and his Democratic party cohorts had cheated the New York City government out of millions of dollars. In one instance Tweed's people listed fifty thousand dollars a day for a plasterer for one month's work on a courthouse. The *Times* and *Harper's* obtained documents proving the schemes. The series of stories and Thomas Nast's cartoon drove the Tweed Ring from power.

This system of corruption prevailed in most major cities at the turn of the twentieth century. When reform moves developed, they were led by journalists and new organizations such as civic leagues. The work of the muckrakers, especially Lincoln Steffens, helped speed the needed changes. This period in American journalistic history, explained in greater detail in Chapter 6, has never been equaled in terms of the influence and power of the press to do good and right wrongs.

The muckraking era established forever the city hall as a permanent newspaper beat. Since then reporters have been there to record the actions of the mayor, the council, and the various departments. They are also there as watchdogs. Whether they know it or not, they are fulfilling the legacy of the muckrakers.

Beginning in the 1960s, a new kind of sub-specialty grew out of local government coverage: urban affairs reporting. The riots in American cities during the mid-1960s called attention to the plight of minorities, particularly blacks, and focused attention on the general decay of the city centers. Newspapers, magazines, and television networks were quick to cover the urban story, even though they had ignored it for years. Ironically, much of the decay was literally right outside their doors. The media first concentrated on the causes of the riots but gradually broadened the coverage to include all aspects of urban decay. Gradually, many of these news organizations lost interest in covering urban affairs as a separate beat, in the same way that presidential candidates used a blighted area like the South Bronx in New York as a backdrop for announcing their new plan to save the cities, then quickly forgot such locales and their citizens after the election.

Now, it is more common for parts of the old urban affairs beat, for example gangs, crime, poverty, and substandard housing, to be covered by reporters on other beats. The urban affairs reporter at a newspaper like the *Los Angeles Times*, for example, concentrates on urban planning and the future of the city and helping readers understand the complexities of the city in which they live.

The 1992 riots in South Central Los Angeles could reawaken media interest in the urban affairs story. The riots began when police involved in the videotaped beating of Rodney King were acquitted by a mostly white jury. The 36-hour rampage left at least 58 people dead, 2,383 injured, and 17,000 under arrest for damage to 5,200 buildings totaling an estimated $1 billion. Unless massive federal aid is injected into Los Angeles and other decaying central cities, however, there is little reporters can do beyond cover the poverty and hopelessness their middle-class readers and viewers soon grow tired of.

In the 1990s, budget shortages will continue to dominate local coverage. Although plagued by overwhelming problems such as the homeless, drug addicts, a rise in crime, a shortage of adequate housing, a breakdown of streets and bridges, inadequate medical facilities, and other problems, most cities are so short of funds that they are nearly paralyzed. These shortages are a direct result of the large cutbacks in the federal funds given to both cities and states during the Reagan Administration. And, with so many central cities populated by the poor people suffering most of the problems — the middle class having fled to the suburbs — city governments are not able to raise taxes to get the funds they need to solve their problems.

Problems and Solutions

It is not an oversimplification to say that no two cities are alike. History, location, economic diversity and composition, and people affect the character and size of all cities. The diversity which results makes it impossible to generalize in any discussion of how to cover local government. Factors true for one city are not present in another.

Fortunately for the purposes of this book only a few kinds of local government structures exist. (Boxes 4.1 and 4.2 describe the basic systems of city and county government in the United States.)

Local government reporters will find themselves covering the same kinds of stories and encountering the same kinds of problems no matter where they work. The differences occur in the size of the city and the scope of the work. A reporter for a small daily will cover all of city government. A reporter for a major metropolitan daily newspaper may be one of ten on the city beat. The problems of covering local government are not unique to that beat. Other beats are as boring in the predictability of events (education) and engender pressure from those in power if stories are unfavorable (business). The difference exists in the scope of the subject matter.

All readers have the potential to be affected by actions of local government. Their property taxes may go up or down. They may not be able to do something they have done before (walk their dog in the park without a leash). The newspaper has the obligation to report what is going on in local government to people who will be affected by these actions.

This need to cover nearly everything is where the boredom comes in. All government actions cannot be made scintillating. But most newspapers feel the obligation to try, and the onus for doing so falls on the shoulders of the local government reporters.

Another big problem on this beat is the pressure that sometimes comes when a reporter does too good a job; often the smaller the town, the greater the pressure. Most local officials are boosters first, great legislators second. They see criticism or the revelation of anything bad as being harmful to the city and its image, no matter whether the story is true. They might talk to the reporter's editor or publisher during a game of golf at the country club, and if that editor or publisher is of a similar booster mentality, a reporter might be asked to ease up or stop doing such stories. If the issue is important enough and the reporter feels compromised enough, he or she may have no choice but to resign.

Beyond these two major problems lurk other potential difficulties. The atmosphere of the local government gets fairly "clubby," especially during private encounters between reporters and council members. Although reporters must work closely with these officials, they must guard against being used by them. It is best, for example, to avoid all social contact with them beyond an occasional business lunch or cup of coffee.

Many local officials get as caught up in the jargon of their jobs as any scientist or other technical person. Reporters must constantly ask for explanations of terms and processes and do necessary background reading to understand what is going on well enough to write about it.

More suggestions on dealing with the local government beat can be found in "Likely Problems and How to Solve Them" later in this chapter.

How to Cover Local Government

The approach to city and county government coverage varies with the size and complexity of the city and county. A large newspaper like the *Los Angeles Times* carries out its city and county coverage with eight people. Most smaller newspapers send only one reporter, augmented by others when the need arises, to keep track of local government events.

Whatever the scope of the beat, however, some factors in approach remain constant:

1. **Establish good sources early.** Good sources are more important on a local government beat than perhaps on any other beat. Because of the need to return again and again for information, a reporter must find out who the best sources are during the first days on the beat. Sometimes these people are obvious (a council member, a county commissioner, and chief aides); sometimes they are not (a city clerk, the mayor's secretary). A reporter needs to develop good rapport with sources and maintain it. A good way to begin this process is to get names from the person who had the beat before and build on that list.

2. **Cultivate these sources constantly.** Once the good sources have been established, a reporter should drop by to see them constantly just in case they have a tip for a story. Some days will yield nothing, but others will be more fruitful. Patience is a virtue in journalism. Another place to renew a relationship with an official is in the corridor during breaks of meetings.

3. **Beware of being used by sources.** Very often, elected officials or other bureaucrats will try to manipulate reporters and get them to cover their special projects. While such projects might be

Box 4.1

How City Government Operates

City governments provide various housekeeping services to citizens of the organized communities within their particular jurisdiction. Essential services that are funded include police and fire protection, a water supply, the collection and disposal of garbage, a sewage system, the maintenance of streets and street lighting, and public health measures for the prevention and detection of infectious and other diseases in restaurants and food markets. City government is also responsible for public education, the costs of which it shares with the state, and the regulation of construction through the issuance of building permits. Even cultural life in the city comes under government jurisdiction; museums, concert halls, swimming pools, parks, and a summer recreation program are all provided, depending on the size and financial resources of the city.

Cities collect taxes, usually in the form of a property tax, to pay for these services. Some cities also levy a sales tax, an income tax, a payroll tax, and occasionally a "nuisance" tax on things such as utilities, banks, hotel room occupancies, auto use, cigarettes, theater tickets, gasoline, and stock transfers to raise extra revenue.

City governments in the United States are set up in one of three forms:

1. Mayor-council is the most widely used system in large cities over one million. It consists of an independently elected mayor, who is the chief executive officer of the city with the responsibility to see that departments operate and ordinances (local laws) are carried out, and a council whose members are also elected. The council has the legal authority to enact regulatory ordinances, establish programs to be administered by the operating departments, appropriate money for city government activities, impose taxes, and condemn property for public use. Most city councils elect a president to preside over meetings.

   Another designation has been made in this system of city government, based on the power granted to the mayor: strong mayor (who has the authority to appoint department heads, establish a budget, prepare and submit ordinances and legislative proposals, and transfer funds from one activity to another); weak mayor (who has none of these powers and occupies a largely ceremonial position with the council doing everything important).

2. Council-manager, adopted in cities from 250,000 to one million, includes a small council and mayor without absolute executive authority. Instead the council appoints a city manager to supervise and direct the operating departments and see that ordinances are carried out. The city manager, who can be removed at any time by the council, is usually a trained professional and not a politician. Council members under this system cannot go to department heads without going through the manager. The manager prepares the city budget, which must be approved by the

council, and attends council meetings where he or she can speak but not vote. Sometimes there is a mayor under this system to preside over council meetings and to act as ceremonial head of the city, but without much day-to-day power.

3. Commission form, which is not as widely used, vests all legal power in a small number of commissioners who govern the town and exercise all legislative power. Each commissioner is the head of a different department or set of related departments. The mayor, who can be elected as such or chosen by the other commissioners, is also in charge of one or more city departments.

newsworthy, a reporter needs to make the decision on coverage, not be coerced into doing so by an official with ulterior motives.

4. **Make the rounds of the beat.** When not meeting a deadline, a reporter should walk around the city hall or county building at least once a week. In doing so, he or she becomes known to people in various government offices, and they may occasionally pass along a tip or an advance copy of a document or an agenda.

5. **Try to make meetings interesting.** It is difficult not to get bored during a meeting of a city council or county commission. The challenge for reporters is to squelch that boredom and pass on the sometimes vital information readers need as citizens. One easy way to do this is to humanize the story by emphasizing the effect on people. Another way is to avoid reporting every detail that goes on during a five-hour meeting. Instead a reporter can pick the five most important subjects and write separate stories on them. One caution: Reporters should be careful to keep track of who is talking during a meeting so that the proper attribution can be given. This is not always easy because of all the people talking, sometimes at once.

6. **Go beyond the official in doing stories.** There is more to local government reporting than a numbing number of meetings, although they do provide most of the official news. Reporters need to go beyond such gatherings whenever possible to bring other aspects of city life to readers: local celebrations, neighborhood activities, new equipment, new systems, people.

7. **Analyze the way things work.** Beyond an organizational chart or textbook understanding of government agencies, a reporter needs to understand how the system functions on a more practical level. This knowledge comes after a reporter begins to cover the beat and has attended meetings and met official sources. "You ask yourself,

Box 4.2

How County Government Operates

County governments take over where those of a city end—at the geographical limit. The average state has sixty-one counties, and the pattern of organization varies widely. Most are presided over by a board of coequal commissioners or supervisors elected to their jobs. There is no separation of powers as in the city and state governments; the executive, legislative, and judicial powers are given to the same people. Smaller counties tend to call their officials "commissioners," and these boards typically have three or five members. Larger counties designate their officials "supervisors," and there are more of them on the board.

In most cases county governments differ from those of cities because they carry out state functions on such matters as courts, tax collection, property assessment, maintenance of health services, provision for public welfare, and collecting official records of property transfer and vital statistics of birth, death marriage, and divorce. County governments are responsible for activities affecting more people over a wider area than their city counterparts.

The commission or board is at the top of the county hierarchy. Its members set the annual budget, levy and collect taxes, approve major purchases, plan and pay for buildings, and fund and maintain roads and highways. The commissioners or supervisors carrying out this work are assisted by an administrative staff. They hire professionals to run the departments reporting directly to them.

The county clerk keeps records of property ownership, liens against property, court judgments, court records, and vital statistics. The health officer spends much of his or her time on preventive medicine, especially in rural areas, and conducts clinics and classes on baby care, venereal disease, and alcohol and drug abuse.

The county treasurer keeps track of the money spent by the commissioners, prepares the annual budget, and audits the books. The assessor evaluates property and determines the work and tax rate. The tax rate is based on the total annual budget of the county, the city, and the school district. In many states the county performs this service for the other two units of government: assesses property, collects the tax payments, and gives each unit its share. Usually this figure is broken down into mills. Each mill is worth one-tenth of a cent, and tax rate totals are reached by multiplying the mill amount by every $100 of assessed valuation. The tax collector then collects taxes.

The county engineer maintains roads, highways, and bridges in the county. The welfare director supervises payments to poor people, quite often using money from state and federal sources.

There is usually a sheriff's department in all counties, and deputies handle crime investigation and prevention and traffic control outside the jurisdiction of cities. This department also runs the the county jail, where suspects are held pending trial.

The district attorney (often called the "D.A.") acts as the attorney for the government within the county, representing it in court cases and investigating crime within that jurisdiction. The D.A. — known in some parts of the country as the county prosecutor or state's attorney — is usually elected. This official works with the sheriff and city police to obtain evidence to convict a person of a crime. The D.A. often has a staff of investigators and detectives to gather this information. In large jurisdictions, D.A.s have a number of assistant district attorneys to help them prepare cases for trial.

'Who runs the city?'" says Boyarsky. "All are run by downtown interests and suburban builders. You've got to understand this and explain it. You do this by describing what happens. For example, a guy gets a subdivision of 600 homes approved by the city council. You find out he contributed to the campaigns of several councilmen." Two examples of subjects that reporters often need to explain are detailed in this chapter: Box 4.3 on bonds and Box 4.4 on land-use planning.

8. **Explain subjects carefully.** Avoid the inevitable jargon of the beat by translating "governmentese" into English. Reporters should never pick up the terminology used by a bureaucrat in explaining something in a story. "Government people use in-house talk," says Boyarsky. "They say things like 'Section 8' and 'leveraging private capital.' It doesn't mean anything. Some of it creeps into copy if you don't make the effort to keep it out." Reporters cannot assume readers have preknowledge of anything.

9. **Conduct interviews carefully.** The interview is the most important part of reporting. Even if a reporter has attended a meeting, he or she will still have questions that can only be answered in a personal interview with the people who know. Reporters should be prepared for anything beyond the quick exchange with a source in the hall. The approach varies with the reporter. Some reporters are always courteous and deferential; others purposefully take a more aggressive approach. Bill Boyarsky combines the two. "If you have both hard, controversial questions and soft ones, you might want to ask the soft ones at the beginning," he says. "If the person is rude, throw your hardball right off to show you are tough. Avoid telephone interviews. They are never as good as personal ones. Go to people's offices at their convenience. See them in their surroundings — what the pictures are on the wall, how they treat their secretary, what the office furniture is like. In our bureau each person has a different technique. A dumb, young boy

Box 4.3

A Word About Bonds

Local and state governments pay for their programs primarily through tax revenues. As costs have increased greatly in recent years, so have demands for tax relief from citizens. Government officials have begun to realize that there is a limit to the tolerance of the public for continual increases in sales, income, and property taxes.

Local governments have had to cut back on services as a result. They have also turned to alternate sources of funding. One widely used method is the sale of bonds.

Like stocks, bonds are sold in public offerings. Individuals and organizations buying the bonds are paid interest on their investment over an extended period of time. The money obtained from such sales are used to finance construction projects and other long-term improvements like parks.

There are four kinds of bonds:

1. *General obligation bonds* require the local government to pledge general revenue to repay the bonds.

2. *Revenue bonds* are paid from income from a certain entity like a water system.

3. *Special assessment bonds* are paid by revenue from a special assessment levied against the property owners who benefit from an improvement such as new sewer line.

4. *Special general bonds* are payable from the revenue of a special assessment. Because of the large amounts involved, they have the added backing of city or county resources as security.

approach is one. I use the 'Columbo' approach.'' (In the television series, Peter Falk plays a seemingly bumbling police lieutenant who pretends not to know anything when he questions suspects in murder cases.)

10. **Remain objective and fair.** It is easy to take sides in covering government stories. There are often ''good guys'' and ''bad guys.'' There is also the temptation to get angry at the inefficiency and waste in government. Reporters must keep their views about what they observe to themselves and let their readers draw their own conclusions from the facts presented to them. To do otherwise is editorializing. ''There are boring stories and a boring routine,'' says Boyarsky. ''You may get bogged down, but you can't bring a spirit of outrage with you on the beat and let it creep into your stories.''

Kinds of Local Government Stories

A number of stories are included in the local government beat:

1. **Meetings.** All local government organizations meet regularly on a weekly, monthly, or even daily basis, and such meetings form the focal point for action. Members debate issues, listen to citizen complaints, and vote on measures. Their actions are newsworthy because they affect the lives of citizens.

2. **City problems.** During these meetings and in interviews and informal chats around the beat, reporters learn about long-term city and county problems, and they need to follow up on these problems in a story or series of stories (budget shortages, breakdowns in transportation and health care, decline of the downtown area, urban renewal, public housing, welfare, gang violence, drug problems).

3. **New programs.** New ways to solve old problems or new funding from the state or federal government agencies to help the city or county are always good stories.

4. **New laws.** What are new ordinances and their effect on the public? What is the background of these laws?

5. **Annual events.** Explanations of the annual budget and profiles of the candidates running for important offices in the local government are always sources of stories.

6. **People profiles.** Interesting people who work in local government—from the mayor or county commissioner to the man or woman who repairs the clock in the courthouse—make good story possibilities.

7. **Tie-ins with national issues.** How are national issues affecting the local scene? Have budget cutbacks in grants to cities and counties crippled local programs? Does a national problem (for example, crime or a dying central city) have a local counterpart?

8. **Environmental problems.** What is the quality of the air and water in the city? How do city officials plan to improve it? Where does the city get its water? What are officials doing to lessen air pollution?

9. **The future of the city.** What do experts see as the future for this city and cities in general? How do their visions match the plans of city officials? Will the city improve or are these plans impossible economically?

10. **The nuances of society.** What factors, individuals, and organizations make the city what it is? This kind of story involves

Box 4.4

Land-Use Planning

Land use has become a major issue in cities and counties across the country as urban and suburban growth has begun to encroach upon rural land, much of it agricultural. The power to decide how land within a city or a county is zoned into housing subdivisions, commercial buildings, office buildings, and factories and how much remains untouched and bucolic is usually vested in a planning commission whose members are appointed by the city council or county commission. Their power is great and so are the pressures on them to make decisions favoring one designation for land over another. What they do determines whether various uses for land are compatible or in conflict with each other.

The decisions made by this commission are usually controversial because they affect the well-being of so many people. Planning and zoning hearings are lively and important sources of news for any newspaper. There is rarely a land-use or planning beat, but city and county government reporters cover the subject enough that extra expertise is required.

After it is set up, a planning commission must first develop a land-use plan for the geographic area over which it has jurisdiction. After the plan has been approved by voters, city council members, or county commissioners, the planning commission must see that it is carried out by meeting periodically to consider requests from those who seek to build or develop land, both in accordance with the plan and at variance with it.

The commission combines administrative and quasi-judicial functions in that it must hear and decide cases that cannot be routinely handled by a regular city or county planning official. The commission recommends a final decision to its parent body, the city council or county commission.

The bulk of reporting about land use takes place at the local level. Reporters are free to go to city hall or the county courthouse and talk to staff members and look at records (building permits and requests for changes to zoning ordinances, called *variances*).

Most of the drama and thus the interest in land use takes place at commission meetings. The commissioners are there to listen to testimony from people for or against the change. The proponents and opponents often bring along supporters who may be quite vociferous in their comments.

Reporters have access to the record of all these hearings and to the commission findings. Reporters can thus follow up on particularly interesting cases to see if the planning commission's recommendation was adhered to by the city council or county commission. In some states a person can appeal an unfavorable decision if certain procedures have not been followed.

The commission's decision is called a "basic finding of fact" and represents the rationale between community land-use policies and the particular verdict on a specific land-use case. In Oregon, for example, the law requires a planning commission to follow established quasi-judicial procedure in its work: the right to a hearing, the right to present and rebut evidence, the requirement that a record be kept, the requirement that adequate findings be made to support the decision reached, and the right to an impartial tribunal. This procedure is designed to prevent the possibility that a public hearings body may make an arbitrary, biased, or otherwise partial decision on a land-use case.

Some states do not make a concerted effort to follow such procedures, although the procedures may be on the books. In many states zoning and the comprehensive plan are completely different things. While the plan is a nice colorful map on someone's wall, a commission makes zoning decisions based on the influence of powerful financial interests rather than the public good.

Reporters who monitor both the hearings and whether the decisions are properly carried out can find valid stories: corrupt officials, the presence of organized crime, danger to the public good (a toxic chemical plant next to a park or a school), disharmonious elements (a mobile home park next to a group of expensive estates), or disruptive elements (a factory with no place for workers to live).

Land-use planning has been resisted in many states because opponents think it imposes government control on their personal freedom of choice. For their part planners and planning commission members consider that they are acting for the public welfare. They contend that land ownership is not the sovereign right of anybody; it is a resource held in common. The divergence of these two points of view makes the conflict, and the conflict makes news.

race, culture, history, business, and any other elements that help explain why the city has evolved into the place it is today.

Writing Local Government Stories

"Writing should be simple and direct," says Bill Boyarsky of the *Los Angeles Times.* "I've found out that some people may be wonderful phrasemakers but say nothing. You very seldom think of great phrases. What makes good writing is the material you get. I pick up a good anecdote and tell it simply. I don't put in a funny line, my anecdote does that."

Boyarsky structures his columns simply: an introduction where he states his theme, a middle where he makes his main point, and an end where he states his opinion.

While news stories on local government cannot be written in quite the same way—certainly they can't include the reporter's opinion—

they will probably be read and understood by readers if they concentrate on people and the behind the scenes maneuvering that make things happen as they do.

HOW THE DEAL WITH GATES WAS STRUCK
By Bill Boyarsky

In this, a background page 1 story detailing how two members of the Los Angeles City Council persuaded controversial Police Chief Daryl Gates to retire, Bill Boyarsky got help from city hall sources he had been cultivating for years. His narrative lead brings readers into the story by giving them insight into the minds of the two councilmen, material he deduced from what they told him.

His transition (graf 2) backs up his suppositions with direct quotes from both.

In graf 3, Boyarsky continues the narrative by summarizing the techniques used ("diplomacy, political sense"), again backing this up with a direct quote (graf 4).

In grafs 5, 6, and 7 Boyarsky gives more details about the deal, fitting in details on the experience of the two councilmen, and alludes to the incident that got the chief into trouble ("beating of Rodney G. King").

1 From the moment they left their homes at the outset of their momentous day until the last triumphant phone call at dusk, Councilmen John Ferraro and Joel Wachs knew they could persuade Los Angles Police Chief Daryl F. Gates to retire only if they could find a graceful way for him to leave.

2 "We wanted to find a way for him to retire with some dignity," Ferraro said. Said Wachs: "The last thing he wanted was to be kicked out."

3 Diplomacy, political sense and an understanding of the chief's volatile psyche guided the two politicians as they crafted an agreement as ambiguous as a Middle East peace treaty—broad enough to allow the chief to call himself master of his own destiny, but still allowing Ferraro to say:

4 "There wasn't any doubt in my mind or Joel's mind that he was going to announce his retirement."

5 Just when he will announce it, of course, is unknown, the ambiguous part of the agreement, the aspect that gives the canny Gates the leverage to make sure that this extraordinary chapter of Los Angeles history—which began with the March 3 police beating of Rodney G. King—is nowhere near its conclusion.

6 Ferraro, a 24-year council veteran, and Wachs, who has served 20 years, are convinced they have a deal.

7 "I think we found an answer," a relieved and happy Wachs told his chief aide, Greg Nelson, Thursday evening.

In graf 8, Boyarsky gives readers a bit of history about the city charter and what the Christopher Commission said about it.

8 It was a potential departure point, not only for Gates, but for sections of the City Charter born amid another scandal—the disgrace of Mayor Frank Shaw, thrown out by recall in 1938 amid charges of corruption. The Christopher Commission concluded earlier this week that those Charter sections not only are outdated, but have contributed to paralysis in city government when it comes to managing the Police Department.

The basic background having been laid out, Boyarsky turns to the heart of his story: the background to the deal itself in grafs 9, 10, and 11. He is able to reconstruct the back-and-forth action because of what the two councilmen told him.

9 Getting to the point Thursday involved a day of delicate negotiations with the proud chief, a man sensitive to slights and determined to stick around long enough to play a major role in reshaping his battered department. By linking Gates' retirement to a special election on Charter reform, they gave him claim to that role.

10 It was a day of telephone negotiations, ending at sunset, with Wachs and Ferraro on the phone in Ferraro's office with Gates, offering the proposal that the chief accepted—a special election in the late fall on the Christopher Commission's reform recommendations, including a term limit for the new chief. With that, Gates agreed to let the retirement process begin.

11 The action took place in Ferraro's office on the mezzanine of City Hall, in a suite filled with mementos of a career in athletics and politics.

He brings readers into the negotiating sessions by giving them details of where the talks took place, over the telephone in the office of one of the councilmen (pictures on the wall, the items on the coffee table).

12 There is a picture of Ferraro, the football All-American, in his early '40's USC uniform; Ferraro the pol, with Frank Sinatra and John F. Kennedy. A Rams football helmet sits on a coffee table. Olympics pins from 1984 are displayed on shelves. This is the office of a man whose life revolved around sports, politics—and his wife, Margaret, whose picture occupies a large space on a table near his desk.

In graf 13, he makes a one sentence transition into a section of the article about the two men.

13 He and Wachs would seem to have little in common.

In the next four grafs, Boyarsky sketches the backgrounds of the two councilmen, their feuds, their similarities.

14 While Ferraro, 57, studies the sports pages, Wachs, 52, is catching up on news of museums, the Music Center and other Los Angeles culture spots. Owner of an extensive art collection, Wachs is the council's greatest supporter of the arts.

15 They once were bitter foes. In the late 1970's, Wachs unseated Ferraro as council president in a move so murderously swift that *The Times*' mid-afternoon edition headline screamed "City Hall Coup." Ferraro nourished his bitterness; and a year or so later organized a coup against Wachs, collecting enough votes to replace him with City Councilwoman Pat Russell.

16 Eventually Ferraro regained his old post. In recent years, these veteran pols have found ways to work together.

17 One other thing they have in common proved crucial this day: they are both among the few members of the council whom Gates, scornful of politicians, trusts. As a friend of Gates said: "Joel sometimes can be an antagonist, but he is looked upon by the chief as a fair-minded man who can reason with council members who won't even talk to the chief. And John is the leader, the president, plus he is a good friends with the chief."

In graf 18, Boyarsky switches to a section on how the two councilmen reached their decision to act, then acted.

18 For months, Wachs recalled Friday, he has been talking long and hard to Gates about the need for the Police Department to change its image. "We've talked about that a lot," he said, "about how there hasn't been a commitment on how you treat people [that is] as great as the [department's] commitment on being incorruptible."

He continues this background in grafs 19-25.

19 Thursday's events began with Wachs and Ferraro reaching the same conclusion on their separate morning drives to work.

20 As Wachs drove in from his hillside San Fernando Valley home, he knew the firestorm at City Hall was out of control. Mayor Tom Bradley and the council were deadlocked over the future of Gates and the Police Department. No other city business was getting done. Tourism, crucial to Los Angeles' economy, was slipping as a result of the King beating. Gates had taken command of the crucial Internal Affairs Division away from Assistant Chief David Dotson in the wake of disclosures that he had frankly criticized the chief in testimony before the Christopher Commission. Gates' move triggered charges of retaliation.

21 Meanwhile, the ranks of those who could offer a solution had thinned.

22 Bradley had removed himself as a potential peacemaker because he supported his Police commission's abortive attempt to put Gates on leave. That maneuver also put the commission out of the picture, unable to fulfill its City Charter role as supervisor of the Police Department.

23 After taking the elevator up to his mezzanine-level City Hall office, Wachs greeted his chief aide, Nelson. "This can't go on this way," he said. "You have any ideas?" Nelson went off to a quiet place in the office and tried to think of something.

24 Ferraro drove in from his home in Hancock Park, the elegant old neighborhood in mid-Wilshire, and went up to his office, down the long hallway from Wachs'.

25 He too was ready to act. Like Wachs, Ferraro had been criticized by civil rights groups for refusing to criticize Gates. In fact, he strongly defended the chief. But he had been impressed by the Christopher Commission Report and was an old friend of the chairman, Warren Christopher.

Having summarized the actions of the men and fitting in colorful details, Boyarsky inserts a quote in graf 26 to authenticate what he had been surmising in the previous paragraphs.

26 "A couple of members had urged me to do something," Ferraro said. "I knew I was in the best position to do something because of my long, strong relationship with Daryl Gates. I've been consistently for him, unlike some of my colleagues."

27 Looking for a solution, Wachs walked down the hall to Ferraro's office. Ferraro, the council president, was pivotal in putting together any plan. Like Wachs, he could communicate with Gates. But their first talk was inconclusive.

In graf 28, he brings the reader into another aspect of the story: the political problems involved, and then details them in grafs 29 and 30.

28 The political problem was daunting.

29 The Christopher Commission Report had proposed the outline of a solution. In one of its most crafty recommendations, the report suggested that Gates remain in office until his successor was chosen, presiding over the beginning of the transition. That opened the door to the possibility of a graceful exit by Gates.

30 But the commission also recommended extensive Charter changes, and these could not be enacted until they were approved by the voters at the next election, and that wasn't until June, 1992. Months of potential turmoil loomed.

In graf 31 comes the moment of truth, which Boyarsky lets one of his sources tell in his own words.

31 Alone in his office, Ferraro telephoned the 64-year-old Gates. "We had a nice, long conversation," Ferraro said. "There was no doubt he wanted to retire in the near future. Then he talked about the process. He didn't want an interim chief. He said he wanted the measures [the Christopher Commission proposals] to run their course" in an election.

32 That was encouraging, but not a solution.

More of the story is told beginning in grafs 33, 34, 35, 36, and 37: one of the councilmen tells two key people. Readers are also reminded that this is being told in chronological order ("it was afternoon").

33 By now, it was afternoon. Ferraro figured he'd better let some others know what he was doing.

34 He called his friend Christopher and offered to drive to the attorney's downtown office to brief him. No, said Christopher. He insisted on driving to City Hall. They talked in Ferraro's office.

35 Then Ferraro briefed the mayor. These two old political pros have had a stormy relationship, but still maintain the old-fashioned civility required to keep the wheels of government rolling. Bradley often walks up to the mezzanine to talk to Ferraro. This time, Ferraro visited him.

36 The mayor sat at his favorite chair next to a coffee table in his large, formal office where he receives guests. Ferraro was on a couch on another side of the table. He told the mayor what he and Wachs were doing. Bradley, he said, listened stone-faced, saying little. He urged Ferraro to go ahead.

37 Go ahead with what? He and Wachs now knew the chief wanted to retire. But only after an election on the Christopher reforms.

More chronology in graf 38 ("after 5 P.M.") . . .

38 By now it was after 5 P.M. Time was running out. Gates was scheduled to fly to North Carolina to address a national meeting of the DARE anti-drug organization he had founded. "The chief had to catch an early evening plane," a friend said. "This all had to be put together, packaged and presented before then."

. . . and deal making in grafs 39, 40, 41, and 42.

39 Ferraro called Wachs. Nobody answered. Most of the office staff had gone home. But Ferraro knew Wachs was in the office. His assistant, Tom LaBonge, hammered on Wachs' door. Wachs appeared.

40 Wachs and Ferraro gloomily looked at an election calendar Ferraro had obtained. No doubt about it, June was too far away.

41 But an idea had been circulating around City Hall, a special election on the Christopher proposals in the Fall. It was just a tentative idea, something discussed in corridors and offices.

42 Wachs mentioned it to Ferraro, somewhat tentatively. But as soon as he spoke the words "special election," the solution came together in Wachs' mind. "That's it," he told Ferraro.

In graf 43, Boyarsky lets his sources pick up the story ("recounting the moment later").

43 Recounting the moment later, Wachs said, "The special made the other things work, it keeps the process from dragging out." A special election would cost more than holding the election in June, but at that moment, Wachs said, "money was irrelevant; if you could bring about peace, it is worth the money."

A final section of the back-and-forth discussion that went on between the councilmen and

44 Ferraro called Gates. "We told him we thought there should be a special election,

the chief begins in graf 44.

the election could take place before the end of the year. He thought that was a good idea."

45 Wachs filled in more details.

46 He said he told Gates that the process included picking a successor to the chief. "He agreed," Wachs said.

47 Ferraro called Christopher, who said he was pleased.

48 Signed, sealed and delivered. Almost.

49 At 7 A.M. Friday, Ferraro's phone rang at home.

50 It was the chief, calling from North Carolina. Reporters were bugging him about him quitting, prompted by a report in the *Times* outlining the chief's willingness to retire.

51 "What's going on?" the chief asked.

52 Ferraro said that he and Wachs were going to announce the special election at a news conference in a couple of hours.

53 "Fine," said Gates. "Just don't announce my retirement."

In the final graf, Boyarsky ties up all the loose ends with a one-paragraph summation of a press conference the two councilmen held to reveal their plan.

54 At the news conference, Ferraro announced the special election plan, but tried to deflect questions about Gates' departure. The chief would address that himself, Ferraro said. Wachs, though, was forthright: Gates had agreed to "pass the mantle to the new chief."

Local Government Reporting: Likely Problems and How to Solve Them

Problem	Solution
1. Dull, boring stories	1a. Humanize subjects.
	1b. Show the impact on average citizens.
2. Pressure from city officials, newspaper editor, and publisher to avoid	2a. Be sure of facts before going ahead with stories.
	2b. Refuse to become a

unfavorable, controversial stories.

chamber of commerce type "booster."

2c. Try to reason with editor and publisher.

2d. Resign, if all else fails.

3. Keeping track of what is going on.

3a. Establish sources in all parts of local government—from high officials to clerks and secretaries.

3b. Cultivate these sources carefully for tips and leaks.

3c. Understand the governmental process.

4. Getting too close to sources.

4a. Never socialize with local officials.

4b. Keep talking about the "proper" separation between reporters and officials.

5. Using too much govern- mental jargon in stories.

5a. Ask sources to explain all unfamiliar terms.

5b. Keep up with trends in government by getting on the mailing lists of organi- zations such as the National Association of Counties, the National League of Cities and the National Conference of Mayors, and by reading publications about city and urban problems.

6. Being closed out of some meetings.

6a. Resist all attempts by knowing and by reciting to officials the state open meeting laws.

6b. Publicize meeting closures.

Summary

Citizens are affected daily by the actions of local governments. Coverage of local government has been a standard journalistic beat since the nineteenth century. The problems of this beat include sometimes boring subject matter and occasional pressure from local officials not to run negative or controversial stories. Reporters on this beat can do a good job by establishing good sources, making daily rounds to keep up with what is going on, writing about meetings in a way that assesses the effect on readers, and analyzing subjects carefully.

Exercises

1. Visit the city hall or county building and make a list of potential sources from among the various department heads working there. Introduce yourself to each of them (or their assistants), and get two ideas for future stories. Compile a list of possible stories from these interviews and rank them according to newsworthy potential. Report your findings to the class.

2. Attend a meeting of the city council or county commission, and make a list of stories that need to be followed up. Select one of those stories, gather material for it, and write it.

3. Attend a meeting of the city council or county commission and write a story. You may do either one long story or a series of shorter ones.

4. Gather the material to write "a day in the life of city hall" by spending time in that building and talking to as many people as possible to learn how the city works.

5. Pick a person doing a routine city or county job and follow them around for a day, reporting on what you see. The job might be: county nurse, county road engineer, garbage collector, animal control officer, building inspector, marriage license clerk.

6. Research the history of an old and decaying building in a downtown area. Trace its past through construction records, building permits, and the recollections of residents; write an article using what you find out.

School Children at FSA Farm Workers' Camp, Caldwell, Idaho, 1941 by Russell Lee. [*Courtesy U.S. Farm Security Administration Collection, Prints and Photographs Division, Library of Congress*]

5

Education

Education is a companion which no misfortune can depress, no crime can destroy, no enemy can alienate, no despotism can enslave.

—Joseph Addison

One Education Reporter

In covering schools in a small community, an education reporter often gets criticized for things over which he or she has no control.

Take Donna Schmidt. The education reporter for the *Tigard* (Oregon) *Times* was in the middle of covering a hotly debated dispute over the redrawing of school district boundaries when her publisher wrote an editorial in favor of a plan that many local parents in the district opposed, in effect, dividing the neighborhood in half.

"I knew I would get creamed when I went out to cover my beat after the editorial," says Schmidt. "I'm the one person people see. Some of them probably think I wrote the editorial." Almost immediately, some parents opposing the boundary change refused to talk to her.

Adds Steve Clark, editor and publisher of the *Times*: "The role of a newspaper is to lead and foster discussion. But this editorial brought many in that neighborhood down on the newspaper—six to eight calls a day, one lady every day. We ended up listening to people saying they would sell their house to move on the other side of the new line and that the new boundary would make one high school for rich kids, the other less desirable. The day after an editorial like that comes out, the reporter on that beat goes out there and listens to people complain."

Eventually, the school board voted for the plan advocated in the editorial. A number of people canceled their subscriptions to the *Times*.

Such are the vagaries of life on a beat that is among the most important on a weekly newspaper like the *Tigard Times*, which serves a community of 31,000 south of Portland, as well as several other suburbs. In a recent telephone survey of its readers, the *Times* discovered that school news, including the school menu for the week, was the topic of most interest.

With advertising revenue down and fewer reporters and news pages available, Clark has restructured the paper to emphasize school news.

"We have to differentiate ourselves from the competition," says Clark. "That means being local—lunch menus, honor roll names, PTA news, school board meetings. None of this is in *The Oregonian*."

Clark thinks all small dailies and weeklies could benefit by emphasizing school news and identifying it as such. On a previous newspaper he edited, he got calls thanking him for increasing school coverage after he grouped all such stories under a "School News" label. The interesting thing was, he had not increased the amount of space or number of stories devoted to education, only their placement.

"Schools touch the communities we serve, more obviously than other, larger communities," says Clark.

This emphasis extends even into headlines. For example, the *Times* editors try to put the name of a school in a headline. They also describe the school and the neighborhood in which it is located. This results in reader identification and interest.

The shift in emphasis also makes Donna Schmidt responsible for her newspaper's most important beat. It is common for the education beat to be crucial on weeklies and small dailies, largely because people realize that education will shape the lives of their children and are eager to be in on as much of the shaping as possible. These parents and other residents in the district also know that much of their property taxes goes to pay for schools. They have a vested interest in keeping up with school news.

For Schmidt, the responsibilities of this important beat translate into a great deal of work. She must keep track of the school board primarily through attendance at weekly meetings and frequent contact with the superintendent. She must also follow news and find features at the nine elementary, two junior high, and one high school. If an issue suddenly becomes hot, such as the boundary dispute or a more recent controversy over censorship of the high school newspaper, she will often write two or three stories on that one issue, along with the more mundane lunch menus and honor roll stories.

"If you are doing your job right on this beat, you should know the teachers, principals, and union people on a first name basis," says Schmidt. "You need to know where to get good tips, good stories. You can't rely on the public information person totally, although the one I work with is good for official details. Parents and kids themselves are also good sources. They are eager to get into the paper."

She keeps up with her beat through constant telephone contact with the district public relations woman and by meeting with teachers, principals, and parents she has cultivated as sources during her three years on the beat.

"The worst way to cover the beat is to continually rely on the telephone," says Schmidt. "You lose sources if you don't meet them, look them in the eye. It's easy to brush someone off. Your stories are better written if you are out in the community. You can't get that passion people often feel [about schools] over the phone. The phone is a good tool, but it's not the only tool."

In Schmidt's view, direct contact with sources is best.

"What it comes down to: you're dealing with people," says Schmidt. "That's why you need to get away from bureaucrats, especially their jargon. There's a lot of it in education and it complicates a story. 'FTE,' 'IB program,' how a tax base differs from a tax rate. If I use it at all, I make sure to explain it."

Schmidt is careful to fill her readers in on background needed to understand the primary issue in the story. For example, when district overcrowding caused the board to vote to restructure into a middle school approach, the reporter made sure to include background on what middle schools are and what that would mean for the students attending them. The overcrowding also raised questions of class size and the length of the school day — issues dealt with in other stories.

"It's a big beat," concludes Schmidt. "Twelve schools means too much to do, not enough of a news hole to put stories in. I turn it all in and talk to my editors about significance. This beat is a good beat. You are not bored. You never know what will blow up. On this beat, your job is to be fair."

Background to Education Reporting

Schools have been a part of American communities since colonial times. Writing about schools on a daily, weekly, or monthly basis for newspapers and magazines is more a twentieth-century phenomenon, however.

At first educators themselves wrote extensively, and what they wrote influenced the structure of how students were taught at all levels of education. Horace Mann, secretary of the Massachusetts Board of Education, was such an educator. Beginning in 1837 Mann led a movement for better teaching and better paid teachers that spread elsewhere. Along with these changes came, for the first time, the gathering of statistics about schools and a discussion of school problems.

Training schools for teachers were also established at Mann's instigation, and equipment was greatly improved. By the mid-nineteenth century, it was a rare town or rural area that did not have at least a one-room school. A feeling that every American citizen should be educated at least through high school was firmly established.

A big boost to public higher education came from the Morrill Act of 1862, which gave federal lands to the states if they would establish colleges teaching courses in agriculture, engineering, and home economics. The Hatch Act (1887) provided federal funds for research and experiment stations, and the later Smith-Lever Act (1914) granted federal support for extension work in agriculture and home economics.

This early government funding in the United States laid the groundwork for the progressive education movement that swept the country at the end of the nineteenth century. Progressive education brought together industrial training, agricultural education, and social education as well as the new techniques of instruction advanced by educational theorists like Mann. Basic to this movement was the belief that children learn best in those experiences in which they have a vital interest and that modes of behavior are most easily learned by actual performance. Progressive education opposed formalized authoritarian procedure and fostered reorganization of classroom practice and curriculum and new attitudes toward the individual student.

John Dewey, another innovative educator, reorganized curriculum and put his ideas into operation at a laboratory school in Chicago where he taught at the University of Chicago from 1894 to 1904. Dewey dominated the progressive movement through his long years (1904 to 1930) as a professor of education at Columbia University and by writing a number of books. His influence led to the abandonment of the authoritarian methods of the past and a growing emphasis on learning through experimentation. In revolt against abstract learning, Dewey considered education as a tool that would enable people to integrate their culture and vocations effectively and usefully.

The principles and practices of progressive education gained wide acceptance in American school systems during the first half of the twentieth century. The movement was not without its critics, however, who faulted the approach because it did not emphasize a systematic study of the academic disciplines. Opposition gradually increased, and the movement declined in the years after World War II, although by then it had transformed American education.

The end of that war also brought another infusion of federal funding so that veterans could continue their education at public expense. Such funding continued after the Korean and Vietnam wars, too.

As theorists and administrators continued to shape the organization and curriculum of American education, a Supreme Court decision affected forever the composition of its student body. In its May 17, 1954 decision in *Brown v. Board of Education* of Topeka, Kansas, the Court set aside a state statute permitting cities with more than fifteen thousand people to maintain separate schools for blacks and whites. The Court ruled that all segregation in public schools was "inherently unequal" and that all blacks barred from attending public schools with white pupils were being denied equal protection of the law as guaranteed by the Fourteenth Amendment. This doctrine was extended to state-supported colleges and universities in March 1956. On May 31, 1955, the Court implemented its 1954 opinion by declaring that the federal district courts would have jurisdiction over lawsuits to enforce the desegregation decision and asked that desegregation proceed "with all deliberate speed."

At the time seventeen states made segregated elementary schools mandatory by law, and four others had laws permitting segregated schools. Discrimination in schools and in other aspects of life was common elsewhere, although not sanctioned by law.

The media covered the desegregation story from those first confrontations at southern schoolhouse doors as governors sought to stop black children — and their escort of federal marshals — from entering.

The story often went beyond educational aspects. Matters of curriculum and learning soon paled beside the sight of a mass of gun-carrying men in uniform escorting a tiny black girl or boy to school. Later, when mobs rioted and integration extended to other aspects of life in the South, reporters risked injury and withstood threats and insults to do their work, which went out of a narrow educational specialty and onto the front pages of newspapers and into the lead position on television news programs.

The desegregation decision set in motion the forces of change that still dominate American education today. After various school systems in the South were integrated during the 1960s, sometimes forcibly by federal troops, this trend spread to the North and West. In city after city, federal judges ordered the busing of children in elementary and secondary schools to achieve integration.

By 1980, more than half of the nation's 40.7 million school children traveled to school by bus. Of this number, about one-twentieth were bused so that schools could be integrated. Such busing quickly became a dominant and sensitive issue in large cities like Boston and Los Angeles where resistance by white parents was high and violence frequent.

Integration first caused white parents to move to the suburbs, leaving behind decaying inner cities and inferior, poorly funded school systems. Busing caused a decline in white support for suburban public schools, as blacks were brought in and white children sent across town to the inner cities where parents feared for their safety. Private — and largely segregated — schools were organized as a response to busing and integration, thus undermining the basic tenet of public education so prevalent in this country for so long.

In the 1990s, many schools reflect the paradoxes of American society as a whole. Strikes have plagued many districts and some colleges; teachers have organized into unions amid worries that there will be little money to give them regular pay raises. Crime and vandalism occur in most big-city schools and smaller ones as well. Drug use is high even among elementary students. The presence of gang members in high schools — carrying weapons and assaulting teachers and other students — has resulted in the need to hire school police to patrol buildings and grounds to keep order.

Absent any increase in federal funding for schools, the push for excellence, especially in math and science, will continue in the

1990s. One proposal that got a lot of support was an increase in days spent in school each year from 180 to 220. Critics of the American secondary education system said that students do not measure up to their compatriots in other countries because they don't spend enough time in school. In comparison, Japanese students go to school 243 days a year and West Germans, 210. Even Russia has a 210-day school year.

Another current dilemma revolves around the failure to accommodate the large numbers of minority students. In 1991, 30 percent of students in public schools — 12 million — were from a minority group. Experts estimate that this figure could reach 40 percent by the year 2000. Twenty-two of the twenty-five largest central city school districts in the United States have a student population that is predominantly minority. The problems inherent in this situation include racism, poverty, language differences, and cultural barriers. When school districts and administrators and teachers fail to deal with these matters — as many do not because of a failure of will and a lack of finances — students suffer.

"Most minority children remain in schools that are separate and decidedly unequal," wrote the members of a 1990 MIT task force in *Education That Works: An Active Plan for the Education of Minorities.* The report went on to note that minority children are victims of low expectations, inadequate school financing, few minority teachers, an over reliance on testing, poorly prepared teachers, and a disregard for language and cultural diversity.

In this regard, a problem exists in school districts in specific parts of the country: the rise in numbers of students who speak no English. This is the case in Miami and all of south Florida due to Cuban refugees; and in southern California and parts of the Pacific Northwest due to illegal aliens from Mexico and all of Central and South America. Since the fall of Saigon to the North Vietnamese in April 1975, 800,000 refugees from Southeast Asia have settled in the United States. California has 40 percent of these Vietnamese, Cambodian, Laotian, and Hmong people; the remainder live in urban areas of Texas, Minnesota, Pennsylvania, and Illinois. These refugees and their parents have had to adjust to vast cultural changes in society in general and schools in particular. The schools themselves have had to assimilate these students and, before they could communicate at all, find teachers who could speak languages not normally taught in the United States

Such special assistance costs money that school districts are finding difficult to raise. Throughout the 1980s, local districts and state governments got less and less financial support from the federal government. Funds were cut for everything from school lunches to loans for college students.

Even if these major, societal-caused problems were solved tomorrow, more fundamental concerns over curriculum, teaching methods, and the process of learning would remain. Such arguments revolve around experimentation versus a "back to basics" approach and an answer to the old question: Why can't Johnny read? In 1983, a report by the U.S. Department of Education, *A Nation at Risk: The Importance for National Reform*, sparked a national drive for educational excellence and resulted in a ranking of states in various categories of educational achievement that provided a standard by which to measure improvement. While this and other studies were a useful way to gain a national perspective on American education, such reports do not pay for teachers or books or police or drug control programs or other solutions to the vexing dilemmas of schools today.

The state of ferment that has existed in education for the past 35 years will likely remain that way.

Problems and Solutions

Although the press has watched the education story with interest for years, it has covered it as a regular beat only since earlier in the twentieth century. The writing of Mann, Dewey, and the other reformers were largely in book form. The major changes taking place in education during the progressive movement were not covered thoroughly, except in articles written by those who participated in it.

Public schools became a regular beat as newspaper editors realized that the public school system was often the biggest thing in town, affecting more lives, employing more people, and costing more tax money than anything else. People took pride in the student athletic teams and hoped for a better life for their children because of what they learned in the schools. This created high reader interest for stories about the district.

Although the subject matter is more pleasant than the often gruesome police beat, and not as complicated as the medical beat, education reporting has its drawbacks.

One problem exists in the attitudes of some of the major sources, the administrators and faculty members of the school unit being covered. They have a kind of "ivory tower mentality" that sometimes causes a communication gap. Some academics — especially on the university level — do not seem to understand what is happening in society beyond the rarified walls of their institutions. They tend to talk down to reporters, for example. They aren't always responsive to questions and may wait for days to return phone calls.

But such lack of responsiveness is rare in secondary education, where most education reporters get full cooperation. One reason is the high value most communities place on their schools. The foundation of American democracy depends on how well educated its citizens are. It is important for newspapers to monitor school districts because so much tax money goes into running them. There is a potential for mismanagement and misuse. Someone needs to keep an eye on them, and that someone is often the education reporter of the local newspaper.

Another problem on the education beat is that major sources often use long and confusing terms. Buildings without steps become "barrier-free modifications," for example. If a reporter has to include such terminology in a story, he or she should explain it immediately afterward.

In much of the country, school systems are tightly organized in a hierarchy extending from federal and state levels down to city and rural districts. This organization gives education a structure, similar to city governments or police departments, that can be fairly easily covered by reporters.

Local school districts form the basic units of the public education system in the United States; however, state and federal agencies supervise them, using the leverage that comes with their funding.

The thousands of school districts in the United States range from complicated systems with hundreds of schools in large cities to small one-room schoolhouses in rural areas. Most states have school districts that are politically and geographically independent of other local units of government. The districts sometimes cut across town lines, although cities usually make up a single district. Even when a school district covers the same area as a city, however, it is usually independent of city officials. Officials are elected independently, and the districts also have their own taxing powers and complete control over their budgets.

School district control is exercised by a school board; members are elected in nonpartisan elections separate from those of other officials and serve without pay. The members are often nominated by a petition of qualified voters.

Boards of five or seven members are common, but small districts sometimes have as few as three. Terms of office range from three to six years and are staggered so that there are always experienced members on the board. School boards are primarily responsible for maintaining the quality of schools.

Because school board members hold other jobs, they hire a superintendent to run the district's schools and to carry out the decisions of the board. The superintendent has as many assistants as the district can afford. Each school is run by a principal and staffed by teachers, all hired by the superintendent with the approval of the board. The board also approves an annual budget, sets the tax rate for property owners who pay for the schools with such taxes, authorizes the purchase of real estate and the construction of new schools and new buildings at old schools, and maintains control over curriculum.

In a growing number of large cities, however, control of schools is being placed in the hands of local committees. The idea behind this shift comes from the view that teachers, parents, and community residents know the needs of schools better than central office administrators and will, as a result, do a better job in managing them. On the negative side is the fact that board members sometimes lack management skills.

In New York, for example, the school system is divided into 32 districts, each with its own board with control over elementary and middle schools. The Board of Education retains authority over high schools. Other cities are trying a similar approach giving local boards of teachers, parents, and business leaders authority over curriculum, the hiring and firing of teachers, textbook selection, and the structure of the school day. This kind of system has led to increased dissension in cities like Chicago, which put a decentralized plan into effect in 1989.

State departments of education, which have final authority and responsibility for the educational system, usually grant much of the power to local boards, whether they be local committees or those chosen city wide. States establish minimum standards, then delegate operating authority to the local boards. These standards include the number of school days required each year, the subjects taught, the qualifications of teachers, the certification of new buildings, and the selection of textbooks.

School financing is within the power of local school boards, although some states now make up the difference between the tax income for schools in a community and the bottom line of the budget. The school districts themselves determine their own budgets and set their own tax rate (an amount that is added to the general tax rate along with the revenue needs of the city and county). This tax rate must usually be ratified by voters in an election. In recent years in smaller districts the amount allocated for school districts is greater than any other governmental entity. This often excessive amount has made school districts the subject of voter wrath; people have taken out their frustrations about all high taxes on the only thing upon which they have a chance to take direct action—the school budget. When tax levies are voted down, school boards have no choice but to cut programs in the budget until voters are willing to pass a new one.

More suggestions on the education beat appear in "Likely Problems and How to Solve Them" later in this chapter.

How to Cover Education

The coverage of education includes the same kinds of "sparring" that exist between reporters and any official agency. Although news consists of both good and bad elements, sources—in education as well as in city, county, and state governments and police departments—want to accentuate the good and ignore the bad.

The board members and the superintendent are all potential news sources. The activities of the district are the subject of weekly or monthly board meetings, and such meetings represent a natural focal point of a newspaper's interest. The sparring in this case usually includes attempts to close the meeting to reporters or make its substance off the record. If the state has an open meetings law, the reporter will be on firm ground in refusing to leave or in agreeing to stay and not take notes. If no such law exists, perhaps the reporter can negotiate with board members or take the controversy onto the editorial pages of the newspaper in an effort to change the policy. (See Appendices A and B on the legal and ethical problems of reporting and Box 6.4 in Chapter 6 on open meetings laws.)

An accommodation must be made because of the importance of school news. In smaller districts, for example, school news sometimes represents as much as 25 percent of a newspaper's content. It is equally important in large cities.

An education reporter will usually deal with the same group of sources: board members and the superintendent, other administrative personnel, teachers, students, and occasionally parents and citizens. Because of this constancy of sources, an education reporter can establish operating methods that will make the job easier:

1. **Meet with key sources regularly.** As soon as a reporter takes over the education beat, he or she should visit the school board president and district superintendent to establish ground rules for coverage. Few officials try to ignore the power of the press in a district because they need to influence public opinion about budget matters

or the school system in general. If officials seem not to know this, a reporter should point it out. The reporter should clearly establish his or her role as a mechanism for informing the public and not as a tool of the district. After a reporter has worked the beat longer, these regular meetings serve to keep lines of communication open and to inform the reporter of what is going on in the district from an official standpoint.

2. **Suggest ways to improve communication.** A reporter might suggest that the school board set up a press table at its meetings and provide advance copies of meeting agendas, reports, and minutes. This helps reporters cover meetings better.

3. **Know the state open meetings law.** Some states have passed laws that prohibit the exclusion of the press from any officially convened meeting. Other states do not have such laws, although organizations often abide by them anyway because they realize the value of openness. A reporter needs to know the law and be prepared to use it as a means to keep all meetings open to coverage. State press associations often print wallet-sized cards containing the actual wording of the law. Usually only personnel matters are subject to closure of a meeting.

4. **Inform sources about the mechanics of journalism.** A reporter should tell board members, the superintendent, principals, teachers, and key students the deadlines of the publication or broadcast stations. A reporter who has developed a good rapport with a source should help that source understand the proper way to write a news release and what constitutes "news" worthy of release. Larger districts have their own public information officers, however, in which case such advice is not necessary and might be resented and ignored.

5. **Learn the background of the district.** An education reporter must fully understand the workings of the school district, its method of financing, its recent history, and its problems. This is best accomplished through background interviews with key sources, a careful reading of past issues of the newspaper, and a candid talk with reporters who have covered the beat in the past.

Kinds of Education Stories

Although education stories vary with the individual districts to be covered, a few subjects are always important:

1. **School board meetings.** Most of what happens in a district is passed upon by the board. Its regular meeting schedule offers a

base upon which to build total coverage. Important sources are usually at meetings, and reporters can talk to them before and after sessions and during coffee breaks. Meetings are sometimes boring affairs with little or no news resulting. Reporters should not be lulled by the dullness, however, and leave early. An unscrupulous board president can save controversial items until late in a meeting. The possibility increases the importance of getting a board agenda in advance. If a reporter must leave to file a story on deadline, he or she should get the notes or a verbal fill-in from other reporters at the meeting. Board stories should be written the same way as any meeting story; select the most important elements for the lead, and deal with all other aspects of the meeting according to their newsworthy quality, at times breaking them into several stories to make the amount of material more manageable.

2. **News of specific schools.** Principals, teachers, and sometimes students are the main sources of these kinds of stories, which can often be written as timeless features. These stories cover interesting student activities, unusual courses, or "unforgettable" teachers. Construction of new schools or fires that destroy old ones are news stories, too.

3. **Important district events.** The annual budget election and contest for school board seats are special events that merit special attention. Stories about the budget election, for example, should explain the budgeting and financing process and analyze major items. School board candidates should be interviewed about their stands on various issues and their past experience. Another special event is a teachers' strike. In this case a reporter must explain the issues and demands on both sides and the ramifications of a strike without, of course, taking sides. If the strike occurs, it should be covered like a regular news event—with sidebar stories on any unique aspects.

4. **Activities of special groups.** The activities of groups such as the teachers' union and the parent-teacher association always make news in a district. The cultivation of sources is particularly important here so that a strike, for example, can be covered fairly from the unofficial as well as the official side.

5. **Activities at other schools and colleges.** Although the local district represents the primary focus of an education reporter's interest, other schools and colleges in the geographic area should not be neglected. Many cities also contain private secondary schools and public and private colleges and universities that merit attention. The kinds of stories and the need to cultivate sources are the same as in the school district. If a large university is located in a city,

however, it may need its own reporter because of its large size and importance as a center of news.

6. **Local angles on national stories.** Education reporters perform a real service to readers when they tie a national issue to the local scene. The presence of a program such as busing, vandalism, teacher abuse, curriculum changes, or textbook censorship usually interests readers. A reporter should keep up on national issues by reading news magazines, big-city newspapers, and such specialized publications as *The Chronicle of Higher Education*.

Writing Education Stories

"Recently, there has been a lot of pressure to write tight," says Donna Schmidt of the *Tigard Times*. "This means you have to digest a lot of information into a short amount of space. My approach to a given story depends on the story.

"What I try to do first is summarize the story in my head, what are the main themes, why am I writing this story, who am I writing for? Sometimes I struggle over the lead, sometimes not. It often depends on how the interview went, what the subject is. I sit there and try to focus on what I am doing."

Before she can start writing any story, however, Schmidt has to get her lead. "If I really get stumped, I actually type 'It was a dark and stormy night' just to get started and relaxed," she laughs. "That usually works. Or, on a feature, I'll write a news lead, then go back and change it later. Maybe I'll think of my lead halfway through. I'll write it and then move it into place."

#1

Donna Schmidt leads with the most important fact: students in a certain area will have to attend a new school. Her transition notes that many parents for the area in question opposed the plans previously.

SCHOOL LINES DRAWN
Bull Mountain Road
to Divide 2 High Schools

By Donna Schmidt of the *Times*

1 TUALATIN — High school students in Tigard who live south of Bull Mountain Road will attend Tualatin High School beginning in September, the Tigard-Tualatin School Board decided last Thursday.

2 Many Bull Mountain parents strongly opposed any plans to send their students to Tualatin High and took their voices to four public hearings on the issue.

In graf 3, using the word "but", she notes how the boundaries were drawn.

Grafs 4 and 5 let her give a quote from the other side.

In graf 6, she brings readers into the meeting site and gives them the feel of the place ("hushed murmurs"), something she expands upon in grafs 7 and 8.

In grafs 10, 11, and 12, Schmidt lets board members express their points of view.

3 But in the end, the board went with plans drawn by a Portland State University demographer it hired last spring to set new boundaries for the district.

4 And the decision frustrated some.

5 "Well, the community that didn't want to be split apart got split three ways and Durham is split again," one frustrated parent called out as she headed to her car.

6 The crowd of about 150 broke out into hushed murmurs in the gymnasium at Bridgeport Elementary School as the decision was announced.

7 "I can't believe it," said June Sulffridge, a Bull Mountain parent who has been outspoken on the issue.

8 "They didn't even talk about any of our concerns—the busing, the safety issues. They didn't address any of them," she said shaking her head.

9 Bull Mountain parents had expressed concerns about long bus rides for students, additional buses on narrow Bull Mountain Road and teen drivers commuting to Tualatin.

10 The decision resetting attendance boundaries, said School Board Chairman Mike Nelson, was the hardest the board had ever encountered.

11 Board member Pat Biggs suggested that students north of Bull Mountain Road be given the choice of attending either Tigard or Tualatin high school. The board did not decide on the choice issue but agreed to discuss it at a future meeting.

12 "I understand Bull Mountain's desire to stay together, but quite frankly there isn't room at Tigard High," board member Rich Carlson said. Carlson added that the safety and busing concerns of parents would be addressed at a later date.

13 Nelson agreed but said he was concerned that if students were given a choice, a blitz from Bull Mountain might quickly fill Tualatin High to capacity. Russ Joki, school superintendent, said a choice option area north of Bull Mountain Road might change year-to-year depending on enrollment figures.

14 "We would hope to honor it every year but the reality is we may not," Joki told the board. A choice zone would also put the burden of transportation to the nearest bus stop on parents, Joki added.

In graf 15, she gives readers who do not know the exact boundaries for the school changes.

15 The new high school boundaries send Tigard students who live south of Bull Mountain Road and west of Pacific Highway to Tualatin High. Durham students east of Southwest 74th Avenue at the railroad tracks, including the Kingsgate neighborhood, also will attend Tualatin High, as well as all students south of the Tualatin River.

In grafs 16, 17, and 18, she presents the viewpoints of students, with the results of a previous student straw vote and a paraphrased quote.

16 Tualatin High opens next fall with freshman through junior classes only. This year's junior class voted Dec. 3 to remain at Tigard High for its senior year.

17 Not all juniors voted, but of those that did only 65 said they favored forming the school's first senior class. Students were also given a tour of the new high school two weeks ago. District officials said they had to have at least 125 seniors to offer a range of courses similar to Tigard High's.

18 Student envoy to the School Board, Chris Backeberg, said the questions generated a lot of discussion among students but that voter turnout was low. Some students said they needed more time to think about it before casting a vote, Backeberg said.

She gives more background in grafs 19-25.

19 Under the new boundaries and with all of the district's seniors, Tigard High is projected to open with 1,693 students.

20 Tualatin High will open with a projected 853 students in three grade levels. Enrollments are expected to balance somewhat the following year with 1,193 at Tualatin High and 1,469 at Tigard.

21 Bull Mountain Road also marks the attendance boundary between Fowler and Twality middle schools. Sixth-, seventh- and eighth-grade students south of Bull Mountain Road will attend Twality when school opens in September with students from Templeton and Durham elementaries. Some C.F. Tigard Elementary students will also attend Twality.

22 And Bridgeport students who live east of Interstate 5 will continue to attend Twality.

23 Fowler Middle School will house students from Metzger and Phil Lewis elementaries, most of C.F. Tigard students and Woodward students north of Bull Mountain Road.

24 Students at Tualatin Elementary, Byrom Elementary and about half of Bridgeport students will attend Hazelbrook Middle School in Tualatin.

25 Minor adjustments to elementary boundaries included sending Bridgeport students who live west of Interstate 5 in an area bounded by Sagert Street, Martinazzi Avenue and Nyberg Road to Byrom Elementary. Bridgeport students who live in Tigard west of the Tualatin River along Pacific Highway will attend C.F. Tigard next year.

She ends her story by using an upbeat quote from the chairman of the school board.

26 At the end of the meeting Nelson thanked parents for their comments during the public hearings.

27 "It's been long and tiring," he said. "We know what the decision is now so let's get on with education. However the decision affects you, you can make the experience positive through your involvement in your child's education," Nelson told the crowd.

#2

ACLU JUMPS INTO SCHOOL FRACAS
First Amendment Violation Alleged
In Two Instances
By Donna Schmidt of the *Times*

This follow-up story to an earlier one about censorship of a local high school paper begins with the news: the American Civil Liberties

1 TIGARD—School officials said this week that an editorial barred from a student newspaper two weeks ago may now be published.

2 But the move is not enough to stop a lawsuit

Union has filed suit against the district.

filed by the American Civil Liberties Union against the Tigard-Tualatin School District.

3 Portland attorney Jonathan Hoffman filed a lawsuit in Washington County Circuit Court on Friday claiming the district violated students' First Amendment rights under both federal and state constitutions.

4 The school district has 10 days to file a response to the charges.

In graf 5, Donna Schmidt gives readers the background to the story, in case they had missed it.

5 The disputed opinion piece written by editors of Hi-Spots, the Tigard High School newspaper, and the suspension of two other students who published an underground newspaper drew the attention of civil libertarians when students cried foul.

In grafs 6 and 7, she tells who the students are and uses a long quote from the ACLU attorney.

6 Hoffman filed the suit on behalf of Shannon Kasten, editor-in-chief of Hi-Spots; Marce Edwards, managing editor of the paper; and Scott Barcik and Tom Jansen, publishers of Low-Spots, an underground newspaper first published last month. All are seniors at the high school.

7 "These students have been punished for acting upon the belief that the expression of their ideas is permissible in a free society. Somehow, they have got it in their heads that they have the right not only to think for themselves but to disseminate and to communicate their thoughts to others. These are hardly radical or revolutionary ideas; they are at the core of our foundations as a free society," Hoffman said at a news conference Friday.

In graf 8, she sums up the issue for readers.

8 The issue centers on whether school officials can punish students for off-campus activities and the degree of control administrators have over student publications.

In grafs 9, 10, and 11 she gives some of the school district's views, noting that officials were not commenting.

9 Superintendent Russ Joki said the administration objected to the use of profanity in Low-Spots and that the paper's articles were "anti-school."

10 Under the advice of the district's attorney, Larry Amburgey, school officials are not commenting on the case until the suit is reviewed and discussed by those named as

defendants in the complaint, said Susan Stark, district spokeswoman.

11   The suit names Superintendent Russ Joki, Assistant Superintendent Al Davidian, Tigard High Principal Mark Kubiaczyk and all School Board members.

In grafs 12-17, Schmidt presents a more detailed summary of the dispute, allowing readers to draw their own conclusions.

12   The dispute arose when Barcik and Jansen solicited articles for the paper from fellow students, the complaint said, and administrators threatened them with disciplinary action if the paper was circulated at school without prior approval.

13   Barcik and Jansen produced and distributed Low-Spots off campus. But when copies of the paper surfaced at school, Kubiaczyk suspended the two for seven days. The suspension was rescinded, and the two students instead were assigned to write 10-page papers on the First Amendment, specifically on freedom of expression.

14   When Hi-Spots editors decided to publish an editorial supporting the unofficial paper as an alternative forum for students, they were told to rewrite parts of the editorial or replace it.

15   Kasten said they were told that Hi-Spots would be confiscated and the paper's funding cut if the editors did not comply.

16   Kasten pulled the editorial, replaced it with red, bold letters accusing administrators of censorship, authorized the printing and then hurriedly distributed it to students before officials could seize the publication.

In graf 17, she gives the ACLU's main contention, detailing the actual complaint in graf 18.

17   The ACLU maintains that underground papers such as Low-Spots are protected under Oregon and federal constitutional law — on and off campus. And that administrators went too far in their efforts to block student opinion in the school-sanctioned Hi-Spots.

18   The complaint asks the court to revoke all disciplinary actions against the students and to bar administrators from interfering with student publications ''which are not obscene, libelous or which do not create an

imminent danger of violence or substantial disruption of school activities."

Lest readers wonder if any of this is about money, Schmidt answers that question in graf 19, expanding on it in graf 20 with a very nice quote that deftly sums up the whole story for readers.

19 The suit also seeks $100 in damages for Jansen and Barcik, the publishing cost of their first edition of Low-Spots.

20 "This case is about principle, not money," Hoffman said.

Education Reporting:
Likely Problems and How to Solve Them

Problem	**Solution**
1. Suspicious school officials who try to hide information.	1a. Explain the need for full disclosure.
	1b. Tell officials the value of open communication to the public via the press (better understanding of school problems and more sympathy in passing budget measures).
	1c. Explain journalistic processes to school officials (deadlines, the difference between straight journalism and public relations, and what news is).
2. One-sided stories with a public relations slant that is too favorable to the district and that ignores real problems.	2. Talk to both sides of any controversy. Make sure not to automatically take the district viewpoint, even though you know it well.
3. Lack of understanding of local and national educational issues.	3a. Try to speak the language of sources by learning the background of issues and the terminology.

3b. Get on mailing lists for newsletters, budgets, and other material.

3c. Establish "unofficial" sources (secretaries and teachers) who know what is going on.

3d. Keep up with national educational issues by subscribing to publications such as *The Chronicle of Higher Education*, *Education Week*, and the *American School Board Journal*. Get on the mailing lists of organizations such as the National Education Association, the American Federation of Teachers, the Association of State Colleges and Universities, the National School Boards Association, the U.S. Department of Education, the state education department, the Senate Committee on Human Resources, the House Committee on Education and Labor, and appropriate state legislature committees.

4. Dull, boring stories that involve only meeting coverage.

4a. Personalize stories by showing the effect on readers.

4b. Take advantage of the potential for features about the wide variety of people and subjects available in any school district.

4c. If meeting stories are too long or involve many subjects, break coverage into several shorter pieces.

Summary

The coverage of education is an essential beat for any publication. In all but large cities, where it competes with many other areas, the school district is an important source of news because it touches so many lives, takes a great deal of tax revenues, and is an employer of considerable importance. Education reporters should cover their beats systematically by attending school board meetings and keeping track of budget elections and teachers' strikes. They need to cultivate both official sources (board members, the superintendent, principals) and unofficial sources (teachers, students, and parents). Stories will range from direct district news to timeless features on unusual courses or teachers. Local aspects of national stories also provide good possibilities. Reporters should learn all they can about the operation of the schools and colleges in their area of coverage, and in turn, they should teach their sources about the way journalism operates so the two can work well together.

Exercises

1. Spend a day as a student (either on the grade school, junior high, or high school level) and write a story about what you do.

2. Spend a day with a classroom teacher in an elementary school and a high school. Write a story that reports what you do and compares and contrasts education on such widely disparate levels.

3. Select a common element of the operation of a school district (buying supplies, cooking for large numbers of people, driving a school bus) and write an in-depth story that tells readers things they never knew.

4. Select a national educational problem (drug use, crime, funding shortages) and interview school district personnel, teachers, students, and parents to get the local angle.

5. Cover a school board meeting and write a story about what goes on. Take notes on everything that happens, making sure to indicate who says what and to spell their names correctly. After

the meeting, ask questions to clarify what is written in your notes. Ask school district officials for any additional material you need to complete the story. As you look at your notes you will have to pick the most important subject discussed—and, perhaps, voted upon—at the meeting to emphasize in the lead. Other subjects may not be covered in as much detail in your story; you may decide to drop a few entirely.

Migrant mother, Nipomo, California, 1936 by Dorothea Lange. [*Courtesy U.S. Farm Security Administration Collection, Prints and Photographs Division, Library of Congress*]

6

Investigative Reporting

*I did not intend to be a muckraker; I did not know I was one till
President Roosevelt picked the name out of Bunyan's Pilgrim's
Progress and pinned it on us; and even then he said that he did not
mean me. Those were important days; we were all innocent folk; but
no doubt all movements, whether for good or for evil, are as innocent
of intention as ours.*
—Lincoln Steffens
.The Autobiography of Lincoln Steffens

One Investigative Reporter

In the summer of 1981, when editors and reporters at *The
Oregonian* in Portland heard that an Indian guru and his followers
had purchased a ranch in central Oregon, they knew a unique story
might be in the offing. That the Bhagwan Shree Rajneesh was
moving his headquarters from a commune in Poona, India, to the
64,229-acre Big Muddy Ranch received national attention. Although
the national story soon ran its course, local media could not ignore
such a bizarre tale.

The bhagwan loved diamond encrusted jewelry and Rolls Royces—he owned more than 80, some of them painted to match his expensive robes. While the bhagwan did not speak in public at first, he allowed himself to be seen on his daily Rolls Royce "drive-bys" which gave his adoring followers glimpses of him.

These followers—called "sannyasins" in Hindi—were mostly Caucasians from Europe and the United States. Many were highly educated and wealthy, yet were willing to adopt Indian names and work 12 hours a day building Rajneeshpuram—a self-sufficient city of 4,500 residents at its peak—from the hardscrabble soil of a failed cattle ranch in a remote and sparsely populated area of the state.

Despite rumors of free love and abundant drugs at the ranch, most Oregonians seemed to adopt a live-and-let-live attitude toward the exotic new residents in those early days.

In 1982, however, the Rajneeshees bought most of the property in the tiny town of Antelope, seven miles away. They took control of that city's government and renamed it Rajneesh. Long time residents were displaced and harassed. Lawsuits were filed against the guru's religious organization and its various corporations. In one, an environmental group said the new city violated Oregon's strict land-use laws. In another, the Oregon attorney general said the city was illegal because it was based on religious control. The bhagwan and his foreign-born followers also began to have trouble with the U.S. Immigration and Naturalization Service.

Early reporting dealt with these and other events as they occurred, but did not go below the surface. Two and a half years after the bhagwan arrived in Oregon, editors and reporters of the investigative team at *The Oregonian* decided to take a closer look at what was going on.

Led by Dick Thomas, an assistant managing editor, the team also included Leslie L. Zaitz and James Long, both longtime investigative reporters on the paper; Scotta Callister, an assistant city editor, as editor and writer and sometimes reporter; and Randy Wood, photographer.

The result of their efforts—which took 13 months to report and write and cost the paper $250,000—was published in a twenty-one-part series from June 30 to July 19, 1985. An examination of their techniques reveals investigative reporting at its best.

Getting Started

As a first step, members of the team decided to follow the money trail, agreeing not to ignore any line of inquiry, going wherever the story led them, according to Thomas. Quickly they were into subjects like membership, finances, the history of the movement, and the problems of the movement, gathering all the paper documentation they could (see Box 6.1).

"We started with no information except clippings from previous news stories on the Rajneeshees that had appeared in the paper since 1981," says Zaitz. "Jim [Long] and I have substantial law enforcement contacts, and we started talking to them: the FBI, the Oregon State Police, and the Oregon attorney general's office. We also filed an early FOI request with 26 federal agencies in both their Oregon district offices and in Washington, DC, for anything they had on the Rajneeshees." (Eventually, the team got help from law enforcement and/or government agencies in Australia, India, Germany, Canada, and England.)

One such FOI request yielded a lot of information from a surprising source. Material from the Bonneville Power Administration, which owned the power lines into the property, revealed the economics of the ranch, the intent of the people there, and their future plans.

(One government agency which had a lot of information on the movement, the U.S. Immigration and Naturalization Service, offered help only reluctantly. Neither Thomas nor Zaitz knows why the INS fought the release of information at all levels, unless, in their view, its officials were trying to cover up their own botched investigation of the Rajneeshees and ineffectiveness in dealing with them.)

A look at depositions for lawsuits in Multnomah County (where Portland is located and where many Rajneeshee-related lawsuits were filed) and in Wasco and Jefferson counties (where the ranch lies) yielded information on the backgrounds of important people and on property transactions. (Under court rules, depositions are available to reporters unless protected by court order.)

A big problem emerged early: the bhagwan's non-Indian disciples had adopted Hindi names. This made it difficult to check the backgrounds of people at the ranch. The team spent a day and a half in the Wasco County Courthouse in The Dalles and half a day in the Jefferson County Courthouse in Madras copying every voter registration card filed by residents of the ranch and of Antelope. Each card listed either given names or parents' names along with the Hindi name.

The reporters later used motor vehicle and immigration records to sort out this confusing mess. Eventually, they put all the names into their computer and used both in their stories (as in "Prem Savita, also known as Sally-Anne Croft").

Box 6.1

How to Look at Records

Investigative reporters call it "the paper trail," the various skeins of information that, when woven together into completed stories, form the fabric of revelation that sets investigative journalism apart. The trail is one of records, and no investigative reporter or public affairs reporter will succeed without learning how to read them. An investigative reporter will spend a great deal more time looking at records and budgets than meeting with secret sources in obscure places.

Examining records is a tedious and time-consuming process and not for everyone. Reporters who like to interview people best should probably avoid this kind of investigative journalism. For those who enjoy this process and do it well, the rewards are great. Donald Barlett and James Steele of the *Philadelphia Inquirer* have won two Pulitzer Prizes largely by examining records. Their 1989 prize was given for their 15-month investigation into hidden tax breaks granted by Congress. Before they interviewed a single source, they spent months looking at Senate Finance Committee lists of those exempted from complying with the law, Securities and Exchange Commission documents, corporation records in state capitals, lawsuits, bankruptcy proceedings, financial disclosure statements by members of Congress, and computer databases of newspapers, magazines and government reports.

Investigative reporter Jerry Uhrhammer thinks that reporters have to take what he calls "a thinking person's approach" to beat coverage and learn how the system operates, whether it's the city hall or county courts. "You need to determine how the money flows," says Uhrhammer, now with the *Morning News Tribune* in Tacoma, Washington. "You need to learn about the laws and regulations under which that system of government operates. You find out how it is supposed to operate so you can recognize when it doesn't. If you know this, then you've got some inkling when there is something wrong. You also need to know where the information is located for the answers you need. There's a paper trail everywhere, especially in government. You need to analyze where the paper trail is and where you penetrate it. Where are the records?"

1. *Financial records.* All corporate entities doing business in a state must file articles of incorporation or partnership papers with the office of the secretary of state and usually the state department of commerce. A company that issues stock must also file a prospectus with the federal Securities and Exchange Commission and the various stock exchanges upon which it is listed. These records yield a great deal of information not contained in the normal annual report, such as names of owners or other names under which the company does business. Records of privately held companies, however, may be impossible to obtain, except in unusual circumstances.

2. *Bids and specifications.* Most states require public bidding for construction projects of a certain amount or higher. Reporters should know

that amount. Projects should also go to the lowest bidder. If not, reporters should find out why. They should also look at specifications to see if they have been rigged to meet the capabilities of one particular company or product. Another area for reporters to watch in this regard is the awarding of contracts on an emergency basis to avoid bidding requirements. In this case the reporter can find something bought on an emergency basis, then compare it to what another city paid for the same item. If the amount is considerably higher, the reporter should begin to ask who might have benefitted financially from the supplier who was awarded the "emergency" contract.

3. *The spending of money*. To find out how a city government or any public agency spends its money, reporters should look at the annual budget in various categories. For example, to find out what is happening with a program, look at what has been allocated to the program and go back to previous years. If a growing (or lesser) amount has gone to the program over the years, a reporter should ask why it is being expanded (or cut back) now. This can be determined by following the "audit trail," the documentation governments always keep to record the spending of money: vouchers, requisitions, checks. For example, to find out how much money a public official spent attending a meeting, a reporter could check bills for airline tickets and hotel and rental car expenses.

4. *Telephone records*. It is a state law in Oregon and many other states that anything to do with a public agency is public, including telephone records. In this instance a reporter can ask to see the toll records for the telephone the official uses. These records indicate what number a person has called; the name can be gained from that, for example, by consulting city directories.

5. *Real estate deeds and mortgages*. Deeds and mortgages establish the ownership of land and other property. They help establish a chronology of what happened in a real estate transaction, especially through dates of purchase and how one piece of property relates to another. In the case of ownership, reporters should look for "dummy" owners, who are fronts for representatives of syndicates or union pension funds. Some states require that reports, listing good points and bad points, be issued before land can be sold. Without this report, the sale is illegal.

6. *Miscellaneous questions*. In addition to checking these records, reporters should be prepared to ask a number of questions, then examine any pertinent documentation. Who controls planning in the city or county? What parts of town have been set aside in the total land-use plan? Who profits from the location of apartment houses and shopping centers? What variances have been granted to building codes, and to whom were they granted? Do those in political favor of officials get away with using inadequate materials or have fewer inspections on building sites? Does anyone get favorable treatment in tax assessment?

(See Appendix C for more information on how to search public records.)

Keeping Track of Material

After three months of material gathering by the reporters, Thomas decided to buy a computer system for the project that would be entirely self-contained and separate from the newspaper's regular system. The growing mound of material was then organized by subject (references to everything in the Rajneesh organization), chronology (key events from the beginning of the movement to the present), and individuals by name (all information on people by given name, Hindi name, place of birth, education, line of work, parents' names).

Each page of each document collected by the team was stamped with a sequential number and indexed in the computer. The notebooks containing the actual documents were stored in the unit's office off of the main newsroom. Later, reports of trips taken by the reporters as well as names gathered in their reporting were also entered into the system. By the summer of 1985, when the series began to run in the paper, the team had collected 25,000 pages of documentation and compiled information on 4,400 people. By spring 1986, the document pile had reached 40,000 pages.

Visiting the Ranch

With this preliminary work behind them, the team was ready to start conducting interviews. In July 1984, Zaitz, Long, and Callister went to the ranch for the first time. "They were pretending to operate as a city, so we knew we could get into city hall," says Zaitz. "We arrived in mid-morning and quickly announced who we were. We pushed for every piece of paper we could get — invoices, minutes of city council meetings. They complied with the requests fairly quickly. We got what we asked for one week later at 25 cents a page."

The reporters decided to go on the regular press bureau tour of the ranch — two hours for $3. Officials told them to return the next morning at 10:30. As they drove to the ranch from Madras, they encountered a Rajneesh road grader blocking the narrow road. A bus had just gone through ahead of them but the grader was now stalled. They waited two hours and got their own special seven-hour tour. (Zaitz speculates that Rajneeshee officials did not want the reporters to learn what regular visitors were told and shown.)

After the tour, the three met with a public relations staff member who told them she knew they were investigative reporters who had been working on a story for three months. "We replied that no story was planned; we were doing research," says Zaitz. "We promised that if we found anything derogatory, they would have every opportunity to respond.''

The team returned two weeks later for a second visit and asked for copies of documents. They took along a portable copier to save time. They encountered some hostility but no resistance, although a Rajneeshee watched which documents they copied.

Reporting Abroad

In mid-December 1984, Zaitz, joined by photographer Wood for one week, went to India to find out why Rajneesh left and details of the movement there. Zaitz spent four weeks in Bombay and Poona, the site of the bhagwan's main commune before he moved to Oregon.

Zaitz's first problem in Bombay was to figure out the government structure to determine what agencies might have the information he sought. He read the telephone books and quite literally guessed which agencies might have something.

''I went over with the assumption that we would not get much,'' says Zaitz, but the police were exceptionally helpful. In Poona, a detective was assigned to get the documents he wanted by the next morning. Other government agencies provided tax records, property records, visa and immigration records.

The same kind of cooperation did not come from the small number of followers keeping the bhagwan's commune running. Zaitz and Wood were treated with suspicion. Zaitz joined Long in London for a week before Long left on a sixty-five day trip to Germany, the Netherlands, Switzerland, and Italy. By then, the word was out about his purpose and he was thrown out of every Rajneesh center in those countries.

Seeing the Key Source

With the bhagwan unavailable for interviews, the key source for the team was Anand Sheela, his personal secretary and the person who ran the day-to-day affairs of the ranch, the commune, and the town. During the guru's three-year period of meditation, she was the only one to whom he talked.

The team had first encountered Sheela's aggressive style in legal depositions she had given in various court cases. She had been highly visible around the state as she attended to the affairs of the movement. She granted media interviews constantly and once had even led members of the Oregon Legislature in prayer. When things started going badly for the movement, she became more publicly hostile in TV appearances where some of what she said had to be bleeped out.

In November 1984, Zaitz returned to the ranch to interview her. He entered the large meeting room and saw Sheela sitting at the end of a long table flanked by a number of her lieutenants. A video crew was recording the proceedings. She told him he was barred from Rajneeshpuram. He left and his relationship with the Rajneeshees went steadily downhill after.

As the team neared publication date, they requested interviews with various Rajneeshee officials and were told to submit questions in writing. They did so but got no response. (Ironically, Rajneeshee leaders continued to cooperate with other *Oregonian* reporters covering daily events at the ranch.)

Interviewing the Disenchanted

Interviews with people who are at odds with the subject of a story have long been a standard investigative reporting technique. This was equally valuable in the case of former sannyasins, but not always easy to do.

Names came from the documents gathered by the team. And, after the series began, the stories generated more leads. People the reporters talked to—both on the telephone and in person— mentioned other people and the list of names grew.

Some former sannyasins were in hiding and afraid. Talking to them took some coaxing. Initial interviews were often done off the record. The reporters talked to some people 100 times or more.

"After we found these people, we had to get them to trust us," says Zaitz. "This required repeated contact and fairly short interviews. We built up their trust in us. It sounds so easy, but they were coming out of an extraordinary experience. We were gentle with them, and we understood how they felt."

A number of sources maintained a loyalty to the bhagwan or to the movement itself. Even though they talked to the reporters, they were torn by their old loyalty.

Writing the Series

After Zaitz and Long returned to Portland from their foreign trips in March 1985, they met with Callister and Thomas and agreed to begin the series by early summer, before the annual festival at

Rajneeshpuram, a 10-day pilgrimage by as many as 15,000 followers from all over the world.

In preparing the series, the three reporters began a process they would follow throughout their work together. First, they discussed what they had and how to break it into manageable chunks. Next, Zaitz and Long used their information to prepare a background memo for each major topic to be covered. The memos included interviews, direct quotes, and excerpts from documents. The two then turned the fact memos over to Callister who started writing the articles, which were then examined by the paper's attorneys, who did not suggest any major changes.

The team worked sixty days without interruption to make the deadline for the series. Zaitz is most proud of the fact that no important point relied on an anonymous source. "Everything was backed up by a document or a person directly quoted, some of them former sannyasins who feared for their lives," he says.

The articles showed that Rajneesh and his followers were in serious legal and financial trouble. The organization was losing members and undergoing various investigations. The series showed the group's problems in India and examined its interlocking financial and religious organization, its leadership structure, and its fund-raising techniques.

After the Series

Reaction to the articles from the Rajneeshees was surprisingly mild. "After the series appeared," says Zaitz, "we received forty-three letters from commune members and organizations saying how boring it was. They also noted that they were not guilty of criminal activity. Interestingly enough, eleven of these people wound up being indicted." In the years since, no Rajneeshee lawsuits have been filed against the newspaper, nor has it gotten demands for retractions.

In the fall of 1985, Rajneeshpuram fell apart. Sheela and three others fled to Europe. They were arrested a month later and returned to Oregon for trial. She was eventually tried and convicted of a number of counts, among them conspiracy, attempted murder, arson, criminal conspiracy, burglary, and conspiracy to commit electronic eavesdropping. She and her key aides spent over a year at a federal prison in California. The bhagwan attempted to flee the country on October 27, 1985 but was arrested and returned to Oregon. He pleaded guilty to federal felony charges on immigration fraud, paid a $400,000 fine and left Oregon for India where he died in 1990.

At Rajneeshpuram, his followers gradually left and the buildings and grounds have been deteriorating. The property was taken over by the mortgage holder and later sold to a developer.

The Dangers of Investigative Reporting

As information from various federal and state investigations of the Rajneeshees surfaced during the fall of 1985, Zaitz discovered that he had been among nine persons targeted for death by a so-called dirty tricks unit at the ranch. Others on the list included the U.S. attorney in Portland, the Oregon attorney general, and several former members of the movement. The members of this group used false identification to buy guns in Texas.

Also in the dirty tricks department, two Rajneeshee members, disguised as cleaning women, entered the *Oregonian* building in May 1985, apparently in an effort to sabotage the computer system used by the investigative team. The women reached the fourth floor where the computer was located but were asked to leave when a night cleaning supervisor did not recognize them.

Zaitz, Long, and Callister were wiretapped when they stayed in cabins at the ranch during a week-long stay early in their reporting. Pay phones in the public areas of Rajneeshpuram were also tapped, and investigators later found twenty tapes of the reporters' conversations.

The Effects of Investigative Reporting

Most investigative series have an impact when they first appear, but do not result in much concrete change. That was not the case with *The Oregonian* series, which marked a turning point in the relationship between the movement and the rest of the state. The citizens of Oregon had gone from mild curiosity over the presence of a reputed "sex" guru who loved Rolls Royces to real concern that the movement had the unlimited legal and financial resources to silence and punish its critics and make good on Sheela's boast about "painting Oregon red," the bhagwan's favorite color. Governor Vic Atiyeh and most top officials seemed powerless to do anything about what was happening.

After the stories appeared, citizens did not have to fear the unknown any more. Facts about the movement were there for all to see. And, too, those facts suggested that there was much less to fear than many had believed. State a. ɔ federal officials also seemed to gain courage they had lacked before, and they pressed their long-standing investigations to conclusion, bolstered now with support from an informed public.

Background to Investigative Reporting

Investigative reporting came to public attention most recently in the Watergate scandal and all the allied improprieties in government and business that resulted from it. Such reporting is a genre that began much earlier, however, at the beginning of the twentieth century.

A group of writers, working first for *McClure's* magazine and others soon afterward, begin to expose for the first time the graft, corruption, and substandard working conditions in business and government all around the United States. Because he was angry at what these writers were doing, President Theodore Roosevelt compared them to the "Man with the Muck-rake" in John Bunyan's *Pilgrim's Progress*, "the man who could look no way but downward with the muck-rake in his hand, who was offered a celestial crown for his muck-rake, but would neither look up nor regard the crown he was offered, but continued to rake to himself the filth of the floor." The name stuck, and they have been called muckrakers in the years since.

No subject was missed by the members of the group, and more and more magazines printed their articles as both a public service and a way to increase circulation.

Lincoln Steffens investigated political corruption in St. Louis, Minneapolis, Pittsburgh, Philadelphia, and New York and in state governments around the country. His articles were later collected in a book, *The Shame of the Cities*. Ida Tarbell delved into the workings of John D. Rockefeller and the Standard Oil Company and exposed unfair business practices that put the company and the Rockefeller family on the defensive. Ray Stannard Baker wrote about child labor conditions and the poor economic status of black people. Upton Sinclair wrote *The Jungle*, a novel about the meat packing industry in Chicago. The unsanitary conditions it portrayed led to passage of the Pure Food and Drug Act.

Other subjects to come under the merciless attention of the muckrakers included the United States Senate, patent medicines, insurance, mining, the Mormon Church, and the courts systems. Many of the articles resulted in the passage of legislation to right the wrongs so well documented. The muckrakers established a tradition that reappears every few decades in American journalism.

This tradition died out as the original writers grew older and some of the publications either went out of business or turned their attention to other subjects. The spirit was resurrected briefly at the time of the "Teapot Dome" scandals in the early 1920s and again more firmly during Watergate in the 1970s.

Without the reporters on the *Washington Post* and other newspapers and magazines, the scandal would not have been revealed. The initial impetus that led to the impeachment hearings in the House of Representatives and President Nixon's eventual resignation in 1974 came from the press.

Modern investigative reporting did not begin with the coverage of Watergate, however. That scandal created the legend of the investigative reporter as American hero. Some newspapers and magazines had been doing this kind of reporting for years, although not always calling it that.

After Watergate, however, publications of all sizes rushed to set up investigative units. Suddenly it was the thing to do. A similar fascination with intrepid investigative reporters in trench coats and slouch hats meeting nameless sources in secret locations attracted record numbers of students to journalism schools—more than could ever get jobs on the relatively small number of publications with investigative units—and inspired several films and television series.

In 1975, a group of like-minded journalists formed Investigative Reporters and Editors (IRE) because they were concerned that hard-earned knowledge gathered separately through their long years of reporting should be shared. The organization, which now has 1,500 working journalists, journalism educators, and students, holds an annual conference and regional workshops, gives awards for outstanding investigative reporting, and publishes *IRE Journal* four times a year in which reporters tell how they wrote a particular story. In 1978, IRE joined forces with the University of Missouri School of Journalism and has had its offices at the university since then. There it maintains an extensive resource library of newspaper and magazine articles, videotapes and transcripts, and books—all on investigative reporting or subjects that have been investigated.

The organization's first activity was also its most well-known. In 1976, after Don Bolles, a reporter for the *Arizona Republic* and a founding member of the IRE, was killed while looking into political corruption and organized crime problems in the state, an IRE team of volunteers went to Arizona to finish Bolles' work. The reporters from twenty-seven newspapers and broadcast stations around the country gathered the material for and wrote a twenty-three part series of articles.

This work by the Arizona Project won a special award from the Society of Professional Journalists and attracted a lot of notoriety—

and several lawsuits — for the IRE. Editors at some large newspapers criticized the series as superficial, sensational, and a new form of what they called "vigilante journalism."

The IRE's efforts to legitimize investigative reporting — along with continually solid investigations by reporters at *The New York Times*, *Washington Post*, *Philadelphia Inquirer*, *Los Angeles Times*, CBS, NBC, ABC, and CNN — established the need for this segment of journalism.

This was especially true in the case of the Iran-contra scandal of 1986-1987, the 1980s equivalent of Watergate. Newspaper and television reporters uncovered many of the related secrets of this complicated series of events in which a small group of White House and CIA officials and arms dealers sold weapons to Iran at inflated prices and used the profits to fund the contra forces then fighting to overthrow the government of Nicaragua, all in violation of the law.

"Investigative reporting is important, because for a person in the press to serve in a watchdog role, that person has got to get below the surface explanations public officials give in press conferences and press releases to give the public an idea of what is happening," says Jerry Uhrhammer, a former president of IRE and member of the Arizona Project and now the investigative reporter at the *Morning News Tribune* in Tacoma, Washington. "I don't believe institutions can investigate themselves. Invariably there is a tendency for them to cover up wrongdoing and corruption so the public doesn't know about it. If the public is going to govern itself, the public has got to be apprised of the facts, good or bad. That is the job of the press — to give them those facts. The importance of investigative reporting in fulfilling this role cannot be understated."

Some editors argue that all reporting is investigative, which indeed it is. Only the TV networks and newspapers in large cities have the resources to devote to full-time investigative reporting in the stringent economy of the 1990s, however. Even at the peak of the investigative reporting frenzy right after Watergate, some small and medium newspapers closed their investigative units or reassigned their investigative reporter when their efforts failed to turn up much material worthy of significant investigation or the expense incurred by pursuing it.

Across the country, investigative reporting has diminished, primarily for two reasons. In the last two or three years, the judicial system has become more active than in the past. Judges, juries, and the public seem more prone to take the side of aggrieved parties against the media. Some awards for libel have been astronomically high and this has frightened even big media companies and slowed their earlier investigative zeal considerably.

Smaller newspapers were chilled by what happened to the Alton, Illinois *Telegraph* in 1980. After a five-week trial, a jury awarded the plaintiff in a libel suit against the newspaper $6.7 million in compensatory damages and $2.5 million in punitive damages. (The suit was settled out of court in 1982 for $1.4 million after forcing the 148-year-old paper into bankruptcy.) What earned this case such attention was the fact that no story was even published. The entire judgment was based on a background memo written by two of the paper's reporters alleging that a local contractor had organized crime connections.

The second reason for a decline in investigative reporting is that there is less public interest in it. Says Les Zaitz: "After Watergate, investigative reporting went wild; anybody and everybody was a target. There was a lot of overreaching and shrill coverage. The mentality developed that if an investigation did not get someone impeached or indicted, it was no good. If you couldn't put someone in jail forget it. There is less public appetite for that sort of thing." The public reacted badly to this overreaction, which may be one reason the media is distrusted and scores low in public opinion polls.

How to Cover the Investigative Beat

Les Zaitz has his own set of rules for investigative reporting:

1. **Be patient.** "One of the greatest weaknesses of a lot of reporters is that they are in too big a hurry to get to the punchline, the conclusion of the story when you find what is to be found," says Zaitz. "If you take shortcuts, you wind up in the wilderness. Of course, the amount of time you take depends on the financial resources of your employer and what your other time commitments are. But even if your reporting only takes a week, you still need the patience to locate documents, then the time to analyze and interpret them so you can form a cohesive picture of whatever you are investigating. You've got to be determined to stick with it and cover all bases."

2. **Act like a human vacuum cleaner in the first period of reporting.** "Even in the early stages, before you know much about what you are looking for, consume all possible facts and documentation," says Zaitz. "You never know when one small fact that at first appears irrelevant will become the one piece that makes your whole story relevant." For example, in the Rajneeshee story, Zaitz and Long spent three hot summer days in two rural court houses photocopying the information on thousands of voter registration cards not really certain at the time how the information

would fit in. "Farther down the road, these cards enabled us to identify the power structure and establish a history of people in control," he recalls. "When you come across things like this, make a copy or take notes, read it through once and save it." (See also Box 6.2 on how to read a budget.)

3. **Organize all documentary material carefully.** "You should catalog everything you get, whether it's property deeds, voter registration cards, correspondence," says Zaitz. "You should label it and organize it in files or three-ring binders. This is true even with smaller investigations. After an interview, I type up a memo that summarizes what I found: on this date I talked to so and so at such and such a place or over the telephone and talked about. . . . I tape key interviews and then type a complete transcript for the file. I tape some phone interviews too. In Oregon and many other states you can do this without telling the other person you are taping. The rule is, one person on the phone needs to know you are taping and that person is you."

4. **Keep a current work list of where you are in the investigation.** "Several times a week, I make a checklist of what I need to do for the story I am working on," says Zaitz. "What questions I still need to ask, what documents I still need to locate, who I still need to call. When you do an investigation, you go in so many different directions, you forget where you are. Keeping track of what you need to do next is crucial to doing a good investigation and working as efficiently as possible." (See Box 6.3)

5. **Keep all your research material even after the story has appeared.** You do this for legal reasons to back up your findings but also, according to Zaitz, because people in one story may turn out to be important in a story later on. "The information you have may make a crucial difference in another story," he says. Old research material can often provide hard-to-get telephone numbers and names of additional sources. For example, Oregon Senator Mark Hatfield was under investigation in 1991 for questions involving his finances. *The Oregonian* could go to Zaitz' analysis of his financial records four years before for additional background information.

6. **The cultivation of sources is fundamental.** "By that, I mean, in the beginning, I'll talk to anybody and everybody," says Zaitz. "Even if it's only off the record, I'll listen to them." As with the collection of documentary material, information from interviews may end up being more important than it seemed at the time of the interview. Zaitz will agree to talk to a source off the record in order to get the information. He then tries to corroborate that

Box 6.2

How to Read a Budget

Reading the budget for a public agency allows a reporter to get a basic idea of how that agency plans to spend the money allocated to it. Although complicated and confusing to the uninitiated, budgets aren't as horrible at closer range.

1. *Remember that a budget has two parts*: revenues (also called income) and expenses (also called expenditures), usually shown in separate categories. The source of that revenue (taxes, fees paid by the public, money transferred from other agencies) will be shown in one column. Expenses (salaries, purchases, payments, construction and maintenance, insurance) will be shown in the other.

2. *Compare this year's figures to last year's figures in each category*. This will enable reporters to find the increases and decreases for various programs. They should look for big increases or big decreases and find out why certain programs have gone way up or way down.

3. *Look more deeply at individual items*. If a city official is asking for funds to hire five more employees, what about the effective use of the two hundred already in that department? Is something that represents a small amount of money really necessary in times of a budget crisis (for example, a parade float or a rifle team), even though that activity might have very vocal supporters?

4. *Look at items in terms of unit costs*. This approach is especially good when perusing school budgets. What is the cost per child, average class size, average daily attendance, and student-teacher ratio? How do these figures compare to past years, and what has been the effect on educational quality? In fire departments, how many firefighters does each company have, and what is the average number of runs per company? Is one overburdened, while another is being underutilized?

5. *Compare all figures to those of other cities*. It is next to impossible for a reporter to know if the figures for staffing in a budget adequately fulfill the needs of that city. A good way to reach a point of comparison is to get figures from adjacent cities, counties, and school districts and those in similar-sized towns elsewhere. Any city, county, or school district that receives federal funds for its programs has access to data on programs of a similar type in every state. Comparisons can be made with these figures.

6. *Examine the number of employees doing what they should be doing*. How many sanitation employees or police officers are actually doing what they were hired to do (picking up trash or walking the beat) as opposed to sitting behind a desk performing largely clerical tasks? How seriously is this affecting performance?

7. *Determine if programs are funded realistically*. Funds requested for

welfare programs should usually be high, because the number of recipients depends on how many are eligible. A low figure will usually mean that the executive will have to come back to the legislature for more money. A different situation exists for new programs. Because it takes a long time to hire people and get going, figures for the first year should be about half the amount needed when the program is fully operational.

8. *Look carefully at revenue sources.* Are they overly optimistic or too pessimistic? Sales taxes, personal income taxes, and business income taxes should usually go up at the same rate inflation does; the exception occurs when the city, county, or state is experiencing unusual growth and prosperity, in which case the rate may increase one-and-a-half to two times the inflation rate. There is, of course, always the danger of economic downturn to cut into tax revenues. Estimates of property tax income, on the other hand, are predictable because the tax rolls are published in advance. In the area of revenue, it is a good idea to note if a one-time source of funds (an influx of federal funds or an unexpected cash balance for a previous year) is being used to balance the budget. What will happen the next year when that money is not available?

9. *Examine the documentation that accompanies most budgets.* This will give reporters the rationale behind the request for more (or, not as frequently, less) money in the coming fiscal year. Do these reasons make sense?

10. *Try to find out as much as possible about individual programs listed in the budget.* How do they relate to other programs in the same branch of government and how does that branch work?

11. *Study the findings of outside budget committees.* In many states, budget committees are required at all levels of government—city, county, school district. Members examine the budget in depth for the governmental organization that will act upon it. The resulting background information can be useful to reporters.

material with someone else who is willing to talk on the record. If he can't, he goes back to the original source to ask that the name be used. "Nine times out of ten," he says, "that person will be willing to do it. I rarely use not for attribution, material with no name. To me, that's a lazy way to do a job. Our Rajneeshee story was a classic case of getting people to talk on the record. The former members were truly fearful for their safety. We talked to them over a long period and they began to trust us. When the time came to publish, we went back to them and only one person in twenty-five absolutely refused to be identified as a source. Doing this really adds credibility to the story."

Box 6.3

How to File an FOI Request

The federal Freedom of Information Act, first enacted in 1966, provides that any person has the right of access to—and can receive copies of—any document, file, or other records in the possession of any federal agency or department. This release may be hampered if the requested information falls into one of the nine categories of exempt material: national defense, internal agency rules, trade secrets, bank reports, invasion of privacy, law enforcement, executive privilege, oil and gas well data, and the so-called "catch all" exemption covering different kinds of information various agencies are allowed to keep secret. After Watergate, Congress amended the FOI in 1974 to make it easier and faster to get to documents. In 1986, the law was changed again altering the law enforcement exemption slightly and establishing a new set of fee provisions which Congress hoped would liberalize the waiver of fees or at least end the practice by which some federal agencies charge exorbitant rates.

1. *Try the direct approach first*. Reporters or anyone else seeking information from government documents should try to get them first by contacting the public information office. It is good to identify yourself as a reporter and offer an explanation of why you want the document.

2. *Don't give up if you are turned down*. If this informal approach fails, talk to the agency's FOI officer (they all have someone so designated) to get what you want without putting your request in writing.

3. *Writing a formal FOI request need not be all that formal*. The request takes the form of a letter to that agency's FOI officer, written as follows:
   a. The first sentence notes that this is a federal FOI request.
   b. The second paragraph asks for copies of the specific document(s) or documents you want, along with identifying names, places, dates.
   c. The third paragraph indicates that you know that certain portions might be exempt but that you expect the agency to send you "all nonexempt portions of the records I have requested, and ask that you justify any deletions by reference to specific exemptions of the FOI Act. I reserve the right to appeal your decision to withhold any materials."
   d. The fourth paragraph indicates your willingness to pay "reasonable" search and duplication fees. It is best to state a total beyond which you want to be notified.
   e. You might also ask for a waiver of fees because you are a journalist (or teacher or book author or student) employed by a designated news organization (or school or publisher) and are planning to use the material in an article (or book or course).
   f. Close by thanking the agency for its response. Mention that you know that the law requires a reply within ten business days.

4. *If a formal request is denied, you can appeal it in writing to the head of the agency.*

5. *After a failure there, you will have to take your case for release to court.*

7. **Learn the system, whatever the "system" is.** "Whenever you are investigating any kind of system, you have to learn the basic mechanics of how that system works," says Zaitz. "If you don't know the process, you won't know any deviation from that process. This means that you learn the laws, administrative rules, and procedures of whatever you are investigating, whether it's a government agency or a charitable foundation. This allows you to draw conclusions based on what you find." For example, for an investigation several years ago into the failure of Oregon's largest bank, Zaitz and Long had to study the regulatory process that controls banks. "We read FDIC quarterly reports for information on subjects like insider trading to find out what the norm could be," continues Zaitz. "This gave us a standard to which we could compare what we were finding." (See Box 6.4 on open meetings and records.)

8. **Avoid cheap shots.** "In any investigation, you ultimately have a target, usually a person," says Zaitz. "It is absolutely essential when your investigation is complete that you lay out your findings for the target before publication to ask, 'What is your explanation?'" Zaitz does this for several reasons: 1) to pick up additional information and documents that could change the direction and even conclusion of the story and make it more solid, and, 2) to be fair. "The target should not read about this on page one for the first time," he says. "Talking to a source upholds basic fairness." Often, Zaitz goes to the key source twice, right at first and then at the end after most of the facts have been dug out. "A lot of investigative reporters make the mistake of not going to the target until the end," he says, "when they're on guard, defensive, and antagonistic. If you talk to them early on, you can get useful background. Sources will very often lie to you then, but you can juxtapose what they tell you in July with what they tell you in September." Zaitz says he seldom encounters anyone who will refuse to talk altogether. "One of the reasons people are involved in the conduct you are investigating is that they think they are smarter than everyone else," he says. "That arrogance brings them to the interview. They conduct a kind of duel with you to talk you out of running the story."

9. **Be fair with readers.** "Just as you should be fair in your treatment of sources, you need to be fair in your treatment of readers," says Zaitz. "If there are holes in the story, tell the reader. Also, be fair in your presentation of evidence. Don't make something worse than it is."

(Zaitz is proof that investigative reporting can best be learned by doing. He got into the field in a rather unconventional way. He was attending college and working on a nearby weekly newspaper when

Box 6.4

A Guide to Open Meetings and Open Records Laws

All 50 states have now enacted open meetings and open records laws, but some are stronger and more effective than others. According to the Society of Professional Journalists, here are some ways to check the strengths and weaknesses of the laws:

Open Meetings

1. *Find out what meetings are covered by the law.* Sometimes sub-committees, advisory boards, and other small bodies are not specified. A key test of a strong law is whether the "public body" definition includes only those entities that receive or expend public funds—it may ignore bodies and local committees that do not spend money.

2. *Scrutinize the exemptions to the open meetings laws.* A long list will mean a weak statute. The most common exemptions deal with personnel, real estate, collective bargaining, security, and legal discussions.

3. *Check the provision for closing a meeting.* How many members are needed to close one? The higher the number, the stronger the law. And, are such notes part of the public record and is an explanation required?

4. *In advance of a meeting, how long does the body have to notify the public and press?* Do emergency meetings provide a loophole to avoid a long notice? Any requirements for them?

5. *Are minutes of meetings public?* Are notes recorded? How much information is required to be included?

6. *Find out about provisions to enforce the law.* Can aggrieved citizens begin an action to enforce the statute? How severe is the penalty for violations—civil or criminal sanctions? Can decisions be voided? Some states allow a judge to nullify actions taken by a public body in an illegal meeting and some laws require it. Who will pay attorney's fees and court costs? If citizens can't be reimbursed, they will not be willing to pursue action.

Open Records

1. *Find out which agencies are covered by the law.*

2. *Check the definition of a "public record."* Strong statutes refer to the physical form of the record, as in "regardless of physical form or characteristic." Weak statutes call public records "those documents required to be kept by law." Strong laws specify records covered as those "made or received in connection with, or relating to law, duty, or public business."

3. *Determine what the exemptions to the law are.* Once again, a long list means a weak law. But so does the broad exemption of nondisclosure

"when it is in the public interest." This allows bodies to determine, on a record-by-record basis, what they will disclose. What is considered to be in the public interest varies from body to body and is sometimes vague. It is common to exempt investment records, trade secrets, information on pending litigation, and records threatening someone's privacy should they be disclosed. The key is whether the exemptions are mandatory for all bodies or can be determined by individual entities.

4. *Find out if the law has both exempt and nonexempt material.* Is public and private information segregated? Strong statutes allow the public to obtain records from which exempted information has been deleted rather than withholding an entire record if even one line has been crossed out.

5. *Examine the state code index for Confidential Information, Private Information, Public Record.* Hundreds of records exempted from disclosure may be scattered throughout each state code and might be missed without a careful check of all categories.

6. *Note the procedure for getting information from an agency.* Long or nonexistent time limits mean a weak law. A strong law is one with a three working-day time limit, plus the requirement that the agency must notify the citizen in writing if a request for a record is denied with information about who made the decision and why and procedure for appeal.

the managing editor of *The Oregonian* invited him to Portland for an interview. He was hired and quit school, never to return. After holding a succession of jobs on the paper—general assignment, night police beat, day police beat—he was assigned to cover the state capital. There he began to do some investigative reporting and this led to a full-time assignment when the newspaper formed its own IR unit in 1982. He has since left to buy his own weekly newspaper in Keizer, Oregon.)

Writing Investigative Stories

"I like investigating reporting so much that I never want to stop and put it all down on paper," says Les Zaitz. "Writing can be just as challenging as finding the deepest darkest secret, however. The challenge comes in digesting the vast amount of material you gather into a few words."

Zaitz begins by sitting down at his computer and writing without referring to notes. "What is this story about?, I ask myself. I think through my fingers onto the scope. Then, I outline the story by writing down the key findings, deciding what order to put them in, and then what evidence I have to back them up. Then, I ask myself, what is the most compelling result? Some investigative reporters never tell readers what they've found, they let the readers guess."

For Zaitz, the key to a good investigative story are the people he writes about: "You've got to have lots of characters, like in a novel. People relate to other people, beyond the organization, statistics and property deeds. How a movement frightened a whole state. How an influential senator accepted questionable gifts. As the evidence unfolds, it helps to have a lot of voices to tell the story."

Good description also helps the reader relate to the characters. "If you describe sources as wearing a pinky ring or having holes in the knees of their jeans or living in a $450,000 house, it tells readers something about them," he says.

Another important writing technique is simplicity. Some investigative reporters make their stories too complicated. For example, in Zaitz's stories on the collapse of the bank, statistics and regulations were prevalent, but he chose to lead with the fact that the bank president approved millions of dollars in loans to a developer and was able to buy prime development land in return. "At some time you have to put in enough facts to give the reader confidence that the story is true," he says. "Don't make broad, sweeping, statements without backing them up. Say 'X occurred because of this.' If a story is really big and complicated, turn it into a series. One story shouldn't go beyond 25 inches. But beware of letting a series run in too many parts. As I look back, the Rajneesh series with 20 parts should have been 10. We worked at it for 13 months and we found it terribly fascinating. We'd say,'Oh, the Rolls Royces. That's interesting. Let's do a story on them.' Or, 'Why are their lawyers so good. Let's do another story.' I don't think even the Rajneeshees found it all *that* fascinating."

HATFIELD FINANCIAL TROUBLES
By Leslie L. Zaitz of the *Oregonian*

The lead summarizes Les Zaitz's major findings in his reporting on the money problems of one of Oregon's U.S. senators. He gathered the material in one day on a trip to Washington, D.C.

1 WASHINGTON—Sen. Mark O. Hatfield and his wife, Antoinette, encountered money trouble in 1982 that was aggravated by their inability to sell a mortgaged Washington building as they assumed new debts.

In graf 2, Zaitz quickly tells readers the source of the information—documents and interviews. "This adds credibility to the account that follows," says Zaitz.

2 Real estate and financial records and interviews showed that the troublesome property was a four-apartment complex, where the Hatfields lived in Georgetown. They put it up for sale in mid-1982 but didn't sell it until 18 months later. The Hatfields shaved $210,000 off their original asking price of $1.1 million before they could get rid of the building at 3051 N St. N.W. in Washington.

3 Antoinette Hatfield said Wednesday that she obtained a bank loan on her own line of credit and "against my property" to finance their $55,000 donation this week to Shriner's Hospital for Crippled Children. The loan was from Pioneer Trust Co, a Salem bank.

4 The donation came just hours before the couple appeared at a Portland news conference Monday to discuss Antoinette Hatfield's acceptance of $55,000 in fees from a Greek financier who had been soliciting her husband's help in promoting a pipeline project across Africa.

5 The Hatfields' personal financial problems, apparently beginning in early 1982, necessitated substantial unsecured borrowing from friends.

6 The Hatfields have refused to discuss their personal finances in any detail, but the senator issued a statement Wednesday repeating earlier denials that they were in financial difficulty.

7 "Our assets always exceeded our liabilities," the senator said. "We could have sold our home at any time in 1982 or 1983 but chose to endure the depressed market conditions in order to receive a fair price on our property."

In graf 8, Zaitz makes the critical link between the timing of the Hatfields' financial troubles and their acceptance of money from a businessman with a somewhat questionable past. Zaitz did this analysis by

8 Records and interviews indicate that Hatfield and his wife's Washington real estate company, Antoinette K. Hatfield Inc., were having financial problems at the time that money from Basil A. Tsakos, then chairman of the Trans-African Pipeline Corp., began flowing to Antoinette Hatfield.

charting the real estate transactions and then charting the timing of the money from the businessman, Basil Tsakos. "This is a basic investigative reporting technique that can prove revealing," says Zaitz.

"Finding a key quotable source (graf 12) builds credibility about the depth of the Hatfields' financial problems," continues Zaitz. "This source, a friend of the Hatfields, would have no reason to play up their troubles."

9   The Hatfields apparently confided their financial troubles to a close circle of five other Washington area couples who meet monthly in prayer meetings. John Dellenback, former Republican Congressman from Oregon and now president of the Christian College Coalition, and his wife, Mary Jane, were in the group.

10   Dellenback loaned more than $250,000 to the Hatfields in February 1982. All but 10 percent of the loan was repaid in the spring of 1984.

11   Dellenback said conversation in the prayer sessions occasionally turned to the couples' personal lives.

12   "We ask, 'Where are you hurting? What's happening in your life? What are you happy about?'" Dellenback said. "It was out of that discussion that Mary Jane and I said, 'We've got some money we don't need right now.'"

13   The senator has reported that the loan was secured by a mortgage on the Hatfield home. No record of such mortgage could be found.

14   Dellenback said he knew one of the problems was the Georgetown building.

15   "They were anxious to sell it," he said.

16   Jeanine H. Arnold, former treasurer and saleswoman for Antoinette Hatfield's company, confirmed that the building had been a burden on the Hatfields' finances.

17   Mortgages on Hatfield properties had been showing up since the early days of 1980. Since that time, the Hatfields have raised close to $1.5 million by selling or mortgaging their major Oregon real estate holdings in Portland and Newport.

From here, Zaitz uses a number of grafs to reveal his findings on the Hatfields' complicated financial situation.

18   Most of the money came from a series of transactions involving the Hatfields' 702 N.W. Westover Terrace condominium and a Newport beach home. The condominium loans were issued by U.S. National Bank of Oregon, whose board of directors included Gerry Frank, Hatfield's chief of staff.

19 The Hatfields paid $391,788 for the Portland condominium on December 28, 1980, apparently financing it with part of a $457,000 mortgage loan from U.S. National Bank that also listed the beach property as collateral.

20 The money was due to be repaid a year later, but the Hatfields on Oct. 9, 1981, got the loan increased by $12,000 and extended for another year. The revision agreement showed that the principal amount of the expanded loan was $469,000.

21 The Hatfields also sold their Newport beach home for $300,000 to Beaverton electronics tycoon C. Norman Winningstad and his wife Delores. The bank reported on Jan. 8, 1982, that the Hatfields had paid off the $469,000 mortgage.

Winningstad, president of Floating Point Systems Inc., said he didn't get the impression that the Hatfields were selling the property under duress.

22 "The reason they wanted to sell it was that Mark didn't like to fly from Washington to Portland and then get in the car and drive two hours to Newport," Winningstad said. "They wanted a place in Portland."

23 On Jan. 5, 1982, the U.S. National Bank advanced the Hatfields $350,000 on a one-year mortgage secured by the Westover condominium. However, the mortgage was revised Jan. 25, 1983, giving the Hatfields another $35,000 and another year to pay.

24 In 1982, Hatfield lent between $15,000 and $50,000 to Antoinette Hatfield Inc.

25 Also in that year Antoinette Hatfield jumped into the Oregon real estate market, opening a Lake Oswego office with Janet R. Skopil, wife of U.S. District Judge Otto Skopil. The partnership, Hatfield & Skopil Inc., was formed June 1, 1982, and dissolved May 12, 1984.

26 A major challenge for Antoinette Hatfield's Oregon partnership came in 1983, when the firm received the exclusive listings for the 21 unsold condominiums in the 56-unit Westover development where they lived. Only one of the units sold — and that one by Cronin & Caplan Inc. — before the Lake Oswego partnership was dissolved, said Rick J. Griebel, public relations manager for the U.S. National Bank of Oregon, which owns the remaining 20 units.

27 In late 1981, the Hatfields borrowed between $15,000 and $50,000 from the Pioneer Trust Co. of Salem. The loan, which was to be paid by the end of 1982, remained on Hatfield's books as a debt into 1983. No record is available on whether that loan has been paid.

28 Throughout 1982, the Hatfields kept up their personal unsecured borrowings. Charles Cook, a family friend from Industry, Calif., made two loans to the Hatfields in August 1982 for amounts between $20,000 and $65,000.

29 Four months after the Cook loan, the Hatfields borrowed from $15,000 to $50,000 from Frank O. Consaivo, a former vice president of Tektronix Inc., who reportedly left Oregon in 1974 to take a job in a Phoenix, Ariz. chemical and pipeline-construction firm. Hatfield has described Consaivo, who is now a self-employed business consultant, as a friend from a Christian fellowship group.

30 During the middle of 1982, Tsakos reportedly began sending checks to Antoinette Hatfield that evidently totalled $55,000.

31 The Senate Ethics Committee and the U.S. Justice Department are investigating the Tsakos payments.

"The following grafs (beginning with 32), as in much of the story, relied on detailed analysis of the annual financial statements that Hatfield must file with the secretary of the U.S. Senate," says Zaitz. "These

32 But while the Tsakos relationship was playing itself out, the Hatfields in mid-1982 changed their real estate portfolio. They paid $195,705 for a house at 639 E. Capitol St. in Washington. The purchase added a $1,916.67 monthly mortgage bill to payments already totaling at least $4,337

public records are often overlooked as sources of information but, in this story, they proved to be a critical resource to trace the Hatfields' problems."

a month. They sold it to a Washington attorney, Jefferson B. Hill, for $240,000, after it sat empty for nearly a year.

33 In 1983, they sold three properties, and the rental income from two others dropped substantially. Hatfield reported that the annual income in 1982 for three apartments in his Georgetown home on N Street was $15,000 to $50,000, but the following year the income was only $2,000 to $5,000. Annual mortgage payments on that property totaled $80,413.16.

34 Income rental property at 3147 Dumbarton St. N.W. declined from between $15,000 and $50,000 in 1982 to $5,000 to $15,000 the next year. The Hatfields are paying $10,842 a year in mortgage payments on that property.

35 As the rental income was dropping, Antoinette Hatfield closed her Washington company. The last employees left in late March, and three months later she went to work as assistant vice president of Samuel P. Pardoe Real Estate.

36 Arnold said the Hatfield company's fortunes were looking up in 1983. She said Antoinette Hatfield didn't close it for financial reasons, but because the chore of selling real estate and managing a company was too much.

37 Dellenback said, "It was not as profitable as she might have hoped."

In grafs 38, 39, and 40, Zaitz discusses the role played by the senator's wife in the couples' financial problems. "By tracing Antoinette Hatfield's activities," says Zaitz, "I shed further light on the Hatfields' financial troubles. The closing of the real estate office is a key event—and her failure to report the closure to the bank is another indication that it was something more than a routine closure. Proxy statements from publicly traded corporations, such as

38 Antoinette Hatfield is a director of United National Bancshares Inc., owner of United National Bank of Washington. William K. Collins Sr., a Washington dentist and board member, said Hatfield never mentioned her March 1983 business closure at monthly board meetings. The holding company's proxy statement dated March 23, 1984, listed Hatfield's occupation as president of her company.

39 The senator's 1983 financial report shows that in February 1983, the Hatfields got between $15,000 and $50,000 from the First Wisconsin Bank of Madison in

in this instance, can provide illuminating details about directors and their other business interests."

Madison, Wis. The interest rate was 1-1/2 percent over the prime lending rate.

40 Two months after selling the empty house on Capitol Street in July, the Hatfields bought a $300,000 house at 119 Second St. N.E. in Washington.

Investigative Reporting:
Likely Problems and How to Solve Them

Problem	Solution
1. Complicated material.	1a. Learn how to read budgets and records and to know what information to look for.
	1b. Develop sources from whom to get records and advice on how to understand them.
	1c. Do background reading in basic accounting practices.
	1d. Prepare carefully for all interviews.
2. Sources who tend to hide everything.	2a. Know if what you want is "gettable" or possible.
	2b. Learn how to use the federal Freedom of Information Act and applicable state laws to get the government documents you need.
	2c. Don't break the law to get information.
	2d. Cultivate sources carefully; try to talk them into revealing what they want to hide.

3. Angry sources who threaten reporters and try to retaliate against them.

3a. Keep your nose clean.

3b. Don't take unnecessary chances with physical safety.

3c. Keep careful records of information used in stories; tape important interviews.

4. Biased reporters who get mad about disclosed information and want to avenge wrongs in print.

4a. Be objective, accurate, and ethical at all times.

4b. Verify all information.

4c. Give both sides of all stories.

Summary

Investigative reporting, which combines the examination of records and budgets with traditional interviews, came to public attention in the Watergate scandal of the early 1970s. It is a kind of reporting, however, that goes back to the muckrakers earlier in this century. The skills of an investigative reporter are specific and somewhat technical. To complete a successful investigation, the reporter must know how to examine financial records, bids and specifications, telephone records, real estate deeds and mortgages, and budgets. He or she needs to be familiar with applicable laws and know how to verify all information. Finally the investigative reporter must conduct his or her work objectively and ethically.

Exercises

1. Go over the case study at the beginning of this chapter and make a list of the steps the investigative reporters followed to get their stories. What would you do differently? Why? Compile your ideas into a 500 word paper to present in class.

2. Write a 1,000 word paper that compares and contrasts the techniques used by the muckrakers with those employed by investigative reporters today.

3. Look at the minutes of student council meetings — or faculty senate meetings — over the past six months and make a list of resolutions passed and actions proposed. Then, interview

appropriate officials to find out what actions were really taken. If not, why not? If so, how have the ideas worked out?

4. Get a copy of the budget for your local school district or city government. Analyze the figures for each segment and compare them with the previous year. Were they up or down? Are there any unusually high (or low) figures? Can you discern any "fat" in the budget? Develop a list of questions and interview appropriate officials for answers. Compile your findings into a 1,000 word story.

5. Ask to see the entertainment budget of your college president. What items are listed? Try to determine the source for funds for these purposes and prepare a list of questions for the official responsible. Compile your findings into a 1,000 word story.

Alternate assignment: Do the same thing with equipment purchased with federal grant money; what is it and what happens to it?

Alternate assignment: Do the same thing with the budget for the athletic department; where does the money come from, how are student athletes treated (financially and academically), and do you detect any waste?

Key Terms for Government and Investigative Reporting

Assessor   The elected official who officially estimates the value of property for taxation.

Attorney general   Chief law enforcement officer of a state or country.

Audit   A formal examination and verification of financial records.

Bankruptcy   The formal condition a person declares when he or she is insolvent and unable to pay bills; a court then administers property which is divided among creditors.

Bid   The written offer to carry out a job at a set price.

Budget   A formal and annual plan of operation by a government agency or a company based on an estimate of income and expenses.

Building permit   A permit by an official agency to construct a building by following certain specifications.

Bureaucracy   A rigid government hierarchy of bureaus, administrators, and lessor officials; often hampered by excessive procedure and detail.

Cabinet   A council advising a president or governor.

Census   A periodic official count of the number of people living in a country.

City commission   The governing body of a city in which elected commissioners actually run the departments.

City council   The main governing body of many cities composed of elected officials.

City manager A professional manager hired by a council to manage the city and run its departments.

Civil service Permanent employees of a government who stay on the job regardless of which elected officials are in office.

Committees Permanent and temporary groups of members of a legislature or the U.S. Congress, divided by subject matter, to prepare legislation and hear testimony on issues facing the state or nation.

Constituent A voter in a district represented by a public official.

County commission The main governing body of the county, which usually has fewer members than a city council.

Deed A document executed under seal and delivered to effect a transfer, as in real estate sold by one person to another.

District The division of a state marked off for administrative purposes; a legislator or member of Congress represents residents.

Fiscal Anything that pertains to the public treasury or revenue.

Fiscal year A twelve-month period covered by a public budget; not necessarily January to December.

Foreign policy The policy of a country toward the rest of the world; set by the president in consultation with the secretary of state.

Gerrymander The act of dividing an area into election districts in order to gain partisan advantage.

Governor Chief executive of a state.

Income tax A tax levied on individual or corporate income.

Invoice A detailed list of services and goods provided.

Land-use planning The systematic planning of how a geographic area (usually a city or county) will be allowed to develop with land set aside for housing, schools, farms, factories, and parks.

Leak The deliberate disclosure of information by a government official to a reporter.

Legislature Governing body of a state.

Lieutenant governor The person second in command of a state.

Line item The distinct entry of an item as it appears on an official budget.

Line item veto A proposal to veto a budget item by item rather than the budget as a whole.

Lobbyist A person hired by a special-interest group to influence the votes of legislators.

Mayor Chief executive and/or ceremonial head of a city.

Mortgage A transfer of real property to a creditor as security for a loan.

Muckraker A reporter who attempts to uncover scandal and corruption.

Paper trail The whole range of paper documentation used by investigative reporters in their work.

Property tax An annual tax on property owned by an individual or a company.

Quorum Number of members required to be present to transact business officially.

Regulatory agencies Agencies on the state and federal levels that regulate key industries in their country (airlines, broadcasting, trade, and power) independent of the legislative branch.

Revenue The income of a government from taxes and other sources.

Revenue enforcement A slightly dishonest term for tax increases.

Revenue sharing A sharing of federal funds with the various state and local governments.

Secretary of state The cabinet member in charge of foreign affairs; a state official often in charge of elections and other administrative matters.

Seniority Rights and privileges granted to legislators and members of Congress based on years of service.

Separation of powers The power of each branch of the U.S. government (executive, legislative, and judicial), granted in the Constitution, to act independently of each other.

Specifications A detailed description of measurements and materials for a proposed building.

State of the Union An annual speech by a president to Congress to outline plans and programs for the coming year.

Sunshine laws Laws requiring that most government agencies open their meetings and records to the public.

Tax A sum of money imposed on income, property, or sales by a government; the source of revenue for a government's programs.

Tax lien The legal claim against a person's property for non-payment of taxes.

Trial balloon The seemingly accidental announcement of a program or decision by a president, governor, or other official to test public reaction; if reaction is negative, the story will be denied; if positive, the story will later be confirmed.

Veto The power that one branch of government has to cancel or postpone the decisions of another branch.

Voter registration The formal process by which people sign up in advance of an election to vote.

Voucher A record of an expense paid.

Zero-base budgeting The process of justifying an entire budget every fiscal year or two rather than dealing only with proposed increases.

Additional Reading in Politics, Government, Education, and Investigative Reporting

Adrian, Charles. *State and Local Governments*. New York: McGraw-Hill, 1976.

Alsop, Joseph, and Stewart Alsop. *The Reporter's Trade*. New York: Reynal, 1958.

Anderson, Jack. *Confessions of a Muckraker*. New York: Random House, 1979.

Barone, Michael, Grant Ujifusa, and Douglas Matthews. *The Almanac of American Politics*. Washington, DC: National Journal, published every two years.

Bernstein, Carl, and Bob Woodward. *All the President's Men*. New York: Simon and Schuster, 1974.

Bloom, Allen. *The Closing of the American Mind*. New York: Simon & Schuster, 1987.

Broder, David. *Behind the Front Page*. New York: Simon & Schuster, 1987.

Bruno, Jerry. *The Advance Man*. New York: Bantam, 1971.

Caraley, Demetrios. *City Government and Urban Problems*. Englewood Cliffs, NJ: Prentice-Hall, 1977.

Cater, Douglass. *The Fourth Branch of Government*. Boston: Houghton Mifflin, 1959.

_____. *Power in Washington*. New York: Random House, 1964.

Congressional Directory. Washington, DC: Government Printing Office, 1809 to present.

Congressional District Data Book & Supplements, Redistricted States. Washington, DC: Government Printing Office, 1961 to present.

County and City Data Book. Washington DC: Government Printing Office, 1952 to present.

Crick, Bernard R. *Political Theory and Practice*. New York: Basic Books, 1973.

Crouse, Timothy. *The Boys on the Bus*. New York: Ballantine Books, 1974.

Dahl, Robert A. *Modern Political Analysis*. Englewood Cliffs, NJ: Prentice-Hall, 1976.

David, Paul T., Ralph M. Goldman, and Richard C. Bain. *The Politics of National Party Conventions*. Washington, DC: Brookings Institution, 1960.

Dewey, John. *Democracy and Education*. New York: Free Press, 1966.

Downie, Leonard, Jr. *The New Muckrakers*. Washington, DC: New Republic Books, 1976.

D'Souza, Dinesh. *Illiberal Educations: The Politics of Race and Sex on Campus*. New York: The Free Press, 1991.

Freedman, Samuel. *Small Victories: The Real World of a Teacher, Her Students and Their High School*. New York: Harper & Row, 1990.

Freeman, Donald, ed. *Fundamentals of Political Science*. New York: Free Press, 1977.

Fulbright, J. W. *The Pentagon Propaganda Machine*. New York: Liveright, 1970.

Germond, Jack and Jules Witcover. *Blue Smoke and Mirrors: How Reagan Won and Why Carter Lost the Election of 1980*. New York: Viking Press, 1981.

Germond, Jack and Jules Witcover. *Whose Broad Stripes and Bright Stars: The Trivial Pursuit of the Presidency 1988*. New York: Warner Books, 1989.

Grant, Daniel R., and H.C. Nixon. *State and Local Government in America*. Boston: Allyn and Bacon, 1975.

Hill, Gladwin. *Dancing Bear: An Inside Look at California Politics.* Cleveland: World Publishing, 1968.

Hofstadter, Richard. *American Political Tradition.* New York: Random House, 1948.

Huff, Darrell and Irving E. Gers. *How to Lie With Statistics.* New York: Norton, 1954.

Kerr, Clark. *The Uses of the University.* Cambridge, MA: Harvard University Press, 1963.

Key, V.O., Jr. *Politics, Parties, and Pressure Groups.* New York: Thomas Y. Crowell, 1964.

Kidder, Tracy. *Among Schoolchildren.* Boston: Houghton Mifflin, 1989.

Kozol, Jonathan. *Illiterate America.* New York: New American Library, 1986.

Lazarfeld, Paul, Bernard Berelson, and Hazel Gaudet. *The People's Choice.* New York: Columbia University Press, 1944.

Lee, Richard W., ed. *Politics and the Press.* Washington, DC: Acropolis Books, 1970.

Lukas, J. Anthony. *Common Ground.* New York: Knopf, 1985.

Machiavelli, Niccolo. *The Prince.* New York: Norton, 1977.

MacNeil, Robert. *The People Machine: The Influence of Television on American Politics.* New York: Harper & Row, 1968.

McGinniss, Joe. *The Selling of the President 1968.* New York: Trident, 1968.

Mandate for Reform. Report of the Commission on Party Structure and Delegate Selection to the Democratic National Committee. Washington, DC, 1970.

Meyer, Philip. *Precision Journalism.* 2nd ed. Bloomington: Indiana University Press, 1979.

Mitford, Jessica. *Poison Penmanship.* New York: Vintage Books, 1980.

Nelson, Jack, and Gene Roberts, Jr. *The Censors and the Schools.* Boston: Little, Brown, 1963.

Plato. *The Republic.* New York: Random House, 1975.

Pollard, James E. *The Presidents and the Press.* New York: Octagon Books, 1973.

Porter, William E. *Assault on the Media: The Nixon Years.* Ann Arbor: University of Michigan Press, 1976.

Ravitch, Diane. *The Schools We Deserve.* New York: Basic Books, 1985.

Report of the National Advisory Commission on Civil Disorders. New York: Bantam Books, 1968.

Reporting the Detroit Riot. New York: American Newspaper Publishers Association, 1968.

Reston, James. *Artillery of the Press.* New York: Harper & Row, 1960.

Rivers, William. *Adversaries: Politics and the Press.* Boston: Beacon Press, 1971.

Scammon, Richard M., and Ben J. Wattenberg. *The Real Majority.* New York: Coward, McCann, 1971.

Smith, Hedrick. *The Power Game.* New York: Random House, 1988.

Steffens, Lincoln. *The Autobiography of Lincoln Steffens.* New York: Harcourt, Brace, 1931.

Stern, Philip. *The Best Congress Money Can Buy*. New York: Pantheon, 1988.

Swados, Harvey. *Years of Conscience: The Muckrakers*. Cleveland: World, 1962.

Thompson, Josiah. *Gumshoe*. New York: Fawcett, 1989.

Ullmann, John and others, eds. *The Reporter's Handbook* 2nd ed. New York: St. Martin's Press, 1991.

White, Graham. *FDR and the Press*. Chicago: University of Chicago Press, 1975.

White, Theodore. *In Search of History*. New York: Harper & Row, 1978.

_____. *The Making of the President 1960*. New York: Atheneum, 1961.

_____. *The Making of the President 1964*. New York: Atheneum, 1965.

_____. *The Making of the President 1968*. New York: Atheneum, 1969.

_____. *The Making of the President 1972*. New York Atheneum, 1973.

Wicker, Tom. *On Press*. New York: Viking Press, 1968.

Williams, Paul N. *Investigative Reporting and Editing*. Englewood Cliffs, NJ: Prentice-Hall, 1978.

Wise, David. *The Politics of Lying*. New York: Random House, 1973.

Witcover, Jules. *Marathon: The Pursuit of the Presidency*. New York: Viking Press, 1977.

III Law

The Law, wherein, as in a magic mirror, we see reflected not only our own lives, but the lives of all men that have been!

—Oliver Wendell Holmes, Jr.

Street meeting, San Francisco, California by Dorothea Lange. [*Courtesy U.S. Farm Security Administration Collection, Prints and Photographs Division, Library of Congress*]

7

Police

I cover crime for The Miami Herald, *daily circulation 438,334. In my sixteen years at the* Herald, *I have reported more than five thousand violent deaths. Many of the corpses have had familiar faces: cops and killers, politicians and prostitutes, doctors and lawyers.*

Some were my friends.

—Edna Buchanan
The Miami Herald

One police reporter
Background to police reporting
Problems and solutions
How to cover the police beat
Kinds of police stories
Writing police stories
Police reporting: Likely problems and how to solve them
Summary
Exercises
Key terms

One Police Reporter

From a friend who is a former New York City homicide detective, Neal Hirschfeld heard about a psychologist who treated police officers with severe psychological problems caused by doing undercover work.

"They wind up like Vietnam vets," says Hirschfeld, until recently a reporter covering crime and police for the *New York Daily News*. "I wanted to do a story because I was intrigued by the subject. I'd been to many press conferences where the cops involved were unveiled for the press but never heard from again. What happens to them when the press conference is over? There had to be more to the story."

He read a series of psychological studies of such police officers, which gave no names. "I tried my contacts all over: NYPD, FBI, the Drug Enforcement Administration, the NY Transit Police and asked if they would let me speak to such a cop," continues Hirschfeld. "They all lied. They said no one had problems. I knew this was not true."

Eventually, a former New York detective he knows mentioned the perfect source for the reporter: a New Jersey state trooper who, at the time, was teaching at the New Jersey State Police Academy. Hirschfeld called the trooper, who agreed to talk after clearing it with the state police public relations department. "He wanted to tell his story so he could put a message out that would help other cops," says Hirschfeld. "Most law enforcement agencies don't help those cops. They peg them as head cases and don't want to deal with the consequences."

Robert Delaney, the New Jersey trooper, had been the key operative in a two-and-a-half-year sting using a fake trucking business to trap forty men for crimes including transportation of stolen goods and bribery. The whole operation went well and Delaney, then still in his 20s, was the star. The difficulties came when the case was over and he had to return to routine duties.

"The psychological problems of going undercover occur because you become so immersed in what you are doing that you actually become friendly with the mobsters you are working with," says Hirschfeld, who gathered the material for his article during six interviews. "Then, when it comes time to arrest these people, you have real conflicts because you think of them as friends, you've been to their houses, know their families. After that, you have to go back to the regular police world and do mundane work and you're like a duck out of water. He had real conflicts with who he was — a cop or a wiseguy? He had divided loyalties."

Delaney had problems when he went to court and had to look at the mobsters and their families. He had problems at home. "When 8 P.M. rolls around, he'd still have these tapping feet and did not want to sit down and read the paper," says Hirschfeld. "He would go into a bar and pull out a bankroll to buy a round of drinks for everyone. His buddy would have to take him aside and tell him, 'That's not federal money, that's your mortgage money.' "

During their interviews, Delaney talked openly with Hirschfeld. The reporter tracked down transcripts of Delaney's appearance before the U.S. Senate Committee on Crime in which he discussed his undercover experiences. The reporter augmented the trooper's story with information from interviews with a New York City undercover cop and a psychiatrist specializing in such cases.

The reporting for the story took Hirschfeld three months, during which time he handled other assignments. It ran in the Sunday magazine of the *New York Daily News* because of its length, too long for the regular paper whose style dictates short stories. The Delaney article won awards from the New York Press Club, the New York Associated Press Association and United Press International. Warner Brothers bought his screenplay of the story, which he left the paper to complete.

By necessity, Hirschfeld interviewed Delaney after the fact, when his undercover operation was long over and he had returned to his old assignment. This was normally not the way the reporter liked to work. When possible, he got directly involved in covering the story, going alone with police on a case, observing what they do.

At the same time, he tried to avoid getting too close to his sources. "I'm interested in police work," he says. "I love hanging around cops. But you do a better job if you're not too close, too beholden to them. I've had lieutenants tell me: 'We know what you want. You need us more than we need you. We can make you or break you. We can manipulate you.' It can happen, it does happen. This is still a competitive newspaper town and if you miss a good story by failing to work with a source, it is embarrassing if someone else gets it."

As much as he needed his sources, Hirschfeld was wary in his dealings with them. "You have to be suspicious of everyone's motivations," he says. "Everyone has ambitions and pet projects, including reporters. Certain people have ulterior motives in everything they tell you, although they aren't going to give you something not true because they realize you're going to check it out. If it doesn't pan out, they realize you're never going to believe them again. They want your attention, your ear. You want to be published. You've got to tread carefully. They know you're desperate for stories, and it's easy for them to play favorites, giving a story to one reporter and not others."

Hirschfeld's awareness of the problem helped him avoid many of its consequences. He preferred to work outside of the dingy press room in police headquarters, whereas five other *Daily News* police beat reporters seldom leave the building. "If you're physically outside the building," he continues, "you can cover a subject and do a better job. You can look at it from a distance, make contact with other sources, be more analytical. When you are obligated to be there, you're too close. If you get to depending on the police department to give you news, you're at a disadvantage."

The separation also explained Hirschfeld's title — criminal justice reporter instead of police reporter. He could cover a broader range of subjects than his colleagues in the police press room. Hirschfeld says his day was never typical, primarily because he didn't work the police beat in the traditional sense.

At times he had to do rewrites of stories telephoned in by other reporters — especially by the older "legmen," who rarely wrote their own stories but often submitted facts over the phone to the city room. Hirschfeld considers such rewriting "the hazard of not looking busy enough at the right time." On smaller papers such positions do not exist. Reporters write their own stories.

His story output varied from one a day to one or two a week in a slow period. On smaller papers a police reporter writes a number of stories a day. Longer pieces take more time. "I'm happiest when I do not have to produce quantity and can spend time on stories," he says. "The editor determines that." His work had to satisfy the metropolitan editor, who is responsible for coverage of the entire city. During his last few years at the *News* he wrote about crime primarily for the Sunday magazine.

"Experience as a police reporter is very good, very helpful to a career," says Hirschfeld, who came to the *Daily News* in 1972 after several years on the *Buffalo Evening News*, "because it's the kind of writing that gets read, especially if you work for a tabloid. If you're writing about the board of education, you really have to do one hell of a job to get it read.

"You get good training in the basics, in learning how to get basic information, because police sources don't spoon-feed you. The longer you do it, the better you get. You learn about the city. It's so big — all those neighborhoods. You learn how the police work, what are the roughest parts of town. You never get bored. A lot of what you get is done by phone. If you're lucky enough to be with the police when something happens, it can be dangerous."

Difficult as it is, police reporting is a valuable part of journalism, in Hirschfeld's opinion. "I'd like to think it's important to *Daily News* readers to know what's going on," he says. "People read police stories, including a lot of cops. The kind of reporting that takes them behind the scenes is more interesting."

The biggest burden reporters like Hirschfeld have to bear is the reputation for exaggeration and fact stretching by the reporters who have covered the beat before them.

"You hear stories of reporters taking certain liberties and making up quotes," he says. "It's called 'piping,' making it up, putting words in a dead man's mouth before he died. I know this happens from my own days on the desk rewriting what the legmen would phone in. I must have had ten stories that included the same quote, 'This is the worst murder I've seen in twenty-five years as a cop.' Younger reporters have less of a tendency to do this."

Hirschfeld thinks police stories are too important to be treated frivolously, especially in a big city like New York. "Police reporting is no longer just cops and robbers," he says. "Police departments are big government agencies spending millions and millions of dollars. Police reporters have got to ask questions that get into other, more complicated stories."

Background to Police Reporting

The coverage of police activities was slow to gain acceptance in American journalism largely because of the experience of English newspapers. The *London Morning Herald* had been one of the first newspapers to run police-court news in the 1820s. Although readers enjoyed such stories, that paper's competitors criticized the practice and refused to imitate it. *The Statesman*, for example, wrote that because of "the absolute indecency of some of the cases which are allowed occasionally to creep into print, we deem it of little benefit to the cause of morals thus to familiarize the community, and especially the younger parts of it, with the details of misdemeanor and crime."

Editors like William Cullen Bryant of the *New York Post* agreed with this point of view, which prevailed for a number of years. The editors of the *New York Sun* and the *New York Transcript* did not. Beginning in 1834 and 1835, they began to run police-court news in their columns.

Although the *Transcript* bragged that it employed two full-time men to attend police courts from 3 A.M. to 8 P.M., the total volume rarely exceeded more than half a column. The material was largely of a statistical nature, however, with little space to tell a story.

James Gordon Bennett, editor of the *New York Herald*, at first publicly decried such coverage, then began to advertise quietly for a police reporter. As he would later do in pioneering coverage of Wall Street, Washington politics, society news, sports, and foreign affairs, Bennett sensed reader interest in a new subject. People were eager to read about human tragedy, he reasoned, so he began to devote more and more space to trials.

The coverage itself was quite unsensational. It followed court procedure with little embellishment from the *Herald* reporters or editors. But the fact that the stories were there caused a jump in circulation.

Bennett himself covered a story that would make him the true father of yellow journalism in the United States sixty years before William Randolph Hearst and Joseph Pulitzer practiced their own brand of sensationalism to increase circulation. With his account of a brutal murder in New York, Bennett not only made crime, scandal, and the underside of life an acceptable kind of story, but also established the reporting of police news as a constant assignment on newspapers everywhere.

The murder of a beautiful prostitute, Ellen Jewett, by a rich and handsome young man, Frank Robinson, was a natural circulation builder. While buyers eagerly snapped up copies containing this story, Bennett decided to do a second one by going to the murder scene himself and describing what he found there. He also included details about the life of Ellen Jewett.

The coverage continued day after day. Readers in New York talked of nothing else. Soon newspapers in Boston, Philadelphia, Baltimore, and Washington reprinted or rewrote the *Herald* articles, thus spreading the sensational story and, in the process, the idea of such coverage on a regular basis.

After a week Bennett was convinced that young Robinson had not killed Ellen Jewett. He passed his doubts along to his readers, suggesting that a rival prostitute had been the murderer in order to do away with a competitor. His detective work took him back to the prostitute's house, where he had a lengthy interview with its madam, Rosina Townsend. On April 16, 1836, Bennett printed their conversation to produce another innovation—the first printed interview.

In later stories Bennett cast doubt on the accuracy of Rosina Townsend's accusation against Robinson. The young man was later found innocent of the murder and vanished. The madam also disappeared, and the real murderer was never apprehended.

When Bennett realized that his readers liked such stories, he decided to continue printing them. He was then locked in a circulation war with his penny press competitors, Benjamin H. Day of the *New York Sun* and later Horace Greeley of the *New York Tribune*, and saw the reporting of police work, crime, and court activity as a way to get more readers from the horde of immigrants then beginning to arrive in the city. At first no case was too sensational, too bizarre, or too sordid for Bennett and Day. Readers willingly plunked down their pennies to read about the underside of life.

Critics complained that the two were ruining journalism, but they continued to publish this kind of story. Soon coverage of police work and courts was an accepted part of every newspaper.

The arrival of William Randolph Hearst in New York in 1895 brought with it a new emphasis on police reporting. The California millionaire was determined to surpass Joseph Pulitzer's *New York World* with his newly purchased *New York Journal*. The inclusion of a great deal of police and crime news was the chief way he proposed to beat Pulitzer.

Hearst had perfected his method of sensational coverage at the *San Francisco Examiner*. Under his ownership that newspaper became, in the words of biographer W.A. Swanberg, "an orchestra composed mainly of horns and drums."

After a young Sunday school teacher, Theodore Durrant, killed two girls at a church, the *Examiner* called it "the crime of the century." One of the paper's "sob sister" reporters, Annie Laurie, wrote about the events in a way that spared no details and was filled with opinion. Artists drew accompanying sketches that depicted the church, the killer, and the victims, particularly their skirts and underwear.

Hearst now transferred this brand of sensational coverage to New York and quickly hired editors and reporters to give him what he wanted and what readers would read. If the masses were stimulated by scandal, sex, and crime, Hearst would give them lurid stories with color illustrations. Hearst so frightened the ailing Pulitzer that Pulitzer directed his editors at the *World* to match the young upstart millionaire crime for crime, lurid detail for lurid detail, lowering himself and his newspaper in the process. Soon New York clubs had banned both newspapers from their staid drawing rooms, and civic groups were asking that they be toned down.

One device used by Hearst to build the circulation of the *Journal* over that of the *World* was the formation of a special "murder squad" of reporters. The group, set up to help the often inept police in their investigations, was sometimes directed by Hearst himself.

He offered liberal rewards for the apprehension of criminals, studied clues, and devised solutions. His reporters were everywhere, much to the dismay of the police. The team did turn up an occasional criminal, however.

Hearst's greatest success as a detective came in the Guldensuppe case in 1897. Guldensuppe was a corpse, or bits of a corpse wrapped in oilcloth and scattered around the East Side of New York. Hearst printed the pattern of the oilcloth in color in his paper and assigned thirty reporters to find the purchaser. One of them traced the oilcloth to a midwife and an accomplice who had cut up poor Guldensuppe in a bathtub and distributed his remains around the city. The *Journal* reported every detail, and Hearst was jubilant.

Hearst was so intent on beating the *World* that he hired extra staff members on the spot if regular reporters were too busy to cover rumored crime stories. If the rumored story did not materialize, the new people would not be recognized in the office. If the story worked out, they would be welcomed triumphantly and kept on the staff.

Hearst reporters regularly posed as city detectives or even federal agents, if necessary. Often the "criminal" was taken to the *Journal* office instead of jail and photographed, interviewed, and asked to confess to whatever the *Journal* wanted a confession for.

In many cases the *Journal* developed stories about an ongoing crime hourly and printed them in successive editions. Ads advised readers not to miss an edition in order to watch crime detection up close. The *Journal* got the entire story, including the confessions. Armed guards rode delivery wagons around the city to keep opposition papers from stealing copies of the newspapers. So eager were readers for the *Journal* that they grabbed copies out of drivers' hands.

Although Pulitzer eventually returned the *World* to a slightly more subdued format, Hearst never did. Indeed he gradually purchased a whole chain of newspapers to give readers throughout the country a steady stream of police, crime, and sex stories. His "sob sister" women reporters and their hard-bitten male counterparts were at every trial and every murder scene from the late 1800s until Hearst's death in 1951.

Other newspaper editors had watched the Hearst-Pulitzer imbroglio at a safe distance. Although they did not wish to join the fray, they saw the value of police and crime news. Such events were a part of the life of every town and city and, thus, were deserving of coverage. The police beat soon became a standard part of every newspaper's operation.

Newspapers emphasized this kind of news to the extent it would be appreciated — and demanded — by their readers. Some newspapers, like the *New York Times*, have always taken an almost sociological approach to police news. If a crime, and investigation, or something involving the police was too big to ignore, that newspaper would cover it. Other newspapers, most notably those in the Hearst chain or tabloids like the *New York Daily News*, frequently emphasized police beat items over other, less sensational news.

That same mix exists today, although the number of newspapers emphasizing the sensational aspects of police beat news has declined greatly. That role is now filled by local television stations and the more sensational tabloids like the *New York Post*.

The field has a better reputation now than in the recent past, when newspapers reporters on the police beat were either fledglings who knew too little or hacks and has beens who knew too much and were jaded and tired. Such people are still around, but in the larger cities they are gradually being replaced by reporters with training in the law and law enforcement. *New York Times* reporter David Burnham, for example, was the person officers David Durk and Frank Serpico called when they wanted to publicize widespread corruption in the New York Police Department in the 1970s. His stories led to the creation of the Knapp Commission and the beginning of police reform.

The coverage of police work and crime is the most thorough on big city newspapers simply because there is more crime to cover. On smaller papers, the police beat is a standard assignment, but often involves one person looking at the record of arrests for the previous twenty-four hours and following up interesting and newsworthy cases.

In a big city, each major newspaper and television and radio station is represented permanently by a reporter or group of reporters. They work in a press room in police headquarters and send their stories to the newsroom electronically. With this big commitment of staff and resources—and because of reader interest—the newspapers will run many more police stories than their counterparts in smaller towns.

Problems and Solutions

But what of the police departments subjected to this reportorial scrutiny?

According to a survey of police chiefs conducted by *American City and County* magazine, the biggest problem for police departments in the 1980s and early 1990s is making the public understand what law enforcement is all about and making officers aware of the image they create. The survey concluded that this public relations problem is greater than more standard and long-standing concerns such as personnel shortages, the lack of funds, and public apathy.

The difficulty from the standpoint of both the police officers and the public comes from the court system. Because of lenient judges, suspects are often released on their own recognizance before they are arraigned. The court system is so slow in many medium and large cities that those released commit several other crimes and are arrested again before the original case comes to trial.

This situation hurts police morale, creating in some officers a feeling of hopelessness. At the same time the public looks at rising crime rates and blames the police, not the clogged court system.

The other major trend nationally among police departments has been a tendency to resort to more force and to purchase more sophisticated equipment. The increased use of force resulted from the turbulent 1960s when ghetto riots and anti-Vietnam War demonstrations hit most American cities. Local police needed help, and they got it as part of the Omnibus Crime Control and Safe Streets Act of 1968, which created the Law Enforcement Assistance Administration (LEAA). Its provisions helped police departments train personnel and purchase equipment.

Since that law was enacted, most medium and large police departments have computers linked with a state data bank or the National Crime Information Center in Washington to determine if an automobile is stolen or a person stopped for questioning is wanted for a crime elsewhere. Many also have a helicopter for night patrol of parks or fast pursuit and sophisticated laboratory equipment for photography and analysis.

Coincidentally, at the same time this federal funding became available, the space program began to decline. As a result, companies that had been manufacturing equipment for space exploration turned their attention to police work with a glittering array of new products: hand-held radiation detectors to search out illegal drugs; electronic scanners to identify gunshot traces; scanning electron microscopes to analyze gun particles wiped from the hands of suspects; hand-held radar units to detect speeders; voiceprint machines to analyze voice patterns on a spectrograph to prove the identity of suspected criminals who use the telephone; the Star-Tron telescope (developed for use on night patrols in the jungles of Vietnam) to see into dark alleys in cities often from helicopters hovering above; and an eighty-thousand dollar emergency vehicle that looks like a tank with one-fourth-inch steel plating and holes through which its crew's M-16 rifles can protrude.

Critics of the police charged that they were overly infatuated with this new equipment at the expense of trying to improve their ability to solve crimes. Police departments replied that the equipment was necessary to perform an increasingly difficult job. The critics deplored the brute force exemplified by such items as the tank. They also castigated police for the organizations of special SWAT (Special Weapons and Tactics) teams—officers with special training in taking a building by force during siege or hostage situations by using powerful weapons and wearing bulletproof clothing.

Beginning the late 1970s, police departments started to recruit more minority officers and to establish better community relations programs in ghetto areas. Departments also tried, for the first time, to detect unstable, brutal, mentally ill, or racist officers or would-be officers and to keep them out of their ranks. As becomes clear later in this chapter, these efforts have not always been successful.

In the mid-1980s, a new factor emerged as a major cause of crime in American cities of all sizes—*crack*, a potent new type of cocaine that was more readily available than the old variety because it was slightly cheaper. Ethnic gangs soon formed to control its distribution. Crimes of other kinds (robbery, murder) occurred as people sought money to buy it or acted under its influence (rape, murder). "One of the big changes in recent years is the public perception that things are out of control," says Neal Hirschfeld, "largely because of crack. There is so much murder, so much random violence. People are being gunned down by random bullets. There has been a big rise in the number of random shootings, of innocent victims caught in the cross-fire because drug gangs pulled guns. Police are like the little Dutch boy with his finger in the dike. There is the sense that crime is rampant."

(Ironically, the dramatic increase in drug-related crime nationwide comes at a time when organized crime is on the decline, primarily because of the Racketeer Influenced and Corrupt Organizations law, first enacted in 1970, which mandated harsh penalties for anyone engaging in a pattern of serious crimes through some business or organization. In city after city, mob bosses were successfully prosecuted under the RICO statute and sent to prison for long sentences. This law has also been used to indict major figures in stock market fraud investigations.)

The startling increase in violent crime—23,200 homicides in the U.S. in 1990—has been combined with severe cuts in city budgets, resulting in fewer police, courts that are overburdened, and prisons that are overcrowded. This state of affairs has created a siege mentality in police departments which, in turn, has caused a rise in police brutality.

The dramatic videotape of Los Angeles police officers beating a black man in March 1991 brought to national attention a problem that had plagued many large cities for several years. At the time of the L.A. incident the U.S. Department of Justice announced that nearly 15,000 complaints of police brutality had been filed with the federal government from 1985 to 1991. A *Newsweek* poll found 62 percent of Americans believed that minority groups suffer at the hands of police. The Los Angeles Police Department got all the notoriety, but few large American cities could deny that they had similar problems.

Experts blamed police brutality on racism, poor training, slack departmental discipline, and a tradition that encourages officers to look the other way when some of their colleagues get violent with suspects. Others warn that the problem stems from political pressures in the drug wars, causing city officials to expect unrealistic results from the cops on the street. The cops, for their part, become frustrated with the never ending cycle of violence and this frustration sometimes reaches the breaking point captured on the videotape.

The furor caused by the incident in Los Angeles resulted in the creation of a special commission to investigate that incident and the general charges of police brutality and racism. Its report issued in July 1991 had implications for police departments all across the United States, many of them faced with the same problems as L.A. The commission found that a significant number of officers use excessive force against Los Angeles residents, a problem worsened by racism and bias in the department. It called for a switch from what it called a "para-militaristic, us-against-them style" to one that is community based with police officers spending less time in their cars and more time interacting with citizens in the community. In what may have been one of the most startling findings of all, the commission noted that L.A. police officers must pass marksmanship tests every two months, but face no psychological testing after they have been hired.

"Too many L.A.P.D. patrol officers view citizens with resentment and hostility," wrote the commission in its report, "too many treat the public with rudeness and disrespect."

The media have been caught in the middle in covering stories like police brutality and the great increase in drug related crime. When a newspaper publishes an editorial that calls for punishment of police officers or the resignation of the chief, its police beat reporter will find it much more difficult to do his or her job because of hostility from police personnel. Sometimes, police reporters sympathize more with police than their editors, creating conflict within the news organization.

When doing the job puts reporters and police at odds, it is the reporters who suffer, however. They must rely on the police for the most precious commodity of all in this kind of beat reporting: access—to records, crime scenes, witnesses and other people to interview. But the public suffers as well when the police and the press, two of the most powerful American institutions, are in conflict.

When they are warring, vital information is not made public. Twenty years ago police reporters in most cities had complete access to every piece of investigative material they wanted. Now it is rare to gain access in most large cities without a lot of digging because of official controls over information. More information is released in states with public records laws, however. And, as Neal Hirschfeld pointed out earlier in this chapter, police officers can reward or punish reporters as they wish. If he or she gets angry at a past story or a critical editorial, a police chief can order officers not to cooperate in releasing information. There is very little a reporter can do but complain, and the chief can hide behind the need for secrecy. Worried over rising crime rates, the public will probably support the chief. Readers usually do not care to hear about the difficulty reporters have in doing their jobs.

In the strange new world of defendant rights, police brutality, and police strikes, the press often gets blamed when a person accused of a crime goes free, a police officer is dismissed for using excessive force, or public opinion turns against officers who strike for higher pay. This blame turns to hatred in many cases, and the ability of reporters to do their jobs becomes nearly impossible.

According to *Police Magazine*, Philadelphia police are subject to disciplinary action if they are seen talking to reporters at the scene of a crime. In San Francisco, in 1979, two former police officers and a former prosecutor were successful in suing the *San Francisco Examiner* for libel. The paper wrote that the three had harassed and coerced a murder suspect, but a jury found in favor of the plaintiffs and awarded them $4.5 million in damages.

Because police have begun to make their jobs so difficult, reporters and the newspapers for which they work have begun to fight back. Two Miami papers sued the public safety director in 1979 for his refusal to release investigative files on alleged police misconduct. In 1979 Los Angeles newspapers filed a lawsuit to force the release of police shooting records back to 1976.

The intensity of the problem varies with the size of the city. Relations are not as strained in smaller towns where the police reporter must worry about getting so close to the chief and officers as to have his or her objectivity tested and questioned.

Most reporters starting out on a police beat on a small or medium paper will not have the problems their battle-hardened colleagues in big cities experience. No matter what the size of the city, however, the potential for difficulty exists because of the built-in adversary relationship between press and police. Both sides try to do their jobs; the press tries to get information that the police want to withhold in order to protect a suspect's rights and to ensure a thorough investigation of crime.

More suggestions for dealing with the problems of the police beat appear in "Likely Problems and How to Solve Them" later in this chapter.

How to Cover the Police Beat

A new reporter on the police beat will get off to a better start by knowing about the problems and trying to contribute to their solution. While working their beats, police reporters walk a thin line between the desire for news of crime and police activities and the need for secrecy in investigations.

Laying the Groundwork

1. **Emphasize the similarities between press and police.** In dealing with police department personnel on the beat, reporters should point out that both institutions — press and police — are large, powerful, operate in a beat system, and influence the lives of a number of people. Both use investigative skills to get the job done. Both are highly secretive and resent criticism. Having an opportunity to point out these similarities might ease tensions. Another argument to use is the public's right to know about what a police department does, particularly since police budgets are paid for with tax dollars.

2. **Overcome the stereotyped points of view.** Police tend to think all reporters are hard-bitten, cynical, and too curious for their own good. Reporters tend to think all police officers are racist, fascist, brutal, and corrupt. Getting together for an occasional cup of coffee or glass of beer might help dispel such myths.

3. **Establish a good relationship with the police chief.** The chief sets the tone for the department. If the chief hates the press, the rank and file officers will hate the press. The relationship in a smaller city begins with a get-acquainted interview after a new reporter joins the beat or a new chief takes over the force. After this, fairness in coverage will suffice until the day comes when the reporter writes a critical story about the chief or a particular officer. If the criticism is warranted, the reporter can be buttressed with that knowledge, and the police chief may respect the reporter for having the courage to print the story. If the chief is corrupt, the story may help ease him or her out of office. If the criticism is without foundation, or if it's true but has no impact, the reporter had best ask for a transfer to another beat or look for another job. In larger cities the chief is a remote figure and unavailable for regular interviews. Desk sergeants and detective lieutenants are the sources to cultivate. Inspectors and deputy chiefs make good contacts as well.

4. **Beware of being "tested."** The men and women in the ranks

of the police department are just as suspicious of reporters as is their chief. Although they might have to work with the press, they don't necessarily like it. They might, for example, show new police reporters the seamier side of the job, such as photos of a murder victim, to see if they have strong stomachs. They might also test reporters to see if they will keep their word; for example, they may deliberately tell reporters something off the record to see if it gets into print. If they don't fail such tests, reporters will be trusted with inside information during investigations.

Working the Beat

1. **Cultivate sources carefully.** Reporters on any beat spend a great deal of time cultivating sources, from the lowest level clerk to the highest official possible. This is especially true on a police beat, where official information may not be provided as it would be on the government or science beat. "When you find people willing to talk," says Neal Hirschfeld, "You've got to convince them it's worth their while or in the public interest for them to do so."

It isn't always as easy as it sounds. Often the people who have the facts for a story don't want to talk. "They are afraid or sensitive or embarrassed," says Hirschfeld. "But you know it is a good story, so you've just got to wait for the spirit to come to them. It amazes me the number of times you get into a story and find people who are willing to help."

Smaller newspapers usually send the police beat reporter to the police station every day to review the "rap sheet" of arrests for the previous twenty-four hours. Few of these items are newsworthy, but the daily visit builds up contacts who may prove valuable when the case merits a story. Such cultivation of sources helps, too, when an important story breaks during the middle of the day. A cooperative police source will call a reporter to offer a tip about something that is about to happen.

2. **Beware of getting too close to police sources.** The acceptance needed to do the police reporting job, however, very often brings with it a closeness to police that borders on patronage. Hirschfeld discussed the problem of getting too close to sources earlier in this chapter. When a reporter is so beholden to a police officer for information that the police person dictates when the information can appear in print, the relationship has gone too far. The only way to avoid this problem is to establish other sources to verify and furnish information and to make it clear to police officials that police reporters are independent agents. When the revelation

of information in a story jeopardizes an investigation, however, that is quite another matter. Each situation should be weighed carefully from ethical and legal standpoints.

3. **Find out about police procedures.** Cooperation by police is imperative on what Neal Hirschfeld calls "nuts and bolts crime stories." It will be easier to do these stories if a reporter learns as much as possible about police procedure. How does the department conduct an investigation? What information can be released about defendants without jeopardizing their rights in court? How can information be obtained when hostages have been taken? How can reporters get through police lines put up around a riot area or the scene of a major crime? In some states a reporter's right to see all arrest records is restricted. Most states limit the information released on juvenile offenders. A reporter new to the police beat must quickly learn the answers to these questions. Boxes 7.1 and 7.2 describe basic police organizations and procedures. The reporter should also be familiar with the definitions provided in "Key Terms for Police Reporting" at the end of this chapter.

If the police department issues any kind of press pass or other credentials, the reporter should obtain one. Most large cities have such an arrangement; most smaller ones do not. If not, it is a good idea to suggest some kind of pass in the initial meeting with the police chief.

4. **Learn how to report a routine crime story.** Once the reporter understands basic police procedures, he or she can cover day-to-day news with police cooperation. "It's kind of tough to avoid official help unless you talk to one of the victims," Hirschfeld says. "On a hard crime story, you have to identify sources and attribute information." On stories concerning the operation of the police department, Hirschfeld tries to verify everything gained from one source with several other sources. He also tries to find out if an official written policy exists. Computer readouts are a particularly good way to get statistics.

"A hard crime story starts with a routine interview where you get the basics — name, time the body was found, what happened," he says. "If they give you a hard time, you can say, 'I don't mean to put you out, but I'm on a deadline.' You play the helpless reporter with the desk sergeant in a precinct. The best thing is to go to the scene. If I had a rule for doing police stories, it would be that it is best to be there, to see things for yourself."

A police story rarely occurs in time to be of benefit to a newspaper's deadline system. "Invariably, a story breaks close to deadline," says Hirschfeld. "There seems to be a delay in notifying the press. Usually there's not enough time to get to the scene, and you have to work the story by phone. Once in a while, every other month, something breaks right.''

For what the police department considers a major occurrence, however, information is transmitted by teletype to each newspaper office in the city. "It might say, '72nd Precinct, report of homicide, two in custody,'" says Hirschfeld, who can then request more details on that crime. On a really newsworthy case, the police department office of public information will call each newspaper, using a special "hot line" to give details.

5. **Away from the flow of news, the best stories come from a reporter's resourcefulness.** The stories Hirschfeld enjoyed most were those in which he originated the idea himself, either through his own ingenuity or because of a tip from a source.

Story ideas might come from informal talks with sources on the beat. "I've heard detectives complain that new procedures are not as good as old ones," he says of one example. "'It is tying our hands,' they say. I hear it a lot, so I check figures from the detective bureau and see that the clearance rate on cases—the percentage they deem solved—has been going down for the past ten years. The next step is to find out why. I talk to the chief, detectives, district attorneys. They think their hands are tied by court decisions that restrict their ability to get statements from those arrested and the fact that overtime is limited. They also blame structural changes in the department that prevent police from really knowing the turf they are responsible for. Last of all, the disintegration of various neighborhoods like the South Bronx and the Lower East Side, has hurt the police. People move so often that witnesses can't be easily located."

In two instances Hirschfeld got tips on possible stories, then had trouble obtaining the corroborating information.

"The impetus for both stories came with the fiscal crisis of 1975," recalls Hirschfeld, "when five thousand cops were laid off. The question was, did the city need a thirty-thousand-man police force? Were they doing police work? If not, why not? How much was being spent on overtime and how many cops were there?"

A companion story covered the number of street officers in comparison to the number of ranking officers. "Why were there so many [ranking officers] when their underlings had been laid off?" asks Hirschfeld, who set out to find out.

Not surprisingly, official sources were uncooperative. "I made the rounds and talked to people but came to dead ends," he continues. "I must have gone to every higher-up, but I couldn't get figures. I

Box 7.1

How Police Departments Are Organized

Any successful police reporter needs to be familiar with basic police procedure and the organization of the police department with which he or she must work.

A police department is usually divided into three main elements: line, staff, and supportive.

Line units do the most visible work of a police department. During patrol, line unit officers do a preliminary investigation of a crime, survey potential hazards, or control crowds. They investigate crimes more fully and arrest suspects, question witnesses, secure evidence, and write reports. These units also regulate vice, that is, prostitution, gambling, illicit liquor and tobacco sales, and narcotics violations. They control traffic and investigate automobile accidents. They protect dependent children and handle juveniles who get into trouble.

Staff functions involve planning, inspection, training, and budget. More specifically, this portion of the department includes personnel and training, planning and research, financial affairs, public relations, community relations, and the enlisting and training of citizens to help with clerical and other duties so police officers can perform line duty.

Supportive units help the other two main areas in the inspection and investigation of personnel and in handling civilian complaints about police mistreatment, vice, or corruption.

A chief usually presides over a police department; assistant chiefs are placed in charge of the three major elements noted above. Sometimes a chief must report to a police commissioner appointed by the major.

A key person in any police organization is the sergeant, the connecting point between the chief and the officers in the ranks.

A good police department operates like a military organization: a strong central authority passing along its orders to those below in a tightly controlled chain of command.

Reporters must also work with law enforcement agencies with more broad jurisdictions. Most of the time this consists of county sheriffs and the state police.

The sheriff is responsible for maintaining law and order in the county. This power is granted by the state. Sheriffs are usually elected to office by voters in the county. Although sheriffs must depend on voter goodwill to stay in office, they must enforce the laws of the state government, an entity controlled from the state capital.

Sheriffs usually exercise civil as well as criminal duties. They call jurors and supervise them during trials, serve subpoenas and other actions of the court, guard prisoners held for court action, and execute civil court judgments (for example, selling the property of someone under judgment of the court). The criminal functions of sheriffs make them the main law enforcement officers in less urbanized counties or rural areas of any county. As such they investigate crimes and do traffic patrol. In larger cities their jurisdictions often overlap those of city police.

State police officers are responsible to the governor. In most states a main duty is to patrol state highways and arrest speeders and investigate traffic accidents. In some states this level of police authority extends to investigation of crime to help local police departments and sheriffs. Well-equipped state police departments have sophisticated crime laboratories for this purpose. Most state police units are organized like the military: a superintendent appointed by the governor is at the top, and divisions headed by captains and staffed by troopers are below.

Occasionally a local police reporter will also come in contact with various kinds of federal police agencies. The Federal Bureau of Investigation maintains offices in all major cities. The Secret Service division of the Treasury Department investigates forgery and counterfeiting. Postal inspectors investigate mail fraud and other postal law violations. The Border Patrol works along the borders with Canada and Mexico. Narcotics and custom investigators work out of large cities as well. These agencies are hierarchical in nature. Reporters can build up sources in the local offices, but control comes from Washington, D.C.

decided I would have to end-run the department and go outside to meet new people."

He went to the office of one of the deputy mayors. A source there showed Hirschfeld a computer readout the size of a telephone book, which broke down every unit in the vast department in terms of who was doing field work, administrative work, and support work. He looked at the document briefly in that office, then requested that police officials let him see a copy, claiming that it was a public document.

"They were surprised I knew about it," he says. "They had a captain sit down and go through a copy with me. I flipped to the end and got the totals. I heard later they were upset that I had known what I was looking for."

He got material for both stories from the document as well as the departmental budget. These showed, he says, "how money was spent, cops deployed, whether too many of them were behind desks, what categories of crime were up or down."

Traps to Avoid

1. **Naming a suspect who has not been charged.** People are sometimes picked up for questioning, detained briefly, and then

released without being charged. A reporter must make sure the suspect was actually booked and either jailed or granted bail before saying so in a story.

2. **Convicting a person before trial.** Under the United States Constitution, a person is presumed innocent until proven guilty in court. If a reporter convicts a suspect of the crime before he or she has gone to trial, the reporter is depriving that person of an important right — and opening the door for a libel suit. This happens when a reporter flatly states in a story that a person is guilty of a crime. The wording of such stories is tricky. The word "alleged" helps lessen the problem but may not be enough to avoid difficulty later. The phrases "arrested on a charge of" and "is charged with committing (or killing)" are often used. Police reporters should read and reread the wording of their stories, particularly the lead — where the crime is outlined.

3. **Misidentifying a suspect.** Police news has a greater potential for libel suits than any other type because of the possibility of misidentifying people arrested for crimes. Such mistakes can subject the reporter and the newspaper to libel suits by those wrongly identified. Careful checking of names and addresses in city directories and telephone books rather than relying only on police records will help alleviate this problem. Such records are often filled out by police personnel in haste and can be full of errors.

4. **Using any information without verification.** The same likelihood of error exists in accepting any information from a police officer and using it in a story without checking it out. Although a detective has the authority of the law behind him or her, that authority does not also confer infallibility as far as accurate information is concerned. Crime scenes are confusing places, and mistakes are made. They do not have to be immortalized in print, however.

5. **Not understanding the state penal code**. This code establishes what constitutes a crime and the punishment for that crime in a state. By being familiar with its provisions, reporters will be able to read a police report and immediately know a crime's magnitude, which is not otherwise distinguishable from others committed during the same time period. Knowledge of the code will also allow reporters to understand police personnel who talk in penal code numbers rather than specify the crimes. If a reporter knows the number of the code section, he or she needs only to find the right volume and turn to the appropriate section for the information desired. If the reporter does not have the correct number, he or she should use the index of the volume that seems likely to contain the

Box 7.2

Standard Police Procedures

No matter the size of the town or city, the responsible police department has much the same goal: enforcing the standards of conduct needed to protect citizens of that community. The department does this by apprehending suspected lawbreakers, who are then prosecuted for their alleged crime in a court system where they are either convicted or set free. If convicted, they are sentenced to jail or prison.

These actions are designed to remove dangerous people from the town or city, to deter others from criminal behavior, and to give society the chance to turn the lawbreakers into good citizens. (Figure 7.1 shows steps in the police process.)

The first step in the police process is the arrest, in which a suspect is taken into custody by police officers because they think that person has broken a law. If they have not seen the act, there may be witnesses who have. At the time of the arrest, or at the police station, the officer must read the defendant his or her rights.

Two U.S. Supreme Court decisions of the 1960s had a profound effect on how police treat those they arrest.

The 1964 *Escobedo* ruling had far-reaching ramifications for defendants. Danny Escobedo had been arrested and released as a murder suspect, then arrested a second time. When he was brought to the police station, he asked to see a lawyer who had previously represented him and who was at the station at that time. The police refused his request. He was then interrogated for a long time with threats, misstatements, and promises intermingled by police. Escobedo made a series of damaging admissions, then confessed. He appealed his conviction because of his denial to counsel, and the case made its way to the Supreme Court. That tribunal found in his favor. According to Justice Arthur Goldberg, evidence may not be used against a defendant in a criminal trial if it was gained in an interrogation "where, as here, the investigation is no longer a general inquiry into an unsolved crime, but has begun to focus on a particular suspect, the suspect has been taken into police custody, the police carry out a process of interrogation that lends itself to eliciting incriminatory statements, the suspect has requested and been denied an opportunity to consult with his lawyer. . . ."

The 1966 *Miranda* decision dealt with the reading of rights, as all viewers of TV police programs and crime films know. Ernest Miranda was arrested for kidnapping and rape at his home in Phoenix, Arizona. At the police station he was identified by the complainant and taken to an interrogation room without being advised of his rights. After two hours of intensive questioning, detectives emerged with a signed confession, which was used as evidence in his trial. Miranda was found guilty, but the Supreme Court reversed his conviction because it said his rights had been violated.

In this decision, the justices required police to inform suspects taken into custody of their rights to remain silent and to consult a lawyer before being interrogated. Failure to follow this procedure could lead to statements made at the time of arrest excluded as evidence at trial.

Because of these two decisions, police now regularly read defendants their rights at the time of their arrest: to remain silent, to refuse to answer any questions, to consult an attorney, and to know that what they say at the time can be used against them in court later. The defendant is also told that an attorney will be provided if the defendant cannot afford one.

In 1981 the *Miranda* decision was reaffirmed by the Supreme Court and actually strengthened. Once a suspect invokes his or her right to remain silent until consulting a lawyer, this right cannot be undone unless the defendant "initiates further communication." In one of the cases considered by the justices, the defendant had requested an attorney but implicated himself in the crime before the attorney arrived. In the other case a defendant had talked to a state-supported psychiatrist, who later testified against him in court. The ruling said suspects do not have to talk to psychiatrists at that point in their incarceration.

By 1984, the conservative tilt to the court was causing *Miranda* to be slightly modified. In one decision the Court said that "public safety" sometimes requires that police question arrested individuals before advising them of their rights. A 1991 ruling, however, seemed to slow the move toward overturning *Miranda* that some court observers have long anticipated: Once an accused person has invoked his *Miranda* right to ask for a lawyer, police cannot resume interrogation without the lawyer being present.

(A hint of toughness to come may exist in three other, non-*Miranda* rulings in 1991. In one, the justices made it easier for police with no warrants to search buses for drugs or to open and examine suitcases or paper bags they find in car trunks. In another, the court allowed prosecutors to use some coerced confessions as evidence against defendants. The third authorized the jailing of individuals for up to 48 hours without a court hearing, during which time police could work to see if there is probable cause for the arrest.)

After being "Mirandized," defendants are searched at the scene of the arrest. At the police station the defendant is searched again in front of the booking desk. His or her property is recorded and placed in an envelope. Also during this booking period the desk sergeant writes the defendant's name, other identification, and the crime for which he or she has been arrested into a master book.

The arresting officer next writes an arrest report, which details the circumstances of the arrest and the alleged crime, on a prepared form in front of the defendant. The officer also asks the defendant to sign a waiver, which allows police to interrogate him or her about the alleged crime.

The defendant is photographed and fingerprinted next; he or she is permitted to make one telephone call before being placed in a detention cell in the police station or the courthouse.

In the next few hours or the next few days, depending on workload, the suspect is taken before a judge, usually in a lower court like a magistrate or justice of the peace. During this appearance, the prosecutor will present a formal complaint, which uses the information obtained in the arrest papers and in interviews with police officers and the victim to charge the defendant with a specific crime.

The defendant will also be advised of his or her constitutional rights, including the protection from self-incrimination. If the defendant has no money, the judge can appoint a public defender at this point. Unless the defendant is convicted of a crime at this point, arrangements for temporary release might be set. This release usually includes the setting of bail, an amount of financial security to be deposited with the court (either from the defendant or a professional bail bondsman) to ensure that the defendant will return for trial. (People who leave anyway are said to "jump bail.") If no bail is deemed necessary, the judge will release the defendant on his or her own recognizance, or promise to appear later.

This first appearance begins judicial inquiry into the case. If the charge is minor and if the court has the jurisdiction, the defendant may be asked to plead. If that plea is guilty, the defendant might be convicted at that point. If the plea is innocent, the defendant will be brought back for trial later.

At this point the police department's role in a case is over, except for the need for the arresting officer to testify at the trial. Court procedure will be discussed in Chapter 8.

information. For example, a legal definition of murder, the various degrees, and the punishment would be in the penal code. If the reporter does not know which volume will be likely to have the desired information, he or she can consult the index for the entire code, which is usually contained in several volumes. The code entries are generally the same in most states. They list: legislative history of the law; cross-references to similar sections; collateral references to specific sections in other legal reference books; other general references like law review articles and opinions of the attorney general; notes of decisions, which are one-paragraph summaries of specific cases with citations; and suggested form, which gives a sample introducing the format of the written procedure described in the statute. Federal laws are also printed in codes that should be studied by reporters covering the courts governed by the laws. All libraries in a state should have copies of that state's codes. Court decisions are listed in books usually called, for example, *California Reports* or *United States Supreme Court Reports*. The listings are by the name of the case (*U.S. v. Smith*) followed by the volume number, the report type (that is, state or federal), the page number, and year of decision. A full listing would read: *U.S. v. Smith*, 117 United States 700 (1937).

6. **Knowing what information to release.** Access to police records, like arrest reports, varies from state to state. If a state has an open records law, the reporter can use so-called police blotter

information as the basis for stories, making sure to verify facts, the spelling of names, and the listing of proper street addresses. In states without such laws, however, a police reporter must rely on cooperation from people in charge of records. If that fails, a reporter — or his or her editor — might take the issue of closed records to the mayor or to readers in a story about the situation. Even public records laws exempt certain information from release, however. Law enforcement agencies are usually allowed to refuse to disclose records of complaints made to them, records of investigations, details of intelligence information, and plans of security procedures. Even states allowing the release of basic jail booking information prohibit the disclosure of information about a person's past criminal record, commonly called a "rap sheet," lest this interfere with the defendant's right to a fair trial. It often is not a crime for a reporter to use such information, only for someone to give it to a reporter. Reporters can obtain such information in other ways: in reports of search warrants or arrest warrants, court records, reports of bail investigations officers, arrest reports incorporated in the court file, and probation reports. (Information on open records laws appears in Chapter 6; details on legal and ethical problems appear in Appendix A and Appendix B.)

Occupational Hazards

1. **Be prepared for a rigorous and often tense occupation.** Police work rarely happens on a schedule that coincides with a reporter's working hours or a newspaper's deadline. This means that police reporters must be healthy and able to work long hours, often late into the night. Police reporters constantly hear about, and observe firsthand, the bad side of life. They see dead bodies and people who have been badly injured. They must sometimes tell a wife or a husband that their mate has died, then ask for a picture. Police reporters can have their own lives threatened or be subjected to bribery. For all its interesting aspects, police reporting is not an easy job.

2. **Don't expect cooperation on a big story after ignoring day-to-day events.** The spirit of cooperation that must exist with sources on any beat must be maintained from day to day with the police. This means that a reporter should do a story on new forensic, investigative, or patrol techniques as well as the hard crime stories so prevalent on the beat. If police sources know a reporter is interested in something other than how badly the department did in capturing a strangler, for example, they will be more cooperative.

On the other hand, the close rapport that might develop between reporter and officer on a routine story one day should not cause the reporter to avoid the disclosure of corruption or incompetence later.

3. **Be prepared for competition from television.** Because of the nature of TV news and the constant quest for high ratings, television reporters in large cities cover the police department in the same way newspapers used to cover them. No robbery or murder seems too insignificant to send an "Eyewitness News Team" racing to the scene, arriving at the same time as police. The more sensational and breathless the story, the higher the viewer interest. Newspapers, on the other hand, are de-emphasizing such treatment for crime stories. Because competition has dwindled in most American cities, the surviving newspapers no longer need rape and murder emblazoned across their front pages to sell papers on the street. When newspapers decide to cover crime stories that are beyond the routine, however, their reporters may find that police officials gravitate toward the camera lenses of TV.

Kinds of Police Stories

The stories gleaned from a police beat will vary with the size and nature of the city involved. Some cities will suffer more of one kind of crime than others. In some large cities there are so many murders and robberies that only an unusual one is newsworthy. In a smaller city one murder can devastate an entire community.

Regardless of the size of a city, however, there are a number of potential stories on the police beat:

1. **Capital crime stories** involve murder, kidnapping, rape, or any other action punishable by death.

2. **Felony crime stories** involve robbery, burglary, larceny, arson, or anything that could lead to a year or more in prison.

3. **Misdemeanor crime stories** detail lesser violations of the law, such as drunk driving, which may be punishable by imprisonment for less than a year and/or a fine. A misdemeanor is usually only a story if something unusual or humorous takes place.

4. **Infractions** are the least serious offenses and often involve motor vehicles; punishment is usually by a fine only. As with misdemeanors, an infraction is rarely a story.

5. **Accidents** are natural police beat stories, especially if they result in serious injury or death; the accidents in this category

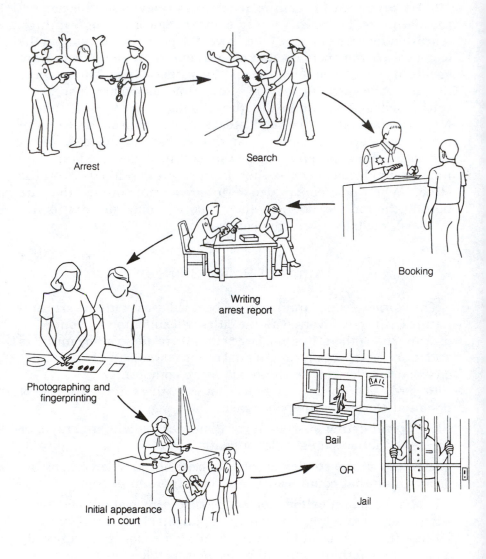

Arrest

Search

Booking

Writing
arrest report

Photographing and
fingerprinting

Initial appearance
in court

Bail

OR

Jail

Figure 7.1 **Steps in the police process**

include those involving automobiles, trains, airplanes as well as suicides, drowning, and rescues.

6. **Fires** are legitimate stories if the damage is great enough to be newsworthy; the number of fire engines responding, the number of people evacuated, and the dollar amount of the damage help make this determination.

7. **Department activities** of both a routine and nonroutine nature make good story possibilities. In this category are stories on how the department conducts an investigation, new techniques, new personnel, and charges of police corruption or police brutality.

8. **The economics of police work** provides material for stories on how the changing economy affects police and the ability to fight crime. This kind of story comes both from within the department (how the adequacy and inadequacy of funding affects staffing and programs) and outside (how recession and layoffs, lack of jobs and housing, and no money for drug treatment causes more crime).

9. **Crime trends** make good stories at certain times of the year in certain cities. If, for example, the city is listed as a major center of drug traffic by a national law enforcement agency or as having a high rate of homicides, both would be good subjects of analytical articles. Shoplifting stories are good at Christmas, and white-collar crime articles are interesting anytime.

10. **Organized crime**, if it exists at all in a city or a state, makes a legitimate subject for an article or series of articles.

11. **Features** about people or unusual aspects of the department break the monotony of the police beat. Such features might include a new chief, a new dog trained to sniff out hidden marijuana caches, the first woman detective, or a newly-designed patrol car.

Writing Police Stories

The basic news story about routine police beat matters should be written in a simple, straightforward manner. The summary lead with its five W's (who, what, when, where, and why) and an H (how) is the best approach. Equally serviceable for the rest of the story is the inverted pyramid style, in which the most important facts are placed first and followed by the other facts in the descending order of their importance.

Neal Hirschfeld's way of writing is probably typical for a big-city police reporter. He says his writing style is dictated in large part by the short, choppy approach of the *Daily News*. "Long stories are rare," he says. "A big story is four takes [manuscript pages]. You really have to write tight. No writer really likes it. If your story gets in and gets space, you figure the editors must like it.

"You can't have a delayed lead. You've got to get to the point immediately and make every quote count. You prune out anything not absolutely essential to the story. This is more so in a tabloid like the *News* than the *New York Times* or the *Los Angeles Times*. You adhere to the old basic—the inverted pyramid. If not, you're not telling the story if it is cut in the middle. You don't know if it has been cut until the paper comes out. If you don't have the kernel of it in the top of the story, it will make no sense if it is cut.

"We try to use more active language. The *News* prides itself on punchy writing. You just get right to the point. You can't dillydally, or you'll fall victim to some editor's pencil.

"If you tell everything first, there's no surprise. But unless you have the space—like in a Sunday magazine piece—you can't resort to tricks. I'm a believer in the very simple sentence, one thought to a sentence. I'm not edited that heavily, probably because I worked on the copy desk and know what editors are looking for.

"Verbs are really good, especially colorful ones, as opposed to lots of adjectives. I really think active verbs help a lot because they pump energy into the narrative and put it into high gear making the story move faster. I hate to read stuff that goes slow.

"Another thing I like to do is to describe things well, with attention to the senses. If you read one of my stories, you not only read it, but you hear it and feel it and smell it.

"As opposed to writing stories from a crime standpoint—so and so was murdered—I spend a lot of time getting inside the heads of my sources, finding out about their worlds, so I can capture it, and see it through their eyes."

Hirschfeld's first story here gives an account of the arrest and trial of two New York prostitutes. The article shows how very simple sentences may be used effectively to present the facts of what is a fairly straightforward news story.

In his second story, a long feature written for the *New York Daily News Magazine*, Hirschfeld spent two weeks with several transit police and their canine partners both on the job and at the dog training compound. To simplify the story, he decided to focus his attention on one such partnership, weaving details of the work of the whole squad around this duo: "I picked these two because I loved the names. Lively and Rommel. Sounds like a comedy team."

#1

WHO'S THAT BIG DUDE?
Father Knick, the Pimp!
By Neal Hirschfeld

Because it is an enterprise story that is less tied to the news than the other story presented here, Hirschfeld's article on the two prostitutes is written in a more unconventional way. The lead is designed to attract attention. Because of its startling nature, however, the lead had to be explained quickly. Hirschfeld does this in the second paragraph with a summary of his investigations on how soon arrested prostitutes are released to return to the street.

1   The biggest pimp in New York City may be the city itself.

2   An investigation by *The News* has found that judges are fining convicted prostitutes routinely, then giving them time to pay the fines. This system quickly returns the prostitutes to the streets to earn the money by the trade they know best.

3   Last year, the courts in lower Manhattan alone levied $275,000 in fines for prostitution.

4   The system of justice, which has been compared with a revolving door, was witnessed first hand by a reporter and photographer from *The News* who accompanied undercover cops as they made two prostitution arrests. The suspects were followed into police stations for booking, into Criminal Court for arraignment, and back out on the street again after they had been fined.

5   The two women, selected at random from the field of streetwalkers by officers of the Manhattan South public morals squad, were unaware that the arrests were being observed by *The News*. After the arrest, the following occurred:

At this point, Hirschfeld uses bullets to summarize the sequence of events in what he calls "revolving door" justice.

6   • The police obtained records showing that one woman had 8 prior arrests and the other had 11 prior arrests. Almost all of the previous arrests were for prostitution or loitering for the purpose of prostitution.

7   • Appearing before different judges, both women pleaded guilty to prostitution. Both received fines.

8   • Both women walked out of the Criminal Court Building less than 24 hours after they had been arrested.

9   • Roughly 48 hours after she had been arrested, one woman was back on a street corner, just one block from the scene of her

arrest. When a *News* reporter approached in a car, she stepped forward and solicited him.

10   The arrests were made the night of Feb. 8 by Detective Arthur Penner and Police Officer William Mulligan of the Manhattan South public morals squad.

11   At 10 P.M., Penner arrested Roberta Jean Browne, 30, on Seventh Ave. near W. 58th St. after she allegedly had offered to perform an oral sex act for $25.

He can use direct quotes and his own observations because he was riding with the arresting officers ("At first, she wept"; "Miss Browne was fingerprinted, processed, and lodged for the night."

12   In his car, on the way to the W. 54th St. station, Penner advised Miss Browne of her rights. At first, she wept. Then she told Penner that if she had been carrying a knife, she would have stabbed him. Finally, she complained, "Why don't you leave me alone? I just came out. I only do two or three tricks a night. I'm no $100 girl."

13   Miss Brown was fingerprinted, processed and lodged for the night at the W. 54th St. station. Penner and Mulligan resumed patrol.

14   At 11:45 P.M., at Park Ave. and 25th St., Mulligan posing as a waiter with a heavy eastern European accent, caught Sally Lewis, 20. Miss Lewis got into Mulligan's car and allegedly offered oral sex for $10.

15   A petite blonde with heavily shadowed eyes, she told the cops that she earns up to $200 a night hustling. At the E. 21st St. station, she rolled up her sleeves, displaying black and blue blotches on the insides of her arms. She said that she is a heroin addict and needs $100 a day to support her habit.

Hirschfeld follows the two prostitutes as they are lodged in jail and taken into court for arraignment.

16   Miss Lewis was lodged overnight at the W. 35th St. station. The next day, Feb. 9, both women were taken into court for arraignment. Their cases were presented by Officers Russell Tonneson and Douglas Richter, acting on affidavits from the two arresting officers.

The short sentences used in Grafs 17 and 18 to describe their trials are good examples of succinct, clear writing.

17   Miss Lewis, represented by a Legal Aid attorney, pleaded guilty to prostitution before Judge Leon Becker. It was her ninth

Hirschfeld includes the time of day in both cases because he is sticking to the theme established in the lead of how quickly prostitutes are back on the street. Also, again following the theme of lenient judges, he lists the names of the judges in both cases.

Hirschfeld continues his narrative in the next graf, noting how he himself ("a *News* reporter") approaches one of the prostitutes forty-eight hours after her first arrest to ask how she got out so fast. He uses a quote ("Oh, it was easy") to reply.

Hirschfeld needs a smooth transition to get readers into the last four grafs of the story, where he details statistics on the low percentage of jail terms among Manhattan prostitutes and reasons for it.

Instead of "According to the Police Department's," he could have started the sentence, "Miss Lewis and Miss Browne were not the only prostitutes to get off lightly." This would have better kept to his theme and his approach of using the story of these two to exemplify the failure to jail all prostitutes.

arrest in two years. She was sentenced to a $250 fine or 30 days in jail and given until March 4 to pay the fine. She walked out of court at 2:45 P.M.

18 Miss Browne, also represented by Legal Aid, pleaded guilty before Judge John Reilly. It was her 12th arrest in less than one year, and her third arrest in February. She got a $50 fine or five days in jail and also was allowed until March 4 to pay the fine. She left court at 8:05 P.M.

19 On the following night, Feb. 10, Miss Lewis was standing at Park Ave. and 24th St., one block from the scene of her arrest 48 hours earlier. When a *News* reporter approached in a car, she solicited him. She was informed for the first time that her arrest had been observed by *The News* and asked how she could return so soon to the streets.

Considers herself Lucky

20 "Oh, it was easy," she replied. "But I was lucky. I had a couple of (outstanding) warrants fall on me. I could have been sent to Rikers Island." The warrants stem from unpaid fines in previous arrests.

21 According to the Police Department's Organized Crime Control Bureau, only 13% of the 2,774 women arrested for prostitution in 1976 in lower Manhattan got jail terms. A majority of the rest received fines, ranging from $10 to $500.

22 Police Commissioner Michael J. Codd says arrests are still needed as a deterrent to the city's being swamped by "wall-to-wall" hookers.

23 Sidney Baumgarten, the mayoral assistant who heads the Midtown Enforcement Project, contended that judges have been reluctant to give out jail sentences that would deter the girls from returning to the streets.

24 By allowing prostitutes time to pay their fines, he added, the judges are merely encouraging them to go back to hustling to earn the fine money.

#2

WALKING THE DOG:
MEET ROMMEL. AND BE COOL.
Rommel's a Little Twitchy.
by Neal Hirschfeld

In his lead, Hirschfeld puts the reader into the dog's mind—at least to the extent that is possible.

1 Lively and Rommel are working the 3 o'clock tour, and Rommel—eyes darting, ears twitching, head snapping at the slightest noise—is even more hyper than usual. Like a coiled-up spring, ready to go . . . boing!

2 Maybe it's just the nasty weather. Maybe it's the soaring crime numbers. Maybe it's the first day back on the job after a weekend off, up at Lively's place upstate. Who can know? Maybe it's some sixth sense that something's about to go down. Whatever. Rommel is wired. He's seriously suspicious of everything.

He gives the readers a good description of what is going on and great direct quotes—both calculated to make readers feel they are there.

3 Jimmy Bogliole, meanwhile, has three farebeats pinned over against a wall. One guy's got a screwdriver, another a pair of pliers. Lively comes in from behind, backing up Jimmy.

4 "Okay, Rommel," Lively murmurs. "Let's go fight crime."

5 "Jackpot!" Jimmy sneers, whipping out his summons book. "Three for the price of one!"

6 Jimmy starts writing it up, one of the farebeats, protesting his innocence, starts to lift an arm—and that's all it takes. Rommel is up, lunging, snarling, baring his teeth, ready to take a chunk of meat. "I ain't gonna do nothin', I ain't gonna do nothin'," the farebeat squeals, shrinking on the spot, popeyed and gulping.

7 Rommel reconsiders. He appears dubious. As the farebeats slink away, summons in hand, Rommel gives them a little farewell growl, just to keep 'em wondering.

8 Scuzzballs . . .

Up to graf 9, however, Hirschfeld hasn't revealed precisely what he is talking about. This is more time than usual, but the space helps build interest. He explains the lead now ("As usual, the Times Square subway station — New York City transit cops . . ."), and that makes what has come before understandable. In graf 9, the reporter gives readers some background on the dog.

Next, he lets the dog's partner talk a bit about Rommel and his "nutty" personality.

9 As usual, the Times Square subway station — New York City transit cops take genuine pride in calling it the world's most dangerous — is crawling with the usual stew of crackheads and muggers. The dregs of the underground. Rommel hates them. You can tell.

10 At home, off-duty, he's a different guy. Lounging around, mellowed out, scarfing up his high-protein dog food, chasing a soccer ball, or just roughhousing with Lively and his wife JoAnne . . . sometimes he even lets Lively's two little nieces play with him. "Uncle Rommel," they call him.

11 Back on "the job," it's another story. "I put on a uniform," Lively says. "And he puts on a uniform."

12 Rommel's always been kind of high-strung. On the days Lively is at his worst — tired, headachy, distracted — Rommel is impossible, like he's been up all night drinking coffee. "Always up, walking under your feet," Lively mutters. "Driving me crazy. Pain in the butt." Lot of cops don't understand how Lively can work with Rommel. In the radio car, Rommel never, ever sits still for a single second. Couple of times he's given Lively a nip himself. "Once he gets going," Lively explains, "if I hold him back, he gets angry. That's the thing with these dogs. When they get it in their mind they're gonna go — they keep going till they get there . . ."

13 He's got a thing about subway doors, too. Likes to bite them. "What can I tell you?" Lively shrugs. "He's a little nutty."

14 Yeah, Rommel is a screwball. Still, Lively would never trade partners. "I said I wanted a dog I could always count on," he says. "And as much as this dog is hyper, I know one thing: I'm always gonna go home safe. I'm not gonna get hurt out there. He's gonna be there when I need him."

This simple sentence makes an excellent transition into a section of the story about their exploits together.

15 And he's been there.

Good descriptions of
incidents follow.

16 Once, on Roosevelt Avenue in Queens, Lively and Rommel were chasing three bruisers who had beaten some poor guy to a pulp with a two-by-four, then stolen all his money. Charging around a corner, they found themselves face to face with their quarry. "Freeze!" ordered Lively, pushing all three up against the bricks. And suddenly, one of the guys came off the wall and rushed Lively. Up went his arm . . . and Rommel was all over him, teeth sunk into flesh, 100 pounds of badass dog taking down an attacker. Who got more polite in a hurry. And once, in the middle of the Times Square platform, one of Lively's buddies got hemmed in by an angry crowd as he tried to arrest a troublemaker: "Let him go! Let him go!" Seeing a brother officer in trouble, Lively marched Rommel straight into the fray. Cavalry to the rescue. Back to back with his buddy, Lively gave Rommel his head. And Rommel cleaned out the entire bunch. "Once he started barking, they were running over each other to get down the stairs," Lively says proudly.

17 "When people see Rommel," he says, "they calm down."

18 Besides riding shotgun for Lively, Rommel's got one of the best noses in the 50-dog transit police canine unit. Last December, after one guy bludgeoned another so badly that the victim needed 80 stitches in his head, Lively and Rommel were sent out to a Queens subway station to assist with the evidence search. Witnesses said the assailant had used a hammer, but damned if any of the cops on the scene could find it. Rommel found it. In no time flat, he rooted it out of the gutter. Picked it up in his teeth, snapped his head back, tossed it straight into the air. Just so Lively and the other cops would get the point.

19 Dog's a piece of work . . .

Background on the cop.

20 Dan Lively, 29 years old and Rommel's partner for three years, had another canine once. But Shep was jittery around trains. Bad habit. He was furloughed out of the

New York City Transit Police Canine Squad and sent to the Jersey City Police Department. No country club, but a little easier on a shepherd's jangled nerves. After that, Lively hooked up with Rommel, wholly by chance. Picked his kennel number out of a hat.

Another one sentence transition — crisp, effective.

21 Lively and Rommel. Canine Unit 33.

Background on the dog.

22 Rommel had been donated to the transit police by a family in Queens. "Probably 'cause he was getting too big," Lively has always figured. At 100 pounds, Rommel is huge, one of the two biggest dogs in the squad; Jimmy Bogliole's got the other one, Rex. Rommel's head is like a block of something. His paws are like baseball gloves. Bones, carriage, champ all the way. His old man, Lively remembers, had been a blue-ribbon winner at a Westminster Kennel Club show.

More on the cop.

23 Lively's had to take plenty of ribbing about Rommel. Especially from his own family — even more especially, because he's from the classic police family. His dad John retired from the city force as a detective sergeant in Jamaica. Two of Lively's brothers, Joe and Mike, retired with line-of-duty injuries. Brother Tom is still on the job, working out of Midtown South.

24 Big John loves to break Lively's chops over Rommel: "Jeez, Danny, if you could teach that dog to write and give directions, you could sit down like the other bugs in the corner, with a cup. You wouldn't have to move at all." But Lively knows he's kidding.

Background on the use of dogs by police in New York, followed by statistics on numbers of dogs and arrests they've assisted.

25 In New York City, the police have used dogs as far back as 1907. Today, the transit cops have their 50 patrol dogs and the city cops keep 26. That's besides the three bloodhounds, the 12 bomb-sniffers, the four drug-sniffers, the two search-and-rescue specialists, and four training animals. Lt. William Pearce commands the city's Police Canine Unit, and his numbers say that last year the patrol dogs participated in 256 arrests and 851 assists. Besides that, they made 118 building searches.

Hirschfeld gives background on the negative part of using dogs.

26   Although police dogs sometimes take heat for alleged unnecessary mayhem, including unprovoked attacks—there was, in fact, a major scandal in Philadelphia a few years ago—such incidents are infrequent in New York, says Pearce. Since 1983, there has been only one recorded instance of an unprovoked attack, when a dog, left alone, went after the kid of some cop's neighbor.

Next comes a graf on how cop and dog bond together.

27   Generally, though, the cops trust their dogs. "What makes the dogs effective," contends Pearce, "is two things—their olfactory sensibility and the bond between the animal and his handler. When they've trained together, worked together, they become partners. They understand each other. They each know their places. If one moves one way, the other automatically knows to go the other."

Why are dogs effective? The reporter answers that question, followed by examples of the effectiveness of dogs in tight situations.

28   Because they are inherently intimidating, the dogs "can defuse a volatile situation in a matter of seconds," says Pearce. "You bring a dog to the scene, it's just like a big cop getting out of a car."

29   Pearce remembers that his people had a hostage-taker holed up in a building once and nobody was close to routing him out. That was until one of the chiefs picked up the megaphone and had a dog bark directly into it. "I'm coming out!" the guy screamed.

Hirschfeld brings in material on other dogs and their cop handlers to broaden the story.

30   The dogs are smart, too. City cop Richie Mulvaney and his shepherd Samson were once doing a basement search with some Emergency Services guys when they came upon a huge puddle of water. Now, Samson was one to play in water, but this time, for some reason, he wouldn't get near the stuff.

31   "What's the matter with the dog?" asked the Emergency Service guys. "Go ahead! Go ahead!"

32   No go. Samson refused to budge.

33 The Emergency Service guys started to laugh. "What's the matter, your dog afraid of water?"

34 That's when one of them spotted the live electrical wire in the puddle. "Hold it!" he shouted. "If you woulda stepped in that . . ."

35 In Brownsville, there's the team of Smokey and Officer Russ Chinnici from the Seven-Three Precinct. They're known, together, as "Hollywood"—in 1988 alone, 36 felony arrests, 16 misdemeanor arrests, 43 felony assists, 5 misdemeanor assists, 442 calls for service, 31 building searches, 20 article searches, three missing persons found, three positive tracks. Smokey once locked onto a suspect's arm as he was pulling a gun on Chinnici. Probably saved his partner's life.

36 "As far as our stats go," boasts Pearce, "we've had more positive results than any police department in the world."

37 Oh, there's contention there, rivalry between the various agencies as to whose dogs are the top dogs, but Lively doesn't get involved with that. "Listen," he says, "every guy out here has to feel his dog is the best on the road. If you don't feel that, then you shouldn't be working with him."

Hirschfeld ends his article in the same rather unconventional way he began it, by describing a moment he himself observed of cop and dog on the job.

38 At the 59th Street Station, a wild-eyed woman with a bag of cookies climbs aboard the Eighth Avenue train. "Oooooh!" she goes. "He's lovely! Can I give him a cookie?"

39 "No, ma'am," says Lively.

40 Rommel yawns.

41 "You sure?" she presses.

42 "No, ma'am."

43 "Well, would you like a cookie?"

44 Uh-oh. Cuckoo time. "Uh, no, ma'am. I don't wanna get fat."

45 "No sugar! I promise!"

46 "No thank you, ma'am."

47 At Times Square, the cookie lady goes one way, Lively and Rommel the other. Whew. "Everyone always wants to give him a biscuit," Lively shakes his head. "That's the first one to offer me a biscuit."

48 Rommel is up on his hind legs, draping those enormous paws over a railing so that he can get a better look at what's going down on the platform below. Couple of folks milling about, but no particular problems, he decides.

49 Suddenly, Lively's portable radio crackles to life. 10-13 . . . Officer in need of assistance. The call that sets every cop's heart to pounding.

As cop and dog disappear, Hirschfeld allows himself to draw conclusions about the danger the two face every day and how they will react to it.

50 "Okay, Rommel, let's go!"

51 And they're off, two bats out of hell, charging up one staircase, then down another, into the passageway linking Seventh Avenue to Eighth . . . Lively sprinting at first, his adrenalin surging, holding the leash, struggling valiantly to keep Rommel at his side; then Rommel surging ahead furiously, joyously, practically dragging Lively behind him; Lively shouting out to passersby to stand clear of this crazy police dog in the full throttle of pursuit; other transit cops huffing and puffing around corners to join the charge; Rommel accelerating into a glorious full gallop now, the way it was always meant for him to run, like a halfback nearing the goal line; and Lively, heart pounding, lungs pumping, legs aching, gasping for each breath—

52 But knowing, as sure as he knows anything, that whatever the two of them find at the end of the passageway, a drunk, a lunatic, a guy with a gun, there is going to be one thing he can count on, and count on absolutely.

53 Rommel will back him up. To the hilt. Just like every other time.

Police Reporting:
Likely Problems and How to Solve Them

Problem	Solution
1. Hostility from police officers.	1a. Establish good relationships with everyone from the police chief to detectives, desk sergeants, and beat cops.
	1b. Point out your desire to be fair and objective; show them stories to prove it.
	1c. Be prepared to be "tested" (given wrong information or shown the "blood and guts" of the beat).
2. Limits to release of information.	2a. Know the state open records law or general policy about release of official information.
	2b. Cultivate sources who will make restricted information available.
3. Getting too close to police sources, so that credibility and objectivity are affected.	3a. Remain objective and fair at all times.
	3b. Don't automatically take the official police point of view.
	3c. Remember the publication, not the police department, pays you.
	3d. Verify all official information.
4. Making mistakes in stories about police procedure or in what information to release.	4a. Learn police procedures and law enforcement techniques by doing background reading and asking basic questions.

4b. Find out what can be used in stories.

4c. Build up a background file of information from publications such as *Police Magazine* and material from the FBI and federal and state justice departments.

4d. Be careful not to name a suspect not yet charged, convict a person before trial, misidentify a suspect, or use information without verification; use the word "alleged" before a person goes to trial.

4e. Be familiar with the state penal code and other civil codes applicable to police work and to appropriate state and federal court decisions.

Summary

Police reporting has been a part of American journalism since the 1820s. Early stories from the police beat were exaggerated and sensationalized in order to sell newspapers. This tendency extended into the twentieth century. Now, however, the proper role of the police reporter is to observe the work of the police and report on the most interesting and newsworthy cases. Problems exist for police reporters: some police officers are hostile toward reporters, some reporters dislike police officers, there is a danger of getting too close to police sources, the hours are long, the stories are sometimes distasteful, and readers of newspapers are too sophisticated to enjoy the "cops and robbers" approach of old-time police reporting. Nevertheless, the police beat is a constant source for news and features in any town. In doing their stories, police reporters need to be careful in gathering correct names, addresses, and details of crimes, lest someone is wrongly accused and sues the paper.

Exercises

1. If local conditions permit, spend a shift with a police officer on duty, either in a patrol car or, if possible, walking a beat. Record what happens and write a chronological account of what life is like on the beat.

2. Research a national crime problem (drugs, gang violence, homicide, rape) and interview local law enforcement officials to see how your city is coping with that problem. Write a story about what you find.

3. Spend an evening in the local police station observing everything that goes on: the sights, sounds, procedures, and mood. Write a story about what you find out.

4. Does your city have a committee or citizen's group to deal with police problems? If so, consult representatives of the group to see what these problems are and how they are handled. If not, find out why not and if there is the need for such an organization.

5. Gather the material for and write a story that deals with the various police jurisdictions responsible for your city: local police, county sheriff, state police, FBI. How do they work and keep out of each other's way?

Key Terms for Police Reporting

Abet   Encouraging and inciting a criminal.

Accessory   A person who has knowledge of a law violation and assists the violator in avoiding arrest, trial, and punishment.

Accomplice   A person equally responsible for an offense considered a violation of the law.

Accused   The defendant in a criminal case.

Alcohol detoxification   Centers run by cities and counties where alcoholics are given the chance to "dry out" and rehabilitate themselves with medical and psychiatric help rather than being sent to jail.

Alias   The false name used by a person escaping law enforcement officers.

Alibi   A statement by a person accused of a crime as to his or her whereabouts at the time the crime occurred.

Anarchist   A person who advocates the violent overthrow of the government.

Arrest   The seizure of a person by legal authority on the suspicion he or she has broken a law.

Arrest report   The first record made by police officers of an arrest.

Autopsy Examination and dissection of a corpse to determine the cause of death.

Bail Property, usually money, given as a surety that a person released from custody will return at a certain time.

Beat Geographic area of a city for which a patrol officer or two patrol officers have responsibility.

Blotter A book or compilation of reports recording arrests as they occur and usually available for perusal by reporters.

Booking The period immediately after arrest during which the charges against a suspect are entered into the police register.

Bunco A swindle or misrepresentation.

Burglary The felony of breaking into and entering a building with the intent to steal.

Cadaver The body of a dead person; a corpse.

Charge The accusation or indictment that a person has committed a crime.

Complaint The formal action against a person by a prosecutor.

Cop Popular slang word for police officer.

Coroner City or county official with the responsibility to look into circumstances of violent or sudden deaths.

Decoy A police officer who poses as someone else in order to catch a criminal.

Detective A person employed to investigate, solve, and prevent crimes.

Entrapment The deliberate attempt by police to get a person to commit a crime.

Evidence Information gathered at a crime scene for later presentation in court.

External control The control of a police department by an outside agency such as a police commission.

Extortion The use of force, intimidation, or abuse of authority against a person to gain money, property, or information.

Extradition The return of a felon by a state or foreign government to the state or country where the felon is wanted for criminal prosecution.

False arrest The unlawful physical restraint of a person in jail.

Felony Offenses such as murder or burglary that are of a graver nature than misdemeanors.

Fingerprinting The impression of the markings of the inner surface of the fingertip in ink for the purposes of identification; no two persons' fingerprints are alike.

Frisking The external patting down of a suspect's outer clothing to search for weapons.

Homicide The killing of one human being by another.

Indeterminate sentence A defendant goes to prison without a set term; that time is set later by a parole board based on the offender's progress toward rehabilitation.

Infanticide The murder of an infant immediately after birth.

Informants   People in the criminal subculture who, because they associate with criminals, may witness crimes and tell police what they know in exchange for money or leniency.

Inquest   A judicial inquiry, especially before a jury, about cause of death.

Intent   The state of mind of a person to commit a particular act.

Internal control   The control of a police department by itself; the chief and assistants set standards and requirements for personnel and select, promote, train, and supervise them.

Jail   City and county facilities administered by local law enforcement agencies for the pretrial detention of suspects in usually substandard conditions with few rehabilitation programs.

Kleptomaniac   One who steals things because of an irresistible, persistent, and abnormal impulse to do so.

Larceny   Nonviolent crime of stealing money or other property from another person.

Malfeasance   Misconduct by someone in public office.

Malice aforethought   The intent to commit an unlawful act.

Malicious   Evil intent or motive to cause injury to another person.

"Mirandize"   Reading a suspect his or her right to remain silent and consult an attorney, immediately after arrest.

Misdemeanor   A criminal offense that is less serious than a felony.

Motive   The emotion, impulse, or desire that causes someone to commit a crime.

Murder   The unlawful killing of a human being with malice aforethought.

Parole   The conditional release of a person from prison before the end of his or her sentence.

Patrol   The practice of passing regularly along a certain beat to maintain order and security.

Patrolman or **Patrolwoman**   The police officer who covers a beat.

Penal code   The state rules for crime and punishment.

Perpetrator   One who commits a crime.

Polygraph   An instrument that records impulses due to changes in certain body activities, while the person being tested is undergoing emotional stress; used by police in detecting lies.

Preventive patrol   Patrols sent out as a deterrent to crime, not a reaction to it.

Prison   A building for the confinement of persons accused or convicted of crimes; prisons usually have rehabilitation programs for the inmates locked up there.

Rape   A sexual act committed by force.

Recidivism   Repeated or habitual relapse into crime.

Recognizance   A written obligation binding a person to appear in court on a certain date; sometimes used in place of bail.

Robbery   The felonious taking of the property of another person by violence or intimidation.

Search   The careful examination of an area or a building by police who are looking for evidence in a criminal case.

Summons   An order to appear before a court as for trial.

Suspect   A person arrested on suspicion of committing a crime.

SWAT   Acronym for Special Weapons and Tactics; a squad of specially trained police officers for use in siege and hostage situations; they usually carry powerful weapons and wear bulletproof clothing.

Tactical groups   Squads of police officers, such as undercover agents and decoys, who work outside normal patrol duties to solve crime in a more aggressive manner.

Ticket   A summons issued for a traffic or parking violation.

Traffic patrol   Police officers who enforce traffic ordinances and assist in accidents and crowd control.

Undercover   Working in secret and often in disguise to gain confidential information during a lengthy police investigation.

Vice   An immoral habit or practice that is also illegal, such as prostitution and gambling.

In front of the courthouse, San Augustine, Texas, 1939 by Russell Lee. [*Courtesy U.S. Farm Security Administration, Prints and Photographs Division, Library of Congress*]

8

Courts

Wherever law ends, tyranny begins.

—John Locke

One Court Reporter

The nine-story Metro Justice Building in downtown Miami houses the second busiest court system in the country, after New York City. In 1990, 160,000 criminal cases went through its grimy jails and overcrowded courtrooms, some going to trial, some to plea bargain.

Criminal circuit court on the fourth floor is the site of the most newsworthy cases. Each of the 238 criminal prosecutors working out of this court deal with a case load of 80 to 150 cases a week. Its twenty-four permanent judges hear cases involving murder, extortion, assault, arson, armed robbery, drugs, prostitution, and all other aspects of life's underside.

It is to this court that Don Van Natta Jr. goes every Monday morning at about 8:30 A.M. "It is a zoo," says Van Natta, criminal courts reporter for the *Miami Herald*. And, happily for Van Natta, it is his zoo. Because Miami is a one newspaper city, he does not have to share his beat with any print colleagues, only broadcasters.

Van Natta begins his week by reading the calendar for each judge's courtroom that week: what cases will go to trial, which ones will be plea bargained, which ones will be postponed. "It is a hectic time but a way for me to schedule my week," says Van Natta. "I sit in on the reading of various calendars just to hear what people say."

The sheer number of cases means that Van Natta must often choose between newsworthy cases based on what he is interested in or what sounds good to his editors. A big murder trial or a novelty case — like the man charged with murder in 1991 for not strapping his baby into a car seat — will always merit coverage. Otherwise, Van Natta says he goes "fishing and shopping. I can't be in all courtrooms so sometimes it's the luck of the draw."

At about 11 A.M., Van Natta moves to the prosecutor's offices on the sixth floor and, quite literally, walks down a long hallway to "pop into each office to ask about interesting cases." He considers this time well spent. "You are being seen, sitting and chatting, and fostering a good relationship," he says. "I'm the only reporter these people see. Being from the only paper can be a detriment. You get lazy. But the flip side to that is that I can go up there and, because the prosecutors are all career-minded, they look good if their names are in the paper. If they feel confidence in me and have a good case, they'll let me know. I feel like a politician, shaking hands, making small talk, asking about children, boyfriends, wives. It became apparent to me my second week on the job that if I spent my time in the *Miami Herald* building, I was not going to get any stories. So I try to see as many people as possible."

By Monday afternoon, Van Natta is usually sitting in a courtroom. "If nothing is going on, I'll go on a fishing expedition," he continues. A next likely destination is the public defender's office on the seventh floor. Here, defendants who cannot afford an attorney get representation from a court-appointed defender. "I don't have the same rapport with this office but I'm trying to foster a better one," he says. "These attorneys are not as forthcoming as the prosecutors. I think it's the style of the chief public defender who is very low key. He does not encourage his people to be up front with reporters."

The ninth floor is home to the organized crime unit which investigates public corruption and police crime. Once again, "I press the flesh and try to drum up stories by talking to prosecutors," he says.

Later in the day he will stop off to see the various personal clerks of judges and those in charge of specific departments. "They always know what's going on," he says. "They'll tell me about something interesting."

Judges are good sources too and Van Natta knows a lot of them. But they are usually occupied in court. When he sees them in the halls they tell him about the hottest trials. "Judges are all elected and very media savvy," he says. "I'll walk into a courtroom and, more often than not, the judge will call a recess within five minutes. He'll call me up to the bench and invite me into chambers. 'This trial is not very interesting, but next week I've got a great case,' he'll say. That's why this job is sometimes so easy and why judges are such great sources."

Van Natta has been in constant motion for hours, walking the long halls of the building, talking and listening, and taking notes. He usually lunches in the cafeteria where he can again sit and talk informally to prosecutors and judges. In this way, he usually picks up information about four or five trials of interest.

Van Natta talks to his immediate boss, an assistant city editor, four or five times a day, to let him know what stories look good. If he doesn't think there is anything of merit he says so. The only time he writes a story without getting his editor's approval is in a fast-breaking news story, like an escape attempt.

On routine days, he will begin writing at about 5 P.M. If he is waiting for a verdict, he can't begin until 7 P.M. or 7:30 P.M. The deadline for the local section is 10 P.M., 11 P.M. for the front page. "One part I hate is waiting for verdicts," he says. "Juries deliberate many hours. They don't like to be sequestered so they stay until they finish. If they get hung up on big legal issues, they may be out until midnight. That's after my deadline but once, in a trial about the burglary of the mayor's home, the verdict came in at 12:10 A.M. and I had five minutes to write the story. Of course, I had already done the 'A' matter ahead of time. You have to learn how to write quickly. Even a jury verdict at 7 or 7:30 leaves you no time to write."

Although there is a media room on the fourth floor of the justice building where the *Herald* has a desk and phone, Van Natta prefers to drive back to the newsroom and write it there. In a late-breaking story, however, he jots down the story in longhand and phones it in.

When he first started on the beat, Van Natta was expected to write two or three stories per day. That was a hard adjustment because his previous assignment at the *Herald* was as an investigative reporter focusing on social issues in the Broward County bureau where he could take two to three weeks to do one story. "I was not used to it," he says.

Now, the paper has changed its philosophy and he may not do

a story a day, unless the trials merit coverage. In June 1991, he began a four-month assignment that preempted the rest of his beat activities. A burgeoning judge's scandal dominated court news in Miami and he wrote thirty separate stories over that period to highlight it for readers.

Most of the time, Van Natta considers coverage of the court beat "the easiest kind. You go into a room and it's like watching a play. The judge is in the center on the bench, the prosecutors are on the left and the defense on the right. Nothing is done behind the scenes. You sit there and take notes of the trial and the verdict. You can almost take old stories and fill in the new details. The challenge comes in doing it in a new way — to find a trend in the law or unique circumstances. At its bare bone, it is very simple. It is easier than covering cops or writing obituaries. In the courthouse, you have to be a good listener."

Given his interest in the law (he attended law school at Boston University for one year after getting his journalism degree there), Van Natta reads judge's opinions and talks to lawyers about legal issues. Beyond that, he does not do much extra homework. "I have a general understanding of criminal law and criminal procedures from my law school courses," he says. "Most trials run very similarly."

When he decides to cover a trial, he goes to the clerk's office to read the files on the case. These files, listed by defendant's name, contain depositions and other information. Although he can't remove the file from the room, he is free to take notes on what he reads or have portions of it copied for use in his story.

Interestingly, the official court record — transcribed verbatim by court reporters hired to record everything said in open court — is not often used. Although everything is taken down on a special machine and available the next day, this transcript is too costly (an average of $400 to $500 per each day of the trial) for the newspaper to purchase on a regular basis.

Van Natta will probably write an advance story for the next edition for the trials he plans to cover and he can usually get all the information he needs from the case files. He will be in the courtroom on Tuesday morning for jury selection but may not actually sit through the entire trial, given the need to keep up with other trials and with his information-gathering rounds in the building.

"Sometimes when I'm making my rounds of trials, I get surprised," he says. "Once, I looked in and the defendant in a petty theft case was bound and gagged. Also, when you see a guy in a bright red jumpsuit it means that he is very dangerous."

Once in a while, on his rounds, even the beat sources will not talk to Van Natta — maybe the case is too sensitive, or someone in the office has fouled up. If he can't find another source and the information isn't in court documents, he may have to abandon the story. Such instances are rare, however.

Van Natta writes four kinds of stories:

- The pre-trial story, in which he states the issues, gives an overview of what happened and quotes the prosecution, defense, and the defendant, if possible. "One nice thing about this beat, everything is out in the open," he says. "Florida has a liberal public records law so that anything a branch of the state government does is open to the public. In the courthouse, everything is open for you, everything is at your fingertips."

- Daily trial coverage, which, as with most large city newspapers, the *Herald* does on major trials, like cop killings, massive sexual abuse, and the like. "This eats up a lot of time, sitting in court from 9 A.M. to 6 P.M.," says Van Natta. "I've done it four or five times but it is frustrating because I feel out of touch when I can't go on my daily rounds. People do get into these stories, follow all the details. There are three or four big trials a week in Miami that, if they occurred anywhere else they'd be covered daily. There are so many murders, so much crime."

- One story on an entire case, which Van Natta calls a "quick hit" and writes about on the day of the verdict. He follows the trial as it plays out — perhaps for as long as two weeks — then writes about it after the verdict. In these kinds of cases, he prepares what he calls "A matter" — that is, background on the case gained in reading the case files — well in advance. Then, on the day of the verdict, he is there to record what happens. "It reads like a tale."

- Trend stories where Van Natta uses a single case to illustrate a trend: "Let's say the defense says his client was using steroids or, after police beat Rodney King in L.A. and I discovered that Miami defense lawyers in police brutality cases were reluctant to go to trial because they thought juries would not be sympathetic with their defendants. These stories are tougher to do because many readers may not care about an archaic legal trend."

Whatever the story, there are no dull days on the court beat in Miami. "There is so much human drama on this beat," says Van Natta. "The court house is a volatile place. On one or two occasions, riots have nearly broken out because of a verdict. The more dramatic the trial, the better the story. There is so much drama in Miami, you look for the truly dramatic. And, there can be drama in a routine robbery trial."

Background to Court Reporting

The coverage of courts in the United States parallels closely the coverage of police discussed in the last chapter. Many New York editors saw early that the public was interested in reading details of trials—the more sensational, the better. They began sending reporters to court trials on a regular basis.

By the turn of the twentieth century, big-city daily newspapers were devoting a lot of attention and space to major trials. This was especially true in New York where William Randolph Hearst and his *New York Journal* were trying to overcome Joseph Pulitzer's *New York World* in numbers of readers. The drama of court, the raw emotion, and often sensational details of the case being tried were too good to pass up. Other New York newspapers and those in other large cities soon followed this trend.

In 1925 the attention of the nation was focused on a small town in Tennessee, where the theory of evolution was debated in the Scopes trial. That year the legislature had enacted a statute prohibiting the teaching of evolution in any secondary school or university in the state.

A group of modernists in Dayton, Tennessee, decided to test the law and persuaded high school biology teacher John Thomas Scopes to permit himself to be caught teaching evolution to his students. He was soon put on trial, and that event captured the attention of reporters, editors, and the public.

The trial soon turned into a carnival, complete with hot dog and lemonade vendors and people selling religious tracts. Hordes of reporters covered the "monkey trial."

Other noteworthy trials followed—such as the trial of the accused anarchists Sacco and Vanzetti and that of Ruth Snyder and her corset salesman lover, Judd Gray, for the murder of her husband. The event that got most of the attention, however, and influenced court coverage for years to come was the 1932 trial of Bruno Richard Hauptmann for the kidnapping and murder of the baby of the famous aviator Charles A. Lindbergh.

More than three hundred reporters, including Walter Winchell, Damon Runyon, Alexander Woollcott, Arthur Brisbane, and Adela Rogers St. Johns and novelists-turned-journalists such as Edna Ferber, Fannie Hurst, and Kathleen Norris, descended on the small town of Flemington, New Jersey, to cover what many newspapers were already calling "The Crime of the Century."

The fifty-room Union Hotel was soon completely full, and townspeople opened their homes to reporters from throughout the United States and abroad. Telephone and telegraph technicians installed equipment in the courthouse so the public could be kept informed during proceedings. Forty telegraph and cable operators were assigned to tiny cubicles in the attic; they were ready, they said, to transmit a million words a day. The press— 150 at a time because of space limitations—observed the trial from an upper gallery at the rear of the courtroom.

From the trial's opening moment on January 2, 1935, the specter of press interference permeated the room. Many reporters had speculated that the spate of publicity would make a fair trial for Hauptmann impossible. The matter came up as the defense questioned the first prospective juror. Had he read the Winchell column in the *New York Daily Mirror*? (Walter Winchell had said in both his column and radio broadcasts that Hauptmann was guilty of the kidnapping and murder.) The prospective juror said he had read Winchell "occasionally" but had not formed an opinion about the case. The jury selection process went on and was completed. The judge tried to keep the proceedings decorous, and the jury was, of course, sequestered during meals and at night and was not allowed to read newspapers or listen to radio broadcasts. They did hear shouts of "Put the Dutchman in the hot seat" as they crossed the street from the courthouse to the hotel.

That the judge managed a degree of decorum was a miracle, given the circus-like atmosphere in the town. Flemington's main street was crowded with sightseers, pickpockets, and hawkers of everything from "certified veritable locks of hair from Baby Lindbergh" at five dollars each to tiny wooden replicas of the ladder the kidnapper had used to reach the baby's window.

The reporters had long before decided that Hauptmann had no chance for acquittal and had begun sending "hold" stories to New York that predicted the trial's outcome. "The butcher of Lindy's baby waits in the death cell/faces a life term/tonight/while outside a heartbroken mother and child sob for a missing father . . .," read one.

As they waited for a verdict, reporters devised ingenious ways to get the word out as quickly as possible. Guards warned those in the courtroom not to try to signal other reporters by hand on nearby roofs. An Associated Press reporter brought with him into the courtroom a shortwave radio set hidden in a briefcase. He had memorized two code signals he would flash to another AP man at the receiver in the courthouse attic. One signal would note that the jury was coming in; the other would indicate the verdict.

When the jury did come in, this system worked perfectly as far as the radio was concerned. The problem was that the receiver operator misunderstood the signal; he decided that the verdict was in and that it had been one of guilty of first-degree murder with a recommendation for mercy, which, under the law, meant a sentence of life imprisonment.

The operator telegraphed, HAUPTMANN FOUND GUILTY, GETS LIFE IMPRISONMENT, thus alerting the world to the jury's verdict prematurely. When the jury foreman announced the actual verdict of guilty with no recommendation for mercy, the AP man in the courtroom once again flashed a signal to his cohort in the attic, who realized his earlier error and sent a new message on the AP wire, HAUPTMANN GUILTY GETS DEATH.

After Hauptmann's appeals were denied by higher courts and the U.S. Supreme Court, his death sentence was twice stayed by the New Jersey governor. All of this attracted much editorial comment and coverage, as did the Lindberghs' decision late in 1935 to move to England with their surviving son, Jon, largely because of incessant hounding from reporters, photographers, and crackpots.

Bruno Richard Hauptmann was executed on April 3, 1936—four years, one month, and two days after he had kidnapped and killed the Lindbergh baby.

The coverage of his trial had not been the finest hour for the American press. Reporters, editors, and especially photographers had shown no remorse in writing about and snapping pictures of the grieving Lindbergh family. Although the judge had forbidden photographs to be taken while court was in session, photographers took them anyway, concealing their cameras in mufflers.

The coverage of the trial led to the passage of Canon 35 of the Canons of Judicial Ethics by the American Bar Association in 1937 which barred the taking of photographs in courtrooms. That canon prevailed for many years and has been lifted only in the past fifteen years.

The print press was not asked to answer for its generally shoddy performance, however.

That call for accountability did not come for another thirty years, when the U.S. Supreme Court handed down its verdict in the *Sheppard v. Maxwell* case. This decision had far-reaching effects on press coverage of murder trials. The Court ruled that the defendant, Dr. Samuel Sheppard, had been deprived of his right to a fair trial because the judge had failed to protect him from the massive and prejudicial publicity that went on during his prosecution. The Court ordered his release from prison.

A look at the case explains why the Court ruled as it did.

Marilyn Sheppard was bludgeoned to death in the upstairs bedroom of the home she shared with her husband in Bay Village, Ohio, a suburb of Cleveland, in July 1954. Sheppard was an immediate suspect in the case. The press reported the coroner's statement on the first day. "It is evident the doctor did this, so let's get the confession out of him," he had said.

Sheppard was interrogated while he was still under sedation in the hospital and recovering from the shock of his wife's death. Before the coroner's inquest, he was frequently and extensively questioned without an attorney being present.

On July 7, the day of Mrs. Sheppard's funeral, a story appeared in a Cleveland newspaper in which the assistant city attorney, who would later be chief prosecutor in the trial, was quoted as being critical of the refusal of Sheppard's family to permit his immediate questioning. From that day, newspaper headlines stressed the doctor's lack of cooperation with police and other officials.

TESTIFY NOW IN DEATH,
BAY CITY DOCTOR IS ORDERED

Newspapers also played up Sheppard's refusal to take a lie detector test.

DOCTOR BALKS AT LIE TEST:
RE-TELLS STORY

Later the headlines became more shrill.

WHY NO INQUEST?
DO IT NOW, DR. GERBER

When the inquest took place, it was broadcast live with many reporters and photographers present. Police searched Sheppard in full view of the spectators. His lawyer was not permitted to ask questions.

By July 20 the headline writers were holding nothing back.

WHY ISN'T SAM
SHEPPARD IN JAIL?
QUIT STALLING,
BRING HIM IN

The story under this second headline called Sheppard "the most unusual murder suspect ever seen around these parts. He is surrounded by a curtain of protection and concealment." That night Sheppard was arrested for murder. He was arraigned without counsel and indicted on August 17.

From this point on, the headlines grew more bold.

SHEPPARD "GAY SET"
IS REVEALED
BLOOD IS FOUND IN GARAGE
DR. SAM FACES QUIZ AT JAIL
ON MARILYN'S FEAR OF HIM

By December, five volumes of such clippings had been accumulated.

In the November election that year the chief prosecutor in the case was a candidate for common pleas judge, and the trial judge was up for reelection. This factor made both of them more strident than they probably normally would have been and apparently more interested in courting press favor.

All three Cleveland newspapers published the names and addresses of prospective jurors, and these people soon began to get anonymous telephone calls and letters and advice from their friends. All jurors had been exposed to the publicity; seven of the ten final jurors subscribed to the Cleveland newspapers.

After the trial began, reporters occupied most of the seats in the courtroom. Indeed the press table was allowed inside the railing that separated spectators from the bench. They sat so close to the defense table, in fact, that Sheppard and his attorney had to go outside to confer. Once there, they were still under scrutiny because the press had been allowed to set up telephone and telegraph facilities.

Not surprisingly, Sheppard was found guilty and sentenced to life imprisonment. His attorneys then set in motion the appeal process that finally freed him in *Sheppard v. Maxwell*.

In its 1966 ruling the Supreme Court cited a number of flagrant examples of prejudicial publicity that were unfair to Sheppard:

1. On October 9 an editorial criticized the defense counsel's random poll of people on the streets as to their opinions of the doctor's guilt or innocence. The poll had been taken to show a reason for a change of venue. The editorial said this poll "smacks of massive jury tampering." The defense attorney dropped the poll idea.

2. On the second day of jury examination, a debate was staged in the courtroom — broadcast live on radio station WHK — during which reporters accused Sheppard's counsel of throwing roadblocks in the way of the prosecution and said the doctor was conceding his guilt by hiring an experienced criminal attorney to defend him. After this broadcast the defense attorney requested a continuance of the trial, but this was denied by the judge.

3. During jury selection, a front-page story had appeared in one of the Cleveland papers with the headline BUT WHO WILL SPEAK FOR MARILYN? Adjacent to a picture of Sheppard were the words, ". . . the face of the accused. Study that face as long as you want. Never will you get from it a hint of what might be the answer."

4. When the jury was taken to view the scene of the murder on the first day of the trial, hundreds of reporters and photographers went along because the time had been announced in advance.

5. On November 19, a Cleveland police officer gave testimony that contradicted details in a written statement Sheppard had made to Cleveland police two days earlier. In a broadcast heard over WHK, a commentator called Sheppard a perjurer and likened him to Alger Hiss being confronted by Whittaker Chambers. The defense asked the judge to see how many jurors had heard the broadcast. He refused.

6. A November 24 story with an eight-column headline, SAM CALLED A JEKYLL-HYDE BY MARILYN, COUSIN TO TESTIFY, spoke of a "bombshell" witness to testify to Sheppard's displays of a fiery temper, to counter the defense contention that the defendant "is a gentle physician with an even disposition." Another defense move for a change of venue was denied.

7. During the five days and four nights of their deliberations, the jurors were sequestered but allowed to make phone calls to their homes. There had been instructions to the bailiff to the contrary. The judge denied a defense motion for a new trial.

The majority opinion, written by Justice Tom Clark, had a great deal to say about the role of the press in a criminal trial:

> The fact is that bedlam reigned at the courthouse during the trial and newsmen took over practically the entire courtroom, hounding most of the participants in the trial, especially Sheppard. . . . The erection of a press table inside the bar is unprecedented. Having assigned almost all of the available seats in the courtroom to the news media, the judge lost his ability to supervise that environment. . . .

> There is no doubt the deluge of publicity reached at least some of the jury. The court lacked power to control publicity about the trial. The carnival atmosphere could easily have been avoided since the courtroom and the courthouse premises are subject to the control of the court.

> As we stressed in Estes[1], the presence of the press at judicial

---

[1] In *Estes v. Texas*, 1965, the Supreme Court had set aside the conviction of Billie Sol Estes for cotton and grain manipulation, despite the absence of any direct show of trial prejudice. "It is true that in most cases involving claims of due process deprivation, we require a show of identifiable prejudice to the accused," said the Court. "Nevertheless, at times, a proceeding employed by the state involved such a probability that prejudice will result that it is deemed inherently lacking in due process." The Court acted even though Estes had been granted a change of venue, the Estes jury saw none of the TV coverage of the trial, and the overall publicity was not as massive as in Sheppard.

proceedings must be limited when it is apparent that the accused might otherwise be prejudiced or disadvantaged.

The courts should have protected witnesses, controlled release of leads, information, and gossip to the press by police officers, witnesses, and counsel for both sides.

. . . Due process requires that the accused receive a trial by an impartial jury free from outside influences. Given the pervasiveness of modern communication and the difficulty of effacing prejudicial publicity from the minds of the jurors, the trial courts must take strong measures to ensure that the balance is never righted against the accused. . . . Of course, there is nothing that proscribes the press from reporting events that transpire in the courtroom. But where there is a reasonable likelihood that prejudicial news prior to trial will prevent a fair trial, the judge should continue the case until the threat abates, or transfer it to another county not so permeated with publicity.

. . . If publicity during the proceeding threatens the fairness of the trial, a new trial should be ordered. . . .

. . . Since the trial judge did not fulfil his duty to protect Sheppard from the inherently prejudicial publicity which saturated the community and to control disruptive influences in the court-room, we must reverse the denial of the habeas petition. The case is remanded to the District Court with instructions to issue the writ . . . that Sheppard be released from custody unless the state puts him in its charges again within a reasonable time.

Since it was issued, this decision has influenced countless judges and reporters. New decisions, discussed later in this chapter, have become equally important to anyone covering trials. They have brought into constant debate the broad issues of a free press and a fair trial. Should the freedom of the press granted in the First Amendment give journalists the right to jeopardize a person's right to a fair trial granted in the Sixth Amendment?

Whether the trials are of local interest or on a national scale — like those of Jack Ruby, the man who shot President Kennedy's assassin; Sirhan Sirhan, the assassin of Robert Kennedy; James Earl Ray, the assassin of Martin Luther King, Jr.; cult leader Charles Manson; the Chicago Seven; the Watergate co-conspirators; Wayne Williams, the man convicted in the Atlanta child murders; and the defendants in the Iran-Contra trials — this concern is the biggest problem of reporters who write about courts.

Problems and Solutions

Courts have long been an established beat in journalism, especially for daily newspapers. There are many reasons for this special status. Local, state, and national courts constitute a structured part of government, hold regular public meetings (trials) that can be covered, and compile a body of information (court records) that can be reviewed and used for reference. The actions of courts affect many people, and the conduct of these people in the courtroom is often dramatic and newsworthy.

By assigning a reporter to keep track of the local courts, a newspaper editor knows that a large portion of predictable news will be gathered. A court reporter can go to the courthouse every day, look at the list of pending trials for those of special interest to readers, attend such trials, talk to court employees, and review records of past trials. Sometimes such access will lead a reporter to good stories outside the court as well.

Television stations have a similar interest, and their reporters can do the same things a print journalist can — although, until recently, they have had to leave their cameras outside the courtroom. Magazines are usually attracted to cases of wider interest and courts of national jurisdiction like the U.S. Supreme Court or federal courts in large cities.

The fascination of the press with courts has increased each year for the past thirty years, spurred by novels, films, and television programs that emphasize the drama of court events. Indeed, the whole panoply of the human condition — poverty, wealth, greed, lust, jealousy, hate, anger, and rage — is played out in most courts every day. A reporter covering the court beat can be assured of getting a reasonably good story nearly every day.

In the late 1980s and early 1990s, the same problems plaguing the police have spilled over into courts at all levels, linked as they are in the criminal justice system. At a time of severe budget cuts in American cities and states, courts have become clogged with so many cases — many of them related to drugs — that the very administration of justice is being hampered. In state after state, people arrested for committing crimes are constantly being set free because the courts lack the judges, court personnel, and jail space to handle them. More often than not these people return to the streets and quickly resume their criminal activity with the knowledge that, even if they are arrested again, they will probably be released yet again.

All aspects of this tragic cycle make good copy for court reporters.

On the surface, covering a courthouse is easy. The people who are good sources work in and around the building and are usually accessible. Trials themselves are normally open, and a reporter can attend one in the same way as a member of the general public. Some courts even provide a table for reporters in the front. The reporter can listen and take notes about what is going on; after the trial is over, he or she can talk to judges, attorneys, and even jurors to clear up any confusion. A transcript of the trial will also be available for review by the reporter later. Many courthouses also maintain good law libraries, and court officials will sometimes let reporters use the books there for reference.

Below the surface, however, things are not quite as placid. The heightened interest in the courts has brought with it greater restrictions by courts on how they are covered. These restrictions constitute the biggest problem for reporters on the court beat and a great threat to press freedom in general.

The problem and the threat have come from actions by various courts, especially the U.S. Supreme Court. Some of these decisions were brought about by a long series of press excesses, beginning with the Hauptmann trial. Some resulted from the anti-press biases of justices and judges during the Reagan-Bush years when more conservatives were appointed.

The roots of this quandary grow out of a potential conflict between two guarantees in the U.S. Constitution: for a free press in the First Amendment and for a speedy and public trial by an impartial jury in the Sixth Amendment. Usually referred to as "free press-fair trial," the clash has become more prevalent in recent years. Both the judges and attorneys on one side and the editors, reporters, photographers, and broadcasters on the other side have sought to ease the problem with varying degrees of success.

No reporter wants to jeopardize the fair trial of another person. No reporter wants to be unduly and unfairly prevented from covering a legitimate story. Although these factors are constant, they are not always compatible.

The problem and the threat are real, and they ebb and flow from year to year and state to state and story to story. The free press-fair trial issue exists in two primary areas: access and contempt.

Access

Reporters cannot cover trials if they are not allowed to do so by judges. After the Lindbergh and Sheppard cases, however, there was greater reluctance to allow uncontrolled coverage.

One response was the adoption by the American Bar Association of "Minimum Standards Relating to Fair Trial and Free Press" in 1968. These standards were based on three years of study by a commission of prominent lawyers and judges under the chairmanship of Justice Paul C. Reardon of the Massachusetts Supreme Court.

Supported by field surveys and consultation with news media organizations and law enforcement officials, the standards were the first comprehensive guidelines to be devised in the free press-fair trial area. They specifically defined the types of nonprejudicial information that can be released for publication to meet the requirements of press freedom.

The report also said that the traditional "screening remedies" — change of venue, continuance, questioning jurors at the start of a trial to determine bias or prejudice, and a judge's instructions to jurors not to read about or discuss the case — "cannot carry the full burden" but are "nevertheless of considerable value."

The committee proposed the use of the contempt power only against a person who disseminated an extrajudicial statement that was "willfully designed" by that person to affect the outcome of a trial and that seriously threatened to have that effect.

During the period from arrest to the end of the trial, the report restricted judges, prosecutors, defense attorneys, police, and court employees from disclosing certain categories of information: 1) prior criminal records, 2) existence or content of a confession, 3) outcome of any examinations or tests, 4) identity of prospective witnesses, 5) opinions as to guilt or innocence, and 6) possibility of a plea of guilty to the offense charged or a lesser offense.

The report permitted authorities to release to the press: 1) the defendant's name, 2) time and place of arrest, 3) resistance, pursuit, and use of weapons, 4) identity of the investigating and arresting officer or agency, 5) description of physical evidence seized, 6) the nature or substance of the charge, and 7) reference, without comment, to public records in the case.

These restrictions apply generally to print reporters, however. Photographers and radio and television reporters have other problems; they have been excluded from the courtrooms of most states for many years. Although this ban affects TV and radio reporters and photographers, it is worth considering in detail here because any restriction threatens press freedom for all.

The ban was a direct result of the Hauptmann trial, as noted before. The accused kidnapper and his attorneys contended that his conviction was the result of prejudice caused by the sensational coverage of his trial, but New Jersey courts rejected this argument, and Hauptmann was executed. The American Bar Association (ABA) had been influenced by this case, however, and sought to eliminate the chance for future press exorbitance. In 1937 the ABA passed Canon 35 of its Canons of Judicial Ethics, "Improper Publicizing of Court Proceedings," which said:

>Proceedings in court should be conducted with fitting dignity
>and decorum. The taking of photographs in the courtroom,
>during sessions of the court or recesses between sessions, and
>the broadcasting of court proceedings are calculated to detract
>from the essential dignity of the proceedings, degrade the court,
>and create misconceptions with respect thereto in the mind of
>the public and should not be permitted.

This canon was later amended to include television and to make
an exception for the naturalization proceedings when immigrants
are sworn in as citizens.

In 1946 radio broadcasts and photography were banned from
criminal cases in federal courts by Rule 53 of the Federal Rules of
Criminal Procedure with the following statement: "The taking of
photographs in the courtroom during the progress of judicial
proceedings or radio broadcasting of judicial proceedings from the
courtroom shall not be permitted by the court."

In 1962 the Judicial Conference of the United States adopted a
resolution extending Rule 53 to any judicial proceeding and what
it called "the environs of the courtroom." It also added television
as part of journalism to be kept out.

According to the Reporters Committee for Freedom of the Press,
a watchdog group, these actions caused all federal courts and courts
in every state but Texas and Colorado to prohibit the televising of
judicial proceedings. But these actions dealt with live coverage and
did not settle the constitutional issue of whether the First
Amendment permitted the presence of print reporters if it excluded
television and radio reporters.

This question was answered in *Estes v. Texas*, the 1965 Supreme
Court decision mentioned earlier in this chapter. The Court agreed
with Estes that he had been deprived of his "due process" right to
a fair trial because of the effects of live television, radio, and
photographic coverage. Activities of TV crews and news
photographers, as well as the presence of their equipment, with
"cables and wires . . . snaked across the courtroom floor," the Court
said, had caused "considerable disruption of the proceedings."

The Court agreed that "maximum freedom must be allowed the
press" but said "its exercise must necessarily be subject to the
maintenance of absolute fairness in the judicial process." Did the
exclusion of TV discriminate in favor of newspaper reporters? "The
news reporter is not permitted to bring his typewriter and printing
press into the courtroom," said the Court, so TV and radio reporters
have the same access.

The court left open the chance for change in this policy when,
in the words of Justice Clark, "the advances in these arts permit

reporting by printing press or by television without their present hazards to a fair trial." But there was little change for a decade, except in 1972 when the ABA slightly modified Canon 35. Section 3A(7) of its new Code of Judicial Conduct provides for a few limited exceptions to the ban if all parties to the case and witnesses agree, nothing is published until all appeals have been exhausted, and the material is used for educational purposes only. These exceptions had no effect on the general public.

With these national bans firm, a few states began to modify their own rules on court coverage. Colorado has allowed the electronic media to attend trials since 1956, although judges must prohibit broadcast or photographing of a juror or witness under subpoena who objects and must get the consent of defendants in criminal trials. With these limitations, live coverage has been permitted in civil and criminal trials and appellate courts proceedings for over twenty years with few objections. According to the Reporters Committee, most defense counsels oppose TV in the courtroom. Thus, cameras are barred in 80 percent of the trials where broadcasting is sought. In 1991, all states but Indiana, Mississippi, Missouri, South Carolina, and South Dakota allowed cameras in the courtroom in either civil or criminal trials or both.

The road to getting such access for photographers and their cameras was long and arduous. It began in Alabama in 1976 with a plan to allow electronic coverage of all courts, including the state supreme court, if all parties in both civil and criminal cases agree. If a witness, a party in the case, or an attorney objects, however, coverage must be suspended.

That same year in Florida, the state supreme court approved a plan to cover one civil and one criminal trial using the Colorado and Alabama approaches of requiring permission of everyone involved. In sixteen months no trial was covered because of the difficulty in getting consent. In 1977 the Florida Supreme Court began a one-year experiment allowing television coverage of any civil or criminal trial or appellate proceeding in the state without the veto power of anyone connected with the case. A judge could block television coverage only if he or she decided that cameras would physically disrupt the trial.

The Zamora trial was the first to be covered under the new rule. One camera and three microphones were operated on a pool basis by local stations in Miami. The court also allowed a still photographer to work in the courtroom. Later surveys and interviews of jurors, witnesses, the defense counsel, the prosecutor, and the judge found that electronic coverage had caused little or no inconvenience or disruption.

This success and the earlier experiences in Colorado and Alabama increased the pressure to adopt similar plans elsewhere. According to the Reporters Committee, most states favor the Colorado-Alabama approach requiring the consent of all concerned; a few states have adopted the Florida plan permitting coverage regardless of objections.

The same liberality does not exist at the federal level, where most members of the U.S. Supreme Court and the majority of federal judges oppose the presence of television, radio, and photography in the courtroom.

In 1980 the Supreme Court agreed to reopen the issue of whether the constitutional right of a defendant to a fair trial is violated if a criminal trial is televised over his/her objections. Two police officers, Noel Chandler and Robert Granger, were arrested by Miami police after they allegedly burglarized a local restaurant, using police squad cars and two-way radios to assist themselves. The policemen objected to the televised coverage of their pretrial and trial proceedings, saying that the very presence of the cameras violated their rights to a fair trial and were psychologically, if not physically, disruptive.

Their objection was overruled in a lower court; the court of appeals declined to rule, saying that the Florida Supreme Court in allowing the experimental program had decided that camera coverage did not violate constitutional rights to a fair trial. It reaffirmed the convictions.

In the meantime, the Florida Supreme Court was completing a review of a petition to make the experimental rule on electronic coverage a permanent one. The Florida Bar Association and the Conference of Circuit Judges of that state opposed the petition. The court ordered a survey to find out the effect of this coverage. The results showed that cameras had little influence on the dignity of court proceedings, scarcely distracted trial participants, and indeed made jurors and witnesses feel more responsible for their actions. The court concluded that the Estes case had referred to the state of television technology as it existed in the early 1960s. Noting that only four of the nine justices in that case had held that cameras violated the right to a fair trial, the Florida Supreme Court said it was free to recognize that the industry had changed.

While the First Amendment did not require the entry of electronic media into judicial proceedings, it said their presence did not abuse defendant's rights. Indeed the exposure of the justice system by TV and photography would bolster faith in the Florida courts. The Florida Supreme Court then approved this change in the state code of judicial conduct:

Subject at all times to the authority of the presiding judge to control the conduct of proceedings before the court, to ensure decorum and prevent distraction, and to ensure the fair administration of justice in the pending case, the electronic media and still photographic coverage of public judicial proceedings in the appellate and trial courts of this state shall be allowed in accordance with standards and technology promulgated by the Supreme Court of Florida.

When the Chandler case reached the Florida Supreme Court, that court dismissed the appeal because of this rule change. The men then took their case to the U.S. Supreme Court, which decided to review as already noted. In their argument Chandler and Granger said the case presented the court with the opportunity to decide whether cameras in courtrooms are consistent with constitutional protections for a fair trial and to consider more fully the constitutional limitations of media access to criminal proceedings in general.

In 1981 the U.S. Supreme Court ruled that state courts have the authority to allow television, radio, and still photography coverage of criminal trials, even over the objection of defendants. In a unanimous decision, the Court said that with the technological advances made in television, its presence in the courtroom does not automatically amount to denial of due process for a criminal suspect. The Court said the only time the presence of television would be banned under the Constitution is if a criminal defendant could show prejudice in his or her specific case, for example, by proving that sensationalized and biased coverage would affect an unsequestered jury. The Court left the decision to admit cameras up to state court systems.

"An absolute constitutional ban on broadcast coverage of trials," wrote then Chief Justice Warren Burger, "cannot be justified simply because there is a danger in some cases that prejudicial broadcast accounts of pretrial and trial proceedings may impair the ability of jurors to decide (impartially) the issue of innocence or guilt. The possibility of such prejudice does not warrant an absolute constitutional ban on all broadcast coverage."

The Reporters Committee says that most members of the print and electronic media are taking a moderate position and that television coverage today is no more intrusive or disruptive than a sketch artist with a crayon or a newspaper reporter with a pad. Many courts use tape recorders, visual demonstration for the jury, and videotaping of depositions; these factors could be used in the argument for electronic coverage. They also make the point that television and photographic cameras pose no due process problem and that states should be as free as Florida to further the First Amendment interests of the public by allowing such coverage of court proceedings. By 1992, the U.S. Supreme Court still prohibited cameras, but six U.S. District Courts and the Court of Appeals in the Second and Ninth circuits volunteered to allow cameras to cover civil proceedings for a test period of three years.

Although the Estes decision, Canon 35, and the other prohibitions pertain to electronic and photographic coverage, six U.S. Supreme Court decisions dealt with the access for all reporters over the past fifteen years.

In 1976 in Nebraska, a judge issued a "gag" order against all press coverage of the trial of a man accused of mass murder. The state press association filed suit, and the case reached the Supreme Court.

The Court's decision in *Nebraska Press Association v. Stuart* overturned the order of the Nebraska judge banning press publication of information obtained in open court, calling it prior restraint and a violation of the constitutional guarantee of freedom of the press. Although Chief Justice Burger cautioned the press on its duty to "protect the rights of an accused to a fair trial by unbiased jurors," his decision in the case allows the press to perform that duty at its own discretion. Even though it rejects the notion that the First Amendment is an "absolute" ban on all court orders against prejudicial publicity, the Burger opinion leaves very little room for such orders.

The decision requires judges to explore all other possibilities before they even consider restraints on press coverage. The ruling also casts doubts on the effectiveness of such controls and discourages their use.

In 1979 the Supreme Court restricted press access to pretrial hearings in criminal cases with its 5 to 4 decision in *Gannett Co. v. DePasquale*. The ruling was highly restrictive of press coverage of all trials because many local judges immediately began to apply the ruling to them as well. Critics called the decision a return to the tradition of the Court of Star Chamber — in which defendants were tried and convicted in secret — in seventeenth century England and a blow to the fundamental assumption of open democracy.

The case stemmed from a routine suppression-of-evidence hearing before a murder trial in Rochester, New York, in 1976. Two men charged with murdering a former policeman had come to court to stop the prosecution from using confessions and a murder weapon they said had been obtained illegally. At the hearing defense attorneys asked Judge Daniel DePasquale to keep press and public out of the court, arguing that adverse publicity would jeopardize their clients' right to a fair trial. The prosecution did not object, so the judge cleared the courtroom.

A reporter for the Gannett-owned *Democrat & Chronicle* and *Times-Union* later challenged the judge's ruling on the basis of the Sixth Amendment (promising the right to a swift and public trial) and the First Amendment (ensuring right to access). The judge saw a "reasonable probability of prejudice" and would not change his ruling. His decision was overturned by a higher court then upheld by another court before reaching the Supreme Court.

In its majority opinion Justice Potter Stewart acknowledged "a strong societal interest" in open trials. The guarantee of a public trial in the Sixth Amendment belongs only to the criminally accused, he said, not to the public itself. He refused to concede that the press or public possesses a constitutional right to attend criminal trials under the First Amendment. Even if such a right did exist, it would have to yield to a defendant's guarantee of a fair trial.

Concurring opinions eased the harshness a bit. Chief Justice Burger wrote that the decision applied only to pretrial hearings and not to trials themselves. Justice Lewis Powell wanted to grant reporters a First Amendment "interest" in attending criminal proceedings, but he noted the need to balance that interest against the risk of unfair publicity.

The dissenting justices worried that lower court judges would use this decision to close courtrooms without good reason. Writing for the minority, Justice Harry Blackmun accused the Court of over-reacting to the risks of prejudicial publicity in the Rochester murder case. News articles about the case had been, in Blackmun's words, "placid, routine, and innocuous. There was no screaming headline, no lurid photograph, no front page overemphasis." He said the Court's decision was an "inflexible rule" that ignores or pays little attention to "the important interests of the public and the press (as a part of that public) in open judicial proceedings." Concluded Blackmun: "The suggestion that there are limits upon the public's right to know what goes on in the courts causes me deep concern."

The press was also deeply concerned about the decision and spoke harshly about it almost immediately. The worries of the dissenting justices about lower court actions soon came true.

According to the Reporters Committee, a circuit court judge in South Carolina excluded the press from a pretrial hearing for a man charged with murder, kidnapping, criminal sexual conduct, and assault with intent to kill. The rest of the public was allowed to stay in the courtroom. The judge admitted he would not have barred the press had it not been for the Supreme Court ruling.

In the same week the New York State Court of Appeals decided that the press could be excluded from a pretrial hearing for a thirteen-year-old boy charged with murder. This was the same court of appeals that acted upon the Gannett case.

In Oneonta, Alabama, a county circuit judge prohibited the *Birmingham Post-Herald* from reporting on the first day of the trial of two men accused of breaking into a farmhouse, killing a married couple, and wounding other family members in a shooting spree. The trial was in the courtroom of another judge.

In the first six months after the decision, 109 similar incidents happened around the country — twenty of them involving actual trials. Interviewed at the Conference of State Chief Justices that summer, Chief Justice Burger insisted that judges who were keeping the public and press out must have misinterpreted the ruling in *Gannett v. DePasquale*. He said the ruling applied only to pretrial hearings, not to trials. Justice Blackmun later said it applied to trials. Other justices commented and added to the confusion.

By the fall of 1979 the justices were apparently feeling the pressure from the Gannett opinion and from their own murky interpretations of it. To clear up the misunderstandings, the Court agreed to hear a similar case. The judge in the trial of a man charged with killing a motel manager agreed to close the trial because of the effects of publicity on the jury. In an earlier trial of the same man, evidence had been improperly admitted, and the judge had reversed the conviction. Two mistrials had followed.

The opinion in *Richmond Newspapers, Inc. v. Virginia* in 1980 greatly eased the fears of the press. In a 7 to 1 decision the Court cleared up the earlier ambiguities, "Absent an overriding interest articulated in findings, the trials of a criminal case must be open to the public."

Even Chief Justice Burger, so long hostile to the press, felt compelled to state his belief in the First Amendment:

> People in an open society do not demand infallibility from their institutions, but it is difficult for them to accept what they are prohibited from observing. When a criminal trial is conducted in the open, there is at least an opportunity both for understanding the system in general and its workings in a particular case.
>
> . . . The First Amendment, in conjunction with the Fourteenth, prohibits government from "abridging the freedom of speech, or of the press; or the right of the people peaceably to assemble, and to petition the Government for a redress of grievances." These expressly guaranteed freedoms share a common core purpose of assuring freedom of communication on matters relating to the functioning of government. Plainly it would be difficult to single out any aspect of government of higher concern

and importance to the people than the manner in which criminal trials are conducted; as we have shown, recognition of this pervades the centuries-old history of open trials and opinions of this court.

The press was jubilant at the apparent change of heart toward the press by the Supreme Court. The Reporters Committee could not decide whether it portended a new era or was merely an isolated victory.

In the meantime, the Gannett decision was still on the books and could still be used to close pretrial hearings. In that event, the Reporters Committee suggested several possible legal actions: 1) fight back, there is a 50 percent chance of winning, 2) fight back procedurally by either objecting on the spot and asking for a postponement, or objecting in writing to the judge if the trial has been closed before the reporter gets inside the courtroom, 3) fight back through an attorney if a trial rather than a pretrial hearing is involved (no matter what the judge says, Gannett applied to pretrial hearings only), 4) point out that Gannett does not affect state common law, constitutions, or laws, and 5) use the following defenses from the Nebraska Press Association case. A judge is not required to follow the "reasonable probability" test but may adopt the "clear and present danger" test in the ABA guidelines. A judge is free to use such less restrictive alternatives to court closure as 1) granting a change of venue if information in an open hearing is prejudicial, 2) conducting an open hearing and then carefully questioning the jury to make sure none had read prejudicial reports, 3) keeping the proceeding open but postponing the trial so that any prejudicial stories will be forgotten, 4) keeping the hearing open no matter what happens if a person is a public official and the crime bears on public duties. (Even the New York Court of Appeals ruling in the Gannett case said the risk of prejudice was overridden by strong public interest in job performance of public employees.)

In 1981, Washington State Superior Court Judge Byron Swedberg told reporters they could cover a trial in his courtroom only if they agreed to abide by the previously voluntary bench-bar-press guidelines his state, like twenty others, had devised. These guidelines would have kept them from reporting on the defendant's prior record or possible confession in advance of jury selection.

Media outlets challenged this rule in court and it was upheld all the way to the U.S. Supreme Court. The decision has been damaging to court access because it allows the government to dictate in advance what can and cannot be written about a trial. It made editors wary of all such guidelines worked out so carefully over the years and resulted in a breakdown of communications between judges and the press.

In 1984, the Supreme Court took two major steps to assure that court proceedings will be open to the press and public. *Press Enterprise Co. v. Superior Court of California* dealt with the jury selection process in a rape and murder trial which a judge had conducted in private for six weeks. The Court ruled that jurors should be picked in the open in most cases. "Openness enhances both the basic fairness of the criminal trial and appearance of fairness so essential to public confidence in the system," wrote then Chief Justice Warren Burger. The Court cited the "community therapeutic" values of openness as well. "Criminal acts, especially violent crimes, often provoke public concern, even outrage and hostility. When the public is aware that the law is being enforced and the criminal justice system is functioning, an outlet is provided for these understandable reactions and emotions."

In *Waller v. George*, the justices said criminal defendants have a constitutional right under the Sixth Amendment to public pretrial hearings. This decision seemed to ease the restrictions of *Gannett v. DePasquale*, which said there was no constitutional right of access to pretrial hearings for the press and public under the Sixth Amendment. Under Waller, judges have to meet these tests before closing a trial: 1) the party seeking to close the hearing must advance an overriding interest that is likely to be prejudiced; 2) the closure must be no broader than necessary to protect that interest; 3) the trial court must consider reasonable alternatives to closing the hearing; and 4) the court must make findings adequate to support the closure.

Another 1984 Supreme Court decision went against the press when justices ruled that a newspaper that is party to a civil lawsuit may be prohibited by a judge from publishing information the paper obtains in pretrial hearings. Courts have increasingly allowed parties in a lawsuit to keep secret the records and information that lawyers exchange in discovery documents before trial. But the validity of sealing pretrial records is more difficult when one party to a lawsuit is a news organization wanting to use documents in a news story.

This decision, based on a case in which the *Seattle Times* and *Walla Walla Union-Bulletin* wanted to publish records obtained during a $14.1 million libel suit against them by a religious group, treats news organizations like any other party in a civil suit. The ruling did not apply to using information obtained from other sources or after it was introduced as evidence in the trial.

Contempt

The other major area of potential press problems with courts is contempt. Here the issue results less from coverage than with the likelihood of reporters getting into trouble with the court for doing their jobs. A reporter could always be held in contempt (and fined or jailed or both) by a judge for disobeying a court order, disturbing the court process, or attempting to influence the decision of a judge or the testimony of a witness. In recent years reporters have gotten into trouble with judges for covering events outside the courtroom more often than for their journalistic activities when court is in actual session. Because judges issue contempt citations, the problem will be discussed here.

The turbulent 1960s and 1970s created the problem. There were more newsworthy events to cover than at any time in history, and reporters were more aggressive in doing so. They also had the improved technology, especially in television news, to get to the turbulence more quickly than before. This put them more frequently at the scene of matters in which law enforcement people were also highly interested.

The result was an inevitable collision course between the public's right to a free, uninhibited, and vigilant press guaranteed by the First Amendment and the right of the government and private litigants to identify and develop evidence on their behalf; the latter right is coupled with the obligation for all citizens to testify when it is necessary for the sake of justice.

Should the work of reporters — especially their notes and source names — be privileged and thus immune from prosecution in the same way that court records, trial transcripts, and congressional debates are? Interviews with sources and the notes from those interviews are among the basic tools of journalism; without them, there would be no profession. If names of sources in controversial stories cannot be kept confidential, reporters would be hard put to find anyone willing to be interviewed. As a result, the flow of information would decline. Also, if reporters are viewed as an arm of law enforcement agencies, both journalism and those agencies will be harmed.

But should one profession be given privileges not granted to other citizens? Wouldn't such protection lead reporters to write more false stories, resulting in more irresponsible reporting and more libel suits?

The U.S. Supreme Court had an answer, and it was not welcomed by the press. In its decision in the Caldwell, Branzburg, and Pappas cases in 1972, the high court went against long accepted practice by denying journalists the right to keep confidential the names of sources used in published or broadcast stories. In the process it struck a blow at the ability of the press to protect notes and source names. The three cases were of similar nature and were linked on appeal to the Supreme Court, where they became known as the "Branzburg" decision.

By a 5 to 4 vote, the justices ruled that journalists can be called before grand juries and compelled to divulge the names of their news sources and answer any questions a jury deems relevant to the matter under investigation.

Wrote Justice Byron White in his majority opinion:

> We do not question the significance of free speech, press, or assembly to the country's welfare. Nor is it suggested that news gathering does not qualify for First Amendment protection; without some protection for seeking out the news, freedom of the press could be eviscerated. But this case involves no intrusions upon speech or assembly, nor prior restraint or restriction on what the press may publish and no expressed or implied command that the press publish what it prefers to withhold. . . . The use of confidential sources by the press is not forbidden or restricted; reporters must remain free to seek news from any source by means within the law. No attempt is made to require the press to publish its sources of information or indiscriminately to disclose them on request.
>
> The sole issue before us is the obligation of reporters to respond to grand jury subpoenas as other citizens do and to answer questions relevant to an investigation into the commission of crime. Citizens generally are not constitutionally immune from grand jury subpoenas. . . . The claim is, however, that reporters are exempt from these obligations because if forced to respond to subpoenas and identify their sources or disclose other confidences, their informant will refuse, or be reluctant, to furnish newsworthy information in the future.

In its decision the Court rejected the claim that reporters were immune from grand jury subpoenas. The ruling is also notable for recognizing, for the first time, a form of constitutional protection for the news gathering process and refusing to concede that that process depends on confidentiality. The decision implied that members of the press are not different from other citizens in their obligation to cooperate with courts and law enforcement officials. In other words, although the Court affirmed reporters' rights to First Amendment protection, it gave them no special privileges.

In a strong dissent, Justice Stewart wrote, "The Court's crabbed view of the First Amendment reflects a disturbing insensitivity to the critical role of an independent press in our society."

Justice White's opinion closed with the assurance that "official harassment of the press undertaken not for purpose of law enforcement but to disrupt a reporter's relationship with his news sources would have no justification."

Almost immediately after the Branzburg decision, judges, lawyers, and grand juries around the country began to subpoena news people. More than thirty-five reporters who refused to disclose the names of sources and give up notes were served with contempt citations in the first year after the ruling. A few were jailed as well.

Things eased on the federal level, however, with the issuance of guidelines for federal grand juries; the guidelines state that the press is not an investigative arm of the government.

In 1973, alarmed by the various contempt citations and jailings of reporters at the time of the Branzburg decision, members of Congress introduced bills to protect journalists and their sources. Because they were designed to protect reporters from interference in the way they do their work, these proposed laws were called "shield laws."

Reporters testifying at congressional hearings pressed for a law that would give them absolute protection from subpoenas of confidential material at federal and local levels. Such an approach was taken by Representative John Moss of California. His proposed law read, in part, "No person shall be required to disclose to any grand jury, or court in the United States, or to the Congress, or to any agency, the source from or through which such persons received information in their capacity as a newsperson."

Such absolute protection was opposed by other representatives as unconstitutional; it would violate the Fifth and Sixth Amendments as they apply to the rights of defendants in trials.

Other proposals took a more narrow approach, protecting reporters within carefully prescribed limits; for example, they would be protected only if they did not have actual knowledge that proved or disproved the commission of a crime charged or under investigation.

The move toward a federal shield law gradually slowed, however, and no such law was ever enacted. The national threat eased as the Nixon administration backed off from its earlier confrontation with the press. When the president was forced to resign, the threat all but vanished on the national level.

It has been a different situation locally, where subpoenas have been issued and reporters jailed regularly. For this reason, twenty-eight states had passed shield laws by 1991.

Even in states with shield laws, however, there is still an argument in differentiating between civil and criminal issues. A reporter can still go to jail for refusing to disclose information to a court in a state with a shield law. Both William Farr and Myron Farber found that out.

Farr, then a reporter for the *Los Angeles Herald-Examiner*, spent forty-six days in solitary confinement in 1971 for refusing to reveal the names of two attorneys who supplied him with documents to verify his coverage of the Charles Manson trial the year before.

Farr agreed to talk to the judge in the case but did so without an attorney. He answered questions only up to a certain point and was cited for thirteen counts of contempt of court as a result. A state court of appeals eventually ordered the judge to vacate all orders against Farr, by then with the *Los Angeles Times*. He was still faced with a $24 million libel suit in connection with the case and thousands of dollars in legal fees.

In Farber's case, a judge in New Jersey jailed him for refusing to surrender notes gathered in writing articles for the *New York Times* about thirteen mysterious deaths in a hospital. His articles caused New Jersey officials to reopen the case and eventually to charge a doctor with murder. When Farber was called to testify in the trial, he refused to answer questions he thought would compromise his sources. The doctor's attorney then subpoenaed his notes, and he refused to give them up. The judge then said he would review the notes to see whether the material was pertinent to the case. The reporter and the newspaper again declined and were cited for contempt of court. After several delays, Farber was jailed and fined $2,000. The *Times* eventually paid $285,000 in fines and more than $200,000 in legal fees. When the doctor was found not guilty by a jury, Farber was released after spending forty days in jail.

In the meantime the case had progressed to the New Jersey Supreme Court, which upheld the reporter's conviction and the fines against the *Times*. A month after Farber's release, the U.S. Supreme Court refused, without comment, to review the case, thus letting the earlier court verdict stand. In 1982, the governor of New Jersey pardoned Farber and remitted $101,000 in fines before he left office.

In addition to its bearing on the protection of sources and notes, the case illuminates the clear clash between the First Amendment guarantee of a free press and the Sixth Amendment's right to a fair trial. The doctor's attorney contended that he needed the notes to prove his client's innocence. The judge supported this argument, despite Farber's insistence that he did not witness a crime or have anything in his notes to establish the defendant's guilt or innocence.

The surrender of his notes, he said, would make him an investigative arm of the government, a role never intended for the press.

For the press, the most chilling aspect of this case was the fact that, because New Jersey had a shield law, Farber and other reporters felt more safe than had they been working in a state without such a statute. This case seriously undermined confidence in a shield law as a source of protection. And, because the doctor was found not guilty, the judge never ruled on the apparent violation of the shield law. The issue remains open. States deal with it case by case. A few reporters still go to jail to protect their notes and sources, at least briefly, every year. In 1989, 4,500 subpoenas were issued by judges to media people seeking source names and notes.

A related case that the Supreme Court did decide to hear involved the police search of a newspaper office. In *Zurcher v. The Stanford Daily* in 1978, the Court by a 5 to 4 vote overturned a lower court ruling to hold that police officers may obtain a warrant to conduct unannounced searches of newsrooms for evidence of a crime, even though they do not suspect anyone connected with the newspaper of wrongdoing. Previously the police had to obtain a subpoena for the material they wanted. A subpoena must specify precisely what is wanted, can be contested in court, and takes longer to obtain than a search warrant.

The case resulted from a 1971 sit-in during which demonstrators seized part of the Stanford University Hospital and injured nine policemen. The *Daily* covered the event. Three days later police obtained a search warrant and arrived at the office of the *Daily* looking for photographs of the clash other than those already published in the newspaper. Only two of the assailants had been identified at the scene, and the police hoped to find out about others from unpublished photographs. They found no new photographs in their search.

The *Stanford Daily* filed suit against the policemen making the search, the chief of police, the district attorney, one of his deputies, and the judge who had issued the search warrant. The grounds for the suit were that the paper's rights under the First and Fourth Amendments had been violated. (The Fourth Amendment protects against unreasonable search and seizure.)

Two lower courts found that the newspaper's constitutional rights had been violated and ordered police to pay attorney's fees. The Supreme Court majority rejected the lower court's contention that a search warrant should be issued in such situations only if there is a "clear showing" that a subpoena ordering the newspaper to give up the material would result in the destruction of the material.

Wrote Justice White:

Properly administered, the preconditions for a warrant—probable cause, specificity with respect to the place to be searched and the things to be seized, and overall reasonableness—should afford sufficient protection against the harms that are assertedly threatened by warrants for searching newspaper offices.

Valid warrants may be issued to search any property . . . at which there is probable cause to believe that fruits, instrumentalities or evidence of a crime will be found. . . . The critical element in a reasonable search isn't that the owner of the property is suspected of a crime but that there is reasonable cause to believe that the specific things to be searched for and seized are located on the property.

The varying definitions of such a "reasonable search" are what worries editors and reporters. What seems reasonable to police might not seem so to journalists. Editors and reporters all over the United States immediately raised the specter of heavy-handed policemen breaking down the doors of newspapers and pilfering files in their search for evidence.

Justice Stewart discussed another problem in his dissent to the majority opinion. He attacked the Court's "facile conclusion" that police searches of news organizations would not seriously burden the "constitutionally protected function of the press to gather news." He argued that if police can search a newsroom, "including, presumably, every file in the office," confidential sources might refuse to talk to the press if they think their statements might fall into official hands. This fear could dry up sources and inhibit the coverage of news.

Soon after the *Stanford Daily* decision, police searches of newsrooms began in various parts of the country; they occurred at a rate of one or two each year, for a total of eighteen up to 1980. At the time of that decision, the Court had invited Congress to enact a statute to limit future unannounced searches. The rash of cases in various states caused pressure to do just that, and President Jimmy Carter signed the statute into law in 1980. Since then, this has not been a big problem.

Under the law's provisions any law enforcement or government official seeking information and material from news people (and authors, scholars, and researchers) must first seek a subpoena specifying the items sought. If the request seems unreasonable to the subpoenaed party, he or she may go to court to challenge the action. The law specifically restricts search warrants against any person who has collected information "with a purpose to disseminate to the public a newspaper, book, broadcast, or other similar form of public communication."

The law restricts "no-notice" search warrant raids—such as the one upheld in the *Stanford Daily* case—by federal, state, and local law enforcement officials.

The law divides information prepared by reporters and editors into two categories: "work product materials" and "non-work product documentary materials." Work product materials are such things as interviews, story drafts, internal memos, and notes. Non-work product documentary materials include documents prepared by a third person and obtained by the press, for example, a ransom note.

The law permits a search warrant for work product materials only if: 1) there is reason to believe the reporter is involved in a crime (other than the possession of the information itself, which is not a crime), 2) the information sought relates to national defense, or 3) there is a reason to believe that "an immediate seizure by search warrant is necessary to prevent the death of or serious bodily injury to a human being."

Search warrants covering documentary materials will be allowed against news people or news organizations under the law for the same reasons as those for work product materials: if that person is suspected of a crime, the information relates to defense, or the search would prevent injury or death. Three other authorizations are permitted: if the materials might be destroyed, if the news organization has refused to obey a subpoena in the past and all court appeals have been exhausted, or if delay "would threaten the interests of justice."

The legal aspects of court reporting and reporting in general, when it involves matters before the courts, obscures the actual coverage of the beat. Reporters can get so entangled in the implications of these various Supreme Court decisions that they are afraid to proceed lest they run afoul of the law. It is not the intention of this chapter to create such fears, only to clarify the problems inherent in doing the reporting job.

Many problems can be eased by knowing how a court works and the laws applicable in your particular state. Another asset is well-informed sources in the courthouse and within the official agencies and law offices that work in the courthouse: judges, clerks, district attorneys, and private attorneys who try cases there.

A summary of the problems of court reporting can be found in "Likely Problems and How to Solve Them" later in this chapter.

How to Cover Courts

The kind of court and the size of the city have some bearing on how a court beat reporter works. There are a number of constants in the process:

1. **Have a basic knowledge of court procedure.** A court beat reporter must know how the court operates. Background reading will help and so will experience. Watching a court in session for a week will help solidify the process in the mind. Many courts also prepare booklets that detail the steps in any trial being held within its jurisdiction. (See Box 8.1 and "Key Terms for Court Reporting.")

2. **Know the difference between civil law and criminal law.** Criminal cases, where the state is the accuser, are generally more newsworthy than civil actions, where a group or individual initiates action. Occasionally a civil case will be interesting if a prominent person or company is involved. Often civil cases merit only brief coverage, if any coverage at all.

3. **Establish and cultivate good sources.** Court clerks, judges' clerks, the court stenographer, defense attorneys, district attorneys, judges, probation officers, and bail bondsmen are all good potential sources.

4. **Take careful notes.** Much of the drama of a trial will be captured by a reporter taking good notes of testimony and capturing the "feel" of the courtroom for readers—startling testimony; good descriptions of attorneys, the defendant, witnesses, the judge, the jury, spectators, the progress of the trial and the outcome.

5. **Review court records for backup.** During the trial a court record is kept by a stenographer (sometimes called a "court reporter") on a special machine. This record is a good backup for a reporter's own note-taking efforts. The problem is that the transcript is not always available when a reporter needs it to meet deadlines and is expensive to purchase.

6. **Know what information to include in stories.** Reporters are free to cover trials in most states. The difficulty comes if they use grand jury information they got in a surreptitious way, confidential records obtained unofficially, or documents taken from the police. (Information on legal problems appears in Appendix A.)

7. **Look for unusual angles.** Such angles could include the nature of the crime or the defendant, the personality of the defense attorney or the district attorney, the strategy of the defense or prosecution, the startling nature of the evidence, or unusual aspects of witnesses or the jury.

Box 8.1

How the Court System Operates

The American court system exists on a number of levels: federal, state, and local. The system is like a pyramid; the final authority rests in the U.S. Supreme Court at the top.

The federal courts consist of the U.S. Supreme Court, the U.S. Courts of Appeal, district courts, and special courts.

State courts include a state supreme court for each of the fifty states, appellate courts, and what are called primary courts, where judicial courses of action are initiated. Some states have two primary court systems, one for civil cases, another for criminal.

Local courts (called district, municipal, or justice courts, depending on the state) hear more minor matters and are usually convened in county seats, although they are still under the jurisdiction of the state court system.

American courts are also defined by their levels of jurisdiction: *Limited jurisdiction* courts cover a particular class of case, usually where the amount of money involved is below a prescribed sum. *Juvenile courts* handle the problems of delinquent or neglected children, including crimes committed by them if they are under the legal age or against them. *Probate courts* rule in wills, estate settlements, adoptions, commitments of mentally defective persons, guardianship of minors, and the administration of trusts. Justices of the peace, county courts, and municipal courts are included here.

Major trial courts go under various names depending on the state involved. They can be called district court, circuit court, superior court, or common pleas court. In such courts the judge and jury (or in a bench trial just the judge) hears evidence to determine the facts of a case and decides on guilt or innocence depending on the trial judge's understanding of the applicable law.

Appellate courts determine whether the trial court committed errors of law (for example, applying the wrong law or making erroneous rulings on the law) and, if so, whether the errors were prejudicial to the original decision.

Courts in the United States operate in much the same way in all parts of the country. A person suspected of a crime is first arrested by police and searched at the scene. The suspect is then taken to the police station for booking. The desk sergeant writes down the person's name, any other identification and details of the alleged crime (date and time), the specific charge, and who made the arrest.

After being photographed and fingerprinted, the defendant is allowed to make one telephone call before being placed in a detention cell in the police station or the courthouse. Unless the person has been accused of a serious crime, he or she is entitled to be released on *bail*, the amount of financial security to be deposited with the court to ensure that the suspect will return for trial.

The suspect must appear before a judge for this determination to be made. During the same appearance a prosecutor will present a formal complaint outlining the information obtained in the arrest and other interviews. The lower court judge makes a decision at this point to grant bail or release the person on his or her own *recognizance*, or promise to appear later.

At this point most states require a defendant to be taken before a magistrate as quickly as possible. In California, for example, the rule is within forty-eight hours after the arrest. Normally this appearance, called an *arraignment*, is before a municipal or justice court judge.

An arraignment is designed: 1) to identify the defendant, 2) to inform him or her of constitutional rights, and 3) to advise him or her of the charges. The judge asks if the defendant can afford an attorney and appoints one if the answer is no. The judge also asks the defendant how he or she pleads — guilty or not guilty.

The plea will have varying ramifications:

1. If the defendant pleads guilty to a misdemeanor, which is a charge not punishable by imprisonment in a state prison, the court may impose sentence during arraignment or the judge may continue the case in order to study a probation report before imposing sentence.

2. Pleading not guilty to a misdemeanor calls for the judge to set a trial date in the municipal or justice court within thirty days after arrest, unless the defendant waives the right to a speedy trial.

3. Pleading guilty to a felony necessitates that the defendant be represented by counsel, unless the judge decides the defendant intelligently and willingly waived the right to an attorney. The defendant who pleads guilty is transferred to superior court for sentencing, and a judge from that court imposes punishment.

4. Pleading not guilty to a felony causes the judge to set a preliminary hearing, normally within ten court days of arraignment, unless the defendant waives the hearing.

A *preliminary hearing* is designed to determine that a crime has been committed and that there is a good reason to believe the defendant committed the crime. The defendant and his or her attorney appear before a judge in municipal or justice court and are confronted with some of the evidence the state has to support the charge. Once the evidence has been presented — with the defendant's attorney allowed to cross-examine witnesses but not present defense witnesses — the judge must decide to either discharge the defendant for lack of evidence or hold for trial in superior court.

A felony case goes to trial in one of two ways: 1) by having the district attorney file an *information*, a document containing the specific charges against the defendant or 2) by a grand jury indictment. If the defendant is bound over to superior court to stand trial, he or she is *re-arraigned*.

Before a criminal trial starts, the defense attorney may file a series of motions with the court to eliminate certain information from consideration (for example, prior conviction or evidence illegally obtained), to set aside the entire trial because of insufficient evidence, to dismiss the case because of lack of a speedy trial, or to gain a hearing as to the defendant's mental competency to stand trial. Once the judge has heard and ruled on all motions, the trial can proceed.

Trial procedures are usually similar in both civil and criminal cases. A judge presides from a large, high desk called a *bench*, rules on various points of law, and makes sure the defendant gets a fair trial. The bailiff keeps order in the courtroom and takes charge of the jury any time any of its members are outside the room. The court clerk gives the oath to each witness called to testify and keeps records of all proceedings. The court reporter records all of the formal proceedings, including witness testimony, objections made to the evidence by attorneys, and the court's rulings on any motions made during the trial. Attorneys are officers of the court working for either the defense or the prosecution.

After pretrial proceedings most attorneys file trial briefs, which detail the facts to be proved and the law applicable to these facts. Sometimes a defense attorney might ask for a *change of venue*, meaning that the trial be moved to another city because the bias and hostility in the current city would render a fair trial impossible.

Both defense and prosecution are entitled to a jury trial, unless either waives this right and asks to have the case heard and decided by a judge. The defendant has a legal right to a jury trial in most civil and criminal cases; he or she does not have an absolute right to waive a jury trial in a criminal case if the judge thinks the defendant is not competent enough to understand the charges or what it means to waive a jury trial. Because the prosecution is also entitled to this right, both sides must agree to waive a jury trial or the jury must hear the case.

Trial by a jury of peers is a long-standing guarantee to every citizen of this country. Jury members are picked from a panel of registered voters chosen at random by court clerks to serve for a set period of time. Most cases are heard by twelve jurors, although a smaller number may be used in a trial for a lesser offense.

Before a trial begins, attorneys for both sides will examine the panel of prospective jurors by asking them questions to determine their fairness and impartiality in reaching a verdict in the case. Do they know the defendant? If the case involves drunk driving, are they against alcohol? What do they think of capital punishment, if the case involves murder? Many such questions are asked before each side is satisfied with the jurors. They will either accept the jurors or challenge them, with or without reason. The judge does not have to accept every challenge and may keep some jurors the two sides wish to exclude.

The trial begins after the jury has been impaneled and sworn in. Both civil and criminal trials begin with the attorney for the side bringing the action—the plaintiff or the state—making a statement to tell the judge and jury about the issues involved in the case and what the evidence will show. Such a statement is not evidence itself, however. After the opening statement by the prosecution, the defense may present its opening statement or wait until the prosecution has completed its case.

The prosecution calls the first witness, who is sworn in by the court clerk and seated in a chair to the right of the bench. When the district attorney or prosecuting attorney finishes direct examination, the defense attorney has the right to cross-examine the witness, usually by isolating each factor of the main examination and trying to get the witness to admit that some of the factors might have been caused by a reason other than what the witness stated. After cross-examination the attorney who originally called the witness can ask questions on re-direct examination, usually to cover new information brought out on cross-examination and to rehabilitate the witness if necessary. This process is repeated for all the witnesses.

At any point in the trial the attorneys for either side may object to any of the testimony based on whether it is admissible or not, that is, whether it pertains to the case. The judge makes this decision. A sustained objection means that an attorney must stop that line of questioning, but an overruled objection allows the attorney to proceed.

Most trials include other evidence besides the testimony of witnesses: written material like letters, deeds, wills, leases, statements; material objects such as weapons or narcotics; things within the knowledge of the court like meanings of words and phrases or existing laws; and presumptions that can be made from particular facts.

Some cases depend on direct evidence, that is, an eyewitness account of events related to the matter on trial. Other cases include circumstantial evidence, or indirect evidence, where the court infers or accepts a fact based on a set of known or proven circumstances. A judge will usually not allow the jury to consider hearsay evidence, untrustworthy statements about third-hand information that cannot be proven in court.

In addition to witnesses who know something about the case by direct knowledge or observation, each side may call expert witnesses to testify about an aspect of the case where their background is important (a handwriting expert or a doctor, for example).

In civil cases the preponderance of evidence must be on one side or the other. In a criminal case the defendant is presumed innocent until proven guilty; therefore, the state must prove guilt to the jury "beyond a reasonable doubt." This requirement means that jurors must be morally certain of their decision in order to prevent conviction and imprisonment of innocent people.

At the conclusion of the plaintiff's case the defense attorney may move for acquittal, alleging that the prosecutor failed to prove the crime occurred or the defendant committed it. Such motions are routine but are seldom granted, unless a significant problem arose in the prosecutor's presentation of the case.

If the motion is denied, the defense may call witnesses and present evidence, and the prosecuting attorney or attorney for the plaintiff will cross-examine the defense witnesses. After both sides have presented their cases, the attorneys will sum up or review the facts and the arguments for the jury or judge.

At this point the judge instructs jury members by defining the issues they must decide and indicating the law that governs the case. The bailiff then takes the jury to the jury room, where it elects a foreman and begins to deliberate. This process may take several hours or several days. If a jury is kept overnight, their lodging and food are provided by the court and they are kept from all outside contact.

After the jury has reached a verdict, the foreman advises the bailiff. He or she then tells the judge who reconvenes court to hear the verdict. In a criminal case the jury may find a person not guilty, guilty, or guilty only of certain charges. It may also find the defendant guilty of a lesser crime than that charged by the prosecution, in which case the penalty would be less. A verdict in a criminal case must be unanimous.

In a civil case the verdict deals with disputed issues or facts, and the jury may make a general finding in favor of the plaintiff or defendant. It may also make a special verdict in which it determines the facts and leaves the judgement up to the court. A three-fourths majority is all that is necessary in a civil suit.

If a jury cannot reach a verdict, it is considered a ''hung'' jury. The judge will declare a mistrial, and the case will be retried later.

After the foreman has announced the verdict, the losing attorney can file a motion for a new trial, which is the same case argued before another jury. This will be granted only on the basis of judge's errors, jury misconduct, or insufficient evidence.

The judge pronounces sentence and the case ends. It can be appealed to higher courts. Sentence may include a fine, one year in county jail, a set period in prison, or a set time on probation.

In the appeal the higher court reviews the actions of the trial court to see whether errors were committed in procedure or interpreting and applying the law. In a civil suit either side can appeal to a higher court. In a criminal case only the defendant can appeal. When the verdict is not guilty, the state cannot appeal because of the rule of double jeopardy. The defendant cannot be tried for that crime again.

The *grand jury* is a special kind of jury convened to hear evidence presented by the district attorney to decide whether the persons accused of a crime should be forced to submit to a trial. Often, such juries are used in important and/or particularly notorious cases. Grand jury members are selected either from regular jury lists or from people thought to be especially well-qualified. The district attorney has cases ready to submit to the grand jury when it meets, and the D.A. will present evidence to support the case and ask for an indictment. Evidence is usually *ex parte* (one-sided), tending only to prove the guilt of the accused, who is allowed to testify along with other witnesses. If that person is indicted, he or she then stands trial before a regular judge and jury.

Kinds of Court Stories

A regular court beat reporter encounters a number of standard stories:

1. **Criminal trials.** The verdict and facts of a criminal trial are usually newsworthy. If the crime is unique or particularly heinous, however, a reporter may want to sit in on the opening and closing statements of attorneys and some of the daily testimony.

2. **Civil trials.** The verdict and facts of a civil case are normally the only aspects meriting coverage. Sometimes details of the people or business involved are interesting, or the amount of the award is high enough to warrant a longer story.

3. **Court procedures.** Once in a while, the way a court works makes a good story. This is especially true if the news peg of a breakdown in the court system applies. Why has this large backlog of cases occurred? A good device here is to follow a case through the courts to see what happens.

4. **Feature stories about people who work in the courthouse.** Interesting people make for good feature material. In such instances, the same rules apply as in any feature: The person should be quotable and have done something newsworthy or of interest to readers, even in a novel or bizarre way.

5. **Investigations into court problems.** Large-scale investigative stories are not different when they specifically deal with court affairs (see Chapter 6). Failure in the court system, corrupt or incompetent judges, an overloaded system, or local angles to national stories all fit into this category.

6. **News of courts.** A number of breaking stories fall into this category. All of them are outside the courthouse: election of judges, court budgets, overcrowded facilities, allocation of funds to build new facilities, and details of such facilities when they are built.

Writing Court Stories

"You have to write fast," says Don Van Natta of the *Miami Herald.* "Homework is important in terms of thinking ahead how to write a story. I sit in trials or in the car or shower and write leads in my head. I always have two leads in mind—acquitted or guilty. I also ponder the way I'll tell the story—that is, what is it about—first to my editor to approve it and then to readers to get them interested in reading it.

"One pitfall of court reporting are tired, dull, stories. 'A jury on Thursday found so and so guilty of first degree murder.' I try to avoid that approach for one that is more dramatic and brings in the victim. Anecdotal leads can be tired too but they work in court reporting.

"There are so many down times in court when you can think of leads. I look for details, like the empty seats in the spectator area. I write the story in a way that makes people sorry they missed the trial, making it as creative and dramatic as possible. I write down the most effective quote and remember the most dramatic moment. I hear it, I see it on the page.

"I write the story like it was a letter to a friend. Sometimes there is so much stuff I don't know where to go.

"What makes good writing is detail. What brand wristwatch the defendant kept looking at, for example. Without such detail, you write a wooden story, a bloodless piece no one will read. When the verdict is read my eyes are darting around the room—the expressions on the faces of jurors, how the defense and prosecution react. My ears are listening for reaction too. My goal is to have something that occurs on Tuesday come alive for readers Wednesday morning.

"The kicker—last paragraph—is as important as the lead. I save my best quotes for last. Some editors don't like that. But sometimes the best detail in the last graf ties everything together, particularly in tale stories."

#1

TARGETED DADE JUDGE
REFUSED ROLE AS SNITCH
By Don Van Natta Jr.
Herald Staff Writer

In his lead for this court beat story, Don Van Natta Jr. uses a dramatic narrative approach that places the reader at the scene. He continues this tack in the transition and paragraphs 3, 4, 5. Also in graf 5 he tells readers what the story ultimately is about by using a colon, followed by an explanation.

1 The telephone at Dade County Judge Harvey Shenberg's house rang at 7:30 A.M. on Saturday, June 8. It was a state agent who said he was in a bind and needed Shenberg's help.

2 The agent asked if Shenberg would sign a search warrant. The judge said OK.

3 Within minutes, two FBI and Florida Department of Law Enforcement agents knocked on Shenberg's door, but they did not have a search warrant for him to sign.

He widens the story in 6 to mention investigations into other judges.

In graf 7, he allows himself the luxury of letting readers know that what they are seeing is exclusive ("pieced together by the *Miami Herald*").

In grafs 8, 9, 10, and 11, Van Natta gives readers background into the probe of the judge.

Throughout the story, Van Natta uses terse, one sentence paragraphs as a technique to move the story effectively ("Shenberg was devastated"). He lays out more background in grafs 12 through 18. His direct, unadorned style gives readers details quickly without letting any extra words get in the way.

4 That was a lie. "Please step outside," one of the agents told the judge.

5 Clad in a bathrobe, the judge was led to one of the agents' cars. Shenberg sat in the back seat and listened to an agent break the news: He was the target of a two-year-old federal and state investigation of Dade's judiciary.

6 By 9 that morning, agents would search the homes and offices of five current and former Dade judges. By noon, the probe would be known all over Miami by its cocky government code name, Operation Court Broom.

7 The early hours of the public investigation were pieced together by the *Miami Herald* from accounts given by five sources close to the probe. In a span of 90 minutes, prosecutors would make Shenberg an extraordinary offer: They wanted him to work as an undercover informant while still sitting on the bench.

8 It was an offer the judge would defiantly refuse.

9 The dramatic chain of events began in the agent's car when the two investigators played a cassette tape for Shenberg on the stereo system. It was a short excerpt of a conversation that Shenberg allegedly had with Miami Beach lawyer and key undercover informant Raymond J. Takiff.

10 The conversation was about a cash bribe.

11 Shenberg was devastated.

12 The agents asked the judge if he would come with them to a nearby hotel to meet with a pair of government prosecutors.

13 He agreed. The agents drove him to the Marriott hotel at Dadeland, 9090 S. Dadeland Blvd. Assistant U.S. Attorney John O'Sullivan and Special Assistant U.S. Attorney Larry LaVecchio waited in a hotel room there for the judge.

14 The prosecutors told Shenberg about some of the evidence state and federal agents had accumulated against him.

15 They then made the judge an offer: Work undercover for the government to help clean up Dade County's dirty judicial system.

16 And the prosecutors named a judge they thought Shenberg could help "bring down:" Dade Circuit Judge Ellen "Maximum" Morphonios, one of Shenberg's dearest friends.

17 Shenberg needed about three seconds to consider the government proposition. His answer: "No Way."

18 O'Sullivan then picked up the telephone and called the U.S. Attorney's office in Miami. "Do the searches," he said.

In graf 19, Van Natta broadens the story a bit to note the wider investigations into other judges.

19 It was the first indication Shenberg had that there were other judges in trouble.

20 Shenberg was driven back to his house. On the way, the agents told him they had a search warrant for him, after all. Chief U.S. District Judge James Lawrence King had signed it.

21 The search warrant was for Shenberg's house.

22 Shenberg's refusal to cooperate had sweeping ramifications: it triggered an alternative plan by agents to serve warrants on four other current and former judges.

23 If Shenberg had agreed to cooperate, those searches would not have occurred and the investigation would have remained a secret, sources said.

24 The order to search the other homes and offices was sent by walkie-talkie to about 80 state and federal agents, including a few who sipped coffee in the parking lot of the Metro Justice Building.

More details follow of the other investigations and what happened—searching judges' chambers and homes.

25 At 9 A.M. sharp, agents began knocking on the front doors of judges Phillip Davis, Roy Gelber and Alfonso Sepe and former judge David Goodhart.

26 At the same time, about 30 agents showed up at each judge's office at the Metro Justice Building. They carried away dozens of cardboard boxes.

In graf 27, he notes the press conference at which the probe was announced. A more mundanely written story would have featured that in the lead.

27 An hour later, Operation Court Broom was introduced into the local lexicon by U.S. Attorney Dexter Lehtinen and State Attorney Janet Reno, who held a 10-minute press conference.

28 Earlier this month, Gelber pleaded guilty to one count of racketeering and accepted a maximum of 20 years in prison. Gelber has given prosecutors essential information about several other targets, including Shenberg, and seven other Miami defense lawyers.

29 Shenberg also allegedly was involved in a murder conspiracy plot with Gelber, sources have said. The take: $50,000.

In graf 30, Van Natta does something not permitted by all newspapers: he speculates. By using the phrase, "It is clear," he is telling readers what he thinks. At this stage, with all his reporting he knows enough to speculate, but some editors would not permit it. He gives the judge's attorney a chance to reply in grafs 32 through 36.

30 It is clear that investigators believed that Shenberg was essential to their efforts to net Judge Morphonios in the corruption probe. Morphonios was subpoenaed and appeared before the grand jury several weeks ago.

31 Her lawyer, Kirk Munroe, said Thursday that Morphonios would not comment because the Florida Code of Judicial Conduct prohibited her from making any statements.

32 On Thursday, Shenberg's lawyer, Stephen Bronis, angrily criticized the government-coordinated "ambush" on June 8.

33 "It was a sneak attack," Bronis said. "It's obvious the furthest thing from the minds of the prosecutors and the agents who devised this scheme was to afford Judge Shenberg any modicum of due process."

34 Bronis said he was not contacted by Shenberg until that afternoon.

35 "It was wrong," he said. "They did everything they could to put as much coercion on him as possible to become an informant."

36 Shenberg's response? "He was shocked and offended. He won't play their game."

His last graf lets readers in on what else Van Natta has found by talking to sources: the judge will be indicted. The reporter has wrapped up this subject neatly for his readers.

37 No one has been charged. However, sources say Harvey Shenberg will be one of the men indicted by the federal grand jury within the next few weeks.

#2

**SPURNED LOVER CONVICTED OF
DROWNING GIRLFRIEND'S 5 YEAR OLD
BOY FOR REVENGE**
By Don Van Natta Jr.
Herald Staff Writer

This story is a good example of the dramatic stories Van Natta finds when he makes his rounds in the Dade County Courthouse. This morality play about a spurned lover and murder is true, but reads as if it were fiction. After a good delayed lead and two other paragraphs to build up suspense, Van Natta explains himself in graf 4. He follows up in 5 with a direct quote from the defendant.

1   It was Valentine's Day 1988, and Guillermo Arbelaez's heart was broken.

2   His roommate and love, Graceila Alfaro, had refused to marry him. Just after midnight, he had spied Alfaro kissing a new suitor.

3   Consumed by jealousy, Arbelaez lusted for revenge.

4   So he kidnapped Alfaro's 5-year-old son, Julio Rivas, a trusting boy who looked forward to being a kindergartner, and drove to the top of the Rickenbacker Causeway.

5   "I took him out of the car, and he put his arms out to me and I threw him," Arbelaez told police later. "I threw him in the sea."

6   A Dade jury convicted Arbelaez of first-degree murder and kidnapping at 9:30 P.M. Tuesday.

Paragraph 6 would have been the lead most reporters would have selected. In a city like Miami, with so many murders, readers might have ignored the story if it had been written in that way.

In graf 7, Van Natta does what he likes to do in such stories: he told readers how the defendant received the verdict.

7   As the verdicts were read, Arbelaez, a 32-year-old native of Colombia, sat ramrod straight, his eyes riveted to the floor.

8   The state is seeking the death penalty. Jurors will return to recommend life in prison or the electric chair to Circuit Judge Allen Kornblum on March 4.

9   "It was a just verdict, and it was a right verdict," prosecutor Sally Weintraub said.

10 Arbelaez's defense lawyer, Reemberto Diaz, vowed to appeal the verdict. His motion to suppress Arbelaez's confessions failed.

In grafs 11 and 12, the reporter gives readers background to the case.

11 Julio's body was found floating in Biscayne Bay, just north of the causeway, at 3:30 P.M. on Feb. 14.

12 Weintraub told jurors Julio trusted Arbelaez, who used to buy him toys and candy, even in the moments just before his death.

13 "This little boy's trust of the defendant was paid for by being murdered," Weintraub said.

14 Arbelaez's defense: It was an accident. He said he was busy fixing the car and the boy fell off the bridge.

15 The jury didn't buy it. The state had accumulated an overwhelming amount of evidence against Arbelaez — much of it from Arbelaez's own mouth.

Beginning in graf 16, Van Natta brings readers into the courtroom by sketching in details on the videotape played for jurors. This also allows Van Natta the rare luxury of letting the defendant tell his own story in chilling detail, a thing the reporter does in alternating paragraphs of direct quote and paraphrase (17-32).

In graf 18 he breaks the narrative briefly to bring readers some courtroom drama he observed himself: the mother of the boy calling the defendant a murderer.

16 Jurors watched a 40-minute videotape of Arbelaez confessing to the crime in harrowing detail.

17 "I didn't know if he had died; I didn't know anything," he told detectives in a videotaped statement. "The only thing I knew was that I threw him."

18 As Alfaro took the stand, she saw several pictures of Julio's body left on the clerk's desk in the courtroom. She pointed at the defendant and screamed, "Murderer! Assassin! You son of a bitch! You killed my beautiful baby!"

19 Arbelaez's troubled conscience inspired him to return from Medellin, Colombia, to face the charges.

20 In an extraordinary series of phone conversations, Miami homicide detective Eddie Martinez persuaded Arbelaez to return to Miami. "I've got to pay for what I did," he said then.

21 Less than two hours after landing in Miami on April 11, 1988, Arbelaez confessed.

22 Arbelaez, a dishwasher who worked two jobs, met Alfaro at the Blanquita Restaurant in Miami, where she worked as a waitress. He gave her generous tips so she would serve him. They became friends.

23 He helped her move into a new apartment. In December 1987, she invited him to move in.

24 He said they had talked of marriage. She said the wedding plans were a product of his imagination.

25 "I loved her," he said in his videotaped confession. "But my friends would tell me that I shouldn't be a dummy, that I shouldn't be stupid, that she was exploiting me."

26 But on Valentine's Day, Arbelaez looked through a key hole as Alfaro kissed a man good night.

27 "I tried to control myself, but was not able to do so," he told detectives. "I did not hit her or anything like that. She said... 'Guillermo, I don't love you. I don't feel anything toward you.'"

28 That night, he slept on the couch.

29 The next morning, he left for work with Julio. "I took him, since I always used to take him for rides. And then it came into my mind that that would be my vengeance.

30 "That she will be sorry for the rest of her life. So then I went to the boy in the car all over, but I was not capable. I did not dare. Until I called her up, and she did not want to (talk) with me.

31 "So then, I went and I dropped him."

32 He picked a spot on Powell Bridge on the Rickenbacker Causeway — the highest point, 70 feet above the water.

In graf 33 Van Natta tells what the little boy was wearing, details sure to make readers sad.

33 When Julio's body was found later, the boy was wearing navy blue shorts, a white T-shirt, socks and sneakers.

In 34 and 35, the reporter presents more damaging details about the defendant.

34 The official cause of death: asphyxiation. However, the medical examiner could not be sure if the boy was choked first or had drowned, or both. The medical examiner also found bruises all over Julio's body.

35 Arbelaez did not bother to watch the boy hit the water. He drove his car to Coral Gables, where he abandoned it. He ran to the home of a friend to plead for help, then flew home to Colombia.

He ends the story with more quotes from the defendant, self-centered, callous quotes which show him still more morose about his lost love than the little boy he killed.

36 Detective Martinez phoned Arbelaez in Medellin. The detective and suspect talked for three weeks. Finally, Arbelaez decided to turn himself in.

37 Why? detectives asked later. "Because there's nothing like peace of mind. To live peacefully. And what I did was not correct, and what she did was not correct either.

38 "And that was very painful for me — to see her in front of me, kissing someone else."

Court Reporting: Likely Problems and How to Solve Them

Problem	Solution
1. Restriction of access to the courtroom.	1a. Know applicable state laws and be prepared to cite them.
	1b. Be prepared to sue (via your newspaper's attorney) for access when the issue is important enough.
2. Contempt power of judges.	2a. Know the appropriate court rulings and abide by them in revealing information gained during reporting.
	2b. Never speak out in court or interfere with the conduct of court business.
	2c. Never try to talk to jurors during a trial lest you be accused of attempting to influence their deliberations.
	2d. Be prepared to go to jail to protect notes and source names (with the backing of your newspaper).

3. Inability to keep up with events on the beat.

    3a. Keep track of upcoming trials via court calendars.

    3b. Cultivate sources for tips on newsworthy trials.

4. Difficulty of understanding court procedures and terms, overall legal issues.

    4a. Study background booklets provided by the court and reference books.

    4b. Sit through several trials in a "dry run" to note procedure.

    4c. Get on the mailing lists of organizations like the American Bar Association, the American Board of Trial Advocates, the Libel Defense Resource Center, the Reporters Committee for Freedom of the Press, the U.S. Department of Justice, the Washington Legal Foundation, your state's attorney general's office and court system to obtain useful background information.

Summary

Coverage of court activities is as old as that of the police work which gives courts their reason for existence. Court reporters experience both advantages and disadvantages as they do their jobs. Their beat is easy to cover logistically in that everything takes place in one building and is generally done in a systematic way. But such reporters have to be careful about the legal implications of what they do. In recent years the issues of access and contempt—and the court rulings that govern them—have hampered the work of court beat reporters, as well as journalists everywhere. When things are going well, reporters write about the verdicts in criminal and civil trials, court procedure, interesting people who work in and around the courthouse, regular court news, and large scale court problems. The writing itself can best be done simply and directly, avoiding legal jargon and emphasizing the people involved.

Exercises

1. Consult court dockets and select five cases that would make good stories. List why you made your selections and the steps you would follow in getting ready to cover the trial.
2. Spend a day with a judge and write a story on the experience.
3. Spend a day with a prosecuting attorney and write a story on the experience.
4. Spend a day with a defense attorney and write a story on the experience.
5. Cover a court trial from start to finish, making sure to take careful notes on everything that goes on. Consult court records and conduct interviews as necessary. For ease of carrying out this assignment, pick a trial that is a fairly simple one lasting one day or less.

Key Terms for Court Reporting

Access Permission for reporters to cover trials.

Action A legal dispute brought into court for trial.

Admissible Evidence allowed to be used in court.

Affidavit A written declaration made under oath as to the facts in a case under trial.

Alleged Asserted without proof; used to describe a person or a crime before proper trial.

Answer The document in which the defendant answers the claims of the plaintiff.

Appeal The review by a higher court of the actions of a trial court for errors that affect the validity of the trial.

Appearance The act of appearing in court.

Appellate A court with the authority to review the decisions of lower courts.

Argument The presentation of the review of evidence and summation at the end of a case; this takes place after all the evidence is in and both parties have rested their cases.

Arraignment The initial appearance of a defendant before a judge to be identified and informed of constitutional rights and charges against him or her.

Arrest The act of seizing a person because of a suspicion that he or she has committed a crime.

Attorney A person whose profession it is to conduct lawsuits for clients or to advise them in legal matters; also called lawyer.

Bail The payment of money by a defendant to ensure his or her appearance for trial.

Bailiff   The officer of the court who maintains order and serves the jury, making sure jurors are not exposed to outside influences during a trial.

Bar   The legal profession.

Bench   The high desk and chair occupied by a judge at the front of a courtroom that symbolizes the authority of the court.

Bench-bar-press guidelines   Informal rules governing media coverage of trials worked out between judges and news organizations.

Brief   A short summary by an attorney of the facts to be proved in a trial and the law applicable to those facts.

Case   A suit or action of law.

Certiorari   A communication from a higher court to a lower court to send up a case for review to see if the court exceeded its authority.

Chambers   An office in which a judge hears matters not requiring action in open court.

Charge to jury   The judge's instructions to a jury about points of law just before the jury begins deliberations.

Circumstantial evidence   Indirect evidence in a trial where the court infers or accepts a fact based on a set of known or proven circumstances.

Civil case   A lawsuit between persons in their private capacities or relations, or when a government sues an individual under the law and is not prosecuting a criminal charge.

Clerk   The officer of the court who keeps all records.

Complaint   The document in which the person who brings the lawsuit sets forth his or her claims against the defendant.

Confession   An admission of guilt by a person charged with a crime.

Contempt   Willful disobedience to, or disrespect of, a court, for which a judge can punish.

Continuance   The postponement of a legal proceeding.

Continue   To keep a matter before a court in a pending status.

Co-respondent   A joint defendant charged with the respondent in a case.

Coroner   A public official with the job of investigating any death not clearly resulting from natural causes.

Corpus delicti   The basic element in a crime, like a death of a murdered person.

Counsel   A lawyer.

Court order   An order by a judge directing that something be done.

Court reporter   The officer of a court who takes down everything that happens in a trial as a permanent record.

Courtroom   A room in which sessions of a law court are held.

Criminal case   Cases in which individuals or organizations are charged with breaking a criminal law; the charges are brought in the name of a government entity, and the jury is asked to return a verdict of guilty or not guilty.

Cross-examination   The questions that a lawyer puts to the opposing party and his or her witnesses.

Defendant   The person in a civil case against whom the lawsuit is brought; in a criminal case the defendant is the person charged with an offense.

Defense A defendant and his or her attorney.

Demurrer The pleading in a case that the facts alleged by an opposing party have not been borne out.

Deposition Testimony written out in a question-and-answer form just as it would have been given in court; taken of a person not able to come into court.

Direct evidence An eyewitness account of events related to the matter on trial.

Discovery Additional information sought by attorneys before a trial begins.

District attorney An officer who acts as the attorney for the government within a specific jurisdiction.

Docket A list of cases in court for trial.

Double jeopardy The rule specifying that in a criminal case no one can be tried for the same crime twice.

Due process A limitation in both the U.S. and the state constitutions that restrains the actions of courts within the limitations of fairness.

Evidence Information presented to a court by one side or the other.

Examination Questions that lawyers ask their own clients and witnesses.

Exhibit An object like a photograph, book, or letter received as evidence in a trial and taken to the jury room during deliberations.

Expert witness A witness who provides information in a trial because of his or her expertise in a field important to the case.

Felon A person who has committed a felony.

Felony Offenses like murder or burglary that are of a graver nature than misdemeanors.

"For cause" Reasons for which a prospective juror can be dismissed involving bias or an inability to be impartial.

Foreman The person who gives the verdict of a jury to the clerk who gives it to the judge.

Grand jury A jury designated to inquire into alleged violations of the law to ascertain whether the evidence warrants trial.

Guilty One of two verdicts in a trial, subjecting a defendant to imprisonment or fine or both.

Habeas corpus A legal means to compel law enforcement officers to bring a charge against an arrested person or release him or her from custody.

Hearsay evidence An off-the-stand statement made by someone who is not in court and therefore not able to take the stand and be questioned; not considered reliable for use in court.

Hung jury A jury whose members cannot agree on a verdict; the case will be retried or dropped.

In camera Actions that take place in the privacy of a judge's chambers.

Indictment The process or document that charges someone with an offense or crime after investigation by a grand jury.

Information A document filed with a superior court by the district attorney that lists a specific crime and the specific law that was violated.

Injunction   A court order requiring a person or corporation to do or refrain from doing a particular act.

Innocent   One of two verdicts in a trial, freeing a defendant from punishment.

Issue   A point in question or matter of dispute in a lawsuit.

Judge   Presiding officer of a court.

Judgment   The judicial decision in a case by a court.

Jurisdiction   The right, power, or authority to administer justice.

Jury   A body of persons sworn to render a verdict in a trial.

Jury panel   The large group of citizens selected from the lists of registered voters from whom individual jurors are picked for trials.

Justice   A judge in a high court.

Juvenile court   Courts that handle crimes committed by, and against, children.

Lawsuit   The prosecution of a claim in a court of law.

Lawyer   A person whose profession is to conduct lawsuits for clients or to advise or act for them in legal matters.

Malice   Evil intent or motive.

Mandamus   A writ from a superior court commanding that a specific thing be done.

Misdemeanor   A criminal offense that is less serious than a felony.

Motion   A proposal made during a trial to change a major aspect of the trial (suppress evidence, set aside information, or dismiss the case).

Motive   The reason a person commits a crime.

Nolo contendere   A defendant's pleading that does not admit guilt but subjects him or her to punishment as though he or she had pleaded guilty.

Oath   A pledge in open court with a hand on the Bible by a witness to tell the truth in testimony.

Objection   A lawyer's formal protest to what the lawyer on the other side has said during questioning in a trial.

Objection overruled   The judge's ruling that the lawyer's objection is not well taken under rules of law during a trial.

Objection sustained   The judge's ruling that a lawyer's objection is well taken under the rules of law.

Open court   The courtroom when a trial is going on.

Opening statement   The first statement by both sides in a trial telling judge and jury the issues in the case and what the evidence will show.

Out of court   Settlement of a matter without going to trial.

Parole   The conditional release of a person from prison prior to the end of a maximum sentence imposed.

Party   A person in a legal dispute.

Peremptory challenges   The ability of an attorney to dismiss a prospective juror without giving a reason.

Plaintiff   The person who starts a lawsuit.

Plea bargaining A practice in which a criminal defendant is allowed to plead guilty to a lesser charge under certain conditions without a trial, usually resulting in a more lenient sentence.

Plead The act of putting forward a plea in court.

Pretrial The period before a trial during which preparations are being made for the trial at the same time motions are being filed to halt it.

Prior restraint A court order banning publication of unpublished material.

Probable cause Reasonable grounds for belief, in a criminal case, that the accused is guilty of a crime; in a civil case that grounds for legal action exist.

Probate The legal process in which a will is proven authentic and valid.

Probation A method of dealing with offenders that allows them to remain free under supervision of a probation officer.

Pro bono publico The willingness of attorneys to work without a fee because they consider the case to be for the public good.

Prosecution The officials carrying out legal proceedings against a defendant.

Re-arraignment The arraigning of a defendant after the preliminary hearing.

Reasonable doubt The guideline that states that jurors must have no doubt that a defendant in a criminal case is guilty.

Recidivism Repeated or habitual relapse into crime.

Record The pleadings, exhibits, and word-for-word record made by the court reporter of all proceedings in a trial.

Remand To send a prisoner back into custody to await further legal proceedings.

Reply The document in which the plaintiff answers any claims made by the defendant in his or her answer to the court.

Rest To conclude the evidence to be introduced in that stage of the trial.

Search warrant A court order permitting an examination of a private dwelling or office by police officials looking for evidence.

Sentence A judicial determination of punishment.

Sequester To keep a jury from outside influences while it is deliberating to reach a verdict in a trial.

Shield law A law that protects reporters from divulging their notes and source names to law enforcement officers.

Striking testimony An order by a judge for the jury to disregard testimony and to have the testimony taken out of the court record.

Subpoena A document issued by a judge and served on a witness to compel his or her appearance in court.

Suit The prosecution of a claim in a court of law; a lawsuit.

Summary judgment A judgment, as in an action for debt, that is entered without the necessity of any jury trial, based on affidavits of the creditors and debtor, that convince the court there is no arguable issue.

Summons An order to appear before a court.

Testimony   The statement made by a witness under oath, usually in court.

Trial   The hearing of evidence and testimony and eventual verdict in a criminal or civil case in a court of law.

Venue   The place where a jury is gathered and a trial is held.

Verdict   The finding made by the jury on the issues submitted to it in a trial.

Voir dire   Preliminary questions and answers put by attorneys to prospective jurors at the beginning of a trial.

Warrant   A legal writ authorizing the police to search, arrest, or seize.

Witness   A person who is present at an occurrence and is able to attest to what took place in a court during a trial.

Writ   A court order requiring a person to do or refrain from doing a specific thing.

Additional Reading on Police and Courts

Adams, Thomas. *Law Enforcement: An Introduction to the Police Role in the Criminal Justice System*. 2nd ed. Englewood Cliffs, NJ: Prentice-Hall, 1973.

Ahern, James F. *Police in Trouble: Our Frightening Crisis in Law Enforcement*. New York: Dutton, 1974.

Anderson, David C. *Crimes of Justice*. New York: Times Books, 1988.

Ashley, Paul P. *Say It Safely*. 5th ed. Seattle: University of Washington Press, 1976.

Bantor, Michael. *Policemen in the Community*. New York: Basic Books, 1965.

Bayler, David. *Police and Society*. Beverly Hills, CA: Sage, 1977.

Bent, Alan E., and Ralph Rossin. *Police, Criminal Justice and the Community*. New York: Harper & Row, 1976.

Brill, Steven and Karen McCoy, eds. *Trial by Jury*. New York: Simon & Schuster, 1990.

Buchanan, Edna. *The Corpse Had a Familiar Face*. New York: Random House, 1987.

Capote, Truman. *In Cold Blood*. New York: Random House, 1965.

Clark, Ramsey. *Crime in America*. New York: Simon & Schuster, 1970.

Cooper, Lynn and Anthony Platt. *Policing America*. Englewood Cliffs, NJ: Prentice-Hall, 1974.

Davidson, Philip L. *SWAT*. Springfield, IL: C.C. Thomas, 1979.

Denniston, Lyle W. *The Reporter and the Law: Techniques of Covering the Courts*. New York: Hastings House, 1980.

Eldefonso, Edward. *Principles of Law Enforcement*. 3rd ed. New York: John Wiley and Sons, 1974.

Franklin, Marc A. *The Dynamics of American Law*. Mineloa, N.Y.: Foundation Press, 1968.

Hirschfeld, Neal. *Homicide Cop*. New York: Berkeley Books, 1982.

Kalmsnoff, Alan. *Criminal Justice*. Boston: Little, Brown, 1976.

Kenney, John P. *Police Administration*. Springfield, IL: C.C. Thomas, 1957.

Kinnare, Adrian. *Policing*. Chicago: Nelson-Hall, 1979.

Kivitny, Jonathan. *Vicious Circles*. New York: Norton, 1981.

Lockhart, William B., Yale Kamisar, and Jesse H. Choper. *Cases and Materials on Constitutional Rights and Liberties*. St. Paul, MN: West Publishing, 1964.

Lynch, Ronald. *The Police Manager*. 2nd ed. Boston: Holbrook Press, 1976.

Maas, Peter. *Serpico*. New York: Viking Press, 1973.

Manning, Peter K. *Police Work: The Sociological Organization of Policing*. Cambridge, MA: MIT Press, 1977.

Menninger, Karl. *The Crime of Punishment*. New York: Viking Press, 1968.

The News Media and the Law. Washington, DC: Reporters Committee for Freedom of the Press. Published five times a year.

Pember, Don R. *Mass Media Law*. 4th ed. Dubuque, IA: Wm. C. Brown, 1987.

Pepinsky, Harold. *Crime Control Strategies*. New York: Oxford University Press, 1980.

Pileggi, Nicholas. *Wiseguy*. New York: Pocket Books, 1987.

Pickerell, Albert G., ed. *The Courts and the News Media*. 3rd ed. San Francisco, CA: Judges Association, 1980.

Silberman, Charles. *Criminal Violence*. New York: Random House, 1980.

Sullivan, John L. *Introduction to Police Science*. New York: McGraw-Hill, 1976.

United States Reports. Washington, DC: Government Printing Office, 1970 to present.

Wambaugh, Joseph. *The Onion Field*. New York: Delacorte Press, 1973.

Woodward, Bob and Scott Armstrong. *The Brethren*. New York: Simon & Schuster, 1979.

IV Science and Medicine

The beautiful thing we can experience is the mysterious. It is the source of true art and science.

—Albert Einstein

Fortune teller at state fair, Donaldsonville, Louisiana, 1938 by Russell Lee.
[*Courtesy U.S. Farm Security Administration Collection, Prints and Photographs Division, Library of Congress*]

9

Science

*To explain the popularity of scientific writing we would probably
have to call upon an essential fact of human nature. People simply
are curious about the world they live in. Perhaps they believe that if
they understand it, they control it; perhaps they enjoy understanding
it just as they would enjoy seeing a good film or listening to a
symphony orchestra.*

—Mary Elizabeth Bowen and Joseph A. Mazzeo
Writing About Science

One Science Reporter

Among ten stories by John Noble Wilford submitted by his editors
at the *New York Times* to the Pulitzer Prize Committee in 1984 for
consideration in the national reporting category was one on how
Pioneer 10 became the first spacecraft to leave the solar system.
Although the judges didn't single out that or any other story in

awarding Wilford's prize, he later heard "that was the one that turned them on."

In retrospect, the longtime *Times* science correspondent thinks he knows why: "I was writing as if I was on board. I try to start all my stories in the most interesting way possible because I don't want to do all of this work without having anyone read it."

The article conveyed to readers the spirit of adventure inherent in the idea of a tiny spacecraft flying out beyond current frontiers to the dark depths of space. In so doing, Wilford transmitted this spirit and excitement to his readers, something he always tries to do. "I guess the little boy still in me comes out," he says. "What interests me, the subjects I gravitate to, I approach from the standpoint of the layman I am. I write my stories in a way that all other laymen can understand."

Wilford expanded upon this idea in the first edition of this book: "The discovery is the most interesting aspect of science reporting. Some of it is the romantic in you. In many senses science is the frontier we're working on these days. There's no more Pacific Ocean or the interior of Africa to explore. Geographically, you have Antarctica and space. Intellectually, you have the frontier of trying to understand nature. . . . Some science writers may be more intellectual. They like the idea of being experts. I don't consider myself an expert. I still consider myself a general assignment reporter who happens to be covering science."

John Wilford did not begin his journalism career as a science reporter. With a master's degree in political science from Syracuse University, he wanted to write about politics. He was hired for a six-month internship by the *Wall Street Journal* and later went full-time.

He left the *Journal* for *Time* and his old love, political writing. But each time the medical writer went on vacation, Wilford was asked to fill in. The same thing happened when the science writer was away.

"The first time I did science writing I found it a lot more fascinating than medical writing," he recalls. "This was the early days of *Gemini* and *Mariner*. Space was bubbling. Within six months I had done four covers, three on space. I got really excited."

After three and a half years at *Time*, Wilford was hired by Harrison Salisbury, a *New York Times* assistant managing editor, to cover the space program from that point in 1965 to the landing on the moon.

At the end of 1973 Wilford was named assistant national editor with the responsibility for running the weekend desk. In 1975 he was named to the position of director of science news. In this job he presided over the creation in November 1978 of a weekly section called "Science Times."

Before this section was started, the newspaper had never had a showcase for science news. Stories were scattered throughout the paper. Although the section was an immediate success, the job of managing it took Wilford away from writing.

"With eighteen columns to fill every Tuesday, I had no time to write," he says. He asked to become a science correspondent and was so named in the summer of 1979. "Once you establish yourself and they [the editors] trust you, you can write a pretty nice ticket for yourself."

In the last five years, he has spent less time on the space program coverage that used to occupy more than half of his time. "In space, I do mostly the science end of missions," he says. "Another reporter tracks the politics of space and many of the actual missions." For example, he covered two missions of the space shuttle in 1991, an April flight during which an observatory was deployed to study gamma rays, and a September flight in which a satellite was deployed in high orbit to study how, where, and why the ozone is created and destroyed. In such instances, he also covers the launch at Cape Canaveral. Unlike the early days of the space program, however, the *Times* does not send a large team of people to record every aspect.

Wilford has been gravitating toward stories in archaeology, paleontology, and astronomy, subjects he thinks include "a sense of exploration. The common thread is exploration, exploring the cosmos or time and space with a sense of history. My main interest is history, which I have enjoyed since college. I got into science writing because of *Sputnik* [the first space satellite launched by the Soviet Union in 1957]. This led me to space exploration and then to exploration in general, which is part of history. I find more continuity to what I'm doing than seems apparent at first glance. I've created my own beat. My beat has evolved as I've evolved.

"I find people genuinely interested in astronomy, archaeology, and paleontology and I think it has to do with a fundamental desire to know who we are and where we come from. It puts into perspective how the whole universe evolved and how species evolved. Archaeology is the history of human civilization. We are all exploring our place in the universe."

Sometimes this interest can take him to some rather remote places which, at first glance, don't seem very scientific.

In June of 1991, Wilford spent a month in Mongolia with a paleontological expedition from the American Museum of Natural History. In this instance, he was on assignment for the *New York*

Times Sunday Magazine, which paid his expenses. The article told the story of how a team of scientists from the museum picked up a search for fossils begun in the 1920s by Roy Chapman Andrews and abandoned for political reasons as Mongolia closed its borders to foreigners after the communists took over in that decade. Wilford traveled to Ulan Bator and out into the Gobi Desert reoccupying old sites and seeing "what it is like to hunt fossils in an exotic land," he says, "how romantic it is and how dreary, tedious, and hard the work is."

Wilford takes the subway from his apartment in Greenwich Village to the Times Building on West Forty-Third Street where he arrives in his office on the fourth floor at about 10 A.M. If he is going to be writing a story that day—for the weekly section or a breaking story—he confers with his editor and then often spends the first two hours on the telephone interviewing sources.

He does most of his reporting on the phone, "because it is more efficient to do it that way. I prefer to travel when possible so every six weeks or so, I take a trip somewhere. If I'm doing a story on the process of science, it's so much better to talk to the scientist in person in a lab or in the field. I feel refreshed and do a better story because I get some of the color instead of generating the color vicariously."

(Ironically, he did the reporting for his Pulitzer Prize-winning story on *Pioneer 10* over the telephone, however. "One of the PR guys at NASA's Ames Research Lab in California called me up the week before and said that *Pioneer 10* was approaching the orbit of Pluto," he recalls. "When it passed that, it would become the first spacecraft to leave the solar system. They were going to have a little ceremony commemorating that and the tenth anniversary of the spacecraft and wondered if I wanted to do a story. That sounded great to me so I called scientists who had been part of the project and who I had interviewed before. I knew these people. I also had my own sense of nostalgia about *Pioneer 10*.")

After completing his telephone interviews, Wilford may consult his files for background or go to the extensive *Times* library. He keeps his files at the office and his home and regularly saves articles and clippings in folders on the broad subjects that interest him— archaeology, space science, the space shuttle. "When I'm doing an archaeology piece, one of the first things I'll do is go to the library and look at the encyclopedia. I'll read whatever I can on whatever I'm writing about, whether it's the archaeology of Troy or the Mayans. I try to do that before talking to the scientists involved to get into the right frame of mind, to get some sense of the background and problems of interpreting what happened in Troy or caused the collapse of the Mayans. What you learn when talking to people and how you advance the story by what you knew before are part of the work and function of a science writer. You extend personal knowledge and pass it on to others."

If he has a story due that day, Wilford begins writing by 1:30 or 2 P.M. Calls from sources he could not reach earlier may still be coming in as he composes. He finishes by 5 P.M. and leaves for home by 7 P.M. The usual deadline for the Tuesday section is the previous Thursday night. It is 5 P.M. for a spot news story. During lulls in the day's routine as he waits for calls or editors to check his copy he thumbs through a number of technical journals, both to educate himself and to get story ideas. For example, a 1991 story on whether the government of Israel was doing enough to preserve the Temple Mount ruins in Jerusalem came from an article in *Biblical Archaeology Review.*

Because he has to get approval from the science section editor before starting a story, Wilford is constantly proposing ideas. "You see something in a journal or a press release from a university or an article in a competing newspaper — there are all sorts of sources for ideas," he says. "When you decide you have an idea whose time has come because of some event or because the paper hasn't done anything on an important subject, the editor relies on you to tell him." Editors may also assign stories based on what they've seen in journals or a competing publication or because of a major news event associated with science.

The science staff meets every Tuesday morning to talk about next week's section. "Each of us tells what we're doing, how and what we plan to do," he says. "We talk about spot stories and talk out our ideas to get feedback and be informed so we don't trample on each other, because several beats overlap."

Most of the time, Wilford himself decides what he will write about. "You turn yourself down," he says. "I reject at least half of the ideas I have before I present them to the editors, ideas I put on the back burner. Sometimes, the editors are cool to an idea or interested in my doing something else. They always jiggle ideas from all reporters. They want a good mix, an article lending itself to illustration, or a news story, or a feature to go at the bottom of the page, and a hard science story and a political piece, and one on medicine."

(In his spare time, Wilford has written five books — covering the Apollo moon landing, mapmakers, dinosaurs, Mars, and most recently, Christopher Columbus on the five hundredth anniversary of his discovery of America.)

Few newspapers in the United States can equal the commitment of the *New York Times* to science coverage. The science news department there consists of a science editor, deputy, assistant editor, an art director, twelve reporters in New York and two in Washington. The staff is responsible for producing a weekly science section every Tuesday and covering breaking science stories as they happen.

Wilford thinks the current decline both in number of specialized magazines devoted to science and in willingness of all but a few large newspapers to hire reporters to cover the subject on a regular basis results from several factors. "The amount of coverage was abnormally high ten or twelve years ago," he says. "We started our section in 1978 and a lot of other newspapers started science pages a year or two after. Time Inc. founded *Discover*. This was probably an overreaction. There wasn't the readership or the advertisers to support them. There has been a retrenchment since then and fewer science publications. It's probably more in tune now with what the public will sit still for. The public has a short attention span, as TV knows and takes advantage of. Most science stories you can't tell in 500 words or one minute on radio or TV. It shows the launch of the shuttle or a problem with some drug and then breezes off to something else. There is a readership for longer, more thoughtful pieces on science and that readership is served by the *New York Times* and a few other publications. There are so many demands on their time, it's hard to get people's attention."

Background to Science Reporting

Even though their lives have been affected by several hundred years of scientific discovery, most people know little about the discoveries of Louis Pasteur, Charles Darwin, Marie Curie, Sir Isaac Newton, Albert Einstein, Jonas Salk, or countless other scientists of the past and present.

The same situation prevailed at the time these scientists were working, largely because the public had heard nothing about them and their work. Except for an occasional sensationally written news story, the press did not cover science.

This omission came about because editors and publishers believed crime stories sold papers and because reporters were often too inexperienced to write about anything else but crime.

Nevertheless, as early as the colonial period, science news did appear now and then in newspapers in the United States. Benjamin Franklin wrote about his electric kite experiment in an issue of the *Pennsylvania Gazette* in 1752. The 1753 edition of his *Poor*

Richard's Almanac contained an article on "How to Secure Houses, etc., From Lightning."

Nearly a century later during the penny press era in New York, editors discovered that some science could sometimes sell papers if it was presented outrageously enough. In 1835, according to journalism professor Hillier Kreighbaum, the *New York Sun* published a series of seven articles on "Great Astronomical Discoveries, lately made by Sir John Herschel at the Cape of Good Hope." The articles, written by Richard Adams Locke, described bat-like men and women who were said to inhabit the moon. The material in the articles was later proven to be fake.

As legitimate scientific and technological discoveries were made, however, they got only brief mention. The first run of Robert Fulton's steamboat from New York City to Albany in 1807, the operation of the first railroad car by steam in Baltimore in 1830, the invention of the telegraph by Samuel F.B. Morse in 1844, and the public display of the first telephone by Alexander Graham Bell in 1876 all got scant attention in the newspapers of the day.

As early as 1860 the *New York Times* was devoting space to the coverage of science; many of the stories were written by John Swinton, one of the paper's editorial writers. In 1860 the newspaper gave three to four columns a day to a meeting of the American Scientists Association at Newport, Rhode Island.

A *Times* competitor was using science news as a way to build circulation. James Gordon Bennett had been the first editor to see the value of police reporting in the pages of the *New York Herald*. His son, James Gordon Bennett, Jr., took over as *Herald* editor and turned his attention to scientific discovery in 1869 in an assignment to his chief foreign correspondent, Henry M. Stanley.

For two years Stanley had been sending interesting stories to the *Herald* from Abyssinia, the Near East, the Balkans, and Spain. On October 16, 1869, he got a terse wire from Bennett: "Come to Paris on important business. J.G. Bennett."

He met his publisher in a hotel suite, and Bennett got right to the point.

"I have important business on hand for you," Bennett told his correspondent. "Where do you think Livingstone is?"

"I really do not know sir."

"Do you think he is alive?"

"He may be, and he may not be."

"Well, I think he is alive, and that he can be found, and I am going to send you to find him."

David Livingstone, a Scotch-Presbyterian missionary and explorer who had kept readers in Europe informed and interested in the results of his travels for thirty years, had dropped from sight earlier that year. He was presumed dead, but no person or group—including the Royal Geographical Society under whose auspices he was exploring—had done anything to find out.

Always able to sense a good story, Bennett decided to fill the void with Stanley's trip. The stunned correspondent protested the difficulty and the cost, but his employer paid no attention. He insisted the reporter go.

Stanley went to Egypt on his way and covered the opening of the Suez Canal on November 17, 1869. He spent thirteen months doing other stories on the Near East and arrived in Zanzibar on the African coast on December 31, 1870. With only eighty dollars and much doubt about whether Livingstone was even alive, Stanley had put together a small expedition by the following March.

The correspondent described his expedition as "a compact little force of three whites, 31 armed freemen of Zanzibar as escort, 153 porters, and 27 pack animals for a transport corps, besides two riding horses."

Despite bouts with fever and warring tribes, the Stanley force pressed on. By September, one of his white companions had died, forty men had deserted, and all but two of the pack animals were dead. After marching south for twenty-six days they heard of a white man, elderly and gray headed, living nearby.

On November 10, 1871, Stanley found Livingstone.

Stanley wrote a series of articles about the explorer and the then unknown interior of Africa. The *Herald* financed Livingstone's explorations for the next year and a half. Until his death in early 1873, Livingstone sent accounts of his travels back to the newspaper.

Bennett's father's rival, Horace Greeley, had long covered science in a less sensational way in his *New York Tribune*. He wrote a series of articles on "What I Know About Farming," and the paper's reporters wrote about other scientific news. After Greeley's death, the *Tribune* began a weekly column called "Science for the People" on March 3, 1877.

On December 21, 1878, the *New York Herald* headlined a great science story: EDISON'S LIGHT. THE GREAT INVENTOR'S TRIUMPH IN ELECTRIC ILLUMINATION. IT MAKES A LIGHT, WITH-OUT GAS OR FLAME, CHEAPER THAN OIL.

In their frenzied competition for circulation in the 1890s, Joseph Pulitzer's *New York World* and William Randolph Hearst's *New York Journal* often used science and pseudoscientific events to attract readers. However, according to Kreighbaum, the exaggeration of this writing caused a setback in science reporting that lasted long afterward. Scientists could not forget—or forgive—the sensationalized treatment of their work in newspapers. The stigma against science writing persisted for years.

Morrill Goddard, Sunday editor of the *World*, who later moved to the *Journal*, had this formula for a Sunday supplement page using science as the subject:

> Suppose it's Halley's comet. Well, first you have a half-page of decoration showing the comet, with historical pictures of previous appearances thrown in. If you can work a pretty girl into the decoration, so much the better. If not, get some good nightmare idea like the inhabitants of Mars watching it pass. Then you want a quarter of a page of big-type heads — snappy. Then four inches of story written off the bat. Then a picture of Professor Halley down here and another of Professor Lowell up there, and a two-column boxed freak containing a scientific opinion, which nobody will understand, just to give it class. (Oliver Carlson and Ernest Sutherland Bates, *Hearst: Lord of San Simeon*. New York: Viking Press, 1936, p. 77.) Reprinted by permission.

The selection of Carr V. Van Anda as managing editor of the *New York Times* in 1904 brought serious coverage of science back to American newspapers. Van Anda and E.W. Scripps of the Scripps-Howard chain were the first modern editors to see the value of science news and the first to give it space.

When he began, Van Anda had trouble getting scientists to agree to be interviewed by his reporters. They had seen their discoveries treated lightly and sensationally in the past. Although Van Anda had respect for science as a subject to be covered, he had few specialized reporters to choose from as he assembled a staff.

The *Times* led in reporting about the opening of the tomb of King Tutankhamen in Egypt in 1922. Van Anda bought the rights of the *Times* of London to print its journalist's account of the entry into the tomb. The managing editor put the story on page one, and it had quite an impact. The account of the king and queen, still reasonably intact after three thousand years, and their jewels and gold furniture made the entire country conscious of King Tut in much the same way that a nationwide tour of some of the tomb's treasures would capture public attention in 1978 and 1979.

Later in 1922 Van Anda assigned reporter Alva Johnston to cover the annual meeting of the American Association for the Advancement of Science in Cambridge, Massachusetts. As science reporters in later years would discover, Johnston had trouble covering the separate sessions that were occurring simultaneously. He ran from one group session to another, grabbing the papers on subjects of the most likely popular appeal. Taking out all the technical words, he turned the papers into newspaper stories.

Without really knowing what he had, Johnston reported the first story in any publication on atomic energy research under the headline: SCIENTISTS WITNESS SMASH-UP OF ATOMS. The story included words like "isotopes" and "alpha particles," all new to the general public.

The series received great readership because it revealed so much information that was new to the general public. And, to show how big a part luck and timing play in journalism, the articles won a Pulitzer Prize for Johnston.

By the early 1930s a small group of science writers was regularly reporting science news for the Associated Press and several New York newspapers. They fought for the time to do their stories and the space in which to print them. It was through their efforts that suspicious and reticent scientists eventually learned to trust the more responsible science writers.

The scientific and technological developments of World War II created a need for more science writers. First radar and then the atomic bomb had to be reported and explained to the general public.

Again the *New York Times* led the way, largely through the work of science reporter William L. Laurence. In April 1945 the reporter disappeared from the newspaper's office without explanation. Because Laurence had written about atomic research as early as 1939, the government asked him to become the historian of the Manhattan Project, the highly secret government unit working to build an atomic bomb. Laurence witnessed many early tests, interviewed all the scientists taking part in the effort, and was aboard the plane that dropped the second bomb on Nagasaki. After months of working in secret, Laurence was able to report one of the biggest science stories of all time.

Continued scientific and technological developments after World War II added to the demand for writers and reporters to explain them to the general public. An early proponent of the need for scientists to communicate details of their work to writers and, eventually, to the public was C.P. Snow, British scientist, novelist, and government official. In a series of influential lectures at Cambridge University in 1959, later collected in a book, *The Two Cultures and the Scientific Revolution*, Snow decried the lack of "our ability to understand, control, and use certain features of the natural world," given the modern dangers brought on by technology. He went on to note the problems that arise when the two cultures of his title — scientists and writers — can't or don't communicate.

"In a time when science is determining much of our destiny," he later wrote in *The Two Cultures: A Second Look*, "that is, whether we live or die, it is dangerous in the most practical terms. Scientists can give bad advice and decision-makers can't know whether it's good or bad. . . . Escaping the dangers of applied science is one thing. Doing the simple and manifest good which applied science has put in our power is another, more difficult, more demanding of human qualities, and in the long run far more enriching to us all. It will need energy, self-knowledge, new skills. It will need new perceptions into both closed and open politics."

Atomic energy started the trend of letting the public in on scientific secrets that would greatly affect their lives, but it was accelerated greatly by the program to place a man on the moon by the end of the 1960s.

Rarely in history had a country put so many of its resources behind a single national effort in peacetime. After the first Soviet sputnik shocked the country into realizing that it might not be first on the moon, the United States government put a great deal of time and money into the space race. The government was joined in this effort by the American media. Never before had so many science reporters been needed to translate the complicated terminology of the space program into understandable language.

On July 20, 1969, when the crew of *Apollo 11* landed on the moon, 3,697 personnel from print and broadcast journalism had been accredited by the National Aeronautics and Space Administration (NASA) to cover the flight. The other manned flights were equally well covered as was its descendant, the space shuttle.

Since the early 1970s the manned space program has declined, NASA's budget has been regularly cut, and the worth of the space program has been questioned. At the same time the number of science reporters in this country has also declined. This decline corresponds directly with the view held by many editors that the public does not want to read about science to the extent that it did during the height of the space program. According to the Newspaper Advertising Bureau, only 11 percent of American daily newspapers have science editors.

This statistic may not reflect the increasing specialization of such technical coverage, however. Some larger newspapers have focused the attention of their specialized reporters as the need has occurred. For example, a newspaper may now assign an environment reporter to cover science news too, or vice versa. A number of newspapers also employ medical reporters who double as science reporters. On smaller papers science may not be covered at all except for running wire service copy, unless the town is the site of a university.

At the beginning of the 1990s, all major daily newspapers in the

United States and the two major news magazines, *Time* and *Newsweek*, had science reporters. The number of science magazines aimed at the general public had declined, however, with the prestigious but difficult to read *Scientific American* at one end and the more prosaic *Popular Science* at the other. *Omni*, which mixes science articles and science fiction, lay somewhere in between, as did *Discover*, which was started by Time, Inc. in 1980 to great acclaim, but later sold to Family Media, which suspended it in 1991. Later that year, the new Walt Disney magazine operation bought it, raising hopes that *Discover* would get another chance to succeed. Another magazine in this category, although not always considered so, is *National Geographic*, which covers many scientific subjects, but with an orientation toward geography.

The situation for science reporting on television is bleaker. Although each of the three networks employs at least one science correspondent, the air time given to stories is skimpy. The tendency seems to be one of having the science specialists available to cover — or at least comment on — major news stories with scientific aspects. In this regard, environment and energy dominate. The one regular science program on television is "Nova," which has a limited audience because it appears on the Public Broadcast System (PBS).

This dearth of science coverage on all but the national level is not for lack of material to write about. Along with atomic power and the space program, the period since World War II has seen many revolutionary discoveries: transistors, lasers, microchips, personal computers, a vaccine to prevent polio, and DNA as a key to human genes.

These great successes have been accompanied, in recent years anyway, by the failure of a number of big science projects. The failures have been significant enough to raise questions about the overall excellence of science in the United States.

The explosion of the *Challenger* space shuttle in 1986 set in motion a series of delayed missions and other failures at NASA, the worst being an error in the manufacture of the $1.5 billion Hubble telescope which caused its images to be blurry. The claim of two University of Utah scientists that they had achieved cold fusion in their laboratory was proven to be false. Several other eminent scientists were caught in misstatements about their work, including Robert Gallo of the National Institute of Health who was involved in a long argument with a French colleague of the Pasteur Institute over who first discovered the AIDS virus. Activists — from pro-life, anti-genetic engineering, and animal rights groups — have sabotaged scientific projects or gone to court to prevent them.

Noted a 1991 *Time* cover story: "In the U.S., the scientific community is beset by a budget squeeze and bureaucratic demands, internal squabbling, harassment by activists, embarrassing cases of fraud and failure, and the growing alienation of Congress and the public. In the last decade of the twentieth century. U.S. science, once unassailable, finds itself in a virtual state of siege."

Problems and Solutions

Whether they are working full-time on the science beat or doing an occasional story in addition to other reporting duties, science reporters face similar problems. The dilemmas of science reporting revolve around the gathering of material and the processing of the material into interesting, factual, and informative articles. The cycle by which a science writer gets leads for possible stories is explained in Figure 9.1.

This sequence of events is no different from that in any story on any subject. The kind of sources and the complicated nature of most of the subject matter, however, often defy easy comprehension.

Sources

Science stories usually come from a personal interview with a scientist or from coverage of a scientific meeting at which research papers are presented. Contact with both kinds of sources often begin with preliminary information.

In the case of the individual scientist, this contact is in the form of a news release about a research project or a telephone call from a public relations person at a lab or university. The news release or the call will alert the science reporter to a story possibility. In another instance, because the science reporter knows about the work of the scientist through general knowledge of the subject, he or she can set up an interview without the prompting of a release or a call from a PR person.

Scientific meetings serve as story sources in a slightly different manner and over a longer period of time than does the interview with a scientist. A science reporter hears about a meeting when he or she receives a news release describing the names of the principal speakers, subjects, and other major events of the meeting. This release gives the reporter an idea of what to expect and enough basic information to prepare a coverage proposal for his or her editor. As soon as the official program has been printed, the public information person in charge of the meeting will send it to the science reporter.

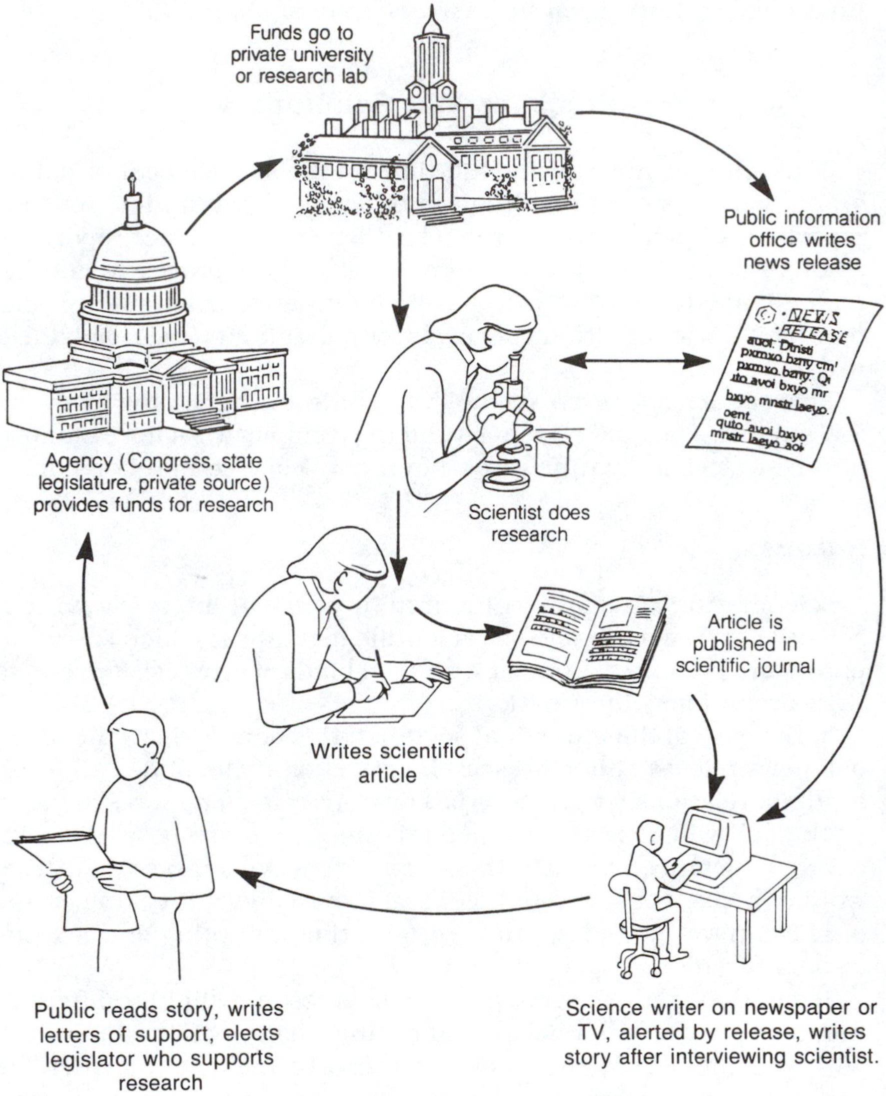
Funds go to private university or research lab
Public information office writes news release
NEWS RELEASE
Agency (Congress, state legislature, private source) provides funds for research
Scientist does research
Article is published in scientific journal
Writes scientific article
Public reads story, writes letters of support, elects legislator who supports research
Science writer on newspaper or TV, alerted by release, writes story after interviewing scientist.

Figure 9.1 **The research cycle**

Well-prepared advanced programs are valuable sources of information because they contain a short synopsis of each paper. Science reporters can use the information in the program to select the papers that seem worthy of coverage. A good PR person can be helpful in this regard by pointing out which papers present anything new and newsworthy. It is to the PR person's benefit to help a science reporter make this determination. No good reporter will be able to devote time and space to a subject that is boring or dated, and a good PR person will know this. A science reporter has to be careful in this regard, however, because scientific research takes place over a long period of time, and a scientist may try to put a new slant to old research each year in a paper to show progress or to renew funding when nothing really new has been found. An alert science reporter will realize this and not be taken in. Every scientific meeting contains these kinds of presentations, despite the best intentions of organizers and PR people.

Once a science reporter arrives at a scientific meeting, he or she must decide how to cover many good sessions when they are going on simultaneously. This can best be done by attending the most interesting ones, sharing information with colleagues, and interviewing scientists about their papers later.

Interviews

An interview with an individual scientist is the best way to gather material for a science story. The scientist is the world's expert on his or her research project, having lived with it day after day for several years. No one else has as much information about the project — information the science reporter needs to write an accurate and complete story.

Several factors work against an easy interplay between the two, however. Many scientists are suspicious of reporters. They or their colleagues have been "burned" by a past association with a reporter. A story was sensationalized or inaccurately reported, and the scientist was embarrassed. No matter that the reporter was untrained in science and bent only on writing a story that would attract attention. Scientists have long memories, and every science reporter who comes in for an interview will remind them of that errant hack who got them into trouble a few years before.

Another problem comes in the peer pressure all scientists feel from other scientists. Scientific research is a very slow, deliberate profession, in which results are arrived at over a long period of time. Few scientists want to reveal results prematurely. They want to wait until they are certain. Journalism does not deal in absolute certainty, only possibilities and promises of certainty. A reporter wants to go into print as soon as possible. If results don't work out or are later altered, that fact can be reported at that time. At least the story will be out — now.

Scientists who think this way will probably get into trouble with other scientists. They will soon be labeled as publicity hungry and perhaps shunned by coworkers. The irony here is that the secrecy imposed upon so much of scientific endeavor limits the public understanding that is so desperately needed to support scientific inquiry both financially and intellectually.

A third factor in this science reporter-scientist confrontation is the requirement by some scientific and technical journals that articles about research results appear in their pages before they go into the popular press. A few even prohibit the mere mention of a subject elsewhere. Because scientists need to publish articles to remain academically certified, they have to agree to cooperate with the journal editors, who themselves seem motivated more by the desire for journalistic exclusiveness than a quest for the sanctity of the scientific process (see Chapter 11).

Some scientists prefer the protected framework of a technical journal, where a number of their peers read the articles in advance and check results, and where the subject is not blown out of proportion, as they sometimes feel it is in the popular press. They resent what they consider premature and sensational reporting of matters before they are precisely sure of results. They decry the reporter's constant search for a "payoff," a result that will be of immediate usefulness and of interest to the public as a consequence. Scientists also worry about the brief space often used to report a story; the technical journals, on the other hand, will give them as many pages as necessary to explain the subject. They also worry because reporters do not let them read the final story before it goes into print or even check back with them about uncertain material. In the eyes of a reporter a word may be changed here and there to make a sentence more readable and understandable. In the mind of a scientist, however, only one thing stands out: "That isn't what I said."

The problems of reporters and scientists dealing with each other have vexed both sides for years. In 1970 thirty-eight scientists and science journalists met at Airlie House in Warrenton, Virginia, to discuss areas of mutual concern under the sponsorship of the Federation of American Societies for Experimental Biology and the National Institutes of Health. Although the meeting took place two decades ago, it still provides a good exploration of the problems between scientists and reporters. Unfortunately, many of the same vexations exist more than twenty years later. And few of the solutions, some admittedly too idealistic to ever work, have been put into practice.

In his opening remarks at that meeting, Arthur J. Snider, science editor of the *Chicago Daily News*, summed up the gaps that exist between the two sides: 1) the lack of access, that is, the tendency of too many scientists to speak only to other scientists and never to the press and the general public; 2) the fragmentation of scientific information into so many narrow disciplines that one source is inadequate and sources from different disciplines disagree; 3) the scientists' use of jargon that obscures and distorts meaning; 4) the scientists' alarm about premature announcement versus the science reporters' need to cover newsworthy items; 5) the lack of accuracy in the translation of a scientist's works into language that a general reader can understand.

Parker A. Small, Jr., a professor of microbiology at the University of Florida College of Medicine, summed up the scientist's point of view:

> The scientist is concerned, quite often over concerned, about sensationalism and premature release of information in the general press, and this clearly inhibits his communication with the journalist. . . . Charles Darwin long ago stated that he cared a great deal about the opinion his fellow scientists had of his work. In my opinion this high regard of, and need for peer approval persists in many scientists today, and is the foundation of much of their fear about lay reports of their work. For example, the "sensational report" of work usually understates or ignores the importance of previous contributors to the subject and as such makes the scientist look to his peers as if he is unaware of the contributions of other scientists, or unwilling to acknowledge his dependence on them. In either case, he loses peer respect. This problem is sometimes compounded by the scientist's ambivalence. On one hand, he would very much like to see his work on the front page of the newspapers. Yet, on the other hand, he is scared stiff it will be misinterpreted and, more important, afraid that even if accurately explained, his colleagues will think less of him. We as scientists must face up to this problem. Many of us have had the experience of having our work reported in an accurate and acceptable way in the lay press, and yet still "caught the raspberries" from our colleagues. I think that is something we as scientists must change.
>
> In addition to the problems presented by the scientist's need for approval by his colleagues and his ambivalence, is his lack of familiarity with the journalist. This results in a lack of

understanding and confidence which can be even further complicated when the scientist finds that the journalist is unwilling to review his article with him before publication. Most scientists would be far more relaxed and cooperative if they understood before the start of the interview the "ground rules" of the interview and especially the reasons for these rules. . . . (Federation Proceedings, Vol. 30, No. 3, May-June 1971, p. 821.) Reprinted by permission.

In the discussion among conference participants, a number of conclusions emerged—some of them practical, some of them overly visionary, few of them now in practice: 1) the scientist has a responsibility to communicate the results of his work to the public as well as to his peers; 2) scientists should take a more active role in criticizing scientific journalism, giving either favorable or adverse comments on science reporting in the general and trade press; 3) scientists need to develop mechanisms that further disseminate the results of their work to the public—for example, local or regional panels of scientists acting as consultants for journalists, or national panels with a similar aim, or ad hoc panels put together by scientific societies on a more formal basis.

The conference closed with a discussion of the responsibilities of the press: 1) science reporters should discuss in advance the ground rules of any interview and the reasons for the ground rules; 2) science articles should contain enough background material to give perspective, clarity, and accuracy; 3) the training process of science writers should be reviewed by the professional science writers' organizations; 4) editors of technical journals need to realize that information presented at open meetings is considered public and can be published in newspapers and magazines without jeopardizing or compromising subsequent publication in the journal; 5) other communicators—like those from television and radio and public information offices at universities and research organizations—need to be included in future discussions.

More suggestions for scientific coverage can be found in "Likely Problems and How to Solve Them" later in this chapter.

How to Cover Science

More practical solutions to the problems of science reporting exist in the manner in which working science reporters like John Noble Wilford conduct their jobs.

1. **A good reputation comes by careful handling of materials.** "Scientists read our stories," says Wilford. "Science

writers get reputations for being trustworthy. If you're careful on one story, you're more apt to get help on another story. It's easier to deal with scientists if you have a reputation of being accurate. A lot of the bad reputation the press gets comes from scientists' dealings with general assignment reporters, people who have neither the background nor the particular interest in the field. Scientists get burned by them. Scientists can tell by your questions if they're dealing with someone who is not going to get it right."

Wilford generally finds scientists receptive to him. "Part of this may be because this is the *New York Times*," he says. "It's easier to open the door if you're from the *New York Times* than the *Sheboygan Gazette*. But science is part of the real world, and the real world is money, and money is Washington, and important people in Washington read the *New York Times*."

2. **Interviews should be planned carefully in advance.** Wilford's preparation for an assignment varies with the assignment. "On space, I don't need as much help as on another subject where I'm going from the standpoint of ignorance," he says. "A lot depends on where the idea came from. Very often the genesis of a story is something that appeared in a journal like *Science* or *Nature*. Another possibility is a press release from a university or government agency." In either of these instances, the background for the interview will come with the reading. He may also check the *Times* morgue (the files of back issues) for other information that might be useful.

He never writes out his questions fully but only jots down three or four things so he won't forget to ask them. "It is a mistake to have a written set of questions," he says. "Questions should follow one from another. If you stick to a rigid list, you let the person feel he's just filling the blanks on your piece of paper."

3. **Knowing the scientist affects the approach.** "If I'm calling someone I already know, I will call out of the blue and ask my questions," he says. "If the subject is space, I probably already know them. When the subject is very much out of the blue, I find it helpful to give them an idea of what I'm doing. Let's say I'm calling a geologist. I say I'm doing a piece and I'd like to talk about geology in general. I let the person know what I'm after so they'll begin to think in those terms. It is also important in the early part of the interview to give the scientist the feeling at what level they should be speaking. For example, I let them know I'm very much new to the subject but give them the feeling I'm not dumb either. A few questions will show him that while I don't know much about magma, I'm not uninformed about the earth's crust."

Because he does 70 percent of his reporting on the telephone, the impression he makes at the start—whether he knows what he wants to ask and asks it—has an important bearing on the end result. "You don't go in person to everyone who contributed to a story," he says. "There is not as much spot news in science as there is in political writing."

4. **Keeping up with science on a general level helps coverage of a specific story and furnishes story ideas.** "There are one or two areas of constant spot news," he says. "A few journals you watch constantly like the *New England Journal of Medicine*, *Science*, and *Nature*. A few government agencies make pronouncements of research results. Because you know other reporters watch the *New England Journal*, as soon as you get a copy, you've got to do your story and be ready to go on the release date."

Wilford also watches important trade publications, which often get an inside track on subjects like space and defense because they cover them so closely. For example, Wilford read in *Aviation Week* about the trip a group of experts from the American Institute of Aeronautics and Astronautics (AIAA) made to China. He called the experts with the help from the AIAA office in New York to get comments on what they had seen. After a day on the telephone he had enough material to write a fairly definitive story on the Chinese space program.

Wilford keeps his own files on many subjects for long periods of time; the files include clippings from other newspapers and magazines and journal articles. He uses that material to prepare story proposals for the director of science news. Because he is the newspaper's expert on the space program, however, he decides what to cover on that subject. "These stories are either dictated by events or are at my suggestions," he says.

With this kind of background, Wilford is able to talk to sources with a combination of confidence and humility. "I say to sources, 'I'm a layman, could you walk me through the steps,' from how to build an airport to how a rocket works," he says. "You have to be modest if you are a science reporter. No one knows everything about everything."

Definitions with which the science reporter should be familiar are contained in "Key Terms for Science Reporting" later in this chapter.

5. **Showing all copy to sources takes too long, but reading certain parts of it on the telephone reduces errors.** Wilford does not show copy to his sources. "You don't have time," he says. "I will read back certain paragraphs I'm worried about. I don't ever read back a whole story. I have read back explanatory paragraphs

to see if I got it right. You occasionally get people who ask if they can review your story, and you have to tell them that is not the way journalism works."

6. **Be careful not to become a "pseudo-scientist."** After a while, an experienced science reporter picks up enough knowledge of science to report and write about many scientific subjects with ease and even without a lot of explanation of difficult terms and processes. There is a danger in this familiarity, however, because it might lull the reporter into thinking he or she is a scientist. When a reporter becomes this "pseudo-scientist," not only will the reporter have abdicated the role as a person probing and questioning, but he or she will have set themselves up for a rather rude awakening. The scientist will never accept a reporter as an equal and will laugh at any who try. And, worse for such reporters is the distinct possibility that they will not get the science story they were after in the first place because they will have become blinded by the aura of science and scientists.

Kinds of Science Stories

The subject of any science story varies with the kinds of scientific work being carried out in the research institution covered by the reporter. Nevertheless, science stories can be categorized as follows:

1. **Research results.** The findings of various research projects constitute the bulk of science beat stories. Gained from news releases and contacts at the institution, the material tells what happened, how the work was done, what its significance is, and the problems encountered and solved.

2. **News of the institution.** Stories about big grants, funding cutbacks, promotions, new building or laboratory construction, management, and other routine happenings are also newsworthy.

3. **Personality profiles.** Features about colorful scientists or institution officials are important parts of the beat. What sets these people apart as scientists and individuals?

4. **Tie-ins with national stories.** Will federal funding cutbacks affect the local institution? Is the local laboratory doing work that is part of a national project?

5. **Explanations of how the scientific process works.** Although they can't be done too often lest they bore readers, stories about the steps in the process of scientific discovery or the steps in an interesting scientific development or experiment make good

background reading from time to time. Explanations of terms are also helpful on occasion—for example, to explain the subject of genetic engineering.

Writing Science Stories

As with most reporters, writing comes sometimes easily for John Noble Wilford and "sometimes with great difficulty. I've got to understand it [the subject of his story] myself. I don't always understand it. What do you do? You've got to be very humble. You say to the source, 'I don't quite understand what you're saying.' You try to get them to go point by point. When they use a big word, you get them to explain it in such a way that readers will understand it."

He explains the technical terms as quickly as possible in a story and tells readers why the subject is important. "This is the way it works," he says of his writing approach. "But I've got to make sure it doesn't read like an encyclopedia. I try to make a narrative out of it. I make sure that in translating technical phrases into English phrases, I didn't simplify too much. A good tool is to find an appropriate figure of speech—something unfamiliar is like something familiar."

"You should keep sentences fairly short because news is supposed to be a little breathless," Wilford says. "Good, muscular English is the best way to write—strong verbs, action verbs. Sentences are best if they march on nouns and verbs rather than adjective or adverbs. The paragraph is an unappreciated structure. So much journalism is using unnatural paragraphs—cut for length, sometimes only one sentence long.

"Trying to have one-thought sentences is very easy. Don't cram too many thoughts into a sentence. It also helps to be a bit slow in understanding things yourself. You know if it took you fifteen minutes on the telephone to understand something, the reader's going to have trouble, too.

"If you make a transition to a narrative form, you will carry the reader better. Use a story to tell a story. One sentence starts it off. A paragraph has a beginning, middle, and end of its own. The end of one paragraph should suggest the transition to the next one. If you do it carefully, you don't need arbitrary, shorthand transitions."

The second story reproduced in this chapter is a good example of the narrative form. It describes a recent development in astronomy within an account of a night spent at an observatory in Arizona.

His Pulitzer Prize-winning story on *Pioneer 10* analyzed here was an instance where the writing came easily. "It was one of those times when you are never able to explain how things worked so well," he says. "That morning, everything clicked. No outline. I didn't consciously write the story beforehand in the 'I am a spacecraft' approach. I knew how I wanted to start it, with the idea of this little vehicle made by man going out so far. I made the decision on how the first two or three grafs would be and this set the theme and tone. The rest of the story flowed from that. When you make those initial decisions, that's where a story takes its own life. By the time you've done that, you've dictated all the decisions."

#1

In his lead, John Wilford uses a storyteller's tone ("far, far away") to bring readers into the adventures of "a hardy little spacecraft." In the next few sentences, he tells them the signifi- cance of what *Pioneer 10* has achieved (no machine has ever gone so far—to the edge of the solar system).

In grafs 2 and 3, he continues to give "gee whiz" elements of the story (the time for messages to get to earth, the difficulty for scientists to discern any- thing). He throws in phrases to keep up the adventure idea ("whispers of dis- covery," "cold and dark and empty").

PIONEER 10 PUSHES BEYOND GOALS, INTO THE UNKNOWN
By John Noble Wilford

1 Out there, far, far away where Earth is a mere pinpoint of light and the Sun is a pale disk of diminishing consequence, a hardy little spacecraft cruises on and on into the unexplored. No machine of human design has ever gone so far. *Pioneer 10* has traveled to the reaches of Pluto, a distance it achieved yesterday, and is advancing toward the edge of the solar system.

2 From out there, now 2.7 billion miles away, *Pioneer*'s eight-watt radio transmitter sends faint messages back to Earth every day, whispers of discovery. The transit time of these reports, traveling at the speed of light, is 4 hours and 16 minutes. And by the time the signals arrive at tracking antennas, they have all but vanished, their strength reduced to 20-billionths of a watt.

3 But scientists with the patience to extract the signals out of the background noise and to decipher their messages are learning for the first time what it is like in the outermost solar system. It is cold and dark and empty, as they knew it must be. A tenuous wind of solar particles, the million-mile-an-hour solar wind, still blows outward. Cosmic rays race inward. A virtual vacuum it may be, but nothingness, it seems, is a relative condition.

In grafs 4, 5, and 6, he forecasts what the spacecraft might do in the future and what it has done since its launch ten years before.

4 If the spacecraft survives long enough and the scientists are clever enough, more exciting discoveries could lie ahead for *Pioneer 10.* It might be able to detect gravity waves, which have been theorized but have never been observed. It might locate the source of the mysterious force tugging at Uranus and Neptune, a gravitational force suggesting the presence of some as yet unseen object—perhaps the long-sought Planet X or a dim companion star to the Sun. The spacecraft may also function long enough to report back the answer to the question, Where does the solar system end and interstellar space begin?

5 "We are constantly entering unexplored territory," says Dr. Aaron Barnes, an astrophysicist at the Ames Research Center in Mountain View, Calif., where the *Pioneer* mission is directed. "We really don't know what we'll learn."

6 Travel was never more broadening. When *Pioneer 10* was launched March 3, 1972, from Cape Canaveral, Fla., no spacecraft had ventured farther than Mars. *Pioneer* made its way safely through the asteroid belt, a region littered with rocky debris between Mars and Jupiter. It flew within 81,000 miles of Jupiter's cloud tops on Dec. 2, 1973, returning the first close-up images of the Sun's largest planet. The picture revealed the cyclonic forces of the Great Red Spot rolling Jupiter's dense hydrogen and helium atmosphere. *Pioneer* made the first detailed observations of Jupiter's powerful radiation belts and discovered that the planet's sphere of magnetic influence extended to the orbit of Saturn, a distance of half a billion miles.

In grafs 7, 8, 9, and 10, Wilford gives readers more about the background of the spacecraft and begins to weave in quotes he has gotten over the telephone from scientists and engineers who worked on the project originally.

7 *Pioneer* had by then accomplished its mission and exceeded its designed 21-- month lifetime. The 500-pound craft had been blasted by Jovian radiation and pelted with micrometeoroids. "No one dreamed then we'd still be hearing from *Pioneer* today," recalls Dr. James A. Van Allen of the University of Iowa, one of the mission's scientists.

8 Still *Pioneer* kept going, its nine-foot dish antenna always cocked in the direction of Earth. It dutifully kept sending home a travelogue on interplanetary space as it crossed the orbit of Saturn in 1976 and the orbit of Uranus in 1979.

9 *Pioneer 10* had now made believers out of its creators, the engineers for the National Aeronautic and Space Administration and the spacecraft manufacturer, TRW Inc. Like the little engine that could, this was the little spacecraft that could probably push on to the frontier of interstellar space and still be living to tell the tale.

10 After more than 11 years in flight, according to Richard D. Fimmel, the project manager at NASA's Ames Research Center, all the craft's scientific instruments, except the magnetometer, are working normally. He estimates that deep-space antennas should maintain communications with *Pioneer* for eight more years, out to a distance of five billion miles. That is when the craft's radio-isotopic power unit will no longer be generating enough electricity for operations.

Leaving Realm of Known Planets

By graf 11, he brings readers back to the present and presents more on the significance of the remarkable *Pioneer 10*.

11 Right now *Pioneer* is, in effect, leaving the realm of the known planets. At 5 P.M. yesterday the craft, traveling 30,613 miles an hour, sped farther out than Pluto. It was then almost 2.8 billion miles from the Sun; Earth is 93 million miles away from the Sun. At the time, however, Pluto was on the other side of the Sun.

12 On June 13, *Pioneer*'s outbound trajectory will cross Neptune's orbit, 2.81 billion miles from the Sun. Normally Pluto is the outermost planet, but because its orbit is highly elliptical, unlike the roughly circular orbits of the other planets, Pluto is now nearer to the Sun than Neptune and will be for the next 17 years.

More "gee whiz" material in grafs 13 and 14 about sending *Pioneer* a message and getting a reply and the scientific data received every day.

13 Each day flight controllers at Ames typically send *Pioneer* a message when they arrive at work. By quitting time eight and a half hours later, which is the round-trip communications time, they receive *Pioneer*'s reply.

14 They also receive about 16 hours of scientific data each day from the spacecraft, mainly information defining the extent and behavior of the heliosphere, the Sun's extended atmosphere. Blowing away in all directions from the Sun is the solar wind, an electrically charged gas composed of protons (hydrogen nuclei) and electrons that stream out from the Sun's corona. The wind carries along with it the Sun's magnetic field.

In graf 15, the reporter uses a meaningful comparison for readers ("blowing a pressure bubble") to describe where the spacecraft is. He sketches in more of the significance of the findings in grafs 16-21 using quotes from experts to help him.

15 It is as if the Sun is blowing a pressure bubble out into space, a tear-shaped magnetic bubble that acts as a barrier against intrusions by most particles from the interstellar medium. The bubble is streamlined by the motion of the solar system through this interstellar gas. At the solar system's leading edge, so to speak, the bubble is blunted. In the opposite direction, the bubble forms a long tail. *Pioneer 10* is traveling down the tail of the heliosphere.

16 Before *Pioneer*, some scientists believed the boundary, the heliopause, might be just beyond Jupiter. But the spacecraft is six times that far out and has yet to encounter the boundary.

17 The spacecraft's instruments indicate the heliosphere "breathes" in and out once every 11-year solar cycle, as reported by Dr. John Simpson, a *Pioneer* experimenter from the University of Chicago. When the Sun is most turbulent, which last occurred in 1980, shock waves from its magnetic storms seem to persist throughout the heliosphere for as long as a year. The effect may be to change the bubble's shape.

18 Moreover, at the time of maximum solar activity, the bubble seems to be more impervious to cosmic rays from out in the galaxy. *Pioneer*'s detectors found the cosmic-ray particles half as numerous then.

19 For the rest of *Pioneer*'s working lifetime, scientists will be monitoring the data for

signs of the boundary crossing. Scientists are not sure what to expect. Dr. Barnes says *Pioneer* would probably encounter changes in the outside temperatures and discernible turbulence as the solar wind was buffeted by the incoming interstellar gases. The speed of the solar wind should drop suddenly from supersonic to subsonic. Dr. Van Allen, however, doubts "anything dramatic" will be observed at the heliopause.

20 Other spacecraft, *Voyager 1* and *Pioneer 11*, may find a sharper boundary. Though not as far from Earth as *Pioneer 10*, they are traveling in an opposite direction, toward the blunt edge of the bubble. Dr. Edward C. Stone of the California Institute of Technology, *Voyager*'s chief scientist, believes the spacecraft should encounter a kind of bow shock caused by the solar wind slamming into the dominant and relatively stationary interstellar environment. It may even be possible to hear the boundary crossing. Energies produced by the interactions may give off whistling noises that *Voyager* will radio back to Earth.

21 Because of its great distance away, *Pioneer 10* could give scientists their first evidence of the existence of gravity waves. According to Einstein's General Theory of Relativity, cataclysms in the universe, collapsing or exploding stars, should send waves of gravitational radiation across the galaxies. Dr. John Anderson of the Jet Propulsion Laboratory says that a painstaking analysis of radio transmissions from *Pioneer* to Earth might reveal the jiggling effects that a gravity wave would have on the craft or Earth itself.

Possible Discovery at the Edge

In graf 22, he describes what the spacecraft's next discovery might be.

22 Accordingly, *Pioneer 10* may lead scientists to the discovery of some massive object toward the edge of the solar system. It may be, as some astronomers suspect, a "brown dwarf" star, a celestial object that was not quite massive enough for its thermonuclear

furnace to ignite. Since most stars are paired, it is not unreasonable to assume that the Sun might have such a dim companion.

23 Or the force could be from a 10th planet, the long-sought Planet X. Evidence assembled in recent years has led several groups of astronomers to renew the search for a large planet out beyond Pluto and Neptune.

By graf 24, he is beginning to wind up and brings readers back to the spacecraft to do so. He notes, in sadness, that it will eventually become "silent and derelict," its radio dead and sensors sightless. In ending this adventurous tale of a valiant and brave little spacecraft he leaves readers with an upbeat thought: the plaque attached to *Pioneer 10* engraved with images of a man and a woman will make it almost eternal.

24 Someday, of course, even the durable *Pioneer 10* will lose touch with those who sent it off on its long journey. The little radio that has already transmitted more than 126 billion bits of scientific data will go dead. Sensors will lose sight of the Sun.

25 Even then, silent and derelict, *Pioneer 10* will cruise on and on, the first human artifact to leave the solar system. About once every million years, as nearly as anyone can calculate such things, the craft might expect to come close to another star system. It might then be found by other intelligent beings.

26 With that eventuality in mind, *Pioneer*'s makers indulged in an act of infinite hubris. They attached a plaque engraved with images of a man and a woman, the location of Earth and some points of basic science — possibly the little spacecraft's ultimate message.

#2

TINY CHIP HELPS HUNT FOR MOONS OF SATURN
By John Noble Wilford

Wilford's dramatic lead immediately captures the attention of readers because of its short, crisp sentences ("Nightfall. It is cold, dry and clear .. Stars appear and fill the sky. . . ."). The reader is with him on the mountaintop.

But what does it all mean? Wilford tells them partially in the second graf by introducing the main source of his story, an astronomer working at the observatory.

1 NIGHTFALL. It is cold, dry and clear atop the Catalina Mountains. A good night, as astronomers say, for "seeing." Stars appear and fill the sky, crisp points of light and smears of cosmic dust, an intimation of infinity.

2 Dr. Bradford A. Smith arrives at the observatory known as Catalina Station (elevation 8,250 feet) around 8 P.M. after a 37-mile drive from the campus of the University of Arizona down in the valley at Tucson. He

unloads a parka, extra sweaters, a supply of computer tapes and a paper bag stuffed with "junk food," all for the night ahead.

By graf 3 he is ready to give readers some science: The subject here is the observation of Saturn by telescope to see if that planet has more moons than was previously thought.

3 Dr. Smith's plan is to observe Saturn, the solar system's most delicately beautiful sight through a telescope. He has reason to believe, based on recent spacecraft data, that Saturn may have several more moons that have gone undiscovered. He wants to find them. And now, tonight and for the next few months, should be the time to look.

Getting an Edge-On View

The scientist thinks he can see them because of Saturn's position (explained in graf 4) and new astronomical technology (explained in graf 5). At the end of this graf Wilford presents the subject of his story: a silicon chip that makes the new observation possible.

4 Once every 13 years, Earth passes through the plane of Saturn's distinctive rings. When this happens, as is happening now, it is possible to view the rings edge-on, which means that they appear as only a faint chalk mark in the telescopic sights. Under these conditions, light reflected off the ice and rocks and whatever else in the rings is minimized and does not wash out the Saturnine neighborhood.

5 Moreover, astronomical technology has moved ahead considerably since 1966, the last time Saturn's rings could be seen edge-on. Attached to the telescope tonight is a camera built around an electronic detector called a charge-coupled device, or C.C.D. It is, Dr. Smith says, "the biggest single advance in astronomy since the invention of the photographic plate back in the 19th century."

In graf 6 he uses the effective technique of comparing a technical item to a more familiar item for clarity. The chip, he writes, is "smaller than a stamp and not much thicker than a piece of photographic film." He goes on in the next graf to discuss its development.

6 The C.C.D. is a rectangular silicon chip, smaller than a stamp and not much thicker than a piece of photographic film. It was developed in the 1960's for the picture telephone, an invention that was shelved. And so was the C.C.D., for a while. Then, NASA got Texas Instruments Inc. to work on an improved C.C.D.

7 The experimental Texas Instruments version that Dr. Smith uses is an array of 250,000 individual microscopic light-sensitive elements, 500 lines of 500 picture elements (pixels) each. When a photon, a

In graf 8 he lets his source explain the chip in direct quotes.

unit of light, hits one of these elements, the energy creates a free electron. The electrons in the many picture elements are read out sequentially to form the picture.

8   "Think of it as an array of little buckets," Dr. Smith explains, holding up a prototype chip. "Five hundred by 500 little buckets sitting there in the silicon, and each bucket, each pixel, will collect some number of electrons in proportion to the light falling on it."

In graf 9 he continues the approach established in the lead — following the astronomer throughout his night at the observatory. ("Dr. Smith greets the other astronomers.") This is the framework from which he digresses at times to expand upon and give background for the new chip.

9   Inside the white dome, up on the observing platform, Dr. Smith greets the other astronomers. They stand in the dim light around the control consoles at the base of the telescope.

In the next seven grafs Wilford reports how the astronomers do their work, almost in a "how-to-do-it" fashion.

10   "It was awful Sunday night, never saw the rings," Stephen M. Larson reports to Dr. Smith. "Better last night, but nothing great. Tonight, it's going to be fairly good. The wind's died down."

11   Wind can mean trouble. Any mixing of hot and cold air causes atmospheric turbulence, a shimmering effect that distorts distant images.

12   One of the first chores is to chill the charge-coupled device. Although temperatures outside — and inside the observatory — hover around freezing, the delicate device must be kept even colder, at a temperature of about 115° below zero Celsius.

13   Eventually, Dr. Smith says, the charge-coupled device will supplant the Vidicon tube in both spacecraft and ground-based astronomy, just as the Vidicon replaced photographic plates and they, a century ago, replaced the astronomers' hand-drawn sketches of the heavens. Among the C.C.D.'s advantages is its efficiency as a collector of light. Its efficiency is better than 50 percent, compared with the Vidicon's 20 percent.

14 Dr. Smith and Mr. Larson, wearing heavy gloves, pour super-cold liquid nitrogen into a container that surrounds the charge-coupled device. This, in effect, all but freezes normal atomic activity in the silicon chip and, therefore, minimizes the spontaneous generation of electrons that would introduce spurious light signals in the image.

15 After the camera is secured to the focal point at the base of the telescope's primary mirror, Dr. Harold J. Reitsema presses a button at the control console and the windscreen and shutter at the top of the dome open slowly, clanking like an electric garage door. There, through the slot, is the starry night. He presses another button and the entire dome rotates a few degrees. The telescope is pointed to the Eastern sky, nitrogen vapors escaping from the camera to give the telescope the appearance of a rocket poised for liftoff.

16 Saturn is not "up" yet and will not be until about 2:30 A.M. So Dr. Ian McLean, a visiting astronomer from the University of Edinburgh, spends the next several hours observing a distant galaxy, an NGC1069. He is studying the polarization of its light in an effort to understand why the galaxy, like many others, has such a bright nucleus compared to its spiral arms.

Wilford brings readers back to the chronology of the night in graf 17 by observing them on their lunch break, during which time they eat spaghetti and "talk astronomy." This very clever construction enables Wilford to digress for the reader and give background in astronomy for the next four grafs.

17 The astronomers take a lunch break shortly after midnight. They leave the dome and walk a short distance down the slope to the dormitory, where they warm up, eat peanut butter sandwiches and canned spaghetti, and talk astronomy. In astronomy, there is some confusion these days about just how many moons are in Saturn's family.

18 Until 1966, the existence of nine Saturnine satellites was well-established, the largest of them Titan, being larger than the planet Mercury. A French astronomer, Anton Dollfus, discovered that year another satellite in the rings. It was named Janus and fittingly it seemed to be two-faced. That is, when the Janus data were re-examined,

Mr. Larson and John W. Fountain, both of the University of Arizona, concluded that two objects — not one — were involved. The second one, still unconfirmed and controversial, was simply designated S-11.

19 Matters grew more confused as *Pioneer 11* flew close by Saturn last September. The spacecraft's imaging system detected what appeared to be another moon. The spacecraft's charged-particle instruments supplied confirming data, but was this a 12th moon or the already hypothesized 11th moon? And where was Janus? It was not seen by *Pioneer 11*.

Telescope Focused on Titan

20 Furthermore, Dr. James A. Van Allen of the University of Iowa, one of the charged-particle experimenters of *Pioneer 11*, reported last month several other "absorption signatures" — sharp drops in the electrons and protons presumably absorbed by a solid object — indicating the possible existence of other small moons near Saturn.

21 Dr. Smith hopes that his ground-based observations will sort out the satellite inventory and provide more accurate orbital plots so that *Voyager 1* will be able to make a more definitive survey during its rendezvous with Saturn next November.

He has them "back in the dome" in graf 22 resuming their work. He uses direct quotes in the next few grafs to tell the reader what they see during three hours of viewing and recording what they see on computer tape.

22 Back in the dome, the astronomers prepare the telescope for Saturn. They replenish the liquid nitrogen around the camera and insert an infrared filter. Dr. Smith, peering through the eyepiece, locates Saturn in the east. There is Mars, ruddy even to the unaided eye below, Jupiter and below Jupiter, at 7 o'clock, Saturn.

23 The telescope is shifted ever so slightly and, there in the eyepiece, is Titan. "You can use Titan for focus," Dr. Smith says to Dr. Reitsema. Titan's light is a coherent point, more suitable than the larger and fuzzier Saturn for focusing.

24 "How's the seeing?" someone asks.

25 "Fair amount of atmospheric excursion," Mr. Larson replies. But the air settles down. "Excursions less," Mr. Larson reports a few minutes later.

26 With Mr. Larson and Dr. Smith taking turns at the eyepiece and with Dr. Reitsema at the controls and Mr. Fountain recording in the log, the astronomers work without ceasing for three hours. They take exposures of 30 seconds, one minute, two minutes and four minutes, all recorded on computer tape. Four fuzzy objects appear on the screen, but they are known satellites, nothing new, no obvious surprises. "If we don't see anything new here," Dr. Smith explains, "it doesn't mean we won't see in when we process the images."

A Business of Patience

Wilford points out that they will not really know what they have seen for several weeks.

27 Discovery in astronomy is seldom immediate. The astronomers at Catalina Station stayed up all night and looked at the neighborhood of Saturn for more than three hours, but it will be several weeks, after much computer-assisted enhancement of the recorded images, before they will know for sure what they have seen — and perhaps discovered.

In the last two grafs Wilford goes back to his main structure of reporting the events of the night and the early morning, making readers feel they are there looking at the "slate blue" sky.

28 Shortly after 6 A.M., the sky brightens to a slate blue. The stars fade back into infinity. But Saturn remains visible for one last look, unmasked, through the eyepiece, a pale yellow like an old and fragile bauble.

His last two sentences are perfect. He returns the reader to the lead ("Nightfall") and completes the circle of the story nicely ("The end of an astronomer's day. Dawn.")

29 Brad Smith walks to the dormitory for some sleep. A dusting of pink appears above the Eastern horizon. The end of an astronomer's day. Dawn.

Science Reporting:
Likely Problems and How to Solve Them

Problem

Solution

1. Difficult material to understand.

1a. Read books and periodicals for background and an understanding of basic terms.

1b. Develop a list of scientists to consult for background information, explanation of terms and processes.

1c. Get on mailing lists of research institutions and companies; appropriate government agencies like the National Science Foundation, NASA, and NOAA (The National Oceanic and Atmospheric Administration); private organizations like the American Association for the Advancement of Science, American Geophysical Union, Federation of Scientists for Experimental Biology, Union of Concerned Scientists; the Senate Committee on Commerce, Science and Transportation, and the House Committee on Science and Technology.

2. Scientists hard to interview (suspicious of reporters and tend to use technical jargon).

2a. Prepare carefully for interviews.

2b. Know enough about the scientist's work to develop intelligent questions.

2c. If all else fails, ask three basic questions that will

evoke enough material from which to write a story: What is the background of your project? What steps did you go through to carry out your research? What is the significance of your research?

3. Scientists refuse to be interviewed because of previous bad experience with a reporter.

3a. Stress public's right to know, especially if the project is publicly funded.

3b. Stress value to public of knowing details of research.

3c. Emphasize need to give you the chance to improve the credibility of all journalists.

4. Inaccurate stories.

4a. Check and recheck all facts and figures.

4b. With especially difficult material, read parts of the story that are unclear to the scientist on the telephone.

5. Dull stories.

5a. Involve readers in the subject by stressing significance to them.

5b. Use meaningful comparisons of a scientific item to a more familiar item, that is, the new device is "bigger than a breadbox."

Summary

Although they have been affected by the work of scientists for several centuries, most people know little about science. It is the job of the science reporter to convey information about scientific discoveries to the public. Beginning in the United States as early as 1752, editors and reporters have tried to tell readers about science, with varying degrees of success. Although a few newspapers like the *New York Times* took a serious approach, most sensationalized science by concentrating on the bizarre and the dramatic. This attracted more readers but alienated scientists for many years thereafter. They resented the fact that reporters and editors viewed their serious work too lightly.

The many scientific advances during World War II, such as the development of atomic energy, and the space program of the 1960s heightened the public's interest in science and created the need for science reporters. The job of the science reporter is interesting and challenging but not without problems. Scientists are hard to interview, and the material to be covered is difficult to understand and convey to general readers. Science stories should be written clearly, concisely, and simply.

Exercises

1. Attend the presentation of a scientific paper by a scientist on campus. Try to get a copy of the paper in advance so you can prepare additional questions to ask the scientist after the presentation, for clarification. Write a story for a general audience.

2. Select a technical article from *Science* magazine and analyze it in the following way: a. determine the subject, source, background to the research, and methodology used; b. select the element that is newsworthy. Then, rewrite the article as a news story for a general audience, using the author of the article as your source. Because you won't be able to interview the scientist, you should use a scientific dictionary to explain all unfamiliar terms.

3. Pick an inanimate object and write a short description of it and how it operates.

4. Interview a scientist at a local university about one of his or her research projects. Ask the scientist to explain the background, methodology, and significance of the work. Write a story for a general audience about what you find out.

5. Write a profile of a scientist and how he or she works. The reporting should involve interviews with the scientist and colleagues, direct observation by you, and background research.

Key Terms for Science Reporting

Aerosol sprays   A liquid substance sealed in a pressurized container for dispersing as a spray or foam. Researchers in atmospheric photochemistry have discovered that the propellants from aerosol spray cans reside for long periods in the atmosphere and circulate to the stratosphere, where they partially destroy the ozone layer and let ultraviolet light from the sun leak down to the earth's surface; this may cause increased skin cancer and possibly destroy microorganisms in the food chain.

American Association for the Advancement of Science   Primary organization of scientists in the United States.

Ancient astronauts   The belief by some scientists that ancient civilizations had contact with extraterrestrial civilizations; they cite archaeological evidence in Egypt, Mexico, and the Easter Islands to prove their point.

Apollo   A three-person spacecraft that traveled to and landed upon the moon.

Asteroid   Any of the thousands of small bodies that revolve around the sun in orbits mostly between Mars and Jupiter.

Astronomy   The science that deals with the material universe beyond Earth's atmosphere.

Astrophysics   The branch of astronomy that deals with the physical properties of celestial bodies.

Atmosphere   The gaseous envelope surrounding the earth or any other celestial body.

Atom   The smallest component of an element having all the properties of the element; consists of an aggregate of protons, neutrons, and electrons.

Atomic energy   Energy released by rearrangements of atomic nuclei, as in nuclear fission.

Biochemistry   The science dealing with the chemistry of living matter.

Biology   The science of life or living matter in all its forms and phenomena.

Biophysics   The branch of biology dealing with the study of biological structures and processes by means of the methods of physics.

Black hole   A region in outer space, hypothetically caused by the collapse of a star, in which the density is so great that even light cannot escape the gravitational force.

Botany   The science of plants and plant life.

Cell   A microscopic plant or animal structure, containing nuclear and cytoplasmic material enclosed by a semipermeable membrane and, in plants, a cell wall.

Chemistry   The science that deals with or investigates the composition, properties, and transformations of substances and various elementary forms of matter.

Chlorophyll   The green coloring matter of leaves and plants; essential in photosynthesis.

Cold fusion   Achieving nuclear fusion — the process by which atoms are fused rather than broken apart as a nuclear reactor does in creating energy — in a test tube; the process usually requires heat of millions of degrees; in 1989, two scientists said they had achieved fusion at low temperature but other scientists were never able to duplicate their results using the technique.

Comets   Celestial bodies moving about the sun; consists of a central mass surrounded by a misty envelope that may form a tail that streams away from the sun.

Computer   An electronic machine capable of accepting and processing data and producing results by carrying out repetitious and highly complex mathematical operations at high speeds.

Cosmology   The study of the origin and general structure of the universe.

Cro-Magnon man   Human being of thirty thousand years ago whose skeletal remains were discovered in 1868; he resembles modern man; six foot or more tall, balanced head, high forehead, large brain, well-developed chin.

Curie, Marie   Polish physicist and chemist who — with her husband, Pierre — was co-discoverer of radium; Nobel prize for physics in 1903 and for chemistry in 1911.

Darwin, Charles   English naturalist who developed the theory of evolution.

Earth   The planet on which humankind lives, third in order from the sun.

Earthquake   A vibration or movement of a part of the earth's surface.

Eclipse   The darkening of the moon's light by the earth's intervention between the moon and the sun; or the darkening of the sun's light by the moon's intervention between the sun and a point on the earth.

Einstein, Albert   American theoretical physicist known for his development of the theory of relativity.

Electricity   A physical agency caused by the motion of electrons, protons, and other charged particles; manifests itself as attraction, repulsion, magnetism, luminosity, and heat.

Electromagnetic   The phenomena associated with the relations between electric current and magnetism.

Entomology   Branch of zoology dealing with insects.

Evolution, theory of   The belief that all living things have acquired their present forms through successive generations; under this theory it is believed that humans are descended from apes.

Extraterrestrial intelligence   The belief that intelligent beings inhabit other planets.

Formaldehyde   A colorless, toxic gas used chiefly in a water or aqueous solution as a disinfectant and preservative.

Fossil fuels   Fuels like oil and coal that are dug from the earth.

Galaxy   A large system of stars held together by mutual gravitation and isolated from similar systems by vast regions of space.

Galilei, Galileo   Italian astronomer, mathematician, and physicist who laid foundations for modern experimental science through his persistent investigation of natural laws; he also greatly enlarged our vision and conception of the universe through construction of astronomical telescopes.

Gemini   The twins, a zodiacal constellation between Taurus and Cancer containing the bright stars Castor and Pollux; a two-person spacecraft designed for orbital rendezvous.

Geography   The science dealing with the earth's surface including such elements as climate, elevation, soil, vegetation, population, land use, industries, or states.

Geology   The science that deals with the physical history of the earth, the rocks of which it is composed, and the physical changes the earth has undergone or is undergoing.

Geophysics   The physics of the earth, including oceanography.

Goddard, Robert   American physicist and rocket expert who completed and successfully fired the world's first liquid fuel rocket in 1926.

Gravity   The force of attraction by which terrestrial bodies tend to fall toward the center of the earth.

Halley's comet   The great comet of 1682, whose orbit was calculated by astronomer Edmund Halley; it returned in 1759, 1910, and 1985.

Helium   An inert, gaseous element used as a substitute for flammable gases in lighter-than-air craft.

Horticulture   The science and art of cultivating flowers, fruits, vegetables, or ornamental plants.

Hydrocarbon   Any compound containing only hydrogen and carbon, like methane.

Hydrogen   A colorless, odorless, flammable gas that combines chemically with oxygen to form water; the lightest of known elements.

Hydrosphere   The water on or surrounding the surface of the earth.

Internal-combustion engine   An engine in which the process of combustion takes place within the cylinder or cylinders.

Jet propulsion   The propulsion of a body by its reaction to a force ejecting a gas or liquid from it.

Jupiter   The planet fifth in order from the sun and the largest in the system.

Laser   An instrument not necessarily larger than a flashlight for producing an enormously intense, pencil-sized, and sharply directed beam of light over long distance; the beam can be used to transport energy, accelerate certain chemical reactions, or carry communication signals.

Light-year   The distance traveled by light in one year; about 5,880,000,000,000 miles.

Malthus, Thomas   English economist and sociologist who contended that poverty and distress are unavoidable since populations increase by geometric ratio and the means of subsistence by arithmetical ratio; as checks on population growth he accepted only famine, war, and disease, but in his revised work he agreed that ''moral restraint'' could slow it down as well.

Manhattan Project Military organization under which the atomic bomb was developed during World War II.

Mars The planet fourth in order from the sun.

Mathematics The systematic treatment of magnitude, relationships between figures and forms, and relations between quantities expressed symbolically.

Mercury The planet nearest the sun and the smallest in the solar system; the name of the first phase of the U.S. space program during which astronauts flew suborbital missions.

Meteor A transient fiery streak in the sky produced by a meteoroid passing through the earth's atmosphere.

Meteorite A meteor that has reached the earth.

Meteoroid Any of the small bodies, often remnants of comets, traveling through space.

Meteorology The science dealing with the atmosphere and its phenomena, including weather and climate.

Methodology A set or system of methods, principles, and rules for regulating a given discipline as in the arts or sciences.

Microbiology The science dealing with the structure, function, and uses of microscopic organisms.

Microscope An optical instrument for magnifying objects that are too small to be seen by the naked eye.

Milky Way galaxy The great system of heavenly bodies that includes the solar system.

Moon Earth's natural satellite; it orbits the earth every twenty-nine and a half days and shines by reflecting the sunlight.

Natural selection A process in nature resulting in the survival and perpetuation of only those forms of plants and animal life having certain favorable characteristics that enable them to best adapt to a specific environment.

Neanderthal man Human being first appearing seventy-five thousand years ago; he was short in stature measuring little more than five feet, with a long and full face, deep-set eyes, and a robust body with deep chest.

Neon A chemically inert gaseous element occurring in the earth's atmosphere; used chiefly for filling electrical lamps.

Neptune The planet eighth in order from the sun.

Newton, Isaac English physicist who formulated the theory of gravitation, which says that all bodies in the universe have a mutual attraction for one another, and the law of motion, which held that 1) a body remains in a state of rest or of uniform motion in straight line unless acted upon by an external force; 2) a change in momentum is proportional to the force; and 3) to every action there is always an equal and opposite, or contrary, reaction.

Oceanography The branch of physical geography dealing with the ocean.

Oxygen Colorless, odorless, gaseous element that constitutes about one-fifth of the air and is the supporter of life and combustion in air.

Ozone layer   The region in the upper atmosphere where most atmospheric ozone is concentrated; it lies about eight to thirty miles above the earth; the maximum ozone occurs at an altitude of about twelve miles.

Pasteur, Louis   French chemist who discovered pasteurization—a partial sterilization of liquids like milk, wine, and beer to destroy disease-causing organisms.

Petri dish   A shallow, circular glass or plastic dish with a loose-fitting cover over the top and sides; used for culturing bacteria and other micro-organisms.

Photosynthesis   The process by which plants convert water and carbon dioxide into carbohydrates, using sunlight as the source of energy and with the aid of chlorophyll.

Physics   The science that deals with matter and energy in terms of motion and force.

Physiology   The science dealing with the functions of living organisms or their parts.

Planet   Any large heavenly body revolving about the sun and illuminated by reflected light.

Plant   Any living organism having rigid cellulose walls, lacking sensory organs and locomotive ability, and living by photosynthesis.

Pulsar   A source of pulsating radio energy located within the Milky Way.

Quasar   One of a number of celestial objects, from four to ten billion light-years distant, that are powerful sources of radio energy.

Radar   A device for determining the presence and location of an object by measuring both the time for the echo of a radio wave to return from it and the direction from which the wave returns.

Radiation   The process in which energy is emitted as particles or waves; radiation sickness can result from too much exposure to radioactive materials.

Radio communication   The transmission of sound and signals through space by means of electromagnetic waves rather than wires.

Radio telescope   A very large instrument for collecting and studying electromagnetic waves from space.

Relativity, theory of   Theory developed by physicist Albert Einstein, which held that matter and energy are equivalent and form the basis for nuclear energy and that space and time are relative rather than absolute concepts.

Rocket   A simple or complex tube-like device containing combustibles that, when ignited, liberate gases whose action propels the tube through the air.

Salk, Jonas   American physician who developed a vaccine against poliomyelitis by cultivating three strains of the virus separately in monkey tissue; the virus is separated from the tissue, stored for a week, and killed with formaldehyde; tests are made to make certain it is dead.

Satellite   A celestial body that revolves around a planet; a manufactured object launched from the earth into orbit around a celestial body for space travel or for sending electronic communication around the world.

Saturn   The planet sixth in order from the sun and second largest in the solar system.

Science   A branch of knowledge or study dealing with a body of facts or truths, systematically arranged, and showing the operation of general laws.

Science fiction   A form of fiction that draws imaginatively on scientific knowledge and speculation.

Solar system   The sun and all the celestial bodies that revolve around it.

Space shuttle   A group of manned spacecraft which can be launched into orbit and returned to earth for reuse after their missions are complete.

Space station   An orbiting artificial satellite from which further space exploration can be taken.

Spectroscopy   A science that deals with the use of the spectroscope, which is an optical device for producing and observing a spectrum of light or radiation from any source.

Stars   Heavenly bodies, except the moon and planets, appearing as luminous points in the sky at night.

Sun   The star that is the central body of the solar system, around which Earth and other planets revolve and from which they receive light and heat.

Sunspots   Dark patches that appear periodically on the surface of the sun and affect terrestrial magnetism.

Television   The broadcasting of images by radio waves to receivers that project them on a picture tube for viewing on a distant screen.

UFO   Acronym for unidentified flying object; thought by some to be from other planets.

Universe   The totality of known or supposed objects and phenomena throughout space.

Uranium   A radioactive, metallic element used in nuclear weapons and as a nuclear fuel.

Uranus   The planet seventh in order from the sun.

Van Allen radiation belts   Two belts, sometimes considered as a single belt of varying intensity, of radiation outside the earth's atmosphere; named for astrophysicist James Van Allen who first interpreted them.

Venus   The planet second in order from the sun and the most brilliant in the solar system.

Volcano   A vent in the earth through which lava, steam, and ashes are thrown up; a mountain formed around such a vent from the materials expelled.

Zoology   The science or branch of biology dealing with animals; the animal life of a particular region.

Dust Bowl farm, Cimarron County, Oklahoma, 1936 by Arthur Rothstein. [*Courtesy U.S. Farm Security Administration Collection, Prints and Photographs Division, Library of Congress*]

10

Environment

One of the duties of the specialist is not to forget. The job of the specialist is to look at consequences, to take an accounting and not be swept away with what is happening today. What makes this job worth doing is not just going day by day by day but in trying to figure out what it means, how it fits together.

—Casey Bukro
Chicago Tribune

One Environmental Reporter

March 24, 1989, four minutes after midnight in Prince William Sound, Alaska.

The silence of the clear, cold night is broken by the groan of tearing metal. The 30,000-ton supertanker *Exxon Valdez* has struck Bligh Reef and crude oil from its fifty-three million gallon cargo is gushing through gaping holes torn along 600 feet of hull into ice-filled waters at the rate of 200,000 gallons a minute. Before the flow is stopped and the oil remaining in its cargo tanks pumped into other vessels, the ship will send eleven million gallons of crude down the Sound — 470 miles in the first fifty-six days alone — contaminating 1,090 miles of shoreline; killing 33,126 birds, 138 eagles, 980 otters; and jeopardizing the area's $100 million fishing industry and Alaska's multi-million dollar tourist industry and future ecology.

An environmental disaster of truly monumental proportions is taking place in one of the country's most pristine states and there seems little that can be done to stop it.

March 30, 1989, mid-day, the tiny airport at Valdez, Alaska.

Casey Bukro, environment writer for the *Chicago Tribune* steps off the regular flight from Anchorage without having figured out his first priority in covering this important story: how to get out to see the rapidly spreading spill so he can fathom its scope and assess its damage.

"I worried about getting out into Prince William Sound during the flight from Chicago to Anchorage," he says. "It's a wild region. Once on the ground, I discovered that it was almost impossible to charter planes and helicopters to get to the Sound because aircraft were in heavy demand by governmental agencies or oil spill response teams. Luckily, I ran into a friend I had met on a previous trip to Alaska. He was a young, idealistic worker for the Alaska Department of Environmental Conservation then. Now he was in charge of transportation for the department, and offered me a seat on a helicopter reconnaissance flight leaving the next day."

Bukro was overjoyed. "This shows the value of making contacts," he says. "You never know who is going to help you later. He remembered I had covered Alaska earlier on other trips and he liked my work. It was luck that it all came together for me but it also shows the value of specialization."

In this instance, the help was crucial to the success of his coverage. Not only would he get a head start on the story — indeed, becoming one of the first reporters on the Sound — but the flight would place him at the scene, quite literally. "This was not an overflight," he continues, "we landed on islands. I have vivid memories of being in oil up to my ankles and looking at what I thought were oil-covered rocks until they moved. They were oil-covered birds, flopping and dying."

The day of his arrival in Valdez, Bukro faced another big hurdle: finding a place to sleep and write. Valdez had grown practically overnight from a sleepy town of 5,000 to a vibrant city of 12,000, with most of the flood of incoming rescue workers, oil company officials, government people, and press trying to find lodging. "People were literally renting out their parked cars," he says. "I called a motel which was full but someone there put me in touch with a family that was willing to rent me a bedroom at $50 a day." He slept there and wrote in the family's kitchen for the first two weeks. Then he traveled to other parts of the state to do additional reporting for two weeks to find, upon his return, that the room had been rented to someone else.

With housing still as tight in Valdez, he rented a space for an air mattress on the living room floor of the same people (also at $50 a day) and wrote his stories at the kitchen table for the remaining two weeks of his stay. "They were very understanding," he says, "of my getting phone calls day and night and tying up the phone when I plugged my laptop computer into it to send in my stories."

In Alaska, Bukro basically reported all day and wrote all night, an exhausting schedule. He wrote his stories on his laptop computer which had a built-in modem that could be connected to the telephone when he was ready to file. The process of filing often took three minutes but the connection was not always good. If there was noise on the line, the machine would shut off automatically. In a few instances, he wrote the story, then called the *Tribune* newsroom and dictated it.

During his first few days on the scene, Bukro concentrated on keeping up with the news, writing one news story a day. When time permitted, he did longer Sunday articles. "At first, I wrote about where the spill was going, what was endangered next," he recalls. "The spill was driven by the wind. I had to figure out where it would go next, where the action was next."

He continued to hitch rides with the Alaska environmental officials. They would land, do their work, and he would ask to remain, whether it was in a small town or an uninhabited region. "I asked to be dropped off and hoped for the best to get back," he continues. "It was risky because there was no guarantee he would get back to pick me up. I could have been stranded, but my first worry was getting the story and taking pictures. There were islands in Prince William Sound with no phone or cab. I was talking to people about how they were fighting the oil and affected by it. In uninhabited areas, it was a wildlife story. One time, to get my return flight, I had to do a story in one-half hour flat. In other places, I would hitch a ride with workers who were cleaning up the beaches."

Bukro's coverage was systematic: he was following the course of the spill by direct observation and writing about what he saw and what people told him. "I tried to tell their stories in human terms," he says. "The oil spill was a story not because we were losing the oil but because the spill told us what is safe and not safe [in the quest for energy] for people, food, and wildlife. There was also interest because Alaska is the last pristine wilderness."

After six weeks, his editors decided that the story had run its course. "You could cover the oil spill forever," he says. "If I had stayed long enough, the oil would have reached the Gulf of Alaska and gone South. Because this was a news story, it was too early to know the long-range consequences."

For Bukro, the Alaska oil spill exemplified the environmental story at its best. "There were the accidental aspects of the story and the effect on people. You were also dealing with oil and oil, when converted to fuel, drives cars. Then you must ask, is there a responsibility [for such accidents] that all people in an industrial society share? Also, there is the matter of describing the unexpected side effects of technology, which we have faith in. The job of the environmental writer is to show how all of this relates: human activity related to economic activity related to what this does to the ecology. What we do, our demands as a society, can result in injury and damage to the environment. The food chain is involved as are people's lives and safety. People are affected, sometimes in unknown ways and with long-term consequences. As a reporter, you sort it out."

Ten years before the Alaska oil spill, in fact, almost to the day, March 28, 1979, he was in Pennsylvania covering the accident at the Three Mile Island (TMI) nuclear power plant. "I was struck in 1989 by the similarities between TMI and the oil spill," he says. "You arrive at a scene of chaos. The spill is more evident because you can see the oil. TMI was more invisible because it was nuclear radiation. You try to make sense of the cause and effects. TMI was more difficult to understand from a technical viewpoint, whereas, in Alaska, a ship runs aground and leaks oil. But the similarities continue in that human errors were involved in both accidents. Both presented the problem of uncertainty as to long-range consequences to people living in an area, and animals, and food sources. Both also involve technology, the dark side of it with people doing the wrong thing."

Covering environmental disasters like TMI or the Alaska oil spill is nothing new for Bukro, who has specialized in the environment at the *Tribune* since 1967. He was named environmental editor in 1970. In that job he was responsible for both national and local environmental coverage. Several years ago he was assigned to the national desk and another reporter was placed on the Chicago environmental beat.

If determining the effects of such disasters on people is his main reporting aim, Bukro has had to learn the technical aspects of the environment as well. "I had to learn the beat," he says. "I learned everywhere I went, not by taking courses, but by asking questions. Nobody ever got a Pulitzer Prize for time spent in class. Great journalists are made on their beats. I approach every source with the idea that I'm a journalist, not a scientist. I ask them what I need to know. In a crisis like TMI, general assignment reporters often are thrown in, and they're hopelessly confused by the technical jargon scientists use. One of the jobs of a specialist is to learn the meaning of that technical language but still report the story in a way that is meaningful to the readers."

Bukro has a master's degree in journalism from Northwestern University, but he never took an ecology or an environment course. "Ecology usually had something to do with biology then, and environment courses weren't even offered then," he says. "They weren't popular as they are now."

Because he had an interest in the environment, Bukro began to write a few stories on water pollution in the mid-1960s. The result was a nine-part series in the *Tribune* on where the city gets its water. After an editor asked him to do a story on the pollution of Lake Michigan, he did another series, "Save Our Lake." This led to a six-month leave of absence from his job as assistant day city editor.

"By Earth Day, April 22, 1970, I had been on the beat for three years," he continues. "At the time there was an explosion of concern for the environment, with 1970 the beginning of the so-called environmental decade. We would make our peace with nature. It sounded good, but it was naive. Three years into this era, the energy crisis hit. Energy is part of this beat, as the flip side to environment. Things changed in regard to the environment when everyone realized that our natural resources were finite."

When Bukro enters the *Tribune's* futuristic-looking city room each day at about 9 A.M., he checks first with the national desk for any stories of a late-breaking nature the editors there might give him. If they have nothing, he goes to his own cubicle to work on his own story ideas.

"As for my cubicle, I'd call it a newspaper clutter motif with stacks of files on my desk," he explains. "Also, I have one bookcase in my cubicle for various reference books within easy reach. Notes hang on my walls for reminders, plus an occasional piece of artwork. One is a piece of tree trunk with oil paintings of two owls looking out of holes in the trunk. They are my companions and are always looking at me. They remind me to be wise."

Bukro's expertise in the environment gives him what he calls "the run of the paper"; that is, the articles he writes are not confined to the news section. He also writes for the newspaper's Sunday magazine, opinion pieces for the op-ed page, or for the business page.

When Bukro thinks it is time for him to do a series of articles on a subject, he goes to the national editor and asks for space and time. "A specialist has to fight for space, for ideas," he says. "Working with other people and their requests, the editor decides. You've got to know when to fight and when to say, 'Ok, I'll do it your way.' You've got to overcome their biases and show them it's a better story than they think it is." He says he still may "lose out to a flashy killing" for a position for his stories on page one.

He originally created his job by showing a interest in a subject that gradually became very newsworthy.

"Obviously I showed an interest in the environment," says Bukro. "If you want to do something special, ask for an assignment, show an interest. Start turning things in. Eventually you may be assigned to the subject. It is a good way to get experience, to let the boss know this is what you want to do. Management is more than willing to give an enthusiastic reporter a chance. It's a self-fulfilling type of thing. You've got to get involved and do it."

And, in spite of spending over twenty years on the beat, Bukro is as interested as when he first started covering this beat. "We can't avoid the environment," he says. "We live in it. One way or the other, we're going to pay attention to it. If we don't and ignore these hazards, the environment has a way of giving us nasty reminders."

Background to Environmental Reporting

Rachel Carson was one of the first harbingers of environmental concern in this country. Long before the press had taken up the cause, she was trying to call attention to the ways in which the environment was slowly being ruined.

Miss Carson, a longtime biologist with the U.S. Fish and Wildlife Service, cited the many perils of using pesticides and herbicides in *Silent Spring* (1962), which first ran as a series of articles in *The New Yorker*.

She began her book with "A Fable for Tomorrow," in which she wrote of a town "in the heart of America where all life seemed to live in harmony with its surroundings." One spring day, however, "a strange blight crept over the area and everything began to change." Chickens, cattle and sheep got sick and died. Farmers and their families became ill. Birds disappeared. Roadside vegetation withered and died; fish died in the streams.

"No witchcraft, no enemy action had silenced the rebirth of new life in this stricken world," she wrote. "The people had done it themselves."

> This town does not actually exist, but it might easily have a thousand counterparts in America or elsewhere in the world. I know of no community that has experienced all the misfortunes I describe. Yet every one of these disasters has actually happened somewhere, and many real communities have already suffered a substantial number of them. A grim specter has crept upon us almost unnoticed, and this imagined tragedy may easily become a stark reality we all shall know.
>
> What has already silenced the voices of spring in countless towns in America? This book is an attempt to explain. (Rachel Carson, *Silent Spring*. Boston: Houghton Mifflin, 1962, p. 3).

The chemical companies that manufactured the products Miss Carson wrote about so eloquently began to attack her even before the book appeared. After reading *The New Yorker* excerpts, one chemical company's general counsel suggested to Houghton Mifflin that it might want to reconsider its decision to publish the book. The publisher hired a toxicologist to verify her findings and went on with its plans to bring out the book.

According to Frank Graham, Jr., in his book *Since Silent Spring*, some companies reportedly told their scientists to look at *The New Yorker* article line by line to find errors. Others in the chemical industry treated her findings as a public relations problem to be handled by the publication of elaborate brochures about the virtues of pesticides and herbicides.

Lost in the controversy was the fact that Miss Carson had not asked that all chemical pesticides be abandoned. Her chief concern was for long-lasting chlorinated hydrocarbon insecticides like DDT. She called for sanity and restraint in the use of shorter-lived pesticides, not their total discontinuance.

Ironically the attacks by the chemical companies, and later some elements of the agricultural industry, attracted more attention to the book than if they had just kept quiet. The book sold a hundred thousand copies in its first few months and was a Book-of-the-Month Club selection.

This notoriety soon brought the subject out of the pages of obscure technical journals. The national press began to cover the story — and quickly chose sides. Newspapers around the country generally supported Miss Carson in editorials and reviews of the book. National magazines did not.

Time noted that, although scientists sympathized with her "mystical attachment to the balance of nature," they (the scientists) worried that "her emotional and inaccurate outbursts . . . may do harm by alarming the nontechnical public, while doing no good for the things that she loves." According to Graham, later articles championing pesticides in *Sports Illustrated*, *Saturday Evening Post*, and *Reader's Digest* were criticized by an official of the National Audubon Society as having been part of "a powerful, public-relations-based attack on *Silent Spring*."

But the press missed the larger story, getting as caught up as it did in the details of the controversy. It largely ignored the questions raised by Miss Carson.

Nevertheless, the book had made its impact on the country. Graham points out that by the end of 1962, more than forty bills had been introduced in state legislatures to regulate pesticide use. Members of Congress were getting interested in the subject as well. The report of a special panel of President Kennedy's Science Advisory Committee examined the values and hazards of pesticides for the first time and recommended closer study of their effects on air, water, soil, fish, wildlife, and humans. The panel's report went on to urge the restriction of wide-scale use of persistent insecticides, except for control of disease, and the ultimate elimination of persistent toxic pesticides. It also called for the initiation of programs to educate the public about the use and toxic nature of pesticides.

Rachel Carson had been vindicated. She died in April 1964, before evidence of what she had warned about had begun to appear around the world almost daily — to be covered by a press that had ignored the subject at the time her book was published.

It took two major environmental disasters, however, to attract the full attention of the press, both print and electronic, to a subject that until then had only briefly piqued their curiosity.

On March 18, 1967, the Liberian supertanker *Torrey Canyon* ran aground on the rocks off the Scilly Isles in the English Channel. The gash in the hull of the immense ship sent 119,000 tons of oil gushing into the water, eventually causing great damage to plankton, fish, and to birds on both the English and French coasts. Phytoplankton, known as the "grass" of the sea, generates at least one third of the world's oxygen through its photosynthesis process and converts the water's nutrients into the sugar, starch, and protein that the sea creates and needs to survive. Zooplankton, the minute organisms that constitute the lower life of the sea, eat phytoplankton; fish, in turn, eat zooplankton. If the phytoplankton are destroyed, as they are in an oil spill, the marine cycle is damaged. Ornithologists later estimated that 25,000 birds died as a result of this disaster. (See Box 10.1.)

In January 1969, an undersea drilling platform off Santa Barbara,

Box 10.1

Ecosystems: Links in a Chain

An ecosystem is the total of all living and nonliving parts of a chain of life in a certain area. There are four primary links in the chain:

1. Nonliving matter is the sunlight, water, oxygen, carbon dioxide, organic compounds, and other nutrients needed by plants to grow.

2. Plants or producers vary in size from tiny phytoplankton in the sea to grass and trees; through photosynthesis, the plants convert carbon dioxide and water into carbohydrates needed by the plants and other organisms in the ecosystem.

3. Consumers are the higher organisms, such as cows and sheep (called herbivores), that feed on the plants; they also include organisms, such as humans and other animals (called carnivores), that eat the herbivores.

4. Decomposers are the bacteria, fungi, and insects that break down the dead producers and consumers and return their chemical compounds to the ecosystems for reuse by new plants.

Growth and decay go on simultaneously and continuously in an ecosystem. They tend to balance each other out over a long period of time, thus keeping the chain in equilibrium. Pollution can disturb this natural process and natural balance; it has done so often in recent years.

California, blew its top and began to leak oil. Before the leak was stopped, it had created a twelve-mile-long oil slick that drifted ashore, fouling beaches, killing fish and ocean organisms, and covering birds with thick gobs of oil.

Local residents saved many birds by washing the oil from their backs. Many of the birds later died. After the leaking well was plugged, Union Oil used a thousand men to spread straw on the water, which absorbed 80 percent of the oil.

The battle to save birds and beaches from the invasion of ruinous oil was a natural story in both the *Torrey Canyon* and Santa Barbara disasters. There was great reader (and viewer) interest in the sight of helpless birds being washed and beautiful sand being fouled with ugly, gooey oil.

But something else happened in both instances: Reporters and editors began to see the environment as a legitimate beat beyond the periodic disasters. Also heightening press interest was the organization of the President's Council on Environmental Quality in 1970.

Beginning in the late 1960s and continuing into the early 1970s, large newspapers, national magazines, and television news departments began to hire new full-time environmental writers and reporters or to assign current staff members to the beat. By the time of the first "Earth Day" on April 22, 1970, the *New York Times* had assigned Gladwyn Hill, its long-time West Coast correspondent, as environmental editor. Both *Time* and *Newsweek* had started weekly sections on the environment. ABC News science editor Jules Bergman switched much of his attention from the space program to the environment. CBS News introduced a regular segment to Walter Cronkite's nightly broadcast, "Can the World Be Saved?" Even the venerable *National Geographic* broke its long-standing policy against covering social problems with a special issue on "Our Ecological Crisis" in December 1970.

In most cases these publications and networks did what the *Chicago Tribune* did with Casey Bukro. They assigned an existing staff member to the environment beat. The new specialists then trained themselves as they went along, covering news events as they happened and planning coverage of overall environmental concerns as they found out about them from expert sources.

Although it was a case of playing journalistic "catch-up" on a story they had ignored for too long, the move of American journalism into the environment was an important one. No longer would readers and viewers miss out on the big story of the ruined environment in America and around the world, its effect on them, and the efforts to ease problems. "Dead" lakes, dead fish, Love Canal, burning rivers — the stories were endless. More recently, the story has shifted to the costs in jobs eliminated and the price increase of products because of government antipollution standards.

Following the oil shortages of the 1970s, energy became an important subject for many large newspapers and TV network news departments, either as part of the environment beat or by itself. (See Box 10.2 for an explanation of energy reporting.)

In recent years, environmental coverage has not been as in-depth as it was in the 1970s following the interest created by the first Earth Day. Large newspapers still employ environment specialists like Casey Bukro, of course, and there is no lack of disasters at home and abroad to write about. The 1980s saw the 1984 Union Carbide disaster in Bhopal, India where 2,000 people were killed in a chemical plant explosion that sent toxic fumes wafting over a populated area, and the 1986 explosion of Reactor No. 4 at the Chernobyl nuclear power station in the Ukraine, USSR, which killed thirty people and exposed as many as 100,000 to varying degrees of radiation. A natural disaster — the 1980 explosion of Mount St. Helens in Washington, was covered extensively.

That does not mean that environmental stories are ignored on the local level. They are just not covered by a full-time environmental reporter but handled by someone who also handles science and medicine or even general assignment. There is no lack of stories to follow, with recycling, landfills reaching capacity, sewage treatment problems, clean water, clean air, and the fear of toxic waste all of concern throughout the country.

Just as the 1972 United Nations Conference on the environment in Stockholm heightened concern about the environment and launched both conservation groups and official agencies in 115 countries, the 1992 United Nations Conference on Environment and Development in Rio de Janeiro brought that subject back to world attention after a number of years of benign neglect, especially in the United States under Presidents Reagan and Bush.

The ten-day Earth Summit, attended by leaders of 120 nations and thousands of representatives from conservation groups, considered the most crucial environmental problems of the day — from deforestation to global warming.

Two factors overshadowed the deliberations. "The rich societies of the industrialized North want everyone to begin being sensible about the environment," editorialized *The New Yorker*. "The people of the Southern latitudes maintain that those who polluted the environment enroute to great prosperity are really asking the less well off to take steps that will keep them that way." The other major issue was the failure of the U.S. government to agree to cut CO^2 emissions to 1990 levels by the year 2000 for fear such a reduction would result in a decline in industrial production and a loss of jobs. A watered-down version was later signed.

Despite interest in the Earth Summit, its power to reignite world-wide interest in the environment to 1970 levels remains to be seen, given other, more economically-oriented concerns, especially in the United States, once the world's environmental/conservation leader.

Perhaps the early days of the environmental movement had a lasting effect: coverage of the environment and the problems associated with it are accepted parts of all media. The stories generated here are not as startling as they once were because journalists on the beat have done a good job of preparing readers.

And, for their part, readers consider the environment and coverage of it important. A 1991 *Wall Street Journal*/NBC News poll found that eight in ten Americans regard themselves as "environmentalists," and half of those say they are "strong" ones. By 53 percent to 34 percent, the respondents said it will take fundamental changes

Box 10.2

Energy Reporting

As a journalistic topic, energy entered the scene when the 1973 Arab oil embargo created immediate shortages of petroleum products in the United States. Caught short by their lack of understanding of the problem, newspapers, magazines, and television news departments rushed to fill the information vacuum.

The major petroleum companies had been warning of an energy crisis for ten years. They said supplies of oil and gas in the United States were declining and the public would have to encourage their search for alternate fuels by paying higher prices. In short, the oil companies had declared the end of the era of cheap energy.

The companies began to reorganize for the change. Seeing the rise of nationalism in the Middle East, the companies went into other parts of the world to search for oil. They also started to branch out into allied fields, such as coal and uranium, and to call themselves energy companies.

When these large companies could not get the press interested in the story, they began to pay for print and television ads that warned of the continuing crisis and detailed what the companies were doing to solve it. The basic message was the need for the public to conserve energy while the oil companies found alternate sources.

The public has not always believed that message, however. Despite all the efforts to convince them otherwise, many people still think that the shortages and the crisis were created by the oil companies to boost profits. This feeling is perpetuated each time the oil companies release their quarterly earnings reports, which always show large increases over previous periods.

In the 1980s, energy gradually disappeared as a separate beat in most large news organizations. It is covered usually as part of the business beat or by environmental reporters as news warrants. This has largely been due to the decline in the power of the Organization of Petroleum Exporting Countries (OPEC), the cartel that brought the world to the point of financial panic with drastic increases in oil prices in the 1970s. Accompanying this was a de-emphasis on energy conservation and government funding for research into alternative fuel sources during the Reagan presidency.

If gas lines reappeared in American cities, widespread coverage of energy as a regular beat would too. The 1990 invasion of Kuwait by Iraq and subsequent Gulf war showed how important—and newsworthy—oil can be.

But there are other aspects to the energy story besides OPEC. The energy beat reporters for national publications and networks cover the activities of government and private companies regularly. By the nature of the subject matter, this approach is generally impersonal. Energy beat reporters on small or medium publications can explore the more personal side of the subject, however. They may be strangers to oil company boardrooms or unfamiliar with the vagaries of Middle East oil politics, but they can show the effect on their readers of high energy costs and new sources of energy in a more compelling way simply because they are closer to those readers and their energy-related problems.

Typical local energy-related stories include local news events, activities of oil companies and public utilities, research into new sources of energy, local energy problems, profiles of people in energy-related jobs, and news of local and state agencies.

in life-style, not scientific advances, to bring dramatic changes in the environment. Sixty-six percent said the environment has gotten worse over the past twenty years.

Problems and Solutions

Given its subject matter and the effect it has on so many people, the environment is a fascinating and challenging subject to cover. But it is also a difficult beat.

"It's hard," says Casey Bukro. "You've got to learn the language of your specialty. Let's say it's water pollution—suspended solids, parts per million, oxygen content. You've got to learn these things."

Bukro considers his environmental beat to include the water, the air, noise, solid waste disposal, and pesticides. "Each of these things has its own language," he says. "Each has to be described in a simple, understandable way. You become versed in a new language that you teach yourself. It's difficult at first. You converse with scientists and specialists. You have to understand what they're saying and translate it. You can't write it as the scientists tell you. They use their own arcane language. They sometimes can't understand each other. Jargon in one area of science may not be known by someone in another area.

"You learn to deal with this problem. You ask them what things mean and to put what they're saying in plain English. Too often specialists try to show off by using technical terms that confuse readers. Scientists often don't know how to communicate. With knowledge gained by experience and reading, a specialized reporter can translate for them.

"The nuclear power people, early on in my coverage, seemed to treat the fact that I had asked questions as an indication I was ignorant. Often technical sources will try to bully a reporter to get out of the interview. If he does that, he's won; the reporter has lost.

Don't let your ego get involved. Don't let the other guy win by [your] not asking a question.

"There is no such thing as a stupid question in journalism, especially if you really don't know the answer. Don't be afraid to ask. If the interviewee won't say, he may not know. If the source says, 'That's a silly question,' say to the source,'If it is, educate me.' Keep it on a friendly plane. If someone really wants to be stubborn, it may not be worth it. Try someone else who is willing to talk."

Bukro says nuclear physicist Edward Teller often takes this kind of approach with reporters. "He is sometimes a little cross and makes you feel you should know this. I've told him, 'I've got a job to do and I need help.' But in general, to hold the attention of somebody like Teller or Einstein, you have to show you know what you are writing about. Teller does get impatient, probably because he hears the same questions all the time. But other times he just gets bored with the interview process, so you have to challenge him. And the reporter can't allow an interviewee to shrug him off, so sometimes you appeal for help. The idea is to do your homework, but persist when the interviewee does not explain things as well as necessary to make the story clear."

Another problem is the emotionalism that is so often a part of environmental reporting, both on the part of the people involved and as a result of the issues. Usually the story involves a confrontation between a powerful "big" (a company or government agency) and a relatively powerless "little" (an individual, an environmental group, an animal, or a plant). Because "big" has the resources to crush "little" easily, reporters must be careful to get both sides of the story and not take "big's" word for everything.

Very often a company or government agency will first try to "kill" the individual or group with kindness, using words like "misguided," "well-meaning," or "under great mental strain" to describe them. If that tactic fails, officials of the government agency or company might call the forces opposing them "crackpots" or a similar term of derision. The agency or company will also have experts to testify on their behalf and official studies available to give to reporters. The individual or group on the other side rarely can afford such help and will only be able to show the damage caused by the particular environmental excess at issue.

In such a highly emotional atmosphere, environmental reporters have a hard time figuring out the truth. They must decide before they write a word. Maybe no one is right totally. The best tactic is to verify the facts and claims of both sides by an outside expert and then present the two points of view equally well. In this way the reader can decide.

To do justice to the environment as an area of coverage, reporters must go all the way and report all sides of every question—again and again. They and their publications and television and radio stations must become platforms for exposure of the stories. Environmental reporters should not spend all their time searching for villains, charlatans, and freaks. They're all there in abundance. Reporters must look beyond them to the truth.

This emotionalism isn't always confined exclusively to sources, according to some critics, who charge that large news organizations in the United States often exaggerate the perils that come from environmental problems. One such critic is Elizabeth Whelan, executive director of the American Council on Science and Health, who decries the scare tactics used by some journalists and authors in explaining the effects of toxic substances. "Daily we are subject to anxiety-producing reports about the 'poisons' in our environment, the threat of premature death, human misery, defective children, or no children at all, caused by our careless use of technology. We are warned that calamity is at our doorstep, fresh out of a sinister test tube, and that we face an impending epidemic of disease and death," she writes in an article in *The Quill.*

Easy as it might be to exaggerate stories—in the copy and in the headlines—environmental reporters and their editors need to avoid such hyperbole. Reporters need also to realize that environmental coverage has changed from its early days.

"Environmental issues have gone from those you could feel, smell, and touch to those that are invisible like radiation and pesticide residue in food," says Bukro. "We are still dealing with long-term consequences but invisible ones, like climate change. It's tough to pin them down. There is also the matter of risk assessment. How much radiation are we willing to take? Is a billion parts of something better or worse than a trillion parts of something? Even if we can measure it, can we understand the meaning?"

Bukro worries about the emotionalism that seems always to be associated with environmental issues. "You have to report what you can prove and watch as the evidence mounts either way. Some things may never be proven, like cancer rates. Even as we are able to measure and detect more, we aren't always sure of the consequences. Here, I am talking about threshold, that is, how much of something is dangerous? The issue for a reporter becomes, who do you believe?"

In deciding, Bukro carefully analyzes the reputation of a technical source. "You look for track records or all you do is report both sides," he says. "You see who, over a passage of time, has been closer to the truth. You find the best informed people and find out what they know. Sometimes, it's not very much. Now, experts are minimizing the dangers of dioxin and saying that the evacuation of Times Beach, Missouri was not necessary. Here the government spent $30 million to buy out property and they say it wasn't necessary? Their answer is it all had to do with what they knew at the time!''

Bukro believes firmly in keeping track of many past stories. "You can't just do it once," he says. "In environmental reporting, you always go back to it because stories involve health and safety and people need to know. You learn to tell old stories in new and interesting ways. But you have to be careful that you don't overplay the story."

Bukro says that "why" and "how" of the old inverted pyramid style of writing are very important in his reporting. "You also have to add 'if,'" he says. "A lot of people call me and say, 'This factory is ruining my health.' It's hard to prove these things, even though they have gone to a doctor and the doctor tells them a toxic chemical has caused this specific disease. People are understandably worried about issues, but if you say that someone is at fault, you have to worry about libel. Beyond the legal aspects, you can't give wrong information where health and safety are concerned, because it alarms people."

In considering current problems of his beat, Bukro concludes by detailing the subjects still to come in the 1990s: leftovers from the 1980s like asbestos, ozone layer depletion, acid rain, damage from emissions, waste disposal, nuclear waste, and overcrowding in national parks; and new concerns such as the effects of pollution in Eastern Europe.

"In the next ten years, this beat will still be propelled by surprises," he continues. "We didn't know about Three Mile Island, Chernobyl, or the Alaska oil spill before they happened. I tend to accept this as business as usual for this beat. The problem is, we [as a country] think we can handle these disasters. It would be wiser to avoid or try to prevent them, rather than wait to see what bites us next."

He thinks present long-range and continuing environmental problems are largely regional: the population explosion in the East, grazing problems in the West, the spotted owl's effect on timber cutting in the Northwest, and agriculture and coal mining in the Midwest.

"Worldwide, we can't forget minorities and the Third World," he says. "The environment has always been considered an elitist story, where rich people do all the talking [about destruction of the rain forests, for example,] and minorities are concerned about housing and jobs. The Third World countries are now saying, 'You made your money and ruined resources to do it, now it's our turn.' We have to help them protect their resources. It's going to be a big issue."

More suggestions for dealing with the problems of environmental reporting can be found in "Likely Problems and How to Solve Them" later in this chapter.

How to Cover the Environment

However slow the press was in recognizing the environment as a legitimate area of coverage, that subject is now firmly established as a beat in medium and large newspapers, many magazines, and on television and radio networks and stations in larger cities.

The environment is an area of coverage with its own set of dilemmas and requirements:

1. **Interviewing sources about difficult subjects.** An environmental reporter needs a new vocabulary even to conduct interviews. After they've gotten the words spelled correctly, reporters have to explain what they mean to the reader. To do so, reporters must probe their sources until they understand what the source has said. If they don't understand the subject at the time of the interview, they are going to understand it even less back in the newsroom sitting before a blank VDT screen.

Casey Bukro considers informed sources an essential tool for doing a good job. "Tips are very important to any reporter," he says. "They know you, see you at hearings, and tell you things." But the cultivation of sources goes beyond chance meetings in corridors. "A specialized reporter must stay on the leading edge of his specialty," he says. "You've got to interview sources constantly, attend hearings, talk to experts. That's how a specialist keeps informed. You talk about the latest developments. These are the things that will be in a book in a year or two. I'm supposed to be right up there with the pioneers. It's one heck of a way to get a good education. Every specialized reporter becomes a well-informed amateur. You read and read and talk to contacts."

2. **Keeping extensive files.** Beyond the interviews with experts needed to do specific stories, environmental reporters need to read extensively in books and technical journals to remain on what Bukro calls "the leading edge" of their subject.

Bukro keeps up in his subject area by talking to people and by reading. "I subscribe to fifty to sixty publications, from technical journals to things put out by the Sierra Club. I wind up reading at home at night." From his reading he finds out about news of significant developments in pollution control, new ideas to handle old problems, story ideas, and new sources.

He saves the articles that interest him—in six filing cabinets at home, three at the office. He files everything by subject matter. It serves as useful background on future stories.

"I can't read it word for word," he says. "If it looks useful, I rip it out and file it. I do what a magazine writer does."

For instance, Bukro had first seen a reference to acid rain in a technical journal. He opened a file on the subject and collected information for several months. Then he conducted several interviews on the subject and eventually wrote a story.

"It's an old magazine writer's trick. You build files before doing serious work," he says. "The files tell me what is known popularly. It's up to me to go beyond that. I try to go further. I ask the question no one has ever asked before, so I'm ahead of what I've read."

3. **Writing to inform readers and keep them interested.** Although the environment is a subject people should know about, its highly technical nature might bore them and thus lose them as readers.

"Writing is important," says Bukro. "It's not enough to know what a scientist is talking about. You need to know how to communicate it in an intelligent way. At times I've gone back to journalism books. The copy desk says it's too technical when I thought I had made it as plain as I could. I feel frustrated. I'd read for a while, trying to get a transfusion of simple things I knew in school but had somehow forgotten. It's easy to get involved in the telling. But it has to be simple and meaningful."

Kinds of Environmental Stories

Although specific stories vary from city to city, there are a number of standard subjects that appear regularly on the environmental beat:

1. **News affecting the environment.**   Actions of local, county, and state agencies that control the environment are always newsworthy. Isolated instances of environmental problems (oil spills, air and water pollution) and solutions to these problems (clean air and water, closing down a polluting plant) also make good stories.

2. **Research results.**   Stories about efforts by researchers at universities or scientific research laboratories to find ways

to ease environmental problems or to predict future problems are good possibilities on this beat.

3. **Personality profiles.**   People in charge of environmental quality make good profile subjects, as do those directly affected by pollution or other environmental control laws.

4. **Major local and regional environmental problems.**   In-depth looks at local, regional, or state environmental problems are always in order. What are the problems? Environmental beat reporters should find out from experts, then start doing stories on all of them. Another good possibility in this regard is to find out who the worst polluters in the city or state are and then write about them.

5. **Tie-ins with national stories.**   A local story that relates to a national story offers a good way to cover this beat. The effect of a new federal or state law or the presence or absence of local suffering from a problem that makes the national news (for example, toxic waste dumping or the failure of a nuclear plant) are good possibilities.

Writing Environmental Stories

"Too many reporters place too much emphasis on reporting and getting the facts and not enough on taking all that reporting and putting it into a story that is readable and interesting," says Casey Bukro. "Writing is often the hardest part of the job. Reporting is like a hunt. It's a lot of fun and exciting in a way you don't get in writing a story. But if you don't do a good job of writing, readers won't read your story.

"You must describe things clearly and tell the story in human terms so it means something to somebody, it is meaningful to readers. You have to get rid of jargon, the fuzzy language in reports and statements by experts.

"In short, you have to make the story sing and doing it fast [on deadline] is difficult. The point is someone has to read it. I strive for simplicity, not because people are dumb. Even smart people without a background [in the technical subject being written about] need to be told why it is important and how it fits together.

"It takes experience. You have to pay your dues and learn how to say it simply rather than using scientific language. You have to translate that for readers. All the things you know about, someday may come into play. A new reporter on the beat is afraid to interpret. A specialist builds confidence. Once you understand, you feel confident.

"A new reporter on the environmental beat should hang loose and get the feel for the subject matter, know it and not be buffaloed by it. You have to take it apart so it makes sense, get people involved. The environment is not a dead subject. It has meaning to someone's life. People can identify with other people and see similarities [to their lives] if you point out the similarities—what happened there, can happen here.

"You do it in a clear, concise style. You can learn a lot by reading other writing, like good science writing, and asking, 'how did they do that?' Writing is hard work. You do it by doing it again and again until you are good at it."

#1

OIL SPILL IS DISASTER FOR WILDLIFE
By Casey Bukro
Chicago Tribune

One of Casey Bukro's original oil spill stories in 1989 describes the effects on wildlife. He begins with a description of a sea otter in normal circumstances.

His transition begins with "but" and tells the reader about an otter suffering from the oil.

1 GREEN ISLAND, Alaska—Normally, a sea otter is a rather charming creature, maybe 30 pounds, the same as a good-sized dog, with large, liquid eyes.

2 But it was awful to see the one Dr. Ken Hill cradled in his arms—gasping, barely alive, its sleek natural coat concealed in a fresh coat of sludgy, stinking black oil.

3 "This is a terrible way to die," said Hill, a bearded young vet from the coastal village of Cordova 50 miles to the north.

In graf 4, he extrapolates from one to discuss the many. His line "an ecological chamber of horrors" sums up the situation aptly.

4 It wasn't just the one otter he was talking about. It was thousands of them, along with countless fish and hundreds of thousands of sea-flying birds like ducks and grebes and cormorants, and loons that cry mournfully in what has suddenly become an ecological chamber of horrors.

In graf 5 he points out the obvious: total effect on all creatures is unknown. Why? the reader might ask.

5 The world will never know how many living creatures died in the slick, syrupy blood of 240,000 barrels of oil that spewed out of the *Exxon Valdez* after it ran aground March 24 in Prince William Sound.

He tells them in graf 6 very simply.

6 The reason is simple. Bodies coated with oil sink, and there are no census takers on the ocean floor.

He amplifies these facts in graf 7 with a "chocolate mousse" analogy.

7 They have a term up here, "chocolate mousse," for oil that has been kicking around in the waves and gets whipped to a froth. There's a lot of mousse in the sound right now.

In grafs 8 and 9 he gives his readers the benefit of his direct observation from the air.

8 It's at the tattered edges of long, iridescent oil stains on the water's surface. The spreading, wind-driven stains now cover about 600 square miles.

9 That makes it the worst and biggest oil spill in the nation's history. But its meaning is best described in small, ugly facts, not large statistics.

In grafs 10, 11, and 12, he continues his vivid description of what he saw on the ground.

10 The Exxon Corp. said at first that it had spied no damage to wildlife, and, in a way, that may be true because from an airplane one can see the slick but can't make out what's happening underneath it or on the shore.

11 Even when a group of scientists took a helicopter to this rocky island to assess the damage, it wasn't immediately apparent.

12 Then, what had at first seemed to be rocks began moving and making feeble noises. Covered with black oil, they were often indistinguishable from rocks. But they were alive — or more precisely, they were dying.

Beginning in graf 13, he brings others into the story to augment his description.

13 Dave Nysewander, a wildlife biologist for the U.S. Fish and Wildlife Service, loped after an otter that had confusedly tried to lick the oil from its coat before heading for the water. It eluded him, but later he successfully went after a limping loon whose cry sounded eerie and pathetic under the bleak Alaska sky.

14 Nysewander, who has been doing research since 1976 on Prince William Sound's sea otters — a population that may be wiped out — echoed the loon's distress.

15 "This was one of my favorite places for beauty and wildlife," he said.

16 He and others estimated that the *Exxon Valdez* oil spill's effect on fish and wildlife will be measured for a least a decade. As they chatted, they were listlessly stared at by birds mired in puddles of oil.

Another source in graf 17.

17 "This ecosystem probably is trashed for 10 years," said Steve Willingham, an environmental engineer for Alaska's conservation department. After surveying damage to other islands in the sound, he said, "We were in tears out there."

Graf 18 is another transition which applies the oil spill disaster beyond the Sound to all of Alaska with the views of scientists (19-22).

18 The truly evil element of what has happened here is the damage to the living dream of Alaska as a last, pristine natural frontier.

19 For the scientists who came to see the nightmarish vision now visible on Green Island—the scientists who say the eagles that nest here will probably die from nibbling on the oil-smeared shore birds that the slick washed up—the dream of Alaska has been dealt irreparable harm.

20 "It makes me angry. I put it in a league with poaching African wildlife, destroying rain forests and urban sprawl," said Bruce Baker, habitat director for the Alaska Fish and Game Department.

21 The normally sparkling air is foul. It smells everywhere like the insides of a car when the crankcase oil is being changed.

22 "I have not seen one bird without oil on it," said Dan Lawn, regional director in Valdez for the state Department of Environmental Conservation. "We're talking about hundreds of thousands of birds."

In graf 23, he amplifies his general observations with details on why the timing of the spill was so bad. He explains this with more detail in grafs 24 and 25.

23 The timing of the oil spill could not have been worse.

24 Migrating birds, 30 species of them, are expected to come winging in during April and May. Where once they found clear shoreline and nesting grounds, now they will find oil.

25 Several hundred fishermen from Cordova—trim, weathered men whose livelihood depends on clean seas—spread floating booms at Port San Juan to block oil from the coastal salmon hatchery there. In these parts, salmon fishing is a $75 million annual business, and millions of salmon fingerlings were to be released soon.

26 The public and private environmentalists who gathered on Green Island are doing their best to make a small dent in the damage.

In graf 27, he brings readers back to his starting point for more descriptions of efforts to save animals and birds.

27 On Friday, they scooped up otters and put them in the sort of cages in which dogs are usually taken to the vet. Loons and ducks were immobilized in plastic bags with their heads sticking out.

This continues in grafs 28, 29, and 30.

28 They all were loaded on to the helicopter for a quick trip back to an animal welfare center in Valdez, where attempts will be made to clean the oil off them so they can be released back into the wild.

29 Once aboard the chopper, their lethargy began to dissipate in the warm air and some grew positively frisky. Ducks squawked, red-eyed loons cried louder and louder, and otters banged against the bars of their cages.

30 But one large otter was pathetically comatose. Licking the oil from his coat, he had ingested it and began excreting it.

Because this is his only story that day—and because the oil spill is on-going—he ends his piece with the latest on what is known.
"Meanwhile" is the transition word to that overall situation. He quotes two sources and a memo to tell readers what he knows in grafs 31 through 36.

31 Meanwhile, the ruptured *Exxon Valdez* lies in the water cross-ways to normal ship traffic. Another tanker lies alongside, siphoning off what remains of its load from the oil fields on the North Slope.

32 Given what is now known, it isn't clear whether the damage could have been contained even if Exxon had moved to do so within the five-hour deadline for action required by the federal government.

33 "We lost all of the oil here in two or three hours after the ship hit," said Steven McCall, U.S. Coast Guard commander in the Valdez area.

34 Still, it isn't as if the alarm hadn't been sounded.

35 An official Alaska state memo in 1976 warned that the contingency plan for an oil spill here, "in almost every major facet, contains mistakes and inadequacies, demonstrates microscopic thinking and, worse, omits major functions that are necessary."

36 "Our worst fears came true," said the memo's author, Randolph Bayliss, then a state official and now an environmental consultant in Juneau. "The plan didn't work."

#2

GREATEST OIL SPILL— HOW TERRIBLE WAS IT?
By Casey Bukro
Chicago Tribune

In July 1991, Bukro returned to Alaska to report on cleanup efforts, more than two years after the spill. His lead tells his readers what this story will be about.

1 ANCHORAGE—The world's longest and most costly oil spill cleanup, in Alaska's Prince William Sound, is drawing to a close after more than two years amid argument over whether it really was an environmental disaster.

In graf 2, he reminds them of what happened and then uses a summary phrase ("black tide") to make his transition from the lead.

2 The black tide from 11 million gallons of oil that spilled on March 24, 1989, is gone— and the life that was snuffed out is beginning to come back sooner than many people expected.

More news of plans in grafs 3 and 4.

3 Exxon Corp. plans to pull its cleanup crews off the rock-strewn beaches on Monday, declaring its work finished at a cost of $2.2 billion to the company.

4 The Alaska Department of Environmental Conservation, the U.S. Coast Guard and Exxon say they'll continue next year to watch for any undetected oil, but the concerted cleanup campaign is over.

In graf 5, he tells readers of an irony he has discovered: the cleanup has created an economic boom whose end has caused uncertainty.

5 It's a strangely guarded time in Alaska. The cleanup has been the highest-priority item on the state's agenda, and the money pumped in to reverse the effects of the spill caused an economic boom that will end now. At the same time, uncertainty remains over the possibility of lingering environmental effects.

6 Experts say there is a tendency to overreact to an oil spill at the beginning and to under-react at the end. So now Alaskans are trying to find the middle ground.

The basic facts of the Alaskan oil spill are widely known:

More basic facts to reacquaint readers with the subject (grafs 7 through 13).

7 The *Exxon Valdez* was steaming away from the Port of Valdez with a full load of oil when Capt. Joseph Hazelwood altered course to avoid icebergs, then went to his cabin.

8 The tanker ripped out its bottom on Bligh Reef.

9 Syrupy black oil smeared 1,244 miles of Alaskan shoreline, engulfing wildlife and killing an estimated 350,000 birds and 3,500 sea otters.

10 Images of struggling, blackened wildlife shocked Americans and triggered tanker safety reforms. Congress passed the Oil Pollution Act of 1990, requiring new safeguards such as double hulls in new oil tankers.

11 Hazelwood was convicted of negligent discharge of oil and acquitted of more serious charges. The National Transportation Safety Board said the captain's drinking, a fatigued and overworked crew and inadequate traffic control by the Coast Guard contributed to the spill.

12 Exxon and the U.S. Justice Department reached a $1 billion settlement, but in April a federal judge in Anchorage rejected it, saying a $100 million criminal fine was too low for the damage the nation's largest oil company had inflicted on Alaska's environment. This case is expected to go to trial in October.

13 State officials say the results of two years of scientific investigations of the spill will not be released until the trial.

In graf 14, he gets to the real meat of the story, now that he has supplied his readers with the necessary background: was the spill an ecological disaster? He asks the question (15) and lets a source answer it in direct quotes (16).

14 At the time of the spill, environmentalists called it an ecological disaster likely to grip Alaska for decades.

15 But was it?

16 "You bet," said Ernie Piper, Alaska's oil spill coordinator. The spill, he says, occurred in a pristine wilderness "unique in the world." It also dominated state environmental activities, allowing other serious matters to go unaddressed.

344   Part IV   Science and Medicine

In graf 17, he brings in his own observations by reporting on his helicopter tour of the Sound.

He continues his observations and includes comments from sources in grafs 18 through 24.

17 A helicopter tour of Prince William Sound July 5 showed no rainbow sheens or black swirls of oil visible on the dark waters.

18 Oil has settled into about 30 underground pockets scattered around the sound. Workers use backhoes to break them open, scattering the oil gravel closer to shoreline so weather and waves can wash the oil away.

19 "The jury is still out" on bioremediation, Piper said, referring to the technique of fertilizing the existing bacteria in the environment to eat and break down the oil.

20 But Andrew Teal, an Exxon oil response supervisor, pointed to barnacles and other forms of life clinging to rocks once covered with oil and said, "From a biological sense, it's a full recovery a lot quicker than people thought."

21 Prince William Sound has always been a harsh environment, he said, and life there is wiped out often, only to make a comeback.

22 "I wouldn't call it a disaster," Teal said of the oil spill.

23 Neither would Coast Guard Cmdr. Ed Page, chief of the marine environmental protection branch in Alaska.

24 The spill was daunting at first, he admitted, but "things are bouncing back much better than I expected."

He sets the scene nicely in graf 25, describing sea lions chasing salmon and a whale spouting in the distance. He then uses several grafs to answer the question of whether the cleanup crews are leaving too soon (grafs 27 through 34) by quoting workers and officials.

25 As Page spoke, sea lions chased a school of salmon just offshore, with squawking sea gulls diving to pick up shreds of the kill. A whale spouted in the distance while a curious harbor seal bobbed to the surface to inspect the work party packing up for the last time.

26 Are the crews leaving too soon?

27 "There's a lot yet to be done," said Bobbi Cross, who has worked on the cleanup for two years and has watched the number of workers dwindle from 1,100 at the campaign's height to 200 today.

28 "I don't know if digging up more oil here would be any good or not," she said. "I do feel we have done some good."

29 Said another worker: "Nature is the only thing that will take care of it in the long run."

30 Otto Harrison, Exxon Alaska's general operation manger, pointed out that no oil spill has ever been worked on this long. "That says some good things about our commitment to stay here to get the job done right," he said.

31 Harrison cited record salmon and herring catches in 1990 as signs of recovery, but critics say Exxon emphasizes good development and ignores the bad.

32 Riki Ott, president of the Oil Reform Alliance, an environmental group in Cordova, Alaska, said Exxon does not mention that salmon fisheries in Kodiak and Cook Inlet failed last year. "They were hammered by the oil," she said.

33 She also referred to unnamed scientists who estimated that some bird populations in Prince William Sound will take 70 years to recover.

34 An Alaskan environment official, L.J. Evans, said: "It's important to come away from this whole experience understanding that nobody wins in an oil spill. There will be oil remaining in some places for a long time."

In graf 35, he notes a factor not always brought out in coverage of the cleanup: it caused harm as it tried to get rid of the oil.

In grafs 36 and 37 he quotes a government official to that effect.

35 One disturbing finding is that the cleanup sometimes caused more damage than the spill, according to the National Oceanic and Atmospheric Administration.

36 "Exxon did everything it could possibly do," said David Kennedy, the agency's chief of hazardous materials response, adding, "They went too far in many cases." For example, the use of hot water sprays often killed wildlife, such as clams, shrimp, fish and snails.

37 "Things are coming back," Kennedy said, "but what is not well known is how the diversity and the ecosystem as it existed before is recovering."

One more question remains (38): the human consequences. He visits a native village to get the answer (40, 41).

38 And what about the human consequences?

39 Chenega, an Alaskan native village hard hit by the oil spill, lives almost entirely on fishing and hunting.

40 Its inhabitants have found much of the wildlife they depend on has disappeared, and it is coming back very slowly.

41 "One of the topics not discussed," said Gail Evanoff, vice president of the Chenega Village Corp., "is people's reliance on the environment. It is okay to be concerned about the birds and animals, but what about us?"

#3

GARBAGE DUMP: FINAL, SMELLY RESTING PLACE FOR LIFE'S DISCARDS
By Casey Bukro
Chicago Tribune

Bukro's wonderfully inventive story on a visit to a garbage dump is something any environmental reporter anywhere could do. He spent time at a local dump and recorded what he saw, adding the slant that any dump "is a shattered mirror of our lives."

He found the things one cannot eat . . . (3)

. . . and the foods, which, we find, give a dump its smell (4-6).

1 A garbage dump is a shattered mirror of our lives.

2 Almost everything heaped and strewn on the ground is recognizable as something that was once sparkling new on a grocery shelf or in a department store. It's the end of the line for what we buy with our hard-earned money so carefully, and what we throw away so carelessly.

3 Tires, shampoo containers, a rumpled sneaker, a plastic baseball bat, tattered rugs and towels, toys, books, bottles and cans, streamers of audio and video tape, wire, sheets and bags of plastic now flapping in the wind, bed springs, refrigerators, panty hose, newspapers, magazines, metal drums, plastic spoons, soiled diapers, light bulbs, paper plates.

4 And then there is the food. It is often unrecognizable, because it is rotting. In the landfill business, food is politely known as a "putrescible."

5 But food helps to give a garbage dump its distinctive odor: Sour, pungent, musty. Sometimes a certain scent will stand out, like coffee grounds. But otherwise the stench is miasmic, as though nature were sending a very strong warning of danger.

But, beyond the smell is something else: "a grotesque crazy quilt" with roaring bulldozers (7) and buzzing flies (8). By this time, the reader feels they're beside the reporter. In grafs 10, 11, and 12 he begins to lay on material facts about trash, which puts the local site in some context.

6 There must be something primal about the smell of garbage; it is so noticeable and so offensive.

7 It's not just the smell. A dump is a grotesque crazy quilt, seemingly devoid of order as trucks arrive all day to dump their loads, followed by roaring bulldozers that spread and flatten the trash before covering it with dirt at the end of a working day.

8 Buzzing flies swarm over the garbage in the summer. In some areas, so do seagulls, wheeling and squealing in unruly clouds.

9 This is a dump, to which each American contributes 3.6 pounds of trash each day.

10 According to the National Solid Wastes Management Association, the total comes to 162 million tons of household garbage yearly.

11 Forty-one percent of it is paper and paperboard. Yard waste accounts for 17.9 percent, metals 9 percent, glass 8.2 percent.

12 Food waste contributes 7.9 percent, plastics 7 percent, wood 4 percent. Rubber and leather account for 2.5 percent, and textiles 1.8 percent.

13 "There's no way to make garbage pretty," said a New Jersey official. "You can bale it and put bows on it, but it's not pleasant."

In graf 14, he puts an element of alarm into the story: beyond the smell is a real threat, due to what has been thrown there (15) and the fact that many dumps are now toxic waste hazards (16).

14 Years ago, the town dump was viewed as a smelly but necessary nuisance.

15 That was before anyone realized that people also throw away motor oil, battery acid, pesticides, cleaning fluids and thousands of other poisonous household chemicals that are picked up by the rainwater passing through the dump on the way to ground-water reservoirs below.

16 As a result, old garbage dumps now account for half of the 1,194 sites designated by the federal government as the nation's most dangerous toxic waste hazards.

17 Americans place "ensuring adequate garbage disposal" third on a list of major problems facing local officials, according to a survey published by the association. Only improving public education and providing affordable housing ranked higher.

People are also a part of a story like this, of course, to allow readers to see them-selves in the same place. So he ends the piece by quoting one worker (20-24), after describing his job.

18 People work in garbage dumps, of course, thousands of people. Given the working conditions, it seems unfair that they don't get much appreciation or recognition.

19 They're people like Joe Lucas of Taylorsville, Ky., who runs a forklift at a landfill in Sulphur, Ky.

20 As a tractor-trailer arrives loaded with garbage, Lucas and three other forklift drivers take turns dashing into the trailer, lifting a bale of garbage and rushing away to deposit it.

21 The charging forklifts pirouette and miss each other by inches in a bellowing dance of garbage, all day long in the stench.

22 How do they stand it?

23 "You get used to it," says Lucas.

24 "But first thing in the morning—that first whiff," he says, shaking his head.

Environmental Reporting: Likely Problems and How to Solve Them

Problem	Solution
1. Complicated subject matter.	1a. Read books and articles for background material, and build reference files.
	1b. Get on mailing lists to receive regular publications of private groups such as the Sierra Club and the National Wildlife Federation; trade associations like the

National Forest Products
Association, the Can
Manufacturers Institute, the
American Gas Association,
and the Atomic Industrial
Forum; government agencies
such as the Environmental
Protection Agency, the
Senate committee on
Environment and Public
Works and the House
Committee on Agriculture,
the Committee on Interior
and Insular Affairs, and the
Committee on Merchant
Marine and Fisheries as well
as local government
agencies and private groups.

1c. Develop two or three
objective sources not allied
to any environmental cause
to go to for guidance and
information.

2. Reluctant sources.

2a. Stress importance of telling
their story.

3. Emotionalism on both
sides of any environ-
mental controversy.

3a. Be scrupulously fair in
detailing the points of view
and facts on both sides so
readers can decide.

3b. Don't be a "pseudo-environ-
mentalist" in your coverage;
that is always taking an
automatic pro-environmental
stance.

3c. Don't get so attached to a
particular story that you
overplay it — for example,
accusing a company of
causing cancer deaths: You
might be sued for libel if
your source's claim was
false, or cannot be proven.

4. Inaccuracy or
   exaggeration.

4a. Check and recheck all facts
    carefully.

4b. Remember that with health
    and safety involved you have
    a responsibility to be
    scrupulously accurate.

4c. Evaluate carefully the track
    record of all sources, official
    or unofficial.

5. Dull, overly technical
   stories.

5a. Involve readers by
    personalizing stories, that is,
    by showing how it affects
    other people with whom
    they can identify.

5b. Explain all technical terms
    quickly, if you have to use
    them at all.

Summary

American journalism's interest in the environment has increased
with public perception of the problems and government and private
actions to correct abuses. Beginning with the crash of the oil
supertanker *Torrey Canyon* in 1967 and the Santa Barbara oil spill
in 1969, the environmental consciousness of the United States has
grown to a greater understanding of the issue. Sensing a good story,
editors began to hire reporters or to assign existing staff members
to cover the environment. Since then, many newspapers, most
national magazines, and television news departments have reported
the subject regularly. As with all specialized areas, the environment
presents special problems to reporters. It is sometimes difficult to
understand the technical terms used by scientists. It is hard to keep
up with all the research going on. Stories have to be written so that
readers are informed in an easily understood manner. The issues
covered in environmental stories are often emotional, but this factor
must not cloud objective reporting.

Exercises

1. How does your town handle its waste? Interview government
   officials and local environmental groups. Spend a day at the
   dump. Write a story reporting your findings.

2. Interview a scientist at a local university who specializes in research to aid the environment. Write a story on your findings.

3. Select an upcoming construction project (a dam, ski area, or resort hotel) in your area, and assess its effect on the surrounding environment. Interview developers, builders, local residents, and government agency personnel for their views, and get details on the finished project and the area as it was before construction. Was an environmental impact statement filed? Were public hearings held? Compile your findings and write an article.

4. Spend a day working in a gas station or at least observing what goes on there in an effort to find out how the energy situation looks from that common point of contact with high prices and scarce supply. Write a story highlighting your findings.

5. Use a news release from a university, government agency, or research laboratory about a new way to save energy or an alternative source of energy as the basis for a story. Be sure to go beyond the release and get facts and opinions from sources opposed to the development. Write a story about your findings.

Key Terms for Environmental Reporting

Acid rain   Sulphur in the air caused by burning coal that comes back to earth in the form of acid rain.

Air shed   A common air supply delineated by arbitrary or convenient borders like an urban area.

Allowable release levels   Levels of nuclear radiation officially accepted as harmless to humans.

Biodegradable   An organic substance that will decay and be absorbed into the environment.

Biosphere   The part of the earth's crust, waters, and atmosphere where living organisms can subsist.

Carcinogen   A substance that tends to produce cancer.

Chlorinated hydrocarbons   Insecticides like DDT that last for years or decades, travel around the world in water and air, and accumulate in hazardous concentrations in animal tissues.

CO_2   Carbon dioxide, a colorless, odorless incombustible gas present in the atmosphere; in recent years, experts have worried that CO_2 levels have grown to harmful proportions because of excessive burning of fossil fuels.

Compost   The mixing of garbage and degradable trash with soil in a pile; the garbage and trash decompose because of bacteria in the soil, thus returning desirable organic material back to nature.

Decibel   The unit of measuring sound intensity, from 0 (the slightest) to 140 (causing the rupture of eardrums).

Decomposers   Living plants and animals, mainly bacteria and fungi, that survive by taking energy from the tissues of dead plants and animals.

Deforestation   The clear cutting of trees which, when done on a vast scale such as in the Amazon Basin, is thought to affect the environment worldwide.

Demography   The science of vital and social statistics of populations like births, deaths, and marriages.

Dioxin   A byproduct of pesticide manufacture that causes cancer and birth defects in certain animals, including, possibly, humans.

Ecocide   The ruination of a whole environmental system, usually through use of pollutants.

Ecology   The branch of biology dealing with the relationship between organisms and their environment.

Ecosystem   A system formed by the interaction of a community of organisms and their environment.

Effluent   The discharge, usually of pollutants, from a self-contained opening like a smokestack, sewage treatment plant, nuclear power plant, or oil tanker into the environment.

Energy cycle   The means by which the sun's energy is passed from one living organism to another or is stored as in oil or coal.

Environment   Everything that surrounds a certain ecosystem.

Environmental impact statement   The study of how a proposed construction project (dam, highway, building) will affect the immediate environment.

Estuary   The area where the waters of a river meet the sea to produce abundant marine and plant life in the lagoons, marshes, and tidal plains.

Eutrophication   The state in which aquatic ecosystems grow old naturally.

Fossil fuels   Combustible energy fuels like coal, oil, and natural gas which come from the earth.

Global warming   A gradual warming of temperatures throughout the world—believed to be caused by deforestation and depletion of the ozone layer—which affects climate, water depth of the oceans, and, ultimately, people everywhere through resultant floods, droughts, and famine.

Greenhouse effect   The reaction that takes place when pollutants in the air absorb infrared or heat rays and prevent the radiation back into space of a certain fraction of the sun's energy.

Herbicide   A chemical substance that kills plants by interfering with the growing process.

Hydrology   The science of the circulation, distribution, and properties of water on the earth.

Insecticides   A chemical used for killing insects.

Inversion   The meteorological action that takes place when a layer of cool air sets on a layer of hot air and prevents the warmer air from rising; if the hot air is polluted, it is harmful to life.

Nitrogen fixation   The process in which bacteria and other soil microorganisms convert atmospheric nitrogen into fertilizer to grow plants.

Nonrenewable resources   Resources like oil and coal that cannot be replaced after they are used.

Ozone layer   The region in the upper atmosphere where most atmospheric ozone is concentrated; it lies from about eight to about thirty miles above the earth; the maximum ozone occurs at an altitude of about twelve miles.

Particulates   Dust and soot in the air.

Photosynthesis   The process by which plants convert water and carbon dioxide into carbohydrates, using sunlight as the energy source with the help of chlorophyll.

Plankton   The microscopic floating plant (phytoplankton) and animal (zooplankton) organisms of lakes, rivers, and oceans that are basic parts of the food chain leading to large fish and aquatic mammals.

Pollution   The action of making something foul or unclean with waste material.

Radioactive   The property of certain chemical elements that causes them to emit radiation as a result of changes in the nuclei of the atoms of the element.

Radioactive waste   Material containing unusable radioactive by-products of the scientific and industrial applications of nuclear energy; since its radioactivity presents a grave health hazard, getting rid of such material is a serious problem.

Rain forest   A tropical forest, usually of tall, densely growing, broad-leafed evergreen trees in an area of high annual rainfall, the destruction of which on a large-scale in the Amazon Basin is believed to influence weather throughout the world.

Recycling   The process of treating or processing used or waste materials like paper to make them suitable for reuse.

Renewable resources   Biological resources that renew themselves by growth and reproduction.

Smog   A mixture of fog and smoke that is hard to breathe because of the presence of pollutants like nitrogen oxide and waste hydrocarbons from automobile exhaust.

Sonic boom   An explosive noise caused by an aircraft flying faster than the speed of sound.

Thermal pollution   The discharge into rivers or lakes of heated industrial waste-water, which destroys plant and animal life.

Toxic waste   Waste from chemical plants and nuclear material producing facilities that is highly dangerous to people and difficult to dispose of.

Wetland   An inland area that is usually wet or flooded; a coastal area like a salt marsh or tidal marsh.

Country doctor and patient in farm home, Scott County, Missouri, 1942 by John Vachon. [*Courtesy U.S. Farm Security Administration Collection, Prints and Photographs Division, Library of Congress*]

11

Medicine and Health

The desire to take medicine is perhaps the greatest feature which distinguishes man from animals.
—Sir William Osler

One Medical Editor

A chance meeting at the Harvard Club in New York with a visiting molecular biologist from New Jersey led medical writer and editor Bill Ingram into one of the most significant stories of his career. By all acceptable standards in journalism and medicine, the story — about a new and controversial AIDS treatment — should have been a big one. But it got little response from anyone; a fact that says a lot about both the journalistic and scientific establishments in this country.

"No one picked it up," says Ingram, editor of *Medical Tribune*, a biweekly medical newspaper for physicians. "No one had seen it in a journal. People in journalism retail what they see in journals. AIDS researchers at NIH are skeptical, so the doctors [involved] can't get in on AIDS research funding. It's too bad, because such attitudes hold back progress."

A closer look at this story, its implications, and the way it was disposed of provide useful lessons for would-be medical writers about the complex world they are entering, a world complicated in more than the difficult medical terms they must use and explain to readers.

Ingram's story detailed the findings of a year-long study of eleven patients in California, all with AIDS. They had been unable to work because of repeated episodes of AIDS-related diseases and were frequently hospitalized for treatment. Although they had been on AZT (the only drug then approved by the Food and Drug Administration for the treatment of AIDS) for two or three years, they were not responding to it and were suffering adverse reactions.

The primary care physician who was treating all eleven patients teamed up with the molecular biologist who was Ingram's main source to work out a research scheme to find a nonpathogenic strain of AIDS for use in treatment of patients. They were joined in their quest by a Los Angeles attorney who raised the funds needed to carry out the program.

To be successful, their case study needed to find someone who had HIV, the virus that causes AIDS, without having gotten the disease itself. They solicited names of possible donors from 1,763 physicians around the world and chose one in Los Angeles from thirty possible subjects. He was both a homosexual and IV drug user who by his own calculations had had well over 500 contacts over a ten-year period, but still did not have AIDS. The chances that a contact would carry the nonpathogenic virus is put at one in 500.

"They discovered when they took blood samples from him and checked the antibody response, he had an atypical response," says Ingram. "They injected the eleven patients with two to three CC's of whole blood from the donor in two infusions and took them off the AZT." A year later—when Ingram found out about the research—four of these patients had had a 90 percent recovery and were back at work, two had died, and three were still fighting off the opportunistic infections that accompany AIDS. "They were in fair condition," he adds, "and would normally be dead without this treatment."

To Ingram, the significance of these findings was clear. "You are using elements of a contagion to destroy a contagion," he says. "I can see the possibilities are enormous. You can treat this highly vicious, treacherous, fast spreading disease by using the disease itself. By using nature's own method, you can counter an epidemic with an epidemic."

In the abstract, it sounded so simple, but as Ingram heard his source's explanation, he realized it was far from that: "The new AIDS treatment, however promising, might never get approval because of stiff resistance by the medical establishment, both other researchers and medical journal editors. And, because of how such matters traditionally work in the United States, this resistance would cause the general media to shun the story and thus, without reader reaction, avoid putting public pressure on the government to fund the new research."

The doctors had submitted a letter about their findings to the British medical journal, *Lancet* and an article to the *Journal of Molecular Biology*, also published in Britain, which accepted it for later publication. *Lancet* thought the findings so explosive that it even masked that letter in early editions sent to the media in the United States. It only showed up later, when copies of the issue began arriving in the United States, too late for the scoop-happy American media. The researchers also submitted an article to the *New England Journal of Medicine*, which showed interest but declined to accept it.

The loss of that imprimatur consigned the subject to secondary status in the eyes of most general media, as will be explained later in this chapter. It only whet Ingram's appetite, however. Yet, his publication reaches 140,000 readers, largely physicians and other health professionals. He gave it big play in his next issue but that was not enough exposure to generate the kind of pressure needed to boost the treatment.

Next to look askance at the two doctors were top AIDS researchers at the National Institutes of Health, the primary focus of both federal research on, and funding for, AIDS. "Of course they hadn't dared to go to NIH before they started," explains Ingram. "They just had to do it on their own. The concept is so shattering and raises so many taboos that they could never have gotten an institution to sponsor them. Any time you give someone a live virus it arouses all kinds of fears. It's so perverse, it's almost immoral."

Once they had results, however, the molecular biologist went to NIH in Washington and tried to get invited to an annual AIDS research conference but met resistance. He ultimately was allowed ten minutes to present the paper, but there was an absolute news blackout on the report. "I'm afraid that he won't be able to get in on AIDS research and, if something comes of all of this, he'll lose all the credit," says Ingram.

The medical editor did not stop after his first story on the research. He did interviews around the world with experts on AIDS to use in follow-up articles. He wrote an editorial about the potential benefits of the new treatment. And then, all he could do was sit back and wait and hope that other coverage would result. The lack of reaction by media and researchers bothers him as a medical journalist who wants his articles to help others.

The World Health Organization Global AIDS Programme eventually judged the research highly equivocal, and did not reply to the researchers' rebuttal. "What happened is an involuntary spontaneous abridgment of the First Amendment," Ingram says. "It shows how establishment media and establishment science, and an uninformed public combine to keep legitimate scientific research out of the public print and public arena. This not only handicaps AIDS research but, possibly, the most basic weapon we possess, a virus with the ability to fight a virus. After all, [Dr. Albert] Sabin showed with his vaccine that a nonpathogenic strain could conquer polio. This work will go on. Nothing can stop it, the work with this AIDS group will go on. But I think other groups should respond and help expand it. I was determined to get recognition for them, to see if their theory works."

Background to Medical Reporting

The history of medical reporting parallels that of science reporting already reviewed in Chapter 9. Early stories in Europe and the United States covered news events with only scant mention of any medical angle.

This account of a plague in Marseilles in 1720 from the *Gazette de Hollande* is typical:

> . . . a hospital in which there are more than 500 dying patients, abandoned without the slightest aid and not even with water to drink, a mass of unremoved bodies between the wards of the hospital; a town stricken and despairing; whole families destroyed; nearly all doctors and surgeons dead, the Brethren and Sisters of Mercy reduced from eighty to four, of whom three have fled; the neighborhood of the town swarming with looters and thieves who rob the farms of the better class and with those latter not knowing how to escape the plague or the robbers.

According to journalism historian Hillier Krieghbaum, Benjamin Harris—publisher of the first newspaper *Publick Occurrences*—included a short medical story in his first issue on September 25,

1690. The account was aimed to quiet "many false reports, maliciously made, and spread among us." The items told of "Epidemical Fevers and Agues" becoming commonplace and warned of an outbreak of smallpox in Boston. Such brief reports were common in early newspapers well into the nineteenth century. Medical writing, however, never reached the sensational stage achieved by science writing.

Gradually, newspapers began to see medicine and health as legitimate areas of coverage. As had happened in science, World War II brought a number of advances in treatment of the wounded and the development and widespread use of new "wonder" drugs like penicillin. The general press began to write about them, but editors soon saw the need to hire or assign special reporters to cover medicine.

The early medical writers were largely general assignment reporters who taught themselves to deal with the difficult words and the medical techniques that were hard to grasp and explain. Soon these big-city newspapers were joined by *Time* and *Newsweek*, which added weekly medicine sections. Specialized magazines like *Medical World News, Medical Economics, Medical Tribune,* and *Today's Health* were founded.

There were many things to write about: the discovery and perfection of the Salk polio vaccine in 1955, increased government spending on medical research, medical aspects of the space program, and successful heart transplants.

In the 1970s the attention of medical reporters turned to the crisis in the health care system in this country. Although doctors in the United States could transplant human hearts, there were not enough doctors willing to work in ghetto areas or poor rural areas. The infant mortality rate was higher than in twelve other industrial countries. Although health in 1970 represented an expenditure of $67.2 million, or 6.9 percent of the gross national product, more than 40 million people never saw a doctor. Moreover, medical costs increased more than 50 percent from 1960 to 1970.

In the 1980s, some medical problems got worse and there were fewer federal funds to help alleviate them. The federal government turned more and more of the funding for Medicaid, the system of providing health care to the poor, over to the states which were already struggling to pay for other programs. This came at the same time that total expenditures for health care increased tenfold from 1970 to $670 million, or 11.5 percent of the gross national product. But, in spite of the vast increase in costs, 30 to 35 million people had no health insurance. Another 60 to 70 million, most with some kind of insurance, couldn't afford to see a doctor because they didn't have the money to pay the deductible.

As the country entered the 1990s, its health care system was in crisis, especially in rural areas where doctors and adequate facilities were in short supply.

In 1991, the infant mortality rate averaged 10 percent in most American cities, higher than twelve other industrialized countries. In New York City alone, the rate was close to 14 percent, higher than such poor countries as Trinidad and Bulgaria.

The costs for caring for AIDS patients alone threatens to break most health care systems. The number of Americans infected with the HIV virus totaled 100,000 in 1981. In 1991, more than 100,000 have died from AIDS and more than one million are infected. An estimate by the World Health Organization puts the number of people with AIDS around the world at eight to ten million, more than half of them in sub-Saharan Africa.

But costs of diseases affecting Americans from a wider spectrum have spiraled even more. The number of people being treated for heart disease and cancer, the two leading causes of death in the United States, has gone up steadily.

Bill Ingram, along with other expert observers of medicine and health care, thinks a crisis in the health care system that started over twenty years ago has never really eased. "Everything that has happened has been technologic," he says. "In 1968, we had heart transplantation for the first time. Coronary artery bypass grafts had already been preferred investigationally. By 1979, we had five-year results on this procedure and were about to get balloon angioplasty, where a balloon is inserted into clogged arteries via a catheter to open them up by removing plaque and improving blood flow, thus preventing heart attacks. Heart transplant success had been good, but cost and availability of donors had limited its use. But heart bypass surgery, where new arteries and veins are constructed to replace diseased ones, by then was commonly done. Angioplasty came in with a roar."

Early success with both heart bypass surgery and angioplasty caused doctors to discover that they must do the interventions again as arteries close: 40 percent of angioplasties have to be redone within five years at a cost of $20,000; once every twelve to fourteen years for bypass surgery at a cost of $38,000, according to Ingram. There are now over 300,000 heart bypass operations per year and over 200,000 angioplasty procedures per year. "That's a lot of procedures," he says. "The fine art of heart replumbing has grown tremendously. But the reliability in both instances has not come up to the level of the ordinary toilet!"

If the health care system has been in crisis for twenty years, a crisis of a more personal kind has befallen medical reporters during the same period. There are fewer jobs available for them. The use of separate health sections in newspapers has decreased by 20 percent in 1991. Medical advertising in specialized medical publications dropped 30 percent that same year. Only large newspapers and news magazines—along with specialized medical trade publications—hire reporters who cover medicine exclusively. More common is to have a science writer who is also responsible for medicine and the environment.

Problems and Solutions

Medical reporters face a number of problems as they cover their beats. Some of these problems stem from the terminology needed to understand the subject matter. Other problems revolve around access to information and the refusal of some doctors to talk. Sometimes, if the finding in a story is critical of their product, advertisers might retaliate or try to interfere with publication.

A reporter will get used to the medical jargon in time. But the tone of words in a medical story and the impression left in the minds of readers are also important. Whatever the disease being written about, there are hundreds, or even thousands, of people suffering from it. They may be literally living on every word in the article, especially if those words promise a cure or new treatment to ease their suffering.

"The biggest Achilles heel of medicine is over-promising," says Bill Ingram. "In the 1980s it was interferon, a so-called miracle cure for cancer patients that was very expensive and had mixed results. Today it's something like a treatment called LAK, which stands for lukocyte-activated killer cells, used in cancer treatment. This has been a tragic disappointment. Or, take the brief furor over the use of the bark from yew trees to make taxol, another cancer drug. It would take five or six one-hundred-year-old yews to get enough bark to treat one patient. This would cause a crisis in the environment. Despite trumpeting in the media, it soon turned out that the same thing could eventually be synthesized and that long-term cure rates for advanced ovarian cancer via taxol were a disaster. Once word of such cures gets out, doctors, hospitals, and even medical writers are besieged by people wanting to be treated by whatever has been publicized. This is all revealed in a flashy way but the results are disappointing and people suffer. A blatant deception is that to join the National Cancer Institute trial, you must just respond to taxol in an 'induction trial.' That guaranteed 100 percent responders in the trial."

One way to avoid this raising of expectations is to be careful in choosing the words for a story. "Medical writers should avoid all adjectives and adverbs that magnify the importance of a subject," says Ingram, "words like "dramatic," "striking," "breakthrough," or those that smack of puffery in a public relations sense — "best," "only," "biggest." But I don't feel a writer should consciously pick and choose language. Medical stories should not be hedged by qualifiers. 'Reported in a study of nine thousand patients at the Mayo Clinic' is direct. If you make that 'a carefully controlled study,' you are implying that only this study was carefully done."

Handling interviews with doctors is another problem for medical writers, but one that can be easily solved with careful preparation. Getting the doctors to talk at all may be a problem, however. Because of the "Ingelfinger rule," doctors are hesitant to release their findings elsewhere before a journal has printed their article. Named for its most ardent advocate, Franz J. Ingelfinger, then editor of the *New England Journal of Medicine*, the rule deals with prior publication of research in the medical press.

Ingelfinger explained the rule in a 1970 article in *Science*: "In general, the *Journal*'s attitude would be influenced in a negative way if the principal ideas of an article, as well as its crucial data and most important figures, had already appeared in a medical news medium — just as the effect would be negative if the identical items had been published by a paradigm of staid medical literature." Thus, a medical research scientist should refrain from cooperating with the press, granting interviews, or furnishing background material. This is true even for work presented at a medical meeting and even though the work, if paid for by government funds, is presumably available to the public.

Although Ingelfinger originally intended the rule to apply only to the medical press, it has since been extended to all media. The distinction has always been lost on most medical researchers anyway. They even assumed it applied to articles they were writing for any medical journal. A study by *Science* found that some researchers refused to divulge article material even though they had no intention of submitting it to the *Journal*. The attitude also affected their contacts with general medical reporters.

Apparently Ingelfinger was motivated by both a desire not to be scooped and a feeling that research results are best if they are not reported prematurely; that is, the scientist's life is one of small advances made year by year, while the journalist is motivated by the need to report something new every day.

The rule was later eased, only to be revived with a vengeance in 1981 by Dr. Arnold Relman, Ingelfinger's successor. At one point, even authors of the *Journal of the American Medical Association* (JAMA) articles thought the rule applied to them until the JAMA editor spoke out against this journalistic straitjacket.

The embargo works like this: medical and science reporters around the United States get air mail copies of the *New England Journal of Medicine* every Tuesday, along with a reminder that information in that issue cannot be reported before 6 P.M. Wednesday, a time critics say is aimed at accommodating television news programs. This means that most Thursday editions of big city papers feature at least one story on a research finding in that week's issue. Thus, both the *Journal* and the researchers get a great deal of publicity, something detractors say is the motivation behind the whole system anyway.

Enterprising reporters can break the embargo by interviewing other people and piecing together enough information to do a story. The Reuters news service did just this in 1988 about a study that said that aspirin prevented heart attacks. The *Journal* immediately dropped the service from its mailing list and the agency was forced to secure a copy by other means until it was allowed back on the list.

Ingram deplores what he calls this "stranglehold" on news, which he says results from the penchant *Journal* editors have for exclusivity. He says lay newspapers, such as the *New York Times* and *Washington Post*, have published articles about the medical news embargo with a strong undercurrent of protest. "Yet these same newspapers slavishly extract an article or two almost every week from the *New England Journal*, many of them arousing false hopes (about possible cures for diseases) and largely incomprehensible to the average patient-reader," he says.

The reluctance to publicize material still prevails among doctors, both in augmenting material in journal articles and in providing information to a reporter who comes up with a story idea independent of any writing by the doctor. Medical reporters should be prepared to give doctors reasons for cooperating with them. A medical reporter should at least be able to get the material on a research project at the same time the journal containing the article appears. That means talking to the researcher in advance and agreeing to embargo the information until a certain date.

"Doctors say they read the *New England Journal*," says Ingram. "How many doctors actually read it is another question." The publication has a certain esteem among doctors, however, and they will fight to get their articles into it. Ingram says he knows of at least one instance in 1969 when a researcher withheld data that would affect the public health because of an article he expected to publish in the *New England Journal*. The researcher was hesitant to tell the Center for Disease Control in Atlanta about hundreds of hospitalized patients who got infections after using a certain medical solution discussed in the manuscript.

Ingram says Relman has given articles on AIDS research the highest time priority in order to get such possibly beneficial findings before the public. "It takes a minimum of a couple of months to get an article into the *Journal*, though, so there is still a lot of delay even with emergency stories."

Relman retired as editor of the *Journal* in 1991 and the new editor promised a re-examination of the rule when he took over.

Another difficulty presents itself when a reporter writes about drugs. If a drug company gets angry at an adverse story about one of its products, it may cancel—or threaten to cancel—all of its advertising in the publication. This can have disastrous economic effects on publications that exist solely on drug advertising. This is not a problem in publications that get advertising from diverse sources. Moreover, the best medical publications resist the outside dominance and stand up for the truth of the story.

A medical reporter under such pressure had best be extra careful that the conclusions in the article are accurate. If the facts are correct and can be substantiated, and a publication still refuses to run the story or an editor bows to pressure and waters down the findings, the medical reporter may have no choice but to resign.

More suggestions for dealing with the problems of medical reporting can be found in "Likely Problems and How to Solve Them" later in this chapter.

How to Cover Medicine

"A good medical story is not unlike any other kind of story," says Bill Ingram. "The only difference is nomenclature, a lot of which you have to look up in a medical dictionary. It is sometimes a good idea to check nomenclature with your sources. Sometimes, words have specialized meanings that escape you and even a dictionary would not be all that helpful. A 1986 AP story, for example, reported that a former Cleveland Browns football player died of a possible cocaine overdose after falling into a coma secondary to a seizure of unknown *ideology*. The right word was *etiology*." (Some of the terms that a medical reporter will need to know are contained in "Key Terms for Medical Reporting" later in this chapter.)

A medical reporter also has to talk to people who sometimes speak in their own arcane language. The willingness of doctors to give information to medical writers can mean the difference between an informative, complete medical story and one that is just the opposite. It can also mean no story at all.

Journal Articles

The biggest source of medical stories in this country is the journal article. Hundreds of such publications appear weekly, monthly, quarterly, or six times a year on subjects ranging from the general to the specific. The doctors and research scientists who write the articles published in these journals do so to inform their colleagues about their work and thus advance medical knowledge. These doctors must also publish in order to get promotions and raises. The articles are a distinct measure of their worth.

Although medical journal articles are often poorly written, they do provide the raw material upon which a medical reporter can develop a story. Such articles are usually organized in a way to present the background, methodology, and conclusions of the research and are fully authenticated by footnotes, charts, and statistics. They also have the correct spelling of difficult medical terms and hard-to-spell drug names.

"Recently, an issue of the *Journal of Pediatrics* contained an article that said that pediatricians can't take care of emergencies and that parents should take their children to an emergency room," recalls Ingram. "This was new information to me and I was able to use it in an article we were doing on the overburdened ER's in the United States."

Many journals will make contents of issues available in advance, as already noted about the *New England Journal of Medicine*. This enables reporters to see articles and do stories on them. Other journals issue news releases about upcoming issues and the American Medical Association even sends video news releases to TV stations.

With the journal article as background, a medical reporter can contact the doctor-author for more information with which to expand the story. Bill Ingram goes beyond that to outside sources. "A lot of researchers cheat at solitaire," he says. "Though the articles are refereed, and there may be peer review, they have sole control over the data of their research. A reporter must be in a position to challenge their extrapolations and look for outright errors in statistics. You check their findings with appropriate federal agencies and other researchers in the same field. You must have the instincts to smell something wrong."

News Releases

After journal articles and follow-up interviews with medical researchers, the next biggest source of stories comes from public relations news releases. Releases should never be run verbatim, but used instead as a source of tips on subjects to be followed up. "These releases tickle your interest, but you run very few of them outright," says Ingram. "Many of the releases today represent an attempt by a medical center to blow its own horn. Often, the releases are about research that is just being run in major journals. You get fooled when you read the release into thinking it is something new, but then in the last graf find that the results are running in the *New England Journal*.

"Releases are a big source of medical news," he continues. "Major PR mills turn them out. We get a foot and a half a week of releases, probably about 750. Someone else screens them and we do find story ideas and material for shorter items. We look for releases on subjects with an event attached—a meeting, a journal article, or a major development. Without that, we aren't interested. A lot of releases give you clues on trends, early information on new discoveries. I admit that I snatch and grab things out of releases. Even when I do a story from a release I check out 90 percent of the information, usually in calls to researchers. Many of the releases are wrong, of course, but many are correct."

Meetings

The third major source of medical stories is the medical meeting. There are several problems associated with the coverage of medical meetings, however. The first is the sheer number of meetings available to cover. There are about 125 major medical meetings a year, and 500 other gatherings that must go unreported in the United States along with an equal number in England, Europe, Mexico, South America, Japan, and Australia.

"Some of the events you hear about are symposia sponsored by drug companies," says Ingram. "There has been a lot of unfavorable publicity on these symposia where the drug company pays to fly the doctor and sometimes his wife to a resort where they'll be captives for a weekend to hear paid researchers delivering papers on a drug or major indications of the use of the drug. We won't cover these but do cover symposia sponsored by universities or research centers or organizations like the American Heart Association."

Deciding to cover a meeting does not solve the problem. "Each meeting may have hundreds of papers presented," continues

Ingram. "It is not uncommon to have 250 papers presented at a major meeting. You must screen the program in advance with the help of medical advisers to find the most promising subjects. But most programs are inadequate, and it is almost impossible to tell what a story is from the title on a program. These titles are notoriously misleading, hackneyed, and ridiculous."

Ingram goes through the abstracts (short summaries) of papers looking for subjects of interest as well as names of researchers he knows and trusts. "If a recognized research scientist has written a paper, something new might be up," he says. But there is another danger to knowing a researcher too well. "Papers are given again and again with only a slight variation on the same subject by the same researcher ad nauseam," he continues. Ingram keeps track of what research scientists write about. "I go by whether I remember that this researcher already has given this paper. I seldom publish the same finding, even if it has been updated, unless five years has elapsed."

After choosing likely research papers and making sure they have not been covered before, Ingram sometimes finds out more about the subject by calling the researcher (the name is on the program) and asking questions. A few organizations make abstracts available in advance of the meeting or print news releases about the subject for a lay audience.

Even with such careful advance preparation, meetings can fail to yield stories. "I feel lucky to get two good stories out of any meeting," says Ingram. "Many produce no story worthwhile in terms of real advances in medicine."

He still sends his reporters to cover meetings, however, because of the lure of the unexpected. "Most good stories at a meeting you discover when you get there and consist of putting two or three papers together or organizing your own thematic story. When I say 'thematic story' I mean a story where you call ten to twelve researchers about a new development or trend and ask their opinion, rather than tying a story to a single news event. Let's say I want to do something on the violence at abortion clinics that has been in the news. I'd call ob/gyn docs all over the country and ask them what they think."

When they do cover meeting sessions, reporters should remember their audience at all times. Unlike the writer for a medical publication, medical writers for a lay audience cannot assume a preknowledge of the subject. "You must be able to describe the medical advance in layman's terms, which means you have to grasp what happened or find someone who can put it all in layman's language for you," says Ingram. "Whereas if you're writing for doctors, they'll have an immediate understanding of what you're writing about. If you're talking to doctors and parroting back, you're not doing the independent work you need. Doctors are very impatient, and it's hard to get good descriptions from them in a short time, like during their presentations at a medical meeting."

Enterprise Stories

Subjects that medical reporters choose to research and write on their own are another category. These are called enterprise stories because of the enterprise reporters display to think of them. "These are the most fun because you decide what to do," says Ingram. "First, you need to be told by a tip that something is happening. A story idea thus springs to life. Needless to say, almost all of the good stories are enterprise stories. Nobody provides a release on the subject or reports it at a meeting. In general, good stories are gotten by hard work, they aren't dropped on your desk. Good stories are developed by phoning everybody involved and checking one against the other. Even a blind pig finds an acorn once in a while."

An example of a recent enterprise idea Ingram had involved Jeffrey Daumer, the Milwaukee man accused of killing and cutting up a number of young men and eating the remains. The coverage reminded Ingram of a book he had read in 1970 by a Harvard neurosurgeon and a Harvard psychiatrist that said that brain injuries might cause a person serious problems later in life. "At the time it was written I decided there just wasn't enough data," he says. "Now, with CAT scans and other diagnostic equipment I thought doctors might be able to profile these people by really looking at their brains. So, I called up one of the authors who told me it could be done but hadn't been. He had even proposed such a study to the National Institute of Mental Health but had been turned down. I'm thinking of doing a whole editorial package on the need for some kind of compulsory examination of people who, say, commit two violent assaults."

Interviews

No matter whether a medical reporter gets a story from a journal, a news release, a meeting, or through his or her own enterprise, the time will come when the appropriate doctor will have to be interviewed, either in person or on the telephone. "The most important part of any medical story is the direct interview with the doctors who have done the research," says Ingram.

However, for many of the same reasons outlined in Chapter 9 about scientists, doctors may not be easy to reach. They are sometimes afraid of being criticized as "publicity hounds" by peers. They may feel their work is not ready to be revealed. Sometimes they have put themselves on a pedestal. "A lot of doctors still think of themselves as men in white as they did in the 1920s," says Ingram.

"Doctors become more inaccessible as time goes on," says Ingram. "Doctors are struggling hard to make a dollar just as other people are. More often than not, however, it's not the doctor but the secretary at the hospital or office that makes them inaccessible."

He tries to convince the secretary to give him the doctor's home number: "If you have a convincing approach, a strong approach, you don't have to say you're a friend of the doctor; the urgency will be evident in your voice. The conviction you have to talk to him will come through. If necessary, I myself have posed as a number of people, including FBI agents."

If that fails, Ingram leaves his own home and office numbers. "I usually get a response," he says, "but it can take days to reach some doctors. I just pursue and pursue until I do. Doctors will call back, but when they finally do, they are often between patients, are about to go home, or have just arrived. It's best to talk to them at home at night."

If he is dealing with a doctor who also does research at a medical research center, Ingram tries to get around the inevitable requirement that the doctor be contacted only through the public relations person. "The easiest thing to do here is to find out if the doctor has a practice in town," he says, "by phoning the area code and getting the number of the office. Then I get the secretary there to give me his number at the hospital. If I can't get the doctor I originally called, I ask to speak to a colleague."

He says it takes twenty-four to forty-eight hours to get in touch with most doctors. He thinks their inaccessibility is a combination of their being pressed for time and a certain disdain for the press. "The cordon around them is much tighter and you just have to be very aggressive in getting them. You have to ring, ring, ring."

Before a medical reporter even tries to get a doctor to agree to an interview, however, he or she must be well prepared with adequate background on the subject of the interview (gained by reading medical journals, back issues of his or her own publication, or medical reference books and texts) and questions either written out or firmly in mind.

"A medical writer does what any good reporter does — he does his homework," says Ingram. "What are the elements of the story? What are the implications for how many people? How much digging do you have to do to make it clear?''

After this careful preparation the next step is to get the doctor to be forthcoming with enough information to do a complete story. ''You have to treat doctors as a news source, as an equal rather than deferring to them, being condescending, or ingratiating yourself,'' continues Ingram. ''Directness is your best friend. You have to level about how much you know and how much you want to learn. You must convey the importance of this very quickly and carefully or you won't get your story.

''It doesn't help to butter up the doctor. He will sense your respect from the knowledge and understanding you bring to your questions. Confessions of ignorance are welcomed by a doctor. Doctors are willing to be teachers. They usually appreciate your own admission of weakness and lack of understanding. They can assume the role of teacher.''

Kinds of Medical Stories

Medical coverage in this country exists on both a national and local level. The source of stories and the inherent problems apply to both levels, although the nature of national coverage gives it a broader range than its local counterpart.

A national newsmagazine, specialized medical publication, or big-city newspaper is concerned with subjects that affect a large number of people, whether that be important research findings, new cures for diseases, trends in medical and health care funding, delivery of health care to ghettos or remote areas, and medical education.

Unless a small city has a large medical research institution or a medical school, the newspaper covering that city would not be interested in the same kinds of subjects. The one exception would be the preparation of a story covering the local angle of a national story.

Nevertheless, smaller daily newspapers and local magazines usually have a medical beat because medicine and health are always of interest to readers. Reporters on this beat must still interview doctors and other sources, review incoming news releases for tips, and keep up with medical journals and specialized publications to know about trends and discoveries that may be applicable to a local story.

Being a medical reporter for a local newspaper is not easy. Such reporters often have to stretch their talents to cover general science stories or environmental developments. There is a distinct link between medical writing and environmental writing on a local level. Because of staff limitations, a duly designated medical reporter will often write about science and the environment in the same way a science reporter will cover medicine and the environment. It all depends on budgets and editorial titles.

Likely subjects of the medical beat on a local level include the following:

1. **Local news of science and health.** "A local medical reporter should concentrate on finding out how well the community is being served by doctors and hospitals," says Bill Ingram. Other good story possibilities might be a new hospital or new equipment at the hospital, rural towns nearby with one doctor or no doctor, personality features on doctors, stories about prominent patients, in-depth articles on diseases in the area, or prevalent social problems like drug addiction or teenage pregnancy. (See Box 11.1 for the restrictions placed on coverage by most hospitals.)

2. **Local health agencies and issues.** Local medical reporters must also cover public health agencies and issues. The need for local and state governments to fund public health agencies grew out of a concern to protect citizens from epidemics several centuries ago. (See Box 11.2.)

3. **Outbreaks of disease.** Cities have long been natural targets for communicable disease. As early as the bubonic plague in London in 1665-1666, the city government marked the houses of those infected with the disease with red crosses. Quarantining the inhabitants in their houses thus became a municipal responsibility. Those without their own houses were isolated in "pest houses." If these people died, the city sent someone to certify their death and to try to determine the cause.

From this humble beginning has come the control of disease as a municipal responsibility. Out of the mid-nineteenth century grew the "filth theory of disease." Experts decided that if sewers were constructed, garbage collected, and sanitation emphasized, health conditions would improve. This became a city or county responsibility, although a counterpart state agency usually has final authority. Health departments were expanded to carry out these tasks, although in the case of garbage, a public works department does the actual collecting.

4. **Medical meetings.** Although local reporters may not be able to cover medical meetings because of limited resources, they should try to do so whenever possible because of the general background they gain and useful sources they meet. "A medical meeting may

Box 11.1

Restrictions on Medical Coverage

In addition to the legal restraints applicable to all reporters, medical reporters face other restrictions when covering patients in hospitals. The restrictions are not part of any law but instead are contained in "codes of cooperation" between hospitals, physicians, and the press. Such codes, which vary in content from state to state, are designed both to protect patients and to ensure coverage.

The Oregon code is typical. It consists of guidelines for hospitals (asking that they appoint public information people to deal with the press), physicians (asking that they cooperate with the press), and news people (asking that they recognize that a patient's health is the first priority, get permission before entering a hospital, and make every effort to get authentic information).

The code restricts access to patients in cases not of public record (patient or family member must give permission). It allows release of some information in cases of public record, that is, those cases reported by fire or police departments, sheriff, medical examiner, or other public authority. In such cases the hospital public information person can reveal name, residence, sex, age, occupation, whether the patient is conscious, statement of condition, and general description of injuries as determined by a physician.

All hospitals use standard definitions to describe a patient's condition:

1. Good—Vital signs (pulse, temperature, and blood pressure) are stable and within normal limits; patient is conscious and comfortable.

2. Fair—Vital signs are stable and within normal limits; patient is conscious but is uncomfortable and may have minor complications.

3. Serious—Vital signs may be unstable or outside normal limits; patient is acutely ill.

4. Critical—Vital signs are unstable or outside normal limits; there are major complications.

The code covers information about police and accident situations, which are the most frequent requests a hospital gets from the press. Release of patient information follows the guidelines noted earlier for cases of public record. The general nature of the accident may be described (automobile, explosion, or shooting) but not the circumstances. The further information that can be given varies with the specific injury categories: fractures, head injuries, skull fractures, internal injuries, unconsciousness, shooting or stabbing, burns, poisoning, battered children, and rape (where a name is never given).

Death is usually not announced by a hospital, but it is public information after the next of kin has been notified. If the death is investigated by the medical examiner's office, inquiries about cause and circumstances should be referred there.

Requests to take photographs are granted only with the written consent of a patient. When the patient is a minor, parental consent must be obtained, too. The physician in the case is informed as well. Requests to interview a patient in custody are granted by the police or government agency concerned. A hospital public information person and a physician can decline to grant permission to interview a patient. A patient can also decline.

Matters change a bit with prominent people. They usually want the publicity. Some have their own public relations people, who can grant requests for interviews. If the person is in serious or critical condition, the hospital will usually issue regular bulletins.

Medical writers should be familiar with state and local codes and abide by them.

Box 11.2

The Typical Health Department

Today's typical health department, which is covered regularly by the medical beat reporter, is presided over by a single director or a board of health composed of citizens of the town (a physician, an engineer, and several lay people are a usual combination). Such departments are responsible for:

1. Communicable disease control, which requires finding the source of an epidemic, isolating those infected, and immunizing others so they won't get it.

2. Sanitary inspection of dumps, swamps (they should be drained), water supplies, retail food establishments and food handlers, local slaughter houses (if not done by the U.S. Department of Agriculture), and milk (for signs of watering, tuberculosis, and typhoid).

3. Public health education about venereal disease treatment, abuse of alcohol and other drugs, maternal and child care, personal hygiene, danger signals of major diseases, and the need for proper preventive medicine.

4. Staff services, which require keeping records of births, deaths, communicable disease, and laboratory analysis.

---

seem unfathomable for a reporter not used to the terms and overall confusion," says Ingram, "but it is worth trying. It's the only way to get your feet wet." If a reporter can't go, the next best thing is to use wire service coverage as a background to doing stories with a local angle.

5. **Medical research findings.** This kind of story is not possible to do unless a medical school or research center is located in the newspaper's coverage area. If so, information about research projects will provide a steady stream of story ideas. If no such institution exists nearby, a medical reporter will be forced to wait for news of major findings to break elsewhere, then follow up with a local angle. (Box 11.3 explains the medical research cycle.)

6. **Drug stories.** Most local drug stories concern abuses, dangers, and efforts to control illegal substances. With this topic, local medical reporters are more lucky than their counterparts on specialized medical publications, who must worry about pressure from drug companies that advertise in the publication. Local sources may get mad about stories, but they usually don't buy advertising space.

7. **Profiles of physicians and other medical personnel.** This kind of story does not differ from a feature on any person, except for the medical angle. A "day in the life" — of a doctor or a nurse or a hospital — is a good approach to take because readers are interested in seeing what a doctor does or how a hospital functions.

Writing Medical Stories

Bill Ingram advocates the following rules for writing medical stories:

1. "Writing is best when it is strong declarative prose with no gimmicks, no attempt to consciously construct a pyramid or a reverse pyramid or a seventeen-word sentence or a striking image or a profundity.

2. "Writing is best when the salient element is clear to the reporter who compiled the facts and did the interview, when the corollary thoughts roll out of the typewriter because that salient set of facts got into the lead. I do think that on a complex story it is a good idea to jot down what you're going to say and the major points you're going to make to save anguish in rewriting.

3. "A good story is already written before it gets into the typewriter, because the facts are understood by the writer. Language is less important. It can be embellished later.

4. "On leads, I wouldn't choose a straitjacket by wanting any particular approach. Some are chronological; some play to the here and now, that is, news oriented. It is important to play your best

Box 11.3

The Medical Research Cycle

Before a drug is ever approved for use by the Food and Drug Administration (FDA), it must undergo a tortuous process of approval that costs a great deal of money and takes a lot of time.

Step 1:   Medical research scientists at a drug company develop a drug that seems to show promise in treating a disease over several years in laboratory tests. They document their findings and work out a plan for trials.

Step 2:   The drug company formally requests permission of the FDA to use animals in further testing. The FDA approves or requests more data.

Step 3:   The drug company conducts tests on animals by using the new drug and carefully recording and analyzing results. This period can last as long as three or four years.

Step 4:   The company compiles its data and formally makes a New Drug Application (NDA) to the FDA.

Step 5:   The FDA considers this animal data, paying careful attention to toxicity rates (fifty percent or more is considered too high).

Step 6:   Included in the NDA is a plan for early clinical open trials in which the therapeutic effects of the drug are tested on humans on a limited basis. If the animal test data is satisfactory, the FDA will approve this limited testing.

Step 7:   The most crucial and costly and time consuming phase comes next. In it, strictly controlled scientific trials of the drug are set up. They may run for six weeks or four years, depending on the drug and the disease.

In the tests, two groups of patients, each with the disease or medical condition, are established. Doctors contact other doctors for patient names; drug companies sometimes advertise for volunteers. The doctors and the patients involved in the study are paid for their work. The patients sign forms releasing the company from liability. The two groups, identical in number, are also matched by sex, health status, age, and even socioeconomic group. For ease of conducting the test and administering the drug, they usually live in the same geographic area. One group is given the drug to be tested, the other a placebo. No one knows who is getting the drug or the "pink pill" placebo, except the administrator of the test. This testing is called "double blind" because the identity of who gets what pill is carefully hidden.

The patients go to the same place on a regular basis to receive their pill. Their reactions are carefully observed and reported to the drug company periodically. A good study will use twelve centers around the country, each with ten to twenty patients. Sometimes, "crossover" testing is done, in which the patients getting the drug are given the placebo after six weeks and vice versa. This is more costly, however, and done less than half the time.

The trials go on until the data shows statistically significant evidence that the drug is working. The FDA uses a "confidence index" level of .005, in other words, success in patients getting the drug .005 percent of the time.

Step 8: The FDA reviews the data and approves the drug or asks for more testing, recalculation of data, or refinement of existing trials.

Step 9: The researchers at the company simultaneously compile their findings into an article which they submit to the appropriate research journal.

The typical research cycle for a drug takes ten years and costs anywhere from $10 million to $20 million.

cards at the outset so readers will jump to page 17 and read the rest of the story. Over the years I've become much less interested in cuteness and imagery than in beginning with clear expression of the strongest point the story is making.

5. "The medical story should be told as sparingly as possible. I like to see stories in the present tense. I think you have a better sense of reality if a story is told as if it is happening."

6. A medical writer should not forget about illustrations. Any article can be enhanced greatly with good illustrations. Indeed a reader may not even understand a subject without a good photograph, drawing, or chart to fit the pieces together. As with their articles, however, many researchers will save the good illustrations for the medical journals. "They will give you inferior or no illustrations," say Ingram. "Without an illustration, a story can be worthless." The best thing for a medical writer to do when a researcher cannot provide an illustration is to get enough information so a staff artist can prepare an illustration.

#1

Medical stories are usually classified as either clinical (about disease, treatment, drugs, or research) or socioeconomic (about societal factors causing disease like poverty and pollution, and the political aspects of medicine). In this clinical story, Bill Ingram begins with a straightforward lead that describes the major finding in the research.

'GOOD' HIV MAY SLOW AIDS
By Bill Ingram

1 Four AIDS patients have regained cell-mediated immune function and are "clinically stable" a year after receiving serum from a long-term asymptomatic donor.

He uses a simple device for his transition, picking up the word "donor" in the lead and beginning the second graf with it.

He goes on to tell the fate of three other patients in the experiment . . . and mentions two who died.

For the first time in graf 4, Ingram backs up what he has thus far summarized with a direct quote from his main source.

Graf 5 continues the quote.

In graf 6, Ingram counters what his main source has told him with a quote from someone who is skeptical.

Grafs 7 and 8 allow Ingram's source to answer his critic.

2 The donor may in effect have "spread" a non-pathogenic or "good" strain of HIV that has dominance over HIV1, according to an investigative team.

3 Three other patients out of 11 who each received a total of 2-3 CC of inoculum in two infusions are in fair condition. They are responding to treatments for "a whole range of recurring infections and complications, many of them pre-existing," said Michael Scolaro, M.D. of Los Angeles, the principal investigator. Two patients are in "poor condition" and two have died.

4 "The four who are stable were suffering weight loss, diarrhea and opportunistic infections a year ago," Dr. Scolaro said. "They were frequently hospitalized. Their physical functioning was 20 percent to 50 percent on the Karnotsky scale.

5 "They had been on AZT from two to three years and either no longer responded to it or were suffering adverse reactions to it. They discontinued it when the trial started. Today they are all back at work. Their functioning on the Karnotsky scale is about 90 percent."

6 "Four improvements do not make a therapy. AIDS is replete with claims like this," commented Donald Francis, a public health expert who is consultant for the Western states for the Centers for Disease Control.

7 "We are not making claims. This is a very preliminary pilot study and these patients should not be considered cured," said Dr. Scolaro. "At 18 month follow-up, we should consider submitting a paper. I wouldn't even think about duplicating the study in other groups now.

8 "But we have had strong immune responses," he said. "Two patients had delayed-type hypersensitivity skin test responses to all eight antigens and the other two to six. Their responses were 'zero' or 'trace' a year ago. Paradoxically, their T-4 cell counts remain low, around a mean of 70."

In graf 9, Ingram brings in a co-investigator on the project to amplify his partner's earlier statements.

9   However, samples from all four and the donor show strong antibody response to the p17 region of the viral core, said co-investigator George Pieczenik, Ph.D., a molecular biologist from New York's Mount Sinai Medical Center.

10   The analysis was done by Steve Alexander, Ph.D., developer of the gradient Western blot-test.

Graf 11 gives that source the chance to amplify his thoughts; although Ingram paraphrases him rather than using direct quotes.

11   Dr. Pieczenik postulates that a selection and competition process at the nucleotide or genotype level predicts "random" changes that could produce a competitive, non-pathogenic virus.

He lets his source continue to amplify his remarks using a paraphrase/quote/paraphrase/quote story structure technique common in news stories.

12   He reasons that a single nucleotide change can make a non-pathogenic strain pathogenic, hence the converse is also possible. He calculates that this change could happen in about one of every 500 AIDS cases.

13   Besides citing findings in the four AIDS patients, Dr. Pieczenik draws parallels from epidemics and uses nucleotide sequencing studies to make his case that non-pathogenic variants could be used to vaccinate as well as treat AIDS patients.

In graf 14, he notes that a journal is considering an article on these findings. This is important information to *Medical Tribune* readers because the results would only be authenticated in their minds if they were published in a reputable journal.

14   His article summarizing his theory of genotypic selection is under consideration by the *Journal of Molecular Biology.*

Ingram brings in other voices in grafs 15, 16, and 17 so as to not appear to be giving a one-sided approach.

15   "I have observed one virus outgrowing another in the tobacco mosaic," said Dr. Aaron Klug, Ph.D., a Nobelist who is chief of Britain's Laboratory of Molecular Biology of the Medical Research Council. "It could apply to HIV. I don't know whether Pieczenik's specifics are correct.

16   "But with success apparent (in the four patients), the work must be pursued. First, it must be determined whether the virus in the donor is dominant and a single strain."

17   "You need a controlled study," said Abraham Karpas, Ph.D., University of

Cambridge assistant chief of hematology research, and developer of passive HIV immunization.

In graf 18, he gives one of his sources the last direct quote, followed by added information on the construction of the study. As with many news stories, this one just ends, without anything dramatic or any attempt to tie it to the lead.

18 "The patients served as their own controls in terms of immune function," said Pieczenik.

19 The donor was selected from 140 case histories after co-investigator Roy Durham solicited 1,763 physicians who treat AIDS. An I.V. drug user as well as an active homosexual, the donor could have had 1,000 exposures to a "good" virus, yet had a T-4 cell count of 1,000.

#2

1991 FOCUS ON NATIONAL HEALTH
By Bill Ingram

To begin this socioeconomic story on what to expect in the year ahead in health care (it ran in *Medical Tribune* in January), Ingram summarized what his sources told him.

His transition continues the summary begun in the lead.

1 The quality of care in this country is uniformly high, and clinical advances this year should push it even higher, according to top health authorities. But the delivery of care is costly and inequitable, the experts agreed.

2 A national dialogue on plans to change the present health care system — or replace it entirely — appears inevitable in the months ahead, though congressional action is not expected.

By grafs 3 and 4, he begins to use the direct quotes from noted medical and health experts who he talked to for this article. He went after variety in his choices: first, the editor of *The New England Journal of Medicine*.

3 "Historic forces are gathering. The handwriting is on the wall," said Arnold Relman, M.D., editor of *The New England Journal of Medicine*. "We are spending vast amounts of money far out of proportion to the value we get. For the first time, the interests of major businesses, unions, consumers and even the medical professions are coalescing. I cannot remember a time when the morale of the profession was lower or when there was more general resentment and frustration.

4 "The system is breaking down. There's no way we can keep an open-ended indemnification system, with each doctor and hospital fighting to get market share."

. . . followed by a congressman who is a psychiatrist (5). . .

5 "The foundation for a national plan has already been laid by DRG hospital payment reform, upcoming physician payment reform and the realization that access must be broadened," said Rep. Jim McDermott, M.D. (D-Wash.), a psychiatrist who is bidding for a role in the reform process. He was just appointed to the House Ways and Means Committee. "I want physicians to be involved in developing a health plan," he said. (See story, page 9.)

. . . and a noted heart surgeon (6). To achieve uniformity in such interviews, everyone is asked the same question.

6 "A national health system doesn't solve the problem," said Michael DeBakey, M.D., heart surgeon and Chancellor of Baylor College of Medicine. "Whatever the plan, if you don't provide the funds, you get de facto rationing . . . reduce the medicine budget and impose more regulations and all you do is decrease accessibility. A certain proportion of patients don't get care and die."

Another source is quoted in grafs 7, 8, and 9 about a major problem—health care delivery.

7 Amid delivery of care turmoil, medicine was seen making steady strides this year. "With heart disease, we will see a shift in prevention strategy," said Antonio Gotto, M.D., chair of internal medicine at Baylor.

8 "In the 1970's, we moved from cigarette smoking to blood pressure. In the 1980's, we moved to cholesterol. Now we have early angiographic evidence that we can halt the progression of atheroma in [many] cases [via diet and exercise, or drugs], and in some cases induce regression.

9 "This gives us options not available before. We're not restricted to one approach. If diet and exercise don't work, we can give drugs. We can identify subsets, find which way to go, and individualize treatment," (see story, page 3). Dr. Gotto said that averting costly interventions would be the payoff of preventive medical management.

Back to an earlier source on the same subject.

10 Dr. DeBakey did not go along with the new strategy. "It's curious," he said "that I have never seen regression in a single patient, and I've looked at thousands of cases [of heart disease], looked at lesions day after day, with cholesterols below 200 mg/dl in a third of the patients. I've followed some patients for 30 years."

In graf 11, Ingram switches to cancer and brings in another source in 12 and 13.

11 In the cancer battle, the expected licensing of hematologic growth factors represents a major advance, according to John Laszlo, M.D., senior vice-president for research of the American Cancer Society.

12 "Very tangible benefits" should attend the use of granulocyte colony stimulating factors," said Dr. Laszlo. By inducing stem cells to "a greater commitment to form granulocytes . . . we can give [substantially] higher doses of drugs and at the same time protect patients from bone marrow toxicity." (See story, page 3.)

13 "With breast cancer, testicular cancer, leukemia and certain types of lymphomas," said Dr. Laszlo, there is a very clear dose-response curve. "The hope here is that the higher doses we can now give might convert people from a complete remission to an actual cure."

Ingram ends his story with a review of what is expected in another big medical problem, AIDS. To do so, he paraphrases the views on the subject of the U.S. surgeon general.

14 No major advances were expected in the control of AIDS, but a shift in epidemiologic emphasis was foreseen. AIDS will be perceived more and more as a heterosexual disease. U.S. Surgeon General Antonia Novello, M.D., said she intends to spend about a third of her time making the public aware of the risk of HIV infection and AIDS in women. In some U.S. subpopulations, the female/male ratio for HIV infection and AIDS deaths approaches the 1/1 ratio typical in Africa.

Medical Reporting:
Likely Problems and How to Solve Them

Problem

1. Doctors difficult to interview (suspicious of reporters, hostile to press, busy, talk in overly

Solution

1a. Gain confidence by a forthright approach.

1b. Explain value of publicity (better public

complicated manner, or
fear peer reaction to
publicity).

understanding and more
grant money).

1c. Ask questions about
anything not understood.

1d. Be persistent in getting an
interview.

1e. Point out that you will try to
get information from other
sources so why not give it to
you to make sure it is
accurately reported.

1f. Try to get information from
other sources: colleagues of
the doctor, experts in the
specialty, etc.

2. Complicated subject
matter.

2a. Have a basic understanding
of medicine gained by
reading textbooks, articles in
medical publications like the
*New England Journal of
Medicine*, the *Journal of the
American Medical
Association*, *Medical World
News*, *Medical Tribune*,
Medical Economics, and
medical coverage in *Time*,
Newsweek, and large daily
newspapers like the *New
York Times*.

2b. Take introductory courses in
physiology, biology, zoology,
epidemiology, and health
administration.

2c. Keep a good medical
dictionary and basic
textbook handy while
writing stories.

2d. Build a file of reference
material of articles clipped
from the above publications
and information gained from
getting on the mailing lists

of state and local medical societies; associations such as the American Medical Association, the American Public Health Association, and the American Hospital Association; the Department of Health and Human Services as well as regional, state, and local health agencies, large pharmaceutical companies; government committees such as state legislative committees, the Senate Committee on Human Resources, and the House Committee on Interstate and Foreign Commerce; local hospitals, research laboratories, and universities doing medical research.

2e. Among researchers and doctors, build a group of experts to call for explanation of complicated terms and concepts.

3. Medical meetings hard to cover (technical papers and simultaneous presentations).

3a. Go over programs in advance with medical experts to decide on significant story possibilities.

3b. Get help from other medical writers to share coverage of sessions.

4. Drug stories leading to advertising pressure.

4a. Try to point out value of full disclosure.

4b. Make sure facts are correct.

4c. Balance coverage by getting material from drug company and from detractors of the drug.

4d. Be prepared to resign if the issue is worth it.

Summary

Medical reporting, which has a similar background and some of the same problems as science reporting, exists on both a local and national level. Local medical reporters, who work primarily for small newspapers and often cover allied beats, write about public health departments, hospitals, and news events. National medical reporters, who work for large newspapers, newsmagazines, and specialized medical publications, cover research findings, new drugs, new techniques of surgery and treatment, and trends in government funding and health care delivery. No matter at what level they work, medical reporters get stories from medical journal articles, public relations news releases, medical meetings, and day-to-day coverage of events on their beat. Each of these sources presents problems to the medical writer. Only the national medical reporter must worry about pressure from advertisers, however. The writing of medical stories necessitates clarity and brevity so that readers understand the complicated subject matter. Medical reporters must be careful not to overemphasize the success of a treatment or a drug, lest sufferers of a disease build up false hopes for a cure.

Exercises

1. Write a story about a local doctor, gathering the material through interviews and personal observations.

2. Write a story about a local pharmacist, gathering the material through interviews and personal observations.

3. Spend the evening in the emergency room of your local hospital and write a story about what you observe and are told.

4. Select a national medical problem as researched in newspapers, magazines, and the medical press and figure out a local angle. Interview appropriate sources and write a story.

5. Obtain a news release from a nearby medical center or university on a research finding. Write a list of ten questions to expand into a story. Make sure you understand all the terms. Arrange an interview with the researcher on the project, and among other questions, ask him or her to explain the background of the project including financial support, the methodology by which it was carried out, and the future significance of the findings. Write an article detailing your findings.

Key Terms for Medical Reporting

Abdomen   The portion of the body between the diaphragm and the pelvis.

Abortion   Premature expulsion from the uterus of a human fetus.

Abstract   A summary of the contents and findings of a scientific or medical article.

Acid   Slang for LSD, a powerful hallucinogenic drug.

Addiction   The state of being addicted to, or physiologically dependent on, a drug; the drug must be administered periodically to prevent the discomfort of withdrawal symptoms.

Adrenalin   A hormone produced by the adrenal glands that causes a rise in blood pressure.

AIDS   Acquired Immune Deficiency Syndrome. A disease of the immune system characterized by increased susceptibility to opportunistic infections like pneumocytis pneumonia, certain cancers like Kaposi's sarcoma, and to neurological disorders; caused by a retrovirus and transmitted chiefly through blood or blood products that enter the body's bloodstream, especially by sexual contact or contaminated hypodermic needles.

Amphetamine   A class of drugs that stimulate the central nervous system; also called "uppers."

Anemia   A condition in which the blood is deficient either in quality or in quantity.

Angina   Any disease characterized by spasmodic, choking, or suffocating pain.

Antibiotic   A substance, like penicillin or streptomycin, derived from various microorganisms and fungi with the capacity to inhibit the growth of or to destroy microorganisms; used in the treatment of infectious diseases.

Antibody   A protein produced in the body to overcome the toxicity of a specific antigen.

Antigen   A substance that stimulates production of antibodies.

Artery   A blood vessel that conveys blood from the heart to any part of the body.

Bacteria   Microscopic and spherical, rod-shaped, or spiral organisms involved in fermentation, putrefaction, and disease production.

Barbiturate   A class of drugs that depress the central nervous system; also called "downers."

Blood   The fluid that circulates in the vascular system of humans and other vertebrates and is necessary for life.

Bone   One of the structures composing the skeleton of a vertebrate.

Carbohydrate   Any class of organic compounds composed of carbon, hydrogen, and oxygen; includes starches and sugars.

Carcinoma   Cancer; a malignant tumor arising from epithelial tissue.

Cubic centimeter   A unit of measure normally used to describe amounts of blood or medication usually expressed medically as "CC."

Cardiopulmonary   Disease that affects the heart and lungs.

Cardiovascular Disease that affects the heart and blood vessels.

CDC Centers for Disease Control, a government laboratory responsible for investigating the causes of epidemics.

Cell The basic structural unit of all organisms, a usually microscopic structure containing nuclear and cytoplasmic material enclosed by a semipermeable membrane and, in plants, a cell wall.

Chemotherapy The treatment of disease, quite often cancer, by chemical compounds like sulfonamides or arsphenamine, which inhibit the life process of disease-causing organisms without injuring the patient's tissues.

Cholesterol An organic fatty alcohol present in bile, blood, and various tissues that can cause heart disease.

Clinical trials Experiments in which new drugs are given to patients and effects observed and recorded.

Coagulation The action of changing from a fluid (like blood) into a thickened mass (like a clot).

Cocaine A short-acting stimulant drug, commonly ingested by sniffing or snorting, less frequently by injection; also called "coke."

Coma Profound unconsciousness.

Contagion The medium in which a contagious disease is transmitted.

Coronary Anything pertaining to the human heart.

Coronary thrombosis A clot in one of the coronary arteries of the heart.

Coroner An officer of a city or county whose job it is to investigate any death not clearly from natural causes.

Corpuscle A blood cell.

Crack Pellet-sized pieces of highly purified cocaine, prepared with other ingredients for smoking. Known to be highly potent and addictive.

Dermatology The field of medicine concerning diseases of the skin.

Diagnosis The process of determining the nature of a disease after examination and analysis.

Dialysis The separation of different components in a chemical solution by diffusion through a semipermeable membrane; used to treat kidney disease.

Dissect To cut, separate, and expose body structures, especially for anatomy study.

DNA Acronym for deoxyribonucleic acid; any class of nucleic acids found chiefly in the nucleus of cells; responsible for transmitting hereditary characteristics and the building of proteins.

Donor A person or animal providing blood, an organ, bone marrow cells, or other biological tissue for transfusion or transplantation.

Drug dependence Reliance on a drug without necessarily being addicted to it.

Dysfunction Partial disturbance, impairment, or abnormality of the functioning of an organ.

Dystrophy A disorder resulting from defective or faulty nutrition.

Electrocardiograph (EKG) An instrument for recording the electric current that originates in the heart muscle.

Electroencephalograph (EEG)   An instrument for recording the electric current that originates in the brain.

Embryo   The early or developing stages of an organism; in humans, the first two months of existence.

Empirical   Something based on knowledge derived solely from experience.

Endocrinology   The field of medicine concerning the endocrine, or ductless, glands (such as the thyroid or pituitary) that secrete hormones directly into blood or lymph.

Epidemic   When disease spreads and infects many persons at the same time.

Epidemiology   The branch of medicine dealing with finding the source and cause of epidemics.

FDA   The Food and Drug Administration, a government agency responsible for protecting the public against impure and unsafe foods, drugs, and cosmetics.

Fever   An abnormal condition of the body, characterized by undue rise in temperature.

Gastrointestinal   Pertaining to the stomach or intestine.

Geriatrics or Gerontology   The field of medicine concerning conditions common among old people.

Gynecology   The field of medicine concerning conditions peculiar to women, especially of the reproductive organs.

Hallucinogen   Any of a group of consciousness-altering drugs that commonly produce hallucinations.

Hashish   A hard, gumlike substance made by extracting active resins from a marijuana plant; when smoked in a pipe, it has more intense effects than marijuana.

Hematology   The field of medicine concerning the blood and the blood-forming organs.

Heroin   An addictive opium derivative that produces a depressed, euphoric feeling after being injected or snorted.

Heroin maintenance   A type of addiction treatment in which heroin addicts are furnished supplies of the drug legally, thus largely eliminating the black market and illicit supply.

HIV   The virus that causes AIDS.

Hormone   An internally secreted compound formed in endocrine organs, which affects the functions of specifically receptive organs or tissues when carried to them by body fluids.

Hypertension   High blood pressure.

Hypotension   Low blood pressure.

Insulin   A protein hormone formed in the pancreas and secreted into the blood, where it regulates carbohydrate metabolism.

I.V.   Abbreviation for intravenous, pertaining to the injection of a substance into the vein.

Kidneys   Two small, oval glandular organs in the back part of the abdominal cavity; their function is to purify the blood of waste products.

LSD Acronym and common name for lysergic acid diethylamide, a powerful hallucinogenic drug.

Lymph A yellowish fluid, containing white blood cells, that surrounds body cells and carries their wastes to the bloodstream.

Malignant The quality of infiltrating, spreading, and causing death; often used to describe a tumor that invades adjacent tissues and spreads to distant parts of the body.

Marijuana A mixture of the dried leaves, stems, and flowers of the Indian hemp plant Cannabis sativa, commonly smoked in crudely rolled cigarettes called "joints" or "reefers"; also called "pot."

Metabolism The sum of all physical and chemical processes by which living organized substance is produced and maintained, and the transformation by which energy is made available for use by the organisms.

Methadone A synthetic narcotic used as a substitute for heroin in addiction treatment programs.

Molecular biology The branch of biology that deals with the nature of biological phenomena at the molecular level through the study of DNA and RNA, proteins and other macromolecules involved in genetic information and cell function.

Morphine An opium derivative commonly used as a painkiller; made by refining raw opium.

Muscle A tissue composed of cells or fibers, the contraction of which produces movement in the body.

Nephritis Inflammation of the kidneys.

Neurology The field of medicine concerning the brain, the spinal cord, and the peripheral nerves.

NIH National Institutes of Health, the primary federal government agency responsible for funding and conducting medical research.

Obstetrics The field of medicine concerning the care of pregnancy, including delivery and aftercare.

Ophthalmology The field of medicine concerning the eyes.

Orthopedics The field of medicine concerning bones, joints, tendons, and muscles.

Pathogenic Capable of producing illness.

Pathology The science of the origin and nature of diseases.

Pediatrics The field of medicine concerning conditions common among children.

Peer review The review by one's peers of work; used in medicine and science as a means to control the quality of both patient care and the reporting of research findings.

Placebo A substance with no medicinal value given to satisfy a patient; often given to one group in a medical study as a means of comparison.

Protocol The plan for carrying out a scientific study or a patient's treatment regimen.

Plasma The fluid portion of the blood in which the corpuscles are suspended.

Platelet Circular or oval disc, found in the blood of all mammals, that affects coagulation.

Prognosis A forecast of the probable outcome of an illness.

Protein Any of a group of nitrogenous organic compounds of high molecular weight that occur in all living cells and are required for all life processes in animals and plants.

Psychiatry The field of medicine concerning the mind and the personality.

Psychosomatic The quality of a physical disorder that is caused or influenced by the emotional state of the patient.

RNA Acronym for ribonucleic acid, any of a class of single-stranded molecules transcribed from DNA in the cell nucleus.

Sarcoma A tumor, often highly malignant, arising from connective or nonepithelial tissue.

Serum Plasma without clotting substances taken from some animals; it can be rendered immune to some disease by inoculation and used as an antitoxin.

Symptom A sign that indicates the presence of a particular disease or disorder.

Syndrome A group of symptoms and signs occurring together to indicate a specific condition or disease.

Tendon A cord of dense, tough tissue connecting a muscle with a bone.

Therapeutics The study of medical treatment of diseases.

Therapy The remedial treatment of a disease or other physical or mental disorder.

Tissue A mass of cells in an animal or plant that form a particular kind of structural material with a definite function.

Toxicity The quality of having the effect of poison; caused by a toxin, a poisonous substance generated by microorganisms, plants, or animals and capable of causing various diseases.

Tracheotomy The operation of cutting into the trachea to allow a person to breathe.

Trauma An injury to the body produced by sudden force.

Trial The process of trying, testing, and gaining proof on the efficacy of a drug before it can be widely used.

Tumor An abnormal or diseased swelling or growth in any part of the body.

Vascular The system in the human body of, or provided with, vessels or ducts that convey fluids like blood or lymph.

Withdrawal The process of ceasing to use a particular drug and the resultant physiological and psychological effects.

Additional Reading in Science, the Environment, and Medicine

Asimov, Isaac. *Asimov's Guide to Science*. New York: Basic Books, 1972.

_____. *More Worlds of Science*. Boston: Houghton Mifflin, 1972.

_____. *Science Past—Science Future*. New York: Doubleday, 1975.

Berkow, Robert, ed. *Merck Manual.* 14th ed. Rahway, NJ: Merck & Company, 1983.

Bernstein, Jeremy. *Experiencing Science.* New York: Basic Books, 1978.

Blakiston's and Gould's Medical Dictionary. New York: McGraw-Hill, 1979.

Bowen, Mary Elizabeth, and Joseph A. Mazzeo, eds. *Writing About Science.* New York: Oxford University Press, 1979.

Bronowski, Jacob. *The Ascent of Man.* Boston: Little, Brown, 1974.

Brown, Harrison. *The Challenge of Man's Future.* New York: Viking Press, 1954.

Burkett, Warren. *Writing Science News for the Mass Media.* Houston: Gulf Publishing, 1973.

Calder, Nigel. *Einstein's Universe.* New York: Viking Press, 1979.

Califano, Joseph A., Jr. *America's Health Care Revolution.* New York: Random House, 1986.

Carson, Rachel. *Silent Spring.* Boston: Houghton Mifflin, 1962.

Cloud, Preston. *Cosmos Earth and Man.* New Haven, CT: Yale University Press, 1978.

Colbert, E.H. *Men and Dinosaurs.* New York: E.P. Dutton, 1968.

Commoner, Barry. *The Closing Circle.* New York: Alfred A. Knopf, 1972.

Control of Communicable Diseases in Man. New York: American Public Health Association, published annually.

Darwin, Charles. *On the Origin of the Species.* Fascimile ed. Cambridge, MA: Harvard University Press, 1964.

Day, David. *The Whale War.* San Francisco: Sierra Club Books, 1987.

DeBakey, Lois. *The Scientific Journal: Editorial Policies and Practices.* St. Louis: C.V. Mosby, 1976.

DeBell, Garrett, ed. *The Environmental Handbook.* New York: Ballantine Books, 1970.

Dorland's Illustrated Medical Dictionary. 26th ed. Philadelphia: W.B. Saunders, 1985.

Ehrlich, Paul R. *The Population Bomb.* New York: Ballantine Books, 1968.

Ehrlich, Paul, A. H. Ehrlich, and J. P. Holdren. *Ecoscience: Population, Resources, Environment.* San Francisco: W.H. Freeman, 1977.

Frank, Phillip. *Einstein: His Life and Times.* New York: Alfred A. Knopf, 1953.

Graham, Frank Jr. *Since Silent Spring.* Boston: Houghton Mifflin, 1970.

Holdren, John, and Philip Herrera. *Energy.* San Francisco: Sierra Club Books, 1971.

Jacob, Stanley W., and Clarice Ashworth Francone. *Structure and Function in Man.* Philadelphia: W.B. Saunders, 1974.

Jungk, Robert. *Brighter Than a Thousand Suns: A Personal History of the Atomic Scientists.* New York: Harcourt, Brace, 1958.

Kean, B. H., with Tracy Dahlby. *M.D.* New York: Ballantine Books, 1990.

Kevles, Daniel J. *The Physicists.* New York: Alfred A. Knopf, 1978.

Leatherwood, Stephen, and Randall R. Reeves. *The Sierra Club Handbook of Whales and Dolphins.* San Francisco: Sierra Club Books, 1983.

Lopez, Barry. *Arctic Dreams.* New York: Charles Scribners' Sons, 1986.

Mandel, Siegfried. *Writing for Science and Technology*. New York: Dell, 1970.

McAlester, A. L. *The History of Life*. Englewood Cliffs, NJ: Prentice-Hall, 1977.

Mostert, Noel. *Supership*. New York: Alfred A. Knopf, 1974.

Mowat, Farley. *Sea of Slaughter*. Boston: Atlantic Monthly Press, 1984.

Musto, David. *The American Disease: Origins of Narcotic Control*. New Haven, CT: Yale University Press, 1973.

Newman, James R. *Science and Sensibility*. 2 vols. New York: Simon & Schuster, 1961.

Reichenbach, Hans. *The Rise of Scientific Philosophy*. Berkeley: University of California Press, 1951.

Rhodes, Richard. *The Making of the Atomic Bomb*. New York: Simon & Schuster, 1987.

Roueche, Berton. *Annals of Epidemiology*. Boston: Little, Brown, 1967.

_____. *A Man Called Hoffman*. New York: Berkley, 1966.

_____. *The Medical Detectives*. New York: Truman Talley/Times, 1981.

Sagan, Carl. *Broca's Brain*. New York: Random House, 1979.

_____. *Cosmos*. New York: Random House, 1980.

Shilts, Randy. *And the Band Played On*. New York: St. Martin's Press, 1987.

Smith, David E., and George R. Gay, eds. *"It's So Good Don't Even Try It Once": Heroin in Perspective*. Englewood Cliffs, NJ: Prentice-Hall, 1972.

Smith, Genevieve Love, and Phyllis E. Davis. *Medical Terminology*. 4th ed. New York: John Wiley & Sons, 1981.

Snow, C.P. *Science and Government*. Cambridge, MA: Harvard University Press, 1961.

_____. *The Two Cultures and the Scientific Revolution*. New York: Cambridge University Press, 1959.

Starr, Paul. *The Social Transformation of American Medicine*. New York: Basic Books, 1984.

Stockton, William. *Altered Destinies: Lives Changed by Genetic Flaws*. New York: Doubleday, 1980.

Sullivan, Walter. *Black Holes*. New York: Anchor Press, 1980.

_____. *We Are Not Alone*. New York: McGraw-Hill, 1964.

Thomas, Lewis. *The Lives of a Cell: Notes of a Biology Watcher*. New York: Viking Press, 1974.

_____. *The Medusa and the Snail: More Notes of a Biology Watcher*. New York: Viking Press, 1979.

Wilford, John Noble, ed. *Scientists at Work*. New York: Dodd, Mead, 1979.

Winter, Ruth. *Cancer-Causing Agents: A Preventive Guide*. New York: Crown, 1980.

V Business

Carlyle . . . spoke in 1850 of the "Respectable Professor of the Dismal Science" and gave to economics a name that it has never quite escaped because it was never quite undeserved.

—John Kenneth Galbraith

General store interior, Moundville, Alabama, Summer 1936 by Walker Evans. [*Courtesy U.S. Farm Security Administration Collection, Prints and Photographs Division, Library of Congress*]

12

Business and the Economy

WALL STREET LAYS AN EGG

—Headline in *Variety* announcing 1929 stock market crash

One Business Reporter

People in journalism don't use the word "scoop" much anymore, considering it about as archaic as manual typewriters or pastepots on the copy desk. But scoop is precisely the word that seems to fit a story Paul Carroll found out about quite by accident.

Soon after the technology reporter for the *Wall Street Journal* arrived in his office on the Tuesday after Memorial Day, he got a call from one of the many sources he had cultivated in his five years

395

covering the computer business. His source said he had a copy of a memo in which IBM Chairman John Akers was highly critical of company employees and blamed them for recent problems.

That message would hardly be news at most American corporations suffering from effects of the economic recession. But for such information to leak out of the button-down world of IBM, where armies of PR people spend a great deal of time keeping their company out of the news, the memo was startling and one Carroll knew he would want to share with *Journal* readers.

"My source, who was from outside of IBM, was pretty casual. He just said, 'By the way, I have my hands on a memo about Akers. Do you want a copy? I'll fax it to you,'" recalls Carroll.

When he had the document in hand a short time later the reporter read through it and called sources at IBM to try to verify it. "They confirmed the veracity of it," he says. "I needed to be sure."

One of his calls was to an IBM public relations person. Even though the *Journal* seldom quotes such a person by name, Carroll needed a quote that would give some balance to the story. "He tried to discount the significance of the memo, saying, 'People may think this is new, but Akers has been talking this way for months,'" continues Carroll. "He tried to make the story sound not as sexy."

These preliminaries done, Carroll told his editor he had the story. This editor said he was going to approach the editors of page one to see if they wanted to use it. At the *Journal*, placement of a story on page one has special meaning. Just three stories a day run on the page, so only subjects of unusual nature get put here. And, unlike the situation on most newspapers, newsworthiness is not the only criteria. The story has to be very special.

As his editor went off to talk to page one, Carroll prepared to write his story. "The memo was fairly short — three pages plus," he says. "But I had a lot of other potentially illuminating documents on IBM I'd been saving up such as materials that top executives had distributed to managers who were supposed to pressure large numbers of employees to quit. I wasn't sure what was in the documents, and, in fact, there wasn't much there, but I flipped through the documents for a couple of hours. I've found you need to have a lot of stuff stockpiled because you never know when something's going to break and you'll need it. I also try to keep things in my head that I know I can use. As I went through the memo I saw that there wasn't much new news, except for the fact that Akers was madder than he was letting on publicly about things such as loss of market share. I decided the interesting thing was that readers would get to hear Akers speaking the way he speaks when he thinks the world is not listening, so I decided to use lots of direct quotes."

Carroll finished writing about 3 P.M. His editor told him that page one was not interested but that the story would appear in the next best location: the first page of section 2. He talked a bit later to the editor handling the story and discussed headlines. Normally, reporters have nothing to do with the writing of the headlines atop their stories. But Carroll had spent his first seven years at the *Journal* in numerous editing jobs, so he'd written his share of heads.

"I wanted to check on the headline because IBM had gotten hacked off in the past over headlines," he says. "The editor hadn't written one yet, but as we chatted something he said made me recall the headline in the *New York Daily News* when President Ford refused to approve loans to the city: FORD TO CITY: DROP DEAD. I jokingly suggested a variation on that and that's what wound up on the story: AKERS TO IBM EMPLOYEES: WAKE UP!"

The reaction from the corporation was mild initially. "The PR guy said he couldn't quibble with the story," says Carroll. "He said it was very fair and reflected their side. But he said that the reaction from people inside the company was, why is this news? He had told them if he were a journalist in my position, he would have done the same thing."

Still, the story on the Akers' outburst marked a kind of watershed for Carroll in his relations with the most important company on his beat. (He also covers Unisys, Xerox, and Computer Associates.) "As other newspapers and even the general interest magazines picked up on the Akers story, IBM returned to the bunker mentality it had been trying to shed," he says.

"With IBM, it's been a long, slow process to get people to open up," he says. "Traditionally, it's been a very bureaucratic, control-oriented company that would make an announcement when it wanted to. They worked super hard to have no pre-emption of their plans. They even use code names with customers so that if anything leaked to the press, they'd track it back to the source. It got kind of silly and with so many names—like Grapefruit, Cherry, Apple, Peach—they'd get confused."

Gradually, as IBM has changed from a company that made all its own components, it has become more difficult for them to keep things quiet. The company now has partners and some of them like to talk to the press. "That makes it harder to control because outside people are more willing to talk," he says.

Carroll has seen a gradual change in the operating methods of IBM PR people as a result. "Five years ago when it was easier to control information, the company hired PR people who tried to keep the press at bay. I'd call for comments on pricing and they'd have a prepared position on pricing and they'd read it to me. They wouldn't go beyond that. They were scared to be quoted by name. If they got me an interview with a company official, they'd want a promise that official would get quoted by name and that it would be a favorable story. They'd pump you before for a list of questions."

Now, much of that has changed for Carroll.

"I've come to an accommodation with them," he says. "They've decided I've been at it a while and understand the issues. They may disagree with what I write but I do see the other side. They prefer the devil they know."

IBM has never been hesitant to complain about *Journal* coverage in general, however. Several years before the Akers story, things got so bad that the company sent a high-level executive to the managing editor to complain and a group of reporters and editors traveled to IBM headquarters in Armonk, New York to sit down with IBM's top six executives and hear criticism, not about a particular error, but coverage as a whole. Things calmed down after that, but complaints have picked up again following the Akers story, and access to senior executives has been curtailed.

"We worry if we don't have people complaining every once in a while," laughs Carroll.

Even though Carroll says he was a "math nerd" in high school and had a "nodding acquaintance" with computers and technology, he found the first six months on his beat difficult. "It took six months to get comfortable, a year to hit my stride," he says. "The first thing I did was to read everything I could get my hands on about computers. I made a list every day of the questions I had. If I didn't understand something someone said in an interview, I'd say, 'Stop. Say that in English!' Every week I would call someone I knew and make him spend an hour answering my questions. I learned, to get people to explain stuff, don't be afraid to ask dumb questions."

Now, working as one of the senior people covering computers in the *Journal*'s New York bureau, in a small cubicle on the tenth floor of Dow Jones headquarters near Wall Street, Carroll has hit his stride. He is well connected to industry sources and has the experience and background to handle the stories on his beat with ease.

"One of the things I like about this job is that there aren't many typical days," he says. "I travel a few days a month. If I'm in the office I arrive about 10 A.M. and spend the first forty-five minutes reading the papers, flipping through the mail, returning phone calls, and figuring out what I'm going to do that day. The big trick on this job is to balance feature writing with spot news. I come in every day planning to work on a feature. Typically, I have one or two features going that I've proposed to page one or the front page of the second section and I'll be working on them. But I have to set them aside if news comes up. I keep my eye on the wires—the PR wire and Business Wire for news releases, the AP for general things, and the Dow Jones ticker for news about my companies and the PIR Wire to see how stocks are behaving. This way I'll know if I have to call people for responses to anything that is announced. I might also call people to find out what is going on."

Carroll does a great deal of reporting by telephone. He attends an occasional press conference for background and leaves the office for face-to-face interviews on longer stories which he has more time to write and where he wants more color than it is possible to get over the phone.

If he is writing a news story, his reporting will be finished by 3 P.M. By 4 P.M. he will have started writing at his computer but might also still be fielding returned phone calls from sources he was unable to reach earlier. By 4:30 P.M., he has begun to turn in the story electronically to his editor. The editor will eventually submit it to the national desk which must begin to make layout decisions for the next day's paper by 5 P.M. He submits his copy take by take, with one "take" or page equaling 300 words. The average news story is two and a half takes or 750 words. (In contrast, a feature will run four takes and a big front-page story six or seven.)

When he has finished the story, he sends it electronically into the system and also walks a hard copy into his superior, a news editor who is responsible for ten technology reporters. Carroll's deadline is 5:30 P.M. for the first edition and, most of the time, he will not deal with his story after that. It will be read by someone on the national desk and then given to a news editor in charge of technology stories. Any of these editors might call him for answers to various questions and they add to the copy. There are usually three or four questions of this kind on every story.

Most days he is finished by 6:30 P.M. The first edition goes to the composing room by 7:15 P.M. Once in a while, if something breaks late, he will rewrite his story for the second edition, but that is rare.

During this waiting period, Carroll sits in his office reading the trade press and his mail. When everything has been cleared on his story, he leaves the building about 7:30 P.M. and takes the ferry to his home in Hoboken, New Jersey across the Hudson River.

Even with five years of cultivating people to call on for comments and tips and verification, Carroll still considers finding good sources his biggest problem. "There are a jillion people who profess to be experts on something, but it is very hard to know who actually knows what they're talking about. It's also tough to figure out what people's biases are and to allow for them in my reporting," he says.

"I wind up talking a fair amount to consultants who talk to customers who get a look at equipment ahead of time. But that turns into cat and mouse too because IBM figures out what's going on."

Securities analysts are another kind of source for him, although not always totally reliable. "They act like they know more than they do," he says. "Even if they sound incredibly sure, I've decided that most people don't know what they are talking about. Former executives at IBM are a fertile area because they still have lots of friends. I go to them to get rumors confirmed or denied."

The reporter has also developed good working relationships with PR people. At IBM, a reporter cannot talk to anyone without going through the public relations department. "Over time, I've gotten them to trust me," he says. "What I want to do is to get PR people to help shape my stories, to confirm what I'd found out anyway. I call and say I'm planning to come out with such and such information and if anything about it is inaccurate it is to the company's advantage to tell me."

Sometimes, Carroll trades information with sources to cultivate them. "I have to be careful because if a story will move the market or the company stock, I have to use it. So, I trade information I can't use, maybe something on reorganization at IBM that's too small to interest *Journal* readers but that might intrigue a source."

In dealing with sources, one big advantage Carroll has over reporters from many other publications is the fact that he works for the *Wall Street Journal*. "I trade on the currency of the *Journal*'s prestige," he says. "I was astonished at how big a deal it is with readers to have their name in our paper. It's ridiculous, but I've talked to people who say their business will double if their name is in print. This is a great advantage to me. If someone has something good, they call me, because the power of being quoted in the *Journal* is so strong."

Background to Business Reporting

The earliest business publications in the United States were called *price-currents*. These periodicals contained a list of commodity price quotations and basic shipping information.

The first in North America was published in Halifax, Nova Scotia, in 1752 by a Philadelphia printer. Another came out in Charleston, South Carolina, in 1774. They were little more than lists of prices and the arrival and departure times of ships, but they were useful to the readers who bought them. The price-current idea spread as trade itself expanded to the commercial centers of Philadelphia, New York, Boston, and Baltimore.

By 1815 a new development emerged: General newspapers were carrying business news because of the financial requirements of merchants, manufacturers, and traders.

The lesson of Baron Rothschild was not lost on other business-men. The French financier arranged for a carrier pigeon to bring him news of Napoleon's defeat at Waterloo in 1815 and then used that knowledge to increase his fortune by buying British govern-ment bonds. This proved that a person could run a business better if he or she knew as much as possible about business and financial news and trends elsewhere.

In that same year a new kind of publication was founded to fill the growing need for business and financial information. *The New York General Shipping and Commercial List* was a step up from the old price-currents, because it also offered commentaries on market conditions and an analysis of commercial problems. With this expanded coverage came a sense of editorial responsibility. Reporting techniques were sharpened, and writing was more like that in regular newspapers. Business news was no longer dull and statistical.

By 1840 the skeleton of the modern American economy was emerging and, along with it, specialized publications to reflect segments of business like banking and finance.

Hunt's Merchants Magazine was founded in 1839 by Freeman Hunt to go beyond the price-currents. Hunt thought every subject of interest to the businessman should be included in his new magazine. This view of business news as being more than short items and statistics was not duplicated for almost thirty years, although newspapers continued to cover the subject to a certain extent.

James Gordon Bennett did for business news what he had done for other specialized subjects: he brought it to the mass reader in the pages of his *New York Herald*, which he founded in 1835. Because Bennett had taught economics, he wrote what he called the "money page" himself, at least in the early days. Such coverage appealed to the merchants of the city who increased their advertising as a result. Other penny press newspapers soon copied the *Herald* and the business page has been a standard part of American newspapers ever since.

The more in-depth coverage of business has been done by specialized magazines and newspapers, however. These publications have long had the expertise and resources to give the most complete coverage to business and the economy.

Business Publications

Wall Street Journal. Two men whose names now dominate business and the economy were responsible for making business a legitimate area for specialized coverage. Charles H. Dow and Edward D. Jones had known each other in Providence, Rhode Island, but came to New York City separately.

Dow arrived first, getting a job as a reporter on mining stocks with one of the daily newspapers. He had the ability to turn routine financial reporting into expert analysis and soon achieved a reputation as a reliable reporter, despite the fact that he took shorthand notes on the cuffs of his shirts.

As Dow's reputation as a good reporter spread, he was asked to join the staff of the best financial reporting organization in the Wall Street area, the Kiernan News Agency. Soon after joining the Kiernan staff, Dow contacted his friend Jones to come to work there, too. The two developed a number of contacts and, as they gained experience, formed their own ideas on the reporting of financial news. In the fall of 1882, they left Kiernan to set up their own firm — Dow, Jones & Company — in a building at 15 Wall Street that housed a soda fountain in the front. The two soon added another partner, Charles M. Bergstresser.

With Jones as the desk man and Dow and Bergstresser as reporters, the service flourished. The reporters gathered the news and gave their completed stories to Jones. He would edit them and dictate them to four or five "manifold writers," who would write the agate-wire stencils on what were called "books of tissue paper with carbon paper between each two sheets." As many as twenty-four copies could be produced in this way, and they were delivered by messengers to clients of the agency. A day's service consisted of eight hundred words.

On November 2, 1883, Dow, Jones & Company began publishing "Customer's Afternoon Letter," which was a recapitulation of the bulletins issued during the day. The company prospered, but with the prosperity came a problem. The handwritten stencils were too slow.

In 1887 the invention of a slotted revolving cylinder to print bulletins faster solved this problem. The bulletins were then delivered by the messengers.

By 1889 Dow, Jones & Company had fifty employees, and its partners decided to turn the letter into a newspaper. Volume 1, Number 1 of the *Wall Street Journal* was the result; a four-page, 15-1/2 x 20-3/4 inch paper with four or five columns per page appeared on July 8, 1889. Advertising sold for twenty cents a line.

The newspaper prospered, but the company was still plagued with the slow distribution of items for its news service. By 1897 the partners had decided they needed a way to provide instantaneous news to all their customers simultaneously. The answer was the "ticker" — a machine, placed in customers' offices, over which the information was transmitted. A hand-wound model was eventually replaced by a series of electrically powered ones.

By this time the company had fallen into the pattern followed today: The news service provided shorter business and financial items to subscribers in other publications and stock brokerage houses; the newspaper furnished more news items and longer analytical articles on a wide range of subjects of interest to people in business.

The *Journal* lost circulation following the 1929 stock market crash because of its close ties to the financial community. Dow, Jones & Company faced the decision of cutting back news coverage and becoming, in effect, a trade paper for the financial community, or broadening its coverage to report both business news and news that affected business. Officials chose the latter course, and what emerged was the newspaper in its present form.

The late Bernard Kilgore, who became managing editor in 1941, did more to influence *Journal* style than anyone since Dow and Jones. He assigned front-page space to stories that could be written in depth and gave reporters several days in which to complete them. Special features of analysis were added, and news of corporate affairs and the stock market was "repackaged" so it didn't dominate the paper.

In 1991 the *Wall Street Journal*, had two million subscribers, making it the largest circulation daily newspaper in the country. Its success is even more dramatic when two factors are considered: The newspaper deals primarily with business and economics, neither of them subjects of general interest, and the *Journal* looks about like it did in the time of Dow and Jones — no photographs and a drab front page with single-column headlines. In recent years it has introduced a few graphics and more attractive layouts on some pages and section fronts.

Several factors account for the *Journal*'s success, however. Its largely professional and high-income readership group is growing. Its main areas of coverage — economics news, the stock market collapse, the junk bond mess, the failure of major brokerage houses, savings and loans failures and their subsequent bailout, and a restructuring of the American economy because of Reaganomics — were all big stories in the 1980s and early 1990s. It also covers subjects of interest to business people like politics and foreign affairs.

Its page one "leaders" provide well-written, in-depth stories on a variety of subjects, not all with a direct connection to business.

The newspaper uses a satellite positioned twenty-two thousand miles over the equator to transmit images of newspaper pages, the ones that look like they are right out of 1889, to the *Journal*'s seventeen printing plants around the country. The fast printing makes the paper available daily from coast to coast.

The newspaper has also prospered because of its definition for stories: "Anything of interest to business leaders." It does not try to compete with local newspapers; it has always thought of itself as a second newspaper. Nevertheless, the major dailies in the United States are increasingly following the *Journal*'s approach.

Forbes. The next national business publication to begin after the *Journal* was *Forbes*, which started in 1917. B.C. Forbes came to America from Scotland and became business and financial editor of the *New York American*. He started the magazine to make use of all the leftover material he couldn't get into his column. The magazine has always covered business in a slightly different way than its rivals. Stories on companies, for example, are less general and offer information to potential investors. It is also more personal because it is still owned by the family of the founder. These two qualities have made its readership base smaller.

On the other hand, *Forbes* has always been more opinionated than its rivals, and this may account for one of the highest renewal rates among business magazines. The flamboyance and outspokenness of the late editor-owner Malcolm Forbes contributed to the special loyalty readers seem to have for the magazine. To Forbes, a story about a company was not a simple rendering of facts but, in the words of financial journalist and teacher Chris Welles, "mini-morality dramas, in which goodness or badness is a function of earnings and return on investment."

Business Week. McGraw-Hill started *The Business Week* just a few weeks before the stock market crash in 1929.

"*The Business Week* herewith makes its first appearance," read a note from McGraw-Hill's president in the first issue, "on a great plan, with a high ambition. Its ambition is to become indispensable — no less — to the businessmen of America. . . . Swiftly, intelligently, tersely, it tells the week's business news, and the news of business. This distinction is not fine-spun. Business news impinges upon business from outside. . . . News of business originates within business. . . ."

Since that first issue appeared, the magazine has been organized like departments in a company — management, finance, marketing, transportation, labor, research. Subject areas such as energy, the environment, and international economics were added later to reflect changes in the world. In recent years it has become much more news-oriented on its cover subjects and lead articles than in the past.

Business Week is a well-designed magazine and highly profitable for McGraw-Hill. It does not cover as many non-business subjects as the *Journal* or orient itself almost exclusively to the investor like *Forbes*. Its strongest points are facts and figures on a broad range of subjects, and they make it of great use to business readers.

Fortune. Henry Luce founded *Fortune* in 1930 because of the great number of stories that could not fit in *Time's* business section each week. Luce also greatly admired the American businessman.

"Business is obviously the greatest single common denominator of interest among the active leading citizens of the U.S.A.," he wrote in the prospectus. "Our best men are in business."

Nobody had ever published a quality periodical devoted exclusively to business. The *Journal* was still in its narrow financial news state, *Forbes* was limited in focus, and *Business Week* was too new to be much competition.

Luce proposed to create what he called a "business literature." The average citizen thought of business as sinister and predatory. Luce would prove otherwise with a luxurious format, superlative illustrations, and good writing. He would give business status, both in its own eyes and in the public's.

The first edition of *Fortune* in February 1930, which sold for the unheard-of price of one dollar a copy, had as its cover a lavish wheel of fortune with a scene of ancient commerce in the background and a scantily clad "Lady Luck" in front. Each of the thirty thousand copies had 184 pages, half of them advertisements. The issue contained articles on meat packing, glass, branch banking, the New York Biltmore Hotel, millionaire-owned islands, and the richest man in the world (Arthur Curtis James).

That issue set the tone for the *Fortune* style: beautiful illustrations and photographs, and long articles with enough space to cover a subject thoroughly. At first the general tone was descriptive and never critical. Later in the Depression, Luce changed the tone of the magazine when he decided there was a need for basic economic reform. Articles even attacked big business from time to time.

As business conditions got better, Luce directed another change: The magazine became more sympathetic toward business and less tolerant of government interference. In recent years it has been moderately conservative.

By the 1970s the lengthy articles and monthly publishing schedule made *Fortune* a bit dated. It could not keep up with the daily *Wall Street Journal*, the bi-weekly *Forbes*, and the weekly *Business Week*. Readers were too busy to wade through page after page of long articles, no matter how complete or how beautifully designed. In 1978 the magazine went to a bi-weekly format. It still looks better than its rivals, but stories are more tightly written and more current than in its monthly format.

Other Business Coverage

As business has come to dominate the day's news, more and more news organizations are covering that subject on a regular basis. The four business publications already discussed have always covered business, finance, and economics. But more general publications began to look carefully at them as soon as the dollar declined, oil prices raised dramatically, inflation increased drastically, interest rates soared, and the nation went into a recession in 1980. Another recession, the budget deficit and lingering effects of Reaganomics, the collapse of the S&L's and restructuring of many brokerage firms, the hostile takeovers of corporations, the weakness in the banking systems—all have maintained readers' interest into the 1990s because they affect the well-being of readers and their pocketbooks (see Box 12.1).

The success of the *Journal* and other business publications caused regular newspapers like the *New York Times* and *Washington Post*, which had devoted more space to sports than to business, to increase the space and resources devoted to the subject.

For example, in 1978 the *Times* began to produce a separate, daily business and financial section with a staff of seventy-five. The *Post*'s expansion began in 1977, when it increased the size of its financial staff to seventeen and added thirty columns of financial news each week. This story has been repeated at daily newspapers in other large cities. Specialized weekly newspapers produced in a magazine style have been started in a number of cities.

Time and *Newsweek* expanded their business and economics sections. Subjects related to those broad categories also appeared on the covers more in the late 1970s and early 1980s than ever before. Regional business magazines have developed and prospered too.

The director of stock market services for United Press International told the *Wall Street Journal* that smaller newspapers had increased their demand for business news. Customers for the Dow Jones News Services and its rival, Reuters' business wire service, have also increased.

Box 12.1

How the Economy Works

Any discussion of the American economy must begin with an explanation of the modern economic cycles.

Step 1: Recovery. The last recession is over, and businesses have begun to expand. They have cut costs greatly. They want to use their factories and machines to full capacity, so they hire more workers to make the products and get their sales staffs to increase their efforts. Retail stores are low on inventories, so they are receptive to the sales people. Consumers are not afraid, so they begin to buy again. Credit loosens up for plants wanting to expand production, stores wanting to buy bigger inventories, and consumers wanting to put purchases on time payments. The federal government has cut taxes and increased its spending. Investors are beginning to buy stocks again, and prices are going up.

Step 2: Increased momentum. Every element—companies, retail stores, consumers, the government—continues to expand. Everyone is confident about the future. With more orders companies increase production, hire more workers, and buy more raw materials. The retail stores buy more products, which are, in turn, purchased by the workers who are making good salaries. With credit easy and income steady, builders borrow more money and construct more. Assured of more tax money in higher wages and increased corporate profits, government keeps spending.

Step 3: Need for restraint. Although still strong, the economy is beginning to show signs of illness. Companies can't keep up with demand for their products, so shortages develop. Prices go up as well. The Federal Reserve has trouble managing the money supply. Demand for credit is increasing and so are interest rates. The Federal Reserve wants to encourage expansion but worries about inflation. The president wants to reduce the budget deficit, but members of Congress do not want to cut back on spending programs that are popular with the public. The Federal Reserve begins to tighten credit, and interest rates go up. Higher interest rates on securities pull money out of the mortgage market, and building begins to slump. Consumers are beginning to reach the limit of their needs and cut back on purchases, leaving more goods in retail stores and less need to order items from manufacturers.

Step 4: Downturn. Because demand for products is going down, manufacturers cut back on production and lay off employees. These employees stop buying all but necessities. Because costs and interest rates are up, new investments are less likely. Many people become pessimistic and stop buying. The recession has begun.

Step 5: Recession. Companies have to sell their extra inventories and cut costs, making sure to pay off debts. A few weak companies go out of business. The president, Congress, and the Federal Reserve are trying to increase demand and make money plentiful. In time the new recovery begins.

The *Journal* story cited the *Ft. Worth Star-Telegram* as typical of the smaller papers expanding their coverage. It doubled the size of its business reporting and editing staff to twelve and increased its daily business news from six columns to an average of twenty-one columns.

More does not necessarily mean better. A great many newspaper business pages reprint news releases from local businesses as a weak lead-in to page after page of stock tables, which few people bother to read. Often, though, a tiny group of devoted stockholders is very vocal when any stock listing is omitted so newspapers are reluctant to drop them. Far too few newspapers examine the businesses in their areas with any depth, however.

Problems and Solutions

In spite of the increased interest in financial news, the business reporter's job is not easy, especially in small and medium sized cities.

Few business communities welcome thorough reporting, preferring instead a kind of chamber-of-commerce look at the products they make and who has been promoted. A reporter who probes too deeply can find himself or herself in trouble with the advertising department of the newspaper, which fears retaliatory cuts by angry advertisers, and the publisher, who does not want to jeopardize friendships with business leaders. There is also the feeling by some newspaper publishers and editors that stories should "boost" the town and "not tear it down," the latter being a euphemism for doing an investigative business story on illegal business practices or any subject treated in a less than laudatory manner.

Business and financial reporters can also inhibit their own coverage. This happens most often when business and financial reporters get too close to their sources.

On no other beat do sources have so much to offer. Detroit automobile manufacturers for many years have made test cars available to auto writers for as long as they wanted to "test" them. The same companies freely gave press discounts when any journalist bought a new car. Reporters can regularly get free rides on corporate jets or stay without charge at resorts. They get gifts of food and liquor at Christmas, although this practice is not as widespread as it once was due to a heightened concern about ethics by both journalists and business people. Corporations sponsor most of the business writing award competitions; this makes it difficult for judges in those contests to make selections of articles that have been critical of big business.

However, the most insidious connection between business and financial writers and the companies and industries they cover is in the area of conflict of interest. Because of their sources and access to details of how companies conduct their affairs, these reporters gain inside information that could be helpful in the buying and selling of stock.

As long ago as 1963 the Securities and Exchange Commission (SEC) questioned press safeguards against such conflict of interest among business writers. In its *Report of Special Study of Securities Market*, the SEC said:

> It remains for the self-regulatory groups, official and unofficial, the business and financial communities, and the press itself to exercise their powers and responsibilities. . . . Not least, the news media and public relations associations could be far more effective than they have been in imposing standards designed to separate corporate propaganda from news, and to control conflicts of interest on the part of writers of financial news.

The SEC went on to detail past actions it considered undesirable. One such practice was that of financial reporters who subscribed to "hot" issues, the stocks that were selling fast and for high rates of return.

> The public eagerly sought stocks in certain "glamour" industries, especially the electronics industry, in the expectation that they would rise to a substantial premium — an expectation that was often fulfilled. Within a few days or even hours after the initial distribution, these so-called "hot issues" would be traded at a premium of as much as 300 percent above the original price. . . . In many cases, the price of a "hot issue" later fell to a fraction of the offering price.

An SEC examination of the distribution list of the underwriters for twenty-two new issues showed that at least eleven financial journalists and publicists received allotments, among them a New York newspaper financial editor, a New York financial columnist, the editor of a nationally circulated business and financial magazine, a television network newsperson, and several financial public relations practitioners.

Two cases in the last twenty years have had a great deal of influence on business and financial journalism.

In one, the senior editor in charge of the business section at *Time* bought stocks in companies about which he or his department was preparing articles. Between August 1957 and April 1971, according to the SEC, this editor had transactions in the stocks of sixty-four companies. Of these, twenty-seven were written about in the business news section of *Time*. In each of the twenty-seven cases he bought the stock a few days or a few weeks before the date of the publication of the articles and usually sold the stock a few days after publication. He held the shares of the companies not written up for a longer time.

The SEC said the editor made a "considerable" profit trading in the companies written about in *Time*, because the price of stock rose sharply after the article appeared in most cases or soon after. *Time*, which did not discover the practice until the editor had left, said it would have dismissed him had his actions been known.

Since the SEC report, national publications dealing regularly in business and financial news have tightened their restrictions to avoid such practices, although the temptation to make fast profits and the chance to do so are still there.

The other and most recent case of this type involved R. Foster Winans, a reporter for the "Heard on the Street" column of the *Wall Street Journal*. He was found guilty in 1985 of securities fraud and conspiracy for trading his advance knowledge of the stocks to be written about in the column, one of the best read features in the *Journal*, to stockbrokers who made as much as $675,000 by trading securities of companies they knew would be featured. Before his activities were discovered and he was fired, Winans himself made $31,000.

At the same time, the SEC filed a civil suit against Winans and others because it is against federal law to profit from advance information that will affect the price of stock. That agency long ago established elaborate safeguards to ensure that all investors have access to the same information at the same time.

Although this case involved only one reporter at the *Journal*, it immediately raised doubts about accuracy and objectivity in all media, especially in the specialized field of business and financial coverage, an area of strong growth for much of the 1970s and early 1980s. With the expanded coverage of routine business news had come a number of "investor advice" and "stock tip" columns that readers liked. It was this kind of feature, however, that got the *Journal* reporter in trouble and raised the specter of ethical transgressions for all business reporters.

The original indictment against Winans included the assertion that financial journalists have a duty to disclose to readers whenever they stand to benefit from price movements in the securities they write about. This alarmed news organizations which worried that such a requirement would give the government power to regulate news gathering and to dictate standards to the media. Although decrying the fraud, these news organizations wanted to police themselves.

Almost immediately, many publications toughened their existing standards. The *Journal* has a three-and-a-half page conflict-of-interest policy employees must follow and requires new staff members to take formal training in ethics. The *New York Times* has a written policy banning stock trading in companies they write about. The *Washington Post* requires all business reporters to outline their stock holdings in a formal letter. *Forbes* and *Business Week* insist on financial disclosure by employees. *Newsweek* forbids editorial employees to own stock in a company they report on, or to invest on the basis of advance knowledge gathered by the magazine.

In spite of such problems, coverage of business is expanding. A 1979 survey of business coverage reported in *Journalism Quarterly* noted that 39.3 percent of newspapers responding have a weekly page, 8.5 percent a weekly section, 28.6 percent a daily page, and 10 percent a daily section. More than three-fourths of the larger papers (fifty thousand and over) have either a daily page (44 percent) or a daily section (33 percent). About half (51 percent) of the newspapers have been providing this kind of coverage for more than five years, and 41 percent have included it for more than ten years.

The most widely covered subject in recent years has been why consumer prices are so high (87 percent) and why there is or is not an energy crisis (78 percent). Of newspapers responding to the survey, 58 percent cover the performance of individual companies in their pages; 30 percent discuss how corporations wield power, 27 percent run exposés on local business, 27 percent report on state business, and 33 percent cover national business. As might be expected, larger newspapers were more likely than smaller ones to run exposés or stories about company performance.

The conclusions of the *Journalism Quarterly* survey — still valid in the 1990s because things have not changed all that much — bode well for business and financial reporting: 1) daily newspapers, especially those over fifty thousand, are becoming more aware of the need for business coverage and are devoting more space to it; 2) dailies are making a greater effort to interpret and explain business news to readers; 3) dailies are expanding their staffs and seeking better prepared persons, although only 40 percent of newspapers responding have a business editor and only 30 percent have a full-time business reporter; 4) most daily newspapers do not accept anything of value that might affect the objectivity of their reporting.

With all this improvement, however, most daily newspapers still devote much less space to business news than to sports, women's issues, and crime.

The decade of the 1980s brought record economic growth through a combination of tax cuts, booming stock market and real estate sales, and deregulation of many businesses. It also brought a number of large acquisitions and mergers as corporations bought other corporations using junk bonds to finance the purchase—and burdening the company that emerged with huge debts which it paid by laying off employees and consolidating operations. Only a few high corporate officials and the brokers and attorneys who helped them set up the mergers made any money on those ventures.

All of these activities made the late 1980s a veritable gold mine for business reporters because of all the subjects to cover. The 1990s are providing an equally abundant number of good business stories for reporters—but on the down side, as the result of a lingering recession (see Box 12.2). Reaganomics has created a budget deficit equal to that acquired by all other presidents combined and brought a halt to most federal government spending for new programs. The mini-stock market crash of 1987 sent the stock market reeling as some fortunes made in the 1980s were lost overnight. The stock market was also shaken in the late 1980s by a series of arrests— and subsequent trials and convictions—of prominent brokers from important firms for *insider trading*, making money by buying and selling stock in companies they had material information about. The junk bond restructuring of corporate America—a scheme developed by some of these brokers—has burdened companies with debt. The rise in competition from Japan, which began in the mid 1980s, has intensified and drastically affected key American industries like automobiles and steel. New competitors will emerge as the European community, a system under which the economics of many countries in Europe are being combined, goes into operation in the early 1990s.

Business reporting, once the graveyard beat on many newspapers and magazines, is no longer one to be avoided. It is interesting and viable and often can be the springboard to other assignments on the newspaper.

A summary of the problems to be encountered in business reporting is contained in "Likely Problems and How to Solve Them" later in this chapter.

Box 12.2

How the Federal Reserve System Influences the Economy

The Federal Reserve System, created by Congress in 1913, was at first set up to ensure the stability of the banking system. But the "Fed," as it came to be called, soon found its powers could have effects that were more broad. Gradually, its policy committee—consisting of the seven Fed governors in Washington and five of its twelve district bank presidents—could take actions that regulated the economy. For example, if they want to ease credit, they can pump more money into the banking system, quite literally by printing more money. This causes the federal funds interest rate—the rate banks charge each other for loans—and other short term interest rates to fall. That, in turn, makes it easier for businesses and individuals to borrow and for the economy to expand.

On the other hand, the Fed can tighten credit by draining money from banks, again, quite literally by printing less of it and having less of it available to spend. This causes short term rates to rise and the economy to slow down. This has long been a strategy for fighting inflation.

The Fed always seems to be walking a tightrope between credit that is too easy and worsens inflation and credit that is too tight and brings on recession.

That is why the chairman of the Federal Reserve System is often in a ticklish position. Although nominally holding a non-partisan post, the chairman has the power to make a president look good because of the control over the economy. For example, former Fed Chairman Paul Volcker is usually credited with easing inflation and boosting recovery by his actions during the 1982 recession.

The Fed breaks the money supply into three categories:

- M-1—cash and balances in checking accounts.
- M-2—M-1 plus money that is less liquid but can still be readily converted into cash like money market funds.
- M-3—M-2 plus assets that are less liquid like large denomination time deposits.
- L—a category of liquid assets such as most securities within eighteen months of maturity.

It determines the amount of money in circulation through its receipt of weekly reports from its 15,000 member banks and many money market funds.

How to Cover Business

As subjects of regular coverage, business, finance, and economics are not different from any technical field discussed in this book. They require good sources, an understanding of unfamiliar terms, and the ability to make a dull subject interesting to readers. A few basic principles will help any business reporter succeed:

1. **Know the key businesses and industries.**   A reporter must find out what businesses and industries dominate the city, county, or region covered by the newspaper or magazine and learn as much as possible about them. What are their products? How many people do they employ? Has business been in decline or doing well? Why? How much impact does each company have on the area's economy? Stories in the newspaper morgue, economic studies by university economists, and background interviews with economists, securities analysts, government officials, and chamber of commerce sources can furnish the needed information. (See Boxes 12.3 and 12.4.)

2. **Build a list of expert sources.**   A good way to keep current about business conditions is to develop a group of business and economic experts who can be interviewed on future stories for comments about trends or specific companies.

3. **Make a list of potential stories.**   A new reporter on the business beat can sit down and probably easily come up with fifty story suggestions as soon as the preliminary work in points 1 and 2 above is complete. Then, interrupted only by breaking news events, the reporter should begin to do the stories systematically.

4. **Keep up with national and state business and economic news.**   All business reporters should read the *Wall Street Journal*, *Sunday New York Times*, *Time*, *Newsweek*, and choose one magazine from *Business Week*, *Fortune*, and *Forbes*. The reporter should also clip and file stories that provide useful background. The largest newspaper in the state and any state magazines should be read and clipped, too. A business reporter should be on the mailing lists of all state agencies, banks, and private research firms that study the economy and business. Their reports can provide valuable background information and an occasional story idea.

5. **Get on mailing lists for news releases and annual reports.** News releases should never be printed as they are received. They are sometimes inaccurate and understandably biased in favor of whatever company has issued them. They should be used as sources for story ideas or as tips to be expanded into a larger story. They sometimes provide good background and should be filed. In large cities, releases come right into the newsroom computer system via one of the PR newswire services. Companies put their releases directly on this wire and reporters can scan them on their screens

Box 12.3

A General Guide to How Business Works

The United States economy thrives largely on a system of private enterprise in which companies large and small hire people to make products or provide services which are then sold to consumers. The majority of organizations in the United States exist to make a profit. Far fewer entities like universities and government-affiliated organizations are nonprofit.

Ownership of the for-profit companies is either *sole proprietorship*, *partnership*, or *corporate*. Partnership has been unpopular in the United States because of the inability of the partners to get along. The divided authority that usually results is its biggest disadvantage. This leaves the corporate mode as the most prevalent: officials reporting to a board of directors.

Profit is the goal of all companies but it is often misunderstood. It can be responsible for a lot of bad that happens. How is it supposed to work? It can be seen as a reward and incentive for good performance, for responding well to customer needs. It can be used as a gauge of how well a business is doing. It is important for the accumulation of capital to keep the business viable and provide jobs for people.

Management is a crucial part of how well companies do. This includes not just top managers but the next generation who will carry the business into the future. In the 1920s, the theory of "scientific management" came into use: increased productivity could be achieved through careful planning. With this came time and motion studies of employees, ways to get the human body to work better. But it tended to make human beings into machines. In the early 1930s, landmark studies began in employee motivation which revealed that temperature and light influenced employee performance. The Hawthorne effect was discovered: workers did best when they were being watched. The human relations movement came next: a happy worker is a productive worker. Under this idea as exemplified by the Mazlo theory, it was felt that business should provide for the needs of its employees to make them happy.

Douglas MacGregor developed a theory which divided employees into two groups: X (people that hate work, are lazy and need to have lots of external control) and Y (people who love to work, are committed to goals, and control themselves). This theory pushed the idea that some people really need to be managed, while others do not.

Next came the Japanese model, the so-called "Theory Z," which looked at companies and employees as part of a lifetime partnership. Most Americans are too independent to subjugate themselves completely to a company; however, a few successful corporations like Hewlett-Packard have made it work.

Marketing is a key part of success for any company: how can its products be sold? In the most prevalent theory, the consumer is king. Products are made to meet consumer needs rather than trying to mold consumer need to fit the products made. Beyond this factor lie concepts like market segmentation (people looked at by age, sex, geographic locations) and target markets (certain segments targeted via advertising or distribution). Distribution is tied closely to marketing because products need to be moved to the people who will buy them. Price is important; it must be right or customers won't buy. Advertising and other promotions are also important to successful marketing. Is the product sold best via mass marketing (most are) or personal selling (usually not except on big ticket items)?

Finance is a crucial part of any business because it looks at sources of funds and how they are used. Obtaining and using funds is central to the decision making of a corporation. Money is expensive to borrow and hard to earn so it needs to be spent wisely. The financial structure of a company usually consists of internal funds (retained earnings, that is profits earned and plowed back into the company; and depreciation, expending of an item as it is used up) and external funds (stock sales to signify ownership and raise money; debt, borrowing via loans or bonds).

and print out only those releases they wish to use. (Reporters should avoid a release that puffs up its subject, as in "Sam's trucking had another good year." But a reporter might take that release and use the basic information, minus the overly optimistic tone, and make it into a useful story relating Sam's trucking to the state of the economy, the trucking business in general, deregulation of the trucking industry, and the company's relationship to the teamster's union local.) Annual reports are equally useful if analyzed correctly; they should be filed for future reference too. (See Box 12.5.)

6. **Attend annual meetings.** Although such events can be boring, they do offer the chance to meet and interview company officials. They also present a potential source of news if dissident stockholders are present to challenge management or if another company tries to vote current officers out of office and acquire control of the company by purchasing a majority of shares of stock. Such proxy fights are usually preceded by a lot of advance warning as both sides present their case in public to justify their action and get more votes.

7. **Keep up with pertinent court cases.** Some business affairs find their way into courts at all levels, and the information presented in such cases can make good stories—bankruptcies, patent infringements, personnel actions, and cases alleging fraud.

8. **Beware of hostility from business.** All the good preparation and story ideas in the world cannot protect a business

reporter from the hostility he or she will encounter from business sources. The problem has several causes.

Much of the bad relationship stems from the post-Watergate revelations of illegal corporate political payoffs, bribes to foreign governments, and secret Swiss accounts and laundered funds. The officials of many large corporations broke the law, and the press, still smelling the blood of high government officials after President Nixon's resignation, pursued the story. This angered many business executives, who had nothing to hide but who thought the press had gone too far. The reasons for the hostility go farther back than Watergate, however.

Many business executives have a conservative political point of view and think many reporters are left-wing liberals. They abhor the carelessness in which business news is gathered and reported. They think that too many reporters refuse to listen to the business side of a story. They think reporters trample on the rights of others to get a story first, then defend what they do by invoking the First Amendment. Another problem comes in the fact that most business people do not understand the way the press and television work. Executives resent spending forty-five minutes with a network television reporter, only to see the interview compressed to thirty seconds. Business executives accustomed to commanding their large corporate empires do not like to be asked unfriendly questions or to be unable to read stories about themselves before the stories go into print. These officials think their words deserve unquestioned acceptance and approval by reporters. They get angry when a reporter asks for specific details. They also worry that information given to a reporter will wind up in the hands of business competitors.

One other factor inhibits business executives and their dealings with reporters. They rely heavily on their legal staffs who have the tendency to block the release of most information.

(A 1981 study of journalists, executives, and PR people conducted for the American Management Association found: one-third believed that media are "always" or "usually" antagonistic toward the business community; most PR directors feel their companies have received favorable media treatment; two-thirds of the journalists and PR directors believe reporters do not research their topics thoroughly; most in each group felt that inaccuracy resulted from sloppiness, not bias; 81 percent of journalists, 79 percent of executives, and 77 percent of PR people believe that fewer than half of all business executives understand the workings of the media, yet 94 percent of CEO's feel they themselves understand the media "fairly well.")

Box 12.4

How to Read Financial Statements

One way to find out more information about a company is to read the financial statements in its annual report. Two such statements, the balance sheet and the income statement, are particularly useful to reporters.

The *balance sheet*, which offers a look at a company's financial health at the time the sheet was prepared, is divided into assets and liabilities. Assets are further divided into three categories: *current assets* (those the company does not expect to hold more than one year such as cash, accounts receivable, and merchandise inventories); *fixed assets* (a tangible element that will be useful for more than one year such as buildings and property); and *other assets* (intangible goodwill the company engenders in the conduct of its business). Depreciation—the loss of value by an asset—plays a part in any discussion of assets. This loss of value can be charged off as an expense, thus reducing the stated value of the asset on the balance sheet. Normally a company figures depreciation by dividing the original cost of an asset into equal parts and charging off these parts each year of its expected life.

Liabilities are either current or long term. *Current liabilities* are those that will be paid off within a year (for instance, money owed to suppliers and estimated tax payments). *Long-term liabilities* are those that will not be paid off within a year. They usually include stockholder equity (the money company stockholders make when the value of stock increases) and owners' equity (the money the business is making for its owners).

The *income statement* details what happened over a period of time to explain some of the differences between several balance sheets. It does so by summarizing revenue and expense accounts in the same way the balance sheet summarizes asset and equity accounts. The income statement is divided into revenues and expenses.

Revenues consist of the amount of money gained from selling the company's products. The selling price, rather than the original cost, is used to make this determination. Sales are *net*, because any discounts or returns and allowances granted to customers have been subtracted from the gross sales. The actual cost of goods sold is deducted from the net sales. This cost is calculated by taking a physical inventory for the year before and recording the purchases made during the year.

Expenses include items like wages and salaries paid, general and administrative expenses, interest expense, and taxes. Gross profit is figured by calculating the difference between net sales and the cost of goods sold. The final expense deduction is for dividends paid to stockholders. The net profit for the year—called *returned earnings*—is what is left over.

Balance Sheet: The Draus Company*

Current Assets:			Current Liabilities:		
Cash	$20,000.		Accounts payable	$10,000.	
Accounts receivable	18,000.		Accrued expenses payable	1,800.	
Merchandise inventory	40,000.		Estimated tax liability	1,800.	
Total current assets		$78,000.	Total current liabilities		$13,600.
Fixed assets:			**Other liabilities:**		
Land	10,000.		Bonds payable		12,000.
Buildings	18,000.				
Less depreciation	5,000.		**Stockholders' equity:**		
Total fixed assets		$23,000	Common stock	$83,000.	
Other assets:			Retained earnings	2,400.	
Goodwill		10,000.	Total equities		85,400.
Total assets		$111,000.	Total liabilities		$111,000.

Income Statement: The Draus Company

Net Sales:		$300,000.
Less cost of goods sold		180,000.
Gross profit		$120,000.
Less expenses:		
Wages and salaries paid	$70,000.	
General and administrative expenses	40,000.	
Interest expenses	1,700.	$111,700.
Net profit before taxes		$ 8,300.
Taxes (paid and accrued)		2,500.
Net profit after taxes		5,800.
Less dividends		4,800.
Added to retained earnings		$1,000.

* The name and figures in this balance sheet are not those of an actual company and are intended only for the purposes of illustration.

9. **Prepare for interviews.** Although one reporter cannot atone for and erase years of distrust and bitterness between business and the press, he or she will greatly ease the encounters with individuals in the business and financial community by being prepared. It is

Box 12.5

Annual Reports and How to Use Them

A recent trend in annual reports across the country has been to increase their lavishness in order to impress other companies and stockholders. Beyond the four-color photographs and well-designed pages, however, lies useful information required by the SEC of all publicly held companies.

The president's letter and review of the year usually take up the first half of the report. All the gloss is in this section, but a careful reading will note any failures of management or an explanation of losses. Management changes will also be revealed. Few companies are straightforward in their annual reports, but some useful information is there. The second half of an annual report contains more solid information, but much of it is in statistical form and thus hard to read.

The following information is required by the SEC and can be helpful in determining how well a company is doing.

1. A brief description of the company's business.
2. A summary of operations for the last five fiscal years and an analysis by management.
3. A breakdown of each segment of business for the most recent five years.
4. The identity and background of directors and officers.

The New York Stock Exchange and the American Stock Exchange require such information as balance sheets; statements of income and retained earnings; statements of sources and applications of funds; the address of the principal office; names and addresses of trustees, transfer agents, and registrars; and number of employees and stockholders.

The SEC also requires each company to prepare for it a more detailed annual report on Form 10-K, which contains additional information on a company. Available to the public and press, this form includes:

1. Balance sheets for the close of the last two fiscal years.
2. Income statements for the last two fiscal years.
3. Statements of the sources and applications of funds for the last two fiscal years.
4. A detailed description of the business, including a five-year summary of revenue.
5. A tabular summary of operations and an analysis by management.
6. The location and general character of important physical properties like plants, mines, and mineral reserves.
7. An analysis of oil and gas reserves, if any.
8. Pending legal proceedings.
9. A list of all parent and subsidiary companies.

A prospectus prepared for potential investors in a company's stock is also useful to read. Such documents are required and include detailed information on the nature of the business, the financial condition of the company, and other facts an investor might want to know in a more expanded form than in the annual report.

insulting to the interviewee to conduct an interview without having read enough background information on the company, general business conditions, and the subject of the interview to ask intelligent questions. Too many reporters go into such interviews with chips on their shoulders. "I am a reporter for an important publication," they seem to reason. "This guy needs me more than I need him." This attitude of arrogance is based on some kind of myth about journalistic supremacy. In reality the approach is unprofessional and counterproductive.

Kinds of Business Stories

In developing a list of story ideas, a business reporter should keep in mind the fact that everything is a business. That idea has made a success of the *Wall Street Journal*, and it will enliven the business and economic coverage of even the smallest newspaper. Business stories will also gain more reader interest if they tell readers how business and economic developments affect them. Some possible business stories include:

1. **News of important local developments.** The lives and livelihoods of men and women and their families are affected dramatically by what happens at the companies which employ them. News of new contracts and expansion, loss of business and layoffs, or changes in management are vital to those readers and need to be covered as they occur. Later, more in-depth analysis pieces can examine the long-term effects of the news developments that have been reported.

2. **Profiles of company presidents or business leaders.** These are best done in the same way any personality profile is done in the rest of the newspaper. The difference here is an emphasis on success or failure, the details of the company or small business, and problems of the particular company and the general industry of which it is a part. It is also important not to make such profiles "puff" pieces that are overwhelmingly favorable and ignore anything negative. Competitors of the person and disinterested observers like stock analysts and economists should be interviewed. Because such articles often include a great deal of information about the company, an interesting variation is the use of a technique borrowed from the national business publications, the corporate strategy story. In this kind of approach the reporter writes about how company officials run the company to make money and beat competitors.

3. **Local tie-ins to national business and economic stories.** If the nation as a whole is in a recession, has the slowdown hit the local area? Why? Why not? If unemployment figures are up or down, what about the local area? Why? Why not? Car sales off nationally? How are local dealers faring? A national strike? What is the local effect? The list of such links is endless. The national wire service story can be run with the local story as a sidebar.

4. **Trend stories.**   A number of stories happen every year and should be covered: high or low retail sales at Christmas, the decline in steel output in the summer, the high cost of electric power consumption in the summer, and the increase in bank loans in the fall.

5. **Survey stories.**   The survey has long been a staple in business and trade publications. This type of story is not one based on the results of a scientific poll with a carefully arranged sample and exact percentage figures. Rather, it is a series of calls to people in the same field who are asked the same list of questions. The resulting story is very unscientific but filled with interesting quotes. If the questioners are carefully selected, such stories can provide valuable insights into local business thought on a subject.

6. **New product stories.**   Every company in the area produces products, and these products make excellent shorter stories. How do they work? What is the market and marketing strategy? What is the background of their development?

7. **Explanations of terms.**   What do the Gross National Product (GNP) and Consumer Price Index really mean? How does the stock market work? How are commodities traded? A story that explains these often heard, but seldom defined, terms and processes would be useful to readers (see Box 12.6).

8. **Hirings and promotions.**   Although the information about people in business will enjoy high readership among these people, it can be boring to everyone else. A newspaper can perform a public service by running such a column, but it should be kept short and avoid "puffery" or gossip. A similar kind of listing for new businesses is preferable to a chamber-of-commerce type story extolling the virtues of each. The firing of a company president or an important personnel change is a big news story.

9. **News of interest to consumers.**   Although many newspapers have cut back on covering the consumer as a separate beat, this kind of story provides a useful addition to a business page. Kinds of stories include comparison shopping, the reporter posing as a

Box 12.6

The Meaning Behind Some Key Economic Categories

Every day, the public is given figures in a number of categories by journalists who don't always explain what they mean. The categories are often used for political purposes, for example, unemployment rates in an election year, without even the candidates who use them understanding their true meaning.

1. The Index of Leading Economic Indicators, published each month by the Department of Commerce, serves as a good gauge of how the economy is doing. The government also uses the index to determine the direction of business activity and employment. A business reporter who understands the index can figure out how the national economy is affecting its local counterpart.

The index, which the department began to use in 1948, is a summary of twelve areas of economic activity, each one averaged according to its importance. The areas are manufacturers' new orders, private housing building permits, daily stock prices, manufactured goods inventories, factory worker layoff rate, the industrial worker workweek average, the nation's money supply, net new business start-ups, shipping rates for finished goods, consumer goods new orders, factory equipment orders, and commodity prices.

The department uses these statistics because they have proven historically to be the most reliable in forecasting business activity. The twelve areas are supposed to indicate general economic activity, although some economists dispute this contention, saying that factors like government spending and balance of payments are also important.

The index has successfully predicted past economic declines. In the 1974-75 recession, for example, the index began going down nine months before the recession actually began. It started to go back up one month before recovery. The index reacted in much the same way during the 1972-1973 recession.

Some economists say the index is more accurate in forecasting the timing of recessions than in predicting how severe they will be.

2. The Dow-Jones Industrial Average, used nightly on the television news programs, tells how the New York stock market is doing and is generally also viewed as an indicator of how the economy is doing. The "Dow," as it is called, consists of stocks of thirty major companies and their total average sales price per share for that day. Although it is widely accepted as a means of predicting the course of the economy because its conclusion is always up or down and can be easily shown on a TV screen with the appropriately directed arrow, the Dow is frequently criticized as being too limited in the stocks represented and misleading in the fluctuations reported.

3. The Wholesale Price Index, prepared monthly by the Bureau of Labor Statistics, mixes the wholesale prices of farm and industrial goods to get an average. This mixing has caused some critics to denigrate its accuracy.

They also criticize its combination of raw materials and finished goods. Supporters say that movements in the index foreshadow changes in consumer prices.

4. The Consumer Price Index measures price increases of a fixed "market basket" of goods and services in five major categories: housing costs (33 percent), food costs (25 percent), health and leisure spending (19 percent), transportation (13 percent), and clothing (10 percent). The Bureau of Labor Statistics selects four hundred items and prices them monthly in eighteen thousand stores and service establishments in fifty-six metropolitan areas. The four hundred include everything from cuts of beef to appliance repairs to the price of toothpaste. Critics contend that the selection is not representative of the average consumer and has not been updated to include areas with dramatic price increases like health care. The index is still widely used, however, to indicate the effect of inflation on prices and to measure the health of the economy.

5. The Unemployment Rate is obtained by dividing the total number of people in the civilian work force—those working or looking for work—by the number of those out of work. The Bureau of Labor Statistics gets its estimates of the total work force and the unemployed from a monthly sample of fifty thousand households. Critics say the rate, depending on how it is analyzed, can give a misleading impression of the job market. When economic conditions are good, for example, jobs expand and people who may have dropped out of the work force may start looking again, thus driving up the unemployment rate. Also, say the critics, it is difficult to define full employment. The goal has been 4 percent since the President's Council of Economic Advisers adopted it in the early 1960s. But since then, more women and younger workers have come into the work force. These two groups change jobs more often and thus have sharply higher unemployment rates than males. The last imponderable is "hidden" unemployed, those who have long since given up looking for jobs. They are never included in the rate figure because they can't be accurately identified and counted.

6. The Gross National Product (GNP), the total output of goods and services, has four major parts: personal consumption (63 percent); new investment in housing and industrial development, and the new increase or decrease in business inventories (16 percent); direct government purchases of everything from ships to school lunches (20 percent); net exports (1 percent). The GNP attempts to measure the performance of the economic system and is considered the best total indicator of the performance and direction of the economy. Economists have long used a 4 percent annual growth rate in the GNP as the norm. However, critics say that GNP figures are not accurate because the statistics collected are not precise (they do not include everything in the economy) and because the effect of inflation is impossible to calculate. (Economists generally believe that if the GNP is down for three quarters in a year, that signifies a recession.)

consumer, investigations into faulty products or business practices, local angles on national consumer stories, and an "Action Line" type column in which the business reporter finds out answers to questions submitted by readers.

Writing Business Stories

"The vast majority of what I write is financial stuff," says Paul Carroll, a technology reporter for the *Wall Street Journal*. "We also do plenty of product stories and our editors encourage us to do gee whiz technology stuff.

"I think of these as straightforward with one theme or, at most, two. I don't tend to use the inverted pyramid. I always want to come up with the most significant fact in the lead but I try to write things essay-like. One reason for this is that a lot of the facts in my stories are known to the people who read my stories. Earnings go out on the wire first thing in the morning and everyone who cares about them will know twenty-four hours before they read my stories, except for people in Omaha with no access to the ticker.

"I strike a balance: basic, barebones facts that I try to put in context, plus analysis that readers haven't gotten with the numbers. The lead contains the main facts plus a clause of significance or interpretation. As I go through the story, I try to add as much perspective as I can to give people a feel for what's going on. Often, that means using a funny anecdote or adding detail in what most would consider to be a dull business story.

"The rule at the *Journal* is that we shouldn't be afraid to say something on our own as reporters. This means that if we know something from our reporting, we don't have to find someone else's mouth to put it into. I may talk to a lot of people but quote only two. I try to quote people only about things that are their province. Who I select depends on the theme of the story. I may also quote someone if he helped me get a scoop on an earlier story, as a way of paying him back and encouraging him to help me again.

"When I start writing, I keep the basic structure in my head. I go until I write a take and then go through that once. When I am finished I do what a friend calls 'a Strunk and White' on a story (refers to the classic style manual *The Elements of Style*, by William Strunk and E. B. White). I was a copy editor so I know enough of *Journal* style that I don't have to look up much. I do get sloppy and often have to take a hard look and tighten things up, define terms, and add descriptive color. I go until I have reached the two or two-and-a-half take limit. If I have a cute or funny item, I use it at the end, but news stories pretty much just end. We don't focus on the end in news as much as on a feature.

"Longer, more complicated pieces, which we have a couple of days to write, are more difficult. On a page one piece that takes two to three weeks to report, you end up with a folder three or four inches thick. I use standard reporter's notebooks on the road or legal pads at the office. I'm not in the habit of recording things because it takes forever to transcribe your notes.

"The first thing I do is to go through the file once and reread everything. I underline things with a magic marker that I might use. I get out a legal pad next and jot down one- or two-word reminders on what's there so I can have the whole representation on one sheet of paper. As I decide on my approach, I reduce that list.

"On another sheet I put down the structure of the story: the lead, the nut graf—the one that summarizes the story as succinctly as possible and lets readers know why they ought to care. Ideally, that graf goes high up in the story, never more than three or four grafs down. Then, I go through and develop the story.

"There used to be a fondness around here for anecdotal leads. But a memo went out three or four years ago that said, 'Let's do something else.' So in the back of my mind when I write is whether I can avoid an anecdotal lead. The page one editor wants drama, conflict, character development in those stories. He wants stories with characters—like in a screenplay. This is not always possible but I have the idea in the back of my head.

"I usually have a lead in mind when I start to write. If I find myself stuck on a lead, I focus on the nut graf. I do this mentally, not committing anything to paper. If I still can't figure out a lead, I use the nut graf as my lead. In the body of the story, I try to toss in something funny. I'm big on jokes and I save them up to use in the appropriate story.

"I've edited a lot and seen a lot of writing. It seems to me that most writing can be improved dramatically by making it tighter, by avoiding passive voice, by not using two adjectives when one will do or two adverbs when one will do, or nothing if you use the right verb in the first place. Most stories jump around too much. If you don't collect all similar parts and use them in one place you need a lot of transitions. If you put all of the same stuff together, things will drop out. The rule some of our editors use is that any story can be cut by ten to fifteen percent and be improved in the process.

"Writing is hard. I'm not the greatest writer. I'm known as a clear writer, not a flashy writer. I don't take big pride in my writing. I'm a competitive person so the reporting is what I like, being out there trying to beat other guys to the story."

#1

AKERS TO IBM EMPLOYEES: WAKE UP!
By Paul B. Carroll
Staff Reporter of
The Wall Street Journal

Paul Carroll uses a good, attention getting lead which makes readers wonder why Akers is "fed up."

1 International Business Machines Corp. Chairman John F. Akers is fed up.

In the transition, Carroll summarizes the public and private views of IBM's chairman and some of his complaints.

2 Although IBM may publicly blame its problems on a slow economy, Mr. Akers is saying the real problem goes far deeper. He is telling IBM managers that IBM has been steadily losing market share to competitors—and that he's tired of it. He is complaining that the quality of IBM products is inadequate. In addition, he is telling managers to fire far more marginal employees.

In graf 3, he gives readers the significance of what they are finding out, letting them in on a secret: that the *Journal* has found something no one else has.

3 While bits and pieces of Mr. Akers's message have made their way outside IBM's walls over the past few months, the most detailed and sternest version yet has surfaced in the form of notes that an IBM manager took at a small-group seminar Mr. Akers addressed a month ago. The manager, Brent Henderson, who wasn't available for comment, apparently thought he was circulating the notes just to people in his area. But, through the magic of IBM's extensive electronic mail network, the word quickly spread through the company.

In graf 4, he quotes directly from the notes for the first time to add authenticity.

4 "We won't rip the IBM company up in a bad economic cycle . . . but after six years with one approach . . . It's time to try another," the notes quote Mr. Akers as saying.

Graf 5 gives context to the revelations. He characterizes Akers' mood ("pique and dismay") and then gives statistics to remind readers that IBM is having problems, quoting figures in his files from a market research firm.

5 Mr. Akers's pique and dismay are surfacing at a time when IBM's reputation for leadership in the computer industry, a key technology for American industrial success in the 21st century, is under broad re-examination. IBM's overall market share world-wide has slipped to about 23% from 37% as recently as 1983, according to the

Gartner Group Inc. market-research firm. The company's reputation as a stock-market leader and growth stock that always rebounds from adversity is also losing currency.

Carroll presents more background in graf 6 about why the IBM chairman is upset.

6 All of that frustrates Mr. Akers, who has been straining to rejuvenate the company since its earnings hit their peak in 1984 but has only managed to stem the speed at which competitors have eroded IBM's proud tradition. Mr. Akers is 3 1/2 years away from IBM's mandatory retirement age of 60 and is starting to talk in terms of what he hopes will be his legacy, so there seems to be a heightened sense of urgency in his statements.

In grafs 7, 8, and 9, he gives readers more direct quotes.

7 Much of what Mr. Akers described would consist simply of communicating that urgency to employees. "The fact that we're losing market share makes me god-dam mad. I used to think my job as a [sales] rep was at risk if I lost a sale. Tell them theirs is at risk if they lose one," Mr. Akers is quoted as saying.

8 "I'm sick and tired of visiting plants to hear nothing but great things about quality and cycle time — and then to visit customers who tell me of problems. If the people in labs and plants miss deadlines . . .

9 "The tension level is not high enough in the business — everyone is too damn comfortable at a time when the business is in crisis."

By graf 10, Carroll lets an IBM spokesman add a cautionary word (the notes aren't verbatim) but confirms their validity.

10 An IBM spokesman, while confirming the basic validity of the notes, cautioned that the notes aren't a verbatim transcript of the meeting. He added that Mr. Akers and others have been delivering stern messages internally for months now. He said the executives aren't merely reacting to the problems IBM disclosed late in the first quarter — problems that meant IBM's operating earnings fell 50% in the quarter and that led securities analysts to expect them to fall about 30% for the full year.

More chance for IBM to have its say in graf 11 . . .

11 The spokesman said the tough messages don't change IBM's position that the

company's prospects will improve once the world-wide economy turns around. He said the messages merely mean that IBM is tired of the loss of market share that has been gradually going on for several years now and feels the need to accelerate its restructuring.

... including a direct quote.

12 "They're intended to be long-term messages that are meant to improve the business, but they're not meant to improve the business next month," the spokesman said.

In graf 13, Carroll broadens the story considerably by summarizing what some outsiders think ("money industry executives") and then quoting one of them directly (14).

13 Still, many industry executives see IBM's problems continuing, and some analysts say the latest round of restructuring is the start of something major.

14 "There is a fundamental rethinking of the business going on," says Steve Cohen, a securities analyst at Sound View Financial Group, Inc. who has been negative on the company for almost a year. "IBM's cost structure presupposes premium pricing." But computer hardware has become so standardized and price wars so severe that "IBM won't be able to get premium prices for who knows how long," Mr. Cohen says. "If that's the case, then the fundamental business model is wrong, and you have to do something about it."

More context by Carroll based on his background knowledge of IBM's problems and what it has already done to solve them (15, 16, 17).

15 In addition, IBM's room to maneuver seems to be getting smaller; simply because it has already done so much. By the end of this year, IBM will have cut its work force to fewer than 360,000 down 47,000 from five years ago. It has moved so many people into new jobs, often in new locations, that two years ago a book on IBM's personnel practices described the IBM restructuring as the biggest movement of people since the troops came home after World War II.

16 While IBM announced another job reduction program in March and hinted that more might be coming, most of its recent moves have just been fine-tuning. It announced a change to its U.S. pension-plan that gives employees modest incentives to retire early. It said it would close most of its U.S.

headquarters operations the week of July 4 so it could save money on air-conditioning, cafeteria costs, and so forth. It told employees they had to start taking the vacation they used to carry over from year to year, so the company can cut the payments it has to make for deferred vacation when people retire. (One side effect of the increased vacation-taking is that IBM has found it can't schedule big meetings on Mondays or Fridays. A consultant who works with IBM has complained that has made life tough because executives at the company are tied up in meetings all day Tuesday, Wednesday and Thursday.)

17   Mr. Akers is quoted as saying at the April seminar that he doesn't see room for major asset sales, given that IBM in March completed the sale of its typewriter, laser-printer and office products businesses.

In graf 18, Carroll offers an additional suggestion (firing people) and his knowledge of company policy on it (19, 20).

18   The one way Mr. Akers might be able to cut employment sharply is through firing—known as MIA, or management-initiated attrition, in IBM-speak. That is a delicate issue at IBM because of its no-layoff tradition and because the distinction between layoffs and extensive firings can be thin, even if the company fires only those it considers to be marginal performers.

19   While it's not yet clear how much firing will pick up, Mr. Akers is quoted as saying at the seminar that "our people have to be competitive, and if they can't change fast enough, as fast as our industry . . . goodbye."

20   He is quoted as saying that only one of every 200 people at an IBM lab was fired last year and as advocating "a forced march on the MIA problem."

In graf 21, Carroll goes inside the company to quote the view of a current employee, anonymously to protect that person's standing.

21   Not everyone, of course, sees things the way Mr. Akers does. One IBMer, reacting on an internal network to the seminar notes, wrote: "I think it is time the people at the top accepted some part of the responsibility for our present problems." He added: "I don't see any sign of that happening." Another complained of the "arthritic bureaucracy"

and said his attempts to circumvent the process were discouraged.

Carroll gives more details on the notes dealing with world competition (23, 24, 25).

22 Mr. Akers singled out parts of the world where IBM was doing much worse than he expected — managing to cover most of the world in the process, according to the notes.

23 He is quoted as saying that four years ago a U.S. sales force of 20,000 delivered $26 billion of revenue, while in 1990 25,000 people produced just $27 billion. "Where's my return for the extra 5,000 people?" he is quoted as asking.

24 Mr. Akers is quoted as saying that IBM has been losing market share in Japan for two years and that first-quarter results were "disastrous" in that country. He is quoted as noting that the European economy is stronger than the U.S. economy and that indigenous European computer makers are faring poorly. "The business benefits should therefore accrue" to IBM, he is quoted as saying. "Where are they?"

25 The notes quote Mr. Akers as saying that "share loss in any sector of the business would not be tolerated."

In graf 26, Carroll begins his ending by taking readers to the beginning of the notes and why their author disseminated them. He finishes that thought by letting the IBM spokesman have the last word.

26 The notes begin with Mr. Akers complaining that his messages get filtered as soon as listeners leave the room. That, Mr. Henderson explains, is why "I left the room with a real sense of obligation to spread his word."

27 The IBM spokesman said that effort was laudable but, with word circulating so widely, added that Mr. Akers might have preferred that his message be communicated "in a more controlled manner."

#2

UNISYS SUSPENDS ITS DIVIDEND ON PREFERRED

by Paul B. Carroll

Staff Reporter of

The Wall Street Journal

This financial story would not even be read by anyone

1 Unisys Corp. suspended the dividends on its preferred stock, retrenching further in its

without an interest in the company. Because only specialists will read it, Carroll uses technical terms without explaining them ("dividends," "preferred stock," "debt load"). The lead is very straightforward. The transition is done by characterizing what was reported in the lead as "the move."

In graf 2 he notes what the action will accomplish and in 3 brings in an outside source for comment.

attempts to deal with its dangerous debt load.

2 The move will save the computer and defense electronics company $120 million a year, giving it more flexibility as it struggles with nearly $3.7 billion in debt. At the same time, the decision underscores the depth of the trouble in which Unisys finds itself because of its overly aggressive expansion campaign in the late 1980's. That can be especially dangerous in the computer industry, where customers depend so much on their suppliers that they get nervous at the first signs of financial troubles.

3 Unisys common stock, which has nearly doubled since Feb. 1 on rumors of possible asset sales, rose a further 50 cents to $4.50 in composite trading on the New York Stock Exchange — but the move left some securities analysts puzzled.

The source's direct quote follows in 4.

4 "You have to wonder what the traders have seen in the past few days that those of us who have been following this for a while haven't seen," said Dan Mandresh, a securities analyst at Merrill Lynch & Co. "You can argue about whether the right price is 2-1/2 or 4-1/2, but nothing has changed" in the past few days to account for the stock price's jump.

Details on how the stock is doing.

5 Unisys Series A preferred had also been climbing recently and was up more than $1.50 at one point yesterday, but it tumbled following the announcement and closed down $3 at $8.

In graf 6, Carroll gives context, telling readers how this is but one problem for the company and detailing them (7, 8).

Litany of Woes

6 The suspension of the dividend adds to the litany of woes that Unisys, Blue Bell, Pa., has had to report in recent months. The

company posted a loss of $436.7 million for 1990, giving it a total loss for the past two years of nearly $1.1 billion, on annual sales of around $10 billion. Although Unisys had predicted several times over the past two years that it would soon return to profitability, the company acknowledged last month that it would lose money again in the first quarter and have a "very difficult" first half.

7   The company suspended its common-stock dividend in September—saving $160 million a year. Shortly thereafter, Moody's Investors Service Inc. downgraded the ratings on Unisys debt to junk-bond levels. In October, Unisys announced it was cutting 5,000 more jobs, bringing to more than 20,000 the number of jobs it has cut out of the 93,000 person work force it had at the beginning of 1989.

8   Unisys is within about $200 million of violating a net-worth covenant in a major bank loan, but its banks have so far been supportive. Unisys also reiterated yesterday that it has begun talking with companies that might buy some of its assets and that it has put more than $1 billion of assets up for sale.

The best solution seems to be selling assets and Carroll writes about that in 10 and 11.

9   Unisys cut its debt by $200 million last year, while also increasing its cash by $400 million, and has said it hopes to cut debt by at least $600 million this year.

10   Unisys hasn't identified what assets it might sell, but the speculation has centered on its $2.5 billion-a-year defense business, its one-third share of a large marketing company in Japan or its Timeplex network business. The company also has plant capacity to sell, because of consolidation among its facilities as it has laid off workers.

11   Unisys has been talking about selling assets for several quarters now, however, and the deteriorating economy has clearly made it more difficult for Unisys to get the sort of prices it wants.

Carroll ends the story with one more worry: the downgrading of the company's bond rating.

12 Moody's, citing Unisys dependence on asset sales, said yesterday that it may downgrade further its ratings on the debt of Unisys and its finance company. Moody's also cut the rating on Unisys preferred to Caa from single-B-3.

Business Reporting:
Likely Problems and How to Solve Them

Problem	Solution
1. Getting too close to sources or accepting gifts, discounts, and other favors.	1a. Be ethical and decline all gifts including free trips on company aircraft.
2. Pressure to write "booster," chamber-of-commerce type stories or to avoid all controversy so as not to antagonize advertisers.	2a. Fight to let the facts speak for themselves.
	2b. Point out that the publication is not an arm of the chamber of commerce.
	2c. Be prepared to resign.
3. Interference from the advertising department when stories are unfavorable to advertisers or potential advertisers.	3a. Stress ethical considerations and the need for full reporting as a service to readers.
	3b. Involve your editor in any battle with the advertising department.
	3c. Make sure facts and figures used in the story are correct; save all source material beyond interview notes as backup.
4. Hostility from business people because of distrust of reporters and fear of revealing information to competitors in stories; resentment of past press treatment of them or business in general.	4a. Explain that you are ethical, honest, and accurate.
	4b. Ask for the chance to prove your ability as a good business and financial reporter.

4c. Prepare carefully for interviews by reading background information on the person and the subject of the interview so you don't waste time by asking uninformed questions.

5. Temptation to benefit financially by writing favorable stories.

5a. Avoid all such temptation.

5b. Don't even check the stock tables at the time you write your story.

6. Dull, boring subjects.

6a. Humanize subjects as much as possible.

6b. Let readers see how the subject affects them.

7. Complicated financial terms.

7a. Ask sources to explain things in everyday language; avoid jargon.

7b. Learn how business and the economy work by taking basic courses and reading textbooks or specialized publications.

7c. Get on the mailing lists of all companies in the area for news releases and other materials and national organizations like the American Bankers Association, American Stock Exchange, Investment Company Institute, Mortgage Bankers Association, New York Stock Exchange, Securities and Exchange Commission, Federal Reserve Board, U.S. Department of Commerce, and the U.S. Department of the Treasury for background publications.

Summary

Business and financial reporting has long been an important part of American journalism. Its popularity has increased in recent years because of the fluctuating U.S. economy, the fluctuating stock market, the S&L crisis, and the energy crisis. Readers and viewers, more personally affected by economic trends than before, are demanding more information. The business reporter can give it to them. Whether working for large or medium newspapers, magazines, or television networks, this specialist will need to understand complicated terms and be able to translate inexplicable business and financial events into language grasped by the public. Business stories come from many sources: news releases, annual reports and annual meetings, new products, trends in industries, personnel changes, and local tie-ins to national stories. No matter how well prepared, however, business reporters often face hostility from the business executives they must interview. Because of past bad experiences with the press and a lack of understanding about how newspapers, magazines, and television news programs work, these executives dislike reporters and may not attempt to hide it.

Exercises

1. Select a public relations news release from a company as the basis for a story. Analyze the release as to the factual, non-biased information it contains. Then make a list of the questions and additional sources of information you would need to write a business story. Report your findings to the class.

2. Select a national business problem and localize it by interviewing company officials and experts about its ramifications in your city or state. Write a story, making sure to tie it in with the national problem.

3. Trace the steps a person has to go through to get a loan at a local bank. Interview bank officials and the person seeking the loan. Write a story using the material you picked up in your reporting.

4. Write a profile of a person in business, keeping in mind the idea that everything is a business. Try to find out profits, problems, and overall business strategy beyond the usual laudatory praise present in most such information gathering.

5. Select a local business problem (decline in downtown area, layoffs of a nearby factory) and do an in-depth analysis of its

causes, the present situation, and possible ways to solve it in the future. This article should involve at least five interviews and library research.

Key Terms for Business Reporting

Annual report   A printed report issued once a year in which a company or other organization reveals financial and other information.

Assets   Property or resources, owned by an individual or company, with positive dollar value.

Balance of payments   The net inflow or outflow of money resulting from the international trade of a nation.

Balance of trade   The difference between the total value of goods imported or exported; if exports are more than imports, a trade surplus results; if they are less, a trade deficit occurs.

Bear market   Slang for the market climate when prices for securities are going down and there are few purchases of them.

Big board   Another name for the New York Stock Exchange.

Blue-chip stock   Common stock of companies that are profitable and pay dividends regardless of economic conditions.

Blue-collar workers   Workers who work in factories or do manual labor.

Bond   A certificate of debt due to be paid by a government or corporation to an individual holder and usually bearing a fixed rate of interest.

Bond rating   The classification of bonds as to their stability and strength.

Book value   The actual value in money of the assets of a corporation minus its liabilities.

Boom   A time of high business activity in the business cycle.

Bull market   Slang for the market climate when prices for securities are rising and purchase of them is at a high level.

Business cycle   The phases of business activity over a long period of time including decline, recession or depression, and recovery.

Capital   Net worth or the amount of assets over liabilities.

Capital gain or capital loss   The profit or loss gained from the sale of a capital asset.

Capitalization   All the securities issued by a corporation.

Cartel   A combination of international corporations within one industry designed to stabilize prices by limiting production and dividing up territory.

Cash flow   The earnings of a corporation after taxes have been paid and dividends disbursed; money that flows into a corporation.

Closed shop   A company or other organization in which only members of a union are hired to work.

Collateral   A security pledge for the payment of a loan.

Commodity   Raw materials (for instance, copper) and provisions (for instance, cotton) quoted on the basis of immediate delivery and for future delivery.

Common stock   Ownership in a corporation, divided into shares of equal value; all common shares confer the same rights to vote on corporation business and to receive equal portions of earnings (see also preferred stock).

Conglomerate   A large corporation that has grown by purchasing and merging with other corporations in many different kinds of business.

Consumer Price Index   A measure of the average changes in prices of four hundred goods and services typically purchased by city families that are said to be representative of all urban places in the country.

Crash   A sudden collapse of the stock market.

Debenture   A corporate bond unsecured by any mortgage and dependent on the credit of the issuer.

Deficit   The money governments, corporations, and individuals spend over that which they collect in a certain period.

Deflation   The economic condition that occurs when prices fall quickly and the pace of business slackens; too many goods, not enough purchasers.

Depreciation   The cost in wear, decay, and obsolescence of any asset.

Depression   A long period of reduced business activity, including low production and a high rate of unemployment.

Discount rate   The interest Federal Reserve banks charge their member commercial banks to borrow funds.

Distribution   The process of locating customers for goods and services and moving such products to them.

Dividend   A sum of money paid to a corporation's shareholders out of its earnings.

Dow-Jones averages   A set of averages of transportation, utility, and industrial stocks that are used to forecast stock market trends.

Dummy   Person on board of directors with no financial interest in the company who represents someone who does have an interest.

Earnings per share   The amount of money earned each year for each share of stock owned by shareholders.

Escalator clause   A clause in a contract or wage agreement that permits automatic increase if prices or costs go up.

Escrow   An agreement involving three parties in which one party acts as custodian for some valuable property received from a second party until a third party has completed an obligation.

Featherbedding   The practice by labor unions of setting pay rates for specified jobs even if those jobs are easier or no longer exist.

Federal Reserve System   The central bank of the United States; its main purpose is the control of the nation's money supply.

Fiscal year   Accounting year rather than the calendar year.

Float   To sell a new issue of securities.

Frozen assets   Assets of a corporation or government that are not readily turned into cash.

Futures   Contracts on commodities in which the seller agrees to deliver a specified amount at a future date.

Greenmail   The practice of buying a large block of company stock in order to force a rise in stock prices or an offer by the company to repurchase that block of stock at an inflated price to thwart a takeover bid.

Gross national product   The market value of the total output of goods and services of a nation.

Growth stocks   Shares in corporations that increase earnings regularly and use profits for research and expansion.

Hedge   To protect against a probable loss by buying or selling items ahead of time.

Holding company   A corporation owning all or most of the stock of one or more operating companies.

Hot issue   A new issue of stock prices below potential value and thus considered a good buy.

Inflation   A rise in prices over an extended period that leads to an increase in the supply of money.

Insider trading   Using inside information about a company illegally to make money by buying or selling its stock before such knowledge has been made public.

Interest   The amount a borrower pays to use a lender's money.

Investment   Capital put into a business over an extended period to receive a moderate return.

Investment banker   A banker who arranges the long-term capital requirements of corporations.

Issue   Stocks, bonds, or other obligations sold for a company and considered among its liabilities.

Junk bond   A corporate bond with a low rating and a high yield, often involving a high risk.

Keynesian economics   The theory that considers wage rates a factor in product demand as well as a cost of doing business; it is used to support wage increases with the explanation that higher wages will increase purchasing power and prevent unemployment and depressions; developed by the British economist John Maynard Keynes.

Legal tender   Coins and paper money that must be accepted by creditors as payment of debts (creditors are not allowed to demand gold instead).

Letters of credit   A means by which a bank can substitute its credit for the credit of its customer.

Lien   A charge against a property in order to force settlement of a debt.

Line of credit   A maximum amount someone may borrow from a bank at any given time.

Liquid assets   Assets that can immediately be turned into cash.

Liquidation   The act of selling securities to get cash or of going out of business by selling all assets.

Long   The state of an investor when he or she is holding securities or commodities and waiting for a price rise.

Manipulation   Any action that causes prices to rise or fall when they would not do so without such action.

Material information Important facts about a company, the public knowledge of which sends its stock up or down.

Merger The joining of two companies, usually by an exchange of stock or a cash settlement.

Monopoly The power to control the prices of an industry; a violation of antitrust laws in most cases.

Multinational corporations Companies that do business in a number of countries.

Negotiable Capable of being traded; usually describes a security that can be sold.

Note Written promise to pay.

Obligation Any kind of indebtedness.

Off-board Transactions in securities not listed on a stock exchange.

Open market A freely competitive market.

Open shop A company in which union membership is not a requirement for hiring.

Option The privilege of buying or selling specified securities or commodities at a set price within a specified time limit.

Over the counter A means to sell large blocks of high-grade listed securities, inactive securities, and those not listed on an exchange; not an organized exchange.

Parent company A company owning enough stocks of another company to dictate control.

Partnership A business owned by a few individuals, each of whom assumes responsibility.

Par value The value printed on stock certificates or bonds.

Personal income Income received by individuals from all sources.

Portfolio The group of securities owned by an individual or a company.

Position The inventory of a trader of stocks or a corporation — whether "long" or "short" of securities and commodities.

Preferred stock Ownership in a corporation; the holders of this stock usually cannot vote their shares as they can with common stock; they receive a fixed dividend before holders of common stock (see also common stock).

Primary boycott The action of workers refusing to do business with their employer.

Prime rate The interest banks charge their best customers for business loans.

Productivity The relationship between quality of goods and services (output) and the amounts of labor, material, and capital (input) needed for the production; measured by output per man-hour.

Prospectus A summary of a company's stock registration statement filed with the SEC; includes information about the company, its operations, its management, and the purpose of the proposed stock issuance.

Proxy A person appointed to represent another person in voting, usually at a stockholders' meeting.

Publicly held company   A company whose stock is sold to shareholders.

Raid   Active and heavy buying or selling of stock.

Rally   A short but spirited upswing in the stock market.

Reaganomics   The economic policies put forth by President Ronald Reagan, especially those emphasizing the supply-side theory.

Real wages   The goods and services a worker can purchase with his or her pay.

Recession   A mild but widespread slowdown in business activity and the economy, resulting in increased unemployment.

Restraint of trade   Interference with free trade; illegal under the Sherman Anti-Trust Act.

Rigging   Manipulation of the sale of any security.

Scab   Someone who crosses a picket line to replace a striking worker.

Seat   A membership in a stock or commodity exchange.

Secondary boycott   The action that occurs when boycotters of a company cause third parties to refuse to do business with their employers.

Securities and Exchange Commission (SEC)   The federal agency that controls operation of stock exchanges, stock brokerage firms, and corporations whose stocks are traded on them.

Security   An evidence of debt or of property, as a bond or stock certificate.

Security analyst   One who analyzes companies in order to recommend that customers buy (or not buy) stocks.

Share   One of the equal parts into which the capital stock of a corporation is divided.

Short   The sale of securities or commodities, which are not owned, in anticipation of buying them at a lower price later.

Sit-down strike   The action of workers going on strike inside a plant.

Speculation   Investing capital in a company to get quick or large returns at some risk.

Squeeze   Combination of a temporary shortage of available funds, borrowing difficulty, and increased interest rates.

Stock dividends   A payment made to stockholders in added shares rather than cash.

Stock exchange   A place where stocks are bought and sold.

Stockholders   People who own common and/or preferred stock; also called shareholders.

Stock market   The trading in securities, especially stocks, throughout a nation.

Street   Popular name for the New York financial district.

Supply-side economics   The theory that large tax reductions will unleash a flood of private investment, work, and savings that will help increase economic growth and lower inflation when combined with reductions in government spending.

Sweatshop   A factory without decent standards of sanitation, safety, and working conditions.

Take-home pay   The amount of pay after all deductions have been made.

Takeover The acquisition or gaining control of a corporation through purchase or exchange of stock.

Tariff Duties or taxes levied by a government on all imports.

Tender offer An offer to buy a large number of shares of company stock to gain control; often the action is not wanted.

10-K A form required by the SEC to be used by a company as its annual report.

Tip An unsupported statement about the possible movement of stock prices.

Took a bath Slang for the investor's fate when an investment turns sour.

Union shop Company in which workers must join a union to stay employed.

Wall Street The heart of the New York financial district; used to describe all financial interests.

White-collar workers Managers and clerical employees of a company.

Working capital A company's investment in short-term assets like cash, accounts receivable, and inventories.

Yield The rate of return on a security.

Additional Reading in Business and the Economy

Berle, Adolph A., Jr. *Power Without Property.* New York: Harcourt, Brace and World, 1959.

Bogart, Ernest L., and Donald L. Kemmerer. *Economic History of the American People.* New York: Longmans, Green, 1946.

Burrough, Bryan, and John Helyar. *Barbarians at the Gates: the Fall of RJR Nabisco.* New York: HarperCollins, 1990.

Dichter, Ernest. *Handbook of Consumer Motivations.* New York: McGraw-Hill, 1964.

Drucker, Peter F. *Management: Tasks, Responsibilities and Practices.* New York: Harper & Row, 1974.

Galbraith, John Kenneth. *The Affluent Society.* Boston: Houghton Mifflin, 1958.

_____. *The New Industrial State.* Boston: Houghton Mifflin, 1967.

Greenwald, Douglas, ed. *McGraw-Hill Dictionary of Modern Economics.* 2nd ed. New York: McGraw-Hill, 1973.

Grunwald, Edgar A. *The Business Press Editor.* New York: New York University Press, 1988.

Iacocca, Lee with William Novak. *Iacocca: An Autobiography.* New York: Bantam Books, 1984.

Kirsch, Donald. *Financial and Economic Journalism.* New York: New York University Press, 1978.

Kohlmeier, Louis M.J. et al. *Reporting on Business and the Economy.* Englewood Cliffs, NJ: Prentice-Hall, 1981.

Leavitt, Harold J. *Managerial Psychology.* 2nd ed. Chicago: University of Chicago Press, 1964.

Moskowitz, Milton, Michael Katz, and Robert Levering, eds. *Everybody's Business: An Almanac.* San Francisco: Harper & Row, 1980.

Packard, Vance. *The Hidden Persuaders.* New York: David McKay, 1965.

Phillips, Kevin. *The Politics of Rich and Poor.* New York: Random House, 1990.

Stabler, C. Norman. *How to Read the Financial News.* New York: Barnes & Noble, 1972.

Steiner, George A. *Top Management Planning.* New York: Macmillan, 1969.

Townsend, Robert. *Up the Organization.* Greenwich, CT: Fawcett, 1971.

White, William H. *The Organization Man.* New York: Simon & Schuster, 1956.

Appendix A
Legal Problems and How to Avoid Them

Like reporters of any kind, public affairs reporters may encounter legal problems in a number of different areas simply by doing their jobs. They can also run afoul of the law through defiance or simple ignorance. This section outlines such problems, ways to avoid them, and the applicable federal and state laws.

Libel

Libel is a defamatory statement about a person that is published and thereby injures that person's reputation. Reporters can get into trouble if their words imply criminality or question morals, sanity, or financial stability or if mistakes are made in stating the facts of stories, for example, misspellings of names or incorrect addresses. If a reporter, editor, and publication lose a suit for libel, they can be sued for damages.

Publications and broadcast stations must be careful in what they print or broadcast about people. No matter what the original intention, the issue is the effect upon those who read, see, or hear it.

There are two kinds of libel: *civil* and *criminal*. Most libel cases fall into the civil category, that is, a story that constitutes a printed or broadcast defamation. Criminal libel, while rare in the United States, results when something written or broadcast leads to a breach of the peace.

To win a civil libel case, a plaintiff must establish that the item in question was published; that he or she was identifiable by others, even if not named directly; that the plaintiff was damaged by the statement; and that the defendant was at fault—that is, he or she published the item knowing it was false (for public figures), or acting negligently in failing to ascertain that the statement was false (private individuals).

If a publication or broadcast station—or any of its employees—loses a libel suit, it must pay damages to the plaintiff. There are three kinds of damages: *compensatory* or general (awarded to the plaintiff who was named in the published or broadcast item; the plaintiff need not prove actual injury); *special* (awarded to the plaintiff who can show evidence of particular loss to reputation, well-being, or profession; this kind of damage can be awarded in addition to general damages); and *punitive* (awarded as a punishment and as an example because the offending publication showed malice in using the libelous item; the plaintiff must show proof of this malice, however).

Applicable Defense and Laws

1. **Truth.**   To prove in court that what was written is true.
2. **Fair comment and criticism.**   To be allowed to make "fair comment" on the performance of actors, sports figures, government officials, and others as long as that comment is without malice and restricted to the person's work.
3. **Privilege.**   To use material in stories that is immune to libel action because it is "privileged." Privileged material includes statements by judges, lawyers, and witnesses in court as long as the court is in session; debates in Congress and state legislatures; and public documents.

Relevant Supreme Court Rulings

1. **Times v. Sullivan, 1964.**   Public figures cannot collect libel damages from journalists unless they can prove that what was written about them was a malicious and deliberate lie and in reckless disregard of the truth.
2. **Rosenbloom v. Metromedia, 1971.**   The *New York Times* rule resulting from *Times v. Sullivan* applies to private individuals engaged in matters of general interest.
3. **Gertz v. Robert Welch, 1974.**   The press does not enjoy the same constitutional insulation from libel suits filed by private citizens as it does in cases brought by public figures.

4. **Firestone v. Time, 1976.** The category of individuals who can bring libel actions as private citizens rather than public figures is broader than indicated in the *New York Times* rule; this is important because private citizens are not required to prove as much as public figures to collect damages for the publication of defamatory falsehoods.

5. **Hutchison v. Proxmire, 1979.** Lower level public employees who sue the press for inaccurate news articles have to show only that the news articles were careless or negligent and do not have to show that the articles were written with malice.

6. **Wolston v. Reader's Digest Association, Inc., 1979.** Persons convicted in courts generally are not "public figures" for purposes of libel actions; this means that most criminal defendants who sue the news media for inaccurate stories about them will have to show only that the reporter was careless rather than either malicious or in reckless disregard of the truth.

7. **Herbert v. Lando, 1979.** The First Amendment does not protect reporters' thoughts, judgments, and newsroom discussions from forced disclosure in libel cases.

8. **Bose v. Consumers Union, 1984.** The Sullivan standards (see #1) requiring public officials to prove malice and "reckless disregard" of the truth are reaffirmed and the role of lower courts in reviewing libel judgments is endorsed. (This appeals power is crucial for the press because more than 80 percent of the libel awards are reversed in appeal.)

9. **Seattle Times v. Rhinehard, 1984.** Judges can bar a news organization from using in a story information it obtained during discovery proceedings in a libel trial it was defending.

10. **Keeton v. Hustler, 1984.** A publisher may be sued for libel in any jurisdiction in which even a small number of publications are available, even if the plaintiff doesn't live in that jurisdiction.

11. **Calder v. Jones, 1984.** A reporter and editor may be sued in any jurisdiction in which it is foreseeable that the plaintiff will suffer damages, even if the reporter never sets foot in that jurisdiction.

12. **Dun & Bradstreet v. Greenmoss Builders, 1985.** Protections provided in Gertz (see #3) apply only when statements are of public concern; this decision also allowed an award of punitive damages without evidence of actual malice.

13. **Philadelphia Newspapers v. Hepps, 1986.** The two-hundred-year-old burden on the media to prove truth in a libel case is removed.

14. **Liberty Lobby v. Anderson, 1986.** The Constitution requires libel plaintiffs to prove at the summary judgment juncture in a case what they must prove at trial: that there is clear and convincing evidence to support their claim and permit a reasonable jury to find for them. (This decision was aimed at disposing of meritless lawsuits before they get very far.)

15. **Falwell v. Flint, 1988.** The First Amendment protects satire and parody even when they cause emotional distress of public figures, just as libelous statements about such persons receive special treatment under the Constitution.

16. **Harte-Hanks Communications, Inc. v. Connaughton, 1989.** The commitment to both the stringent proof standard required of public officials under *Times v. Sullivan* (see #1) and the exacting standard of judicial review required by Bose (see #8) is reaffirmed.

17. **Milkovich v. Lorain Journal Co., 1990.** The First Amendment does not make the news media immune from libel lawsuits based on statements of opinion. Opinions expressed in newspaper columns and editorials and television and radio commentaries are entitled only to the constitutional protections that the news media already receive for stories based on facts, and not more.

18. **Masson v. New Yorker, 1991.** Public figures cannot win damages for libel based on a writer's use of altered quotations unless there were significant changes in the meaning of what they said and plaintiff can prove the meaning was changed.

Ways to Avoid Libel

1. Be fair and accurate in reporting at all times.

2. Agree to check the facts of any story a person claims libeled him or her; do this politely but without admitting error.

3. Do not discuss the story or the reporting of it with the person who is complaining.

4. Print clarifications willingly and in a prominent place in the newspaper or magazine to explain and clarify the facts that are in question; only in extreme circumstances print retractions which actually admit error and "take back" the original story.

5. Consult an attorney from the moment the person complains about the alleged libel.

6. Consult the Reporters Committee for Freedom of the Press, 1735 "I" Street, N.W., Suite 504, Washington, D.C. 20006, a voluntary association of reporters and editors working to protect the interests of journalists; it provides libel defense to journalists in freedom of the press and FOI cases.

Contempt and Confidentiality

A reporter has always been subject to a judge's contempt ruling for disobeying a court order, disturbing the court process, or attempting to influence a judge's decision or witnesses' testimony.

Beginning in the 1970s, however, contempt was used increasingly to compel reporters to disclose the names of sources and turn over their notes to law enforcement and other government agencies. Both source names and notes are crucial to the successful practice of journalism. Reporters consider any infringement upon either a violation of their First Amendment rights. The law enforcement and other government officials think their need for information from any source takes precedence over any right of the press to gather news. The Supreme Court has tended to support the officials in several decisions.

Applicable Laws

1. **Branzburg v. Hayes, 1972.**   Journalists do not have the right to keep confidential the names of sources of information used in published or broadcast stories.

2. **Zurcher v. The Stanford Daily, 1978.**   Police officers may obtain a warrant to conduct unannounced searches of newsrooms for evidence of a crime, even though they do not suspect anyone connected with the news organization of wrongdoing; previously police had to go through the longer legal process of getting a subpoena specifying what they wanted.

3. **Shield laws.**   The Branzburg decision led to the enactment of shield laws in a number of states. A move to pass a federal shield law died out, however. In essence, a shield law protects reporters from having to disclose interview information or source names unless they have personal knowledge that proves

or disproves the commission of a crime charged or under investigation.

4. **Farber case.**   Reporters in states with shield laws felt safe in conducting their jobs, at least until the Farber case. In 1978, Myron Farber, a *New York Times* reporter, was jailed by a New Jersey judge for refusing to surrender notes gathered in writing articles about thirteen mysterious deaths in a hospital in that state. The judge did so despite the fact that New Jersey has a shield law. Later the U.S. Supreme Court let stand a New Jersey Supreme Court decision upholding contempt of court citations against Farber and the *Times*. The reporter was eventually released. Shield laws still exist in many states, but reporters are less certain of their protection after the Farber case.

5. **Privacy Protection Act, 1980.**   The *Stanford Daily* case had a happier outcome for the press. In 1980, President Carter signed the Privacy Protection Act making it:

> . . . unlawful for a government officer or employee, in connection with the investigation or prosecution of a criminal offense, to search for or seize any work product material possessed by a person reasonably believed to have a purpose to disseminate to the public a newspaper, book, broadcast, or other similar form of public communication . . . but this provision shall not impair or affect the ability of any government officer or employee pursuant to otherwise applicable law, to search for or seize such materials if . . . there is probable cause to believe that the person possessing such materials has committed . . . the criminal offense to which the materials relate . . . [and] . . . there is reason to believe that the immediate seizure of such materials is necessary to prevent the death of, or serious bodily injury to, a human being.

6. **Cohen v. Cowles Media Co., 1991.**   The First Amendment does not protect the news media from lawsuits for damages for breaking promises of confidentiality to news sources.

Ways to Avoid Contempt Problems

Subpoena, request to testify:

1. Never appear voluntarily as a witness.
2. Be careful in disclosing any information about a story to an attorney even in an informal way.
3. Notify your editor immediately if you get a subpoena, but do not contact the attorney involved; the newspaper's attorney

should make the contact to find out the nature of the proceeding and the testimony sought.

4. Do not agree to produce material before any court appearance.

Subpoena, factual testimony:

1. Seek to have the newspaper's attorney petition the court to quash the subpoena because it would jeopardize the reporter's future work and relationship with sources.

2. Go to court—if you have to go—with an attorney.

Subpoena, source names and notes:

1. Notify your editor and the newspaper's attorney as quickly as possible.

2. File any petition to quash the subpoena immediately.

3. Do not discuss anything about the case with anyone, especially with the attorney issuing the subpoena.

Search warrant:

1. Assert First Amendment right to the officers arriving to search the offices of the news organization.

2. Step aside and allow them to search without necessarily volunteering to show them the location of what they want.

3. Make a list of any items taken by police in their search.

Privacy

The foundations of privacy laws have their roots in the U.S. Constitution. Although the word "privacy" does not appear in that document, the Supreme Court has consistently interpreted the Constitution to grant individuals a right of privacy based on the First, Fourth, Fifth, Ninth, and Fourteenth Amendments. Despite this broad support, privacy is an area with few legal precedents, far less well-defined than libel, for example.

As it has evolved over the years, the right of privacy is considered to be the right of a person to be left alone to enjoy life without his or her name, visage, or activities becoming public property, unless he or she relinquishes that right. This privacy—for living persons only—is protected from invasion by newspapers, magazines, books, television, radio, photographs, motion pictures, creditors, and wiretappers.

The laws generally cover invasion in one of four ways: 1) intrusion (unreasonably intruding upon the solitude of another by physical or other means); 2) publicizing private matters (revealing in print or broadcast something about the private life of a person that offends ordinary sensibilities); 3) publicizing in a false light (writing something about a person that puts them in a "false light," that is, contrary to the truth); 4) appropriation (using a person's name, likeness, or personality for advertising or commercial purposes without his or her consent).

Applicable Defenses

1. **Consent.**   To prove that a person consented to the invasion of his or her privacy. Verbal consent is not enough; the person must give it in writing.
2. **Newsworthiness (public figures).**   To show that the person in question is a public figure or public official. Courts have agreed that such a person invites public interest and must accept even unwelcome publicity.
3. **Newsworthiness (private individuals).**   To prove that a private individual was involved in a matter of public interest. Unwarranted and unauthorized exposure of the private affairs of a private citizen, offensive to ordinary sensibilities and without legitimate interest to the public, can be deemed an invasion of privacy.
4. **Constitutional privilege.**   To show that the alleged invasion of privacy in a "false light" was not carried out with the knowledge that it was false or untruthful. This defense resembles the constitutional proof requirements for public officials and public figures in libel law.

Applicable Laws

1. **Time v. Hill, 1967.**   *The New York Times* rule must be applied to privacy cases where the publication is false or fictitious, testing whether the falsehood was intentional and calculated.
2. **Cantril v. Forest City Publishing Company, 1974.**   A person's claim that a story "contained significant misrepresentations" was upheld by the Supreme Court, putting the press on notice that it would be punished when it was careless in reporting facts.
3. **Cox Broadcasting v. Martin Cohn, 1975.**   The press has the right to carry news stories about open records used in open court hearings, because "the commissions of crimes, prosecutions resulting therefrom, and judicial proceedings arising

from prosecutions are events of legitimate concern to the public. . . ."

4. **B.J.F. v. Florida Star, 1989.**   Privacy suits should be decided on a case-by-case basis without a national standard and all fifty states are invited to shape their own privacy laws. The decision should not be interpreted to mean "that untruthful publication is automatically constitutionally protected, or that there is no zone of personal privacy within which the state may protect the individual from intrusion by the press. . . ."

Ways to Avoid Privacy Problems

1. Do not publicize matters about the private life of someone that would be offensive to a "reasonable person," even if what is printed is true.
2. Do not publicize matters that put another person in a false light.
3. Do not physically intrude into a person's solitude or seclusion.
4. Do not appropriate the name or likeness of another person for benefit or advantage.

Access

Without the opportunity to cover court proceedings, examine public records, attend meetings of governmental bodies, and review arrest records, reporters cannot do their jobs. All of these areas can be grouped collectively under the broad category of access. (Chapter 8 covers this subject more completely.)

Courtrooms: Applicable Laws and Rulings

1. **Canon 35, American Bar Association Canons of Judicial Ethics, 1937.**   The taking of photographs in courtrooms was banned, because it "detracted from the essential dignity of the proceedings, degraded the court, and created misconceptions with respect thereto in the mind of the public. . . ." This was later extended to television.
2. **Rule 53, Federal Rules of Criminal Procedures, 1946.** Radio broadcasts and photography were banned from criminal cases in federal court.
3. **Judicial Conference of the United States Resolution, 1962.**   Rule 53 was extended to any judicial proceeding and

to the "environs of the courtroom"; television coverage was also prohibited.

4. **Nebraska Press Association v. Stuart, 1976.**   Judges must explore all other possibilities before even considering attempts to keep the press from covering a trial at all; this eliminated so-called "gag" orders.

5. **Gannett Company v. DePasquale, 1979.**   Judges have broad discretion to exclude the public and the press from criminal pretrial proceedings.

6. **Richmond Newspapers v. Commonwealth of Virginia, 1980.**   The First Amendment guarantees the right of the public and the press to attend criminal trial proceedings, except in the most unusual circumstances.

7. **Chandler v. Florida, 1981.**   State courts have the authority to allow — even over the objection of the defendant — television, radio, and still photography coverage of criminal trials. (Even with this ruling, many states still prohibit cameras and tape recorders in the courtroom.)

8. **Press Enterprise Co. v. Superior Court of California, 1984.**   A court order closing the jury selection process in a rape-murder case was invalid.

What to Do When Faced with Closed Courtrooms

1. Notify your editor and the newspaper's attorney.
2. Object to the closure in writing if you learn of it in advance, asking to be heard with your attorney.
3. Request through your attorney that your objection to the court closure be heard in public, and try to get it into the record.
4. If the court will not listen to the arguments of your attorney, ask the court to postpone further proceedings until application can be made to a higher court.
5. Request a copy of the order closing the proceedings; if it is not in writing, ask that a written order and your objection be entered into the court record.
6. If the hearing is under way, ask the sheriff or bailiff to carry to the judge your written objections and a request for your admittance.
7. Do not try to get into a closed courtroom or refuse to leave when asked to do so by a judge.

8. Do not consent to a judge's agreement to let you into the court if you agree not to publish anything.

9. You can publish anything about the closed hearing you obtain from other sources.

10. Have your attorney file the appropriate motion to get the court opened up.

Public Records: Applicable Laws and Regulations

1. **The Freedom of Information Act, 1966 (Amended 1974 and 1986).** "Any person" may have access to all records of all federal agencies, unless these records fall within one of nine categories of exempt information that agencies are permitted but not required to withhold. (The nine categories are: national security, internal agency rules, information specifically exempted by dozens of other federal laws already on the books, trade secrets, executive privilege, invasions of privacy, law enforcement investigations, bank reports, and oil and gas data.)

2. **State Public Records Laws.**   Most states have some kind of public records law, some more restrictive than others. The laws usually specify types of public records (for example, vouchers and receipts relating to the spending of public money, official files and memoranda, and "writings" — books, papers, maps, and photographs), rules of inspection, reasons for denial of access, and the fees to be charged to photocopy the desired records.

   In both federal and state public records laws, the copying charge can be prohibitive and indeed be the factor that denies access. The laws usually do not state an exact amount, only a "reasonable" one. One agency's definition of "reasonable" may not coincide with that of a reporter trying to make copies, especially of a long document at five dollars a page. (See Chapter 6.)

What to Do When Faced with Closed Court Records

1. Request access to the records in writing to the judge who closed them; identify the documents as specifically as possible; you do not need to state a reason, however.

2. If the request is denied, ask the judge to put the denial and the reasons in writing.

3. Have your attorney appeal any denial to the next highest court.

4. If you come into possession of a sealed court document from another source, you may print it; you should be prepared, however, for a later request to disclose your source.

What to Do When Faced with Closed Federal Agency Records

1. Try to get the documents you want informally through the public information office of the agency.

2. If that fails, request the documents in a simple letter that states what you want as specifically as possible.

3. If the request for documents is denied (by law, it must be within ten days), reasons must be given.

4. File an appeal of any denial to the head of the agency involved (answerable within twenty days).

5. If this appeal is upheld, file a complaint in federal district court.

What to Do When Faced with Closed State Agency Records

1. Know the procedure and the laws about public records in your state.

2. Request the specific information you want with the appropriate agency head.

3. If this request is denied, ask in writing what law is being used and the reasons; have your attorney file an appeal in court.

Open Meetings: Applicable Laws and Regulations

1. **Federal Open Meetings Act of 1976.**   Any agency meeting that results in the "disposition of official agency business" must be open to "public observation." A meeting need not be open to the public if the subject matter deals with secret, personnel, trade secret, financial, or currency speculation information; accuses someone of a crime; invades someone's privacy; or interferes with law enforcement.

2. **State Open Meetings Laws.**   Many states have passed open meetings laws requiring proper notice (usually at least twenty-four hours) and minutes available in several days. There is a provision for closed executive sessions to consider personnel

matters, legal advice, private records, and labor negotiations. (See Chapter 6.)

What to Do When Faced with Closed Meetings

1. State your objection to a closed meeting, and ask that your objection and the reasons for the closure be recorded in the minutes.

2. If the meeting closure violates the state open meetings law, advise everyone at the meeting that the action is in violation of the law.

3. If the meeting is already closed, send a written objection into the meeting via someone going into the room, and request that the objection be entered into the minutes.

4. Do not volunteer to leave the meeting; let an official public body order you to leave.

5. If ordered to leave, do not refuse but ask that a vote be taken about closing the meeting.

6. Do not agree to off-the-record remarks during a meeting or not to report certain portions of the meeting.

7. If a public meeting goes into executive session, ask that the head of the agency state reasons for doing so and that these reasons be recorded in the minutes.

8. If you are excluded, ask for a transcript or copies of the minutes in writing.

9. In some states, if you are wrongfully kept out of a meeting, you may void any action taken in your absence and secure an injunction against future violations of the state open meetings law.

10. You may use information about a closed meeting obtained from other sources.

Arrest Records: Applicable Laws and Regulations

1. **Crime Control Act, 1973.** This act required the Law Enforcement Assistance Administration (LEAA) to promulgate regulations to maintain the accuracy, security, and privacy of all criminal history record information and to provide a mechanism by which an individual believing his or her criminal record information is inaccurate can review, challenge, and if necessary, correct it.

2. **LEAA Regulations, 1975 and 1976.** These regulations required each state to prepare and submit for approval a Criminal History Record Information Plan.

3. **State Regulations.** Although they vary in specifics, most state plans allow law enforcement agencies to release information contained on posters, announcements or lists identifying fugitives; original records like police blotters; court records of public judicial proceedings; published court or administrative opinions and public administrative and legislative proceedings; traffic records; and announcements of executive clemency. Although agencies may disclose criminal history record information about a current offense, they can only confirm the existence of such a record if it relates to the above subjects and if the reporter specifies the date of arrest. Agencies may not release information about a juvenile unless ordered by a court to do so.

What to Do When Faced with Closed Arrest Information

1. Know the state and local rules pertaining to such information.
2. Protest in writing and in person if a law enforcement agency tries to close records in the categories noted earlier.
3. If that fails, have the newspaper's attorney protest the closure to court.

Key Legal Terms

Access   The right to cover trials.

Civil libel   A defamatory statement about a person that is published and thereby injures that person's reputation.

Contempt and confidentiality   Willful disobedience or disrespect to a court, for journalists the failure to surrender notes and source names.

Copyright   The exclusive right, granted by law for a certain number of years, to make and dispose of copies of literary, musical, or artistic work.

Criminal libel   A defamatory statement that, when printed, results in a breach of the peace.

Damages   The money award to winning plaintiffs in libel cases to compensate them for their injury.

Defenses   Reasons given in a libel suit to explain a defendant's action.

First Amendment The First Amendment to the United States Constitution, which reads, "Congress shall make no law respecting an establishment of religion, or prohibiting the free exercise thereof, or abridging the freedom of speech, or of the press; or the right of the people to assemble, and to petition the Government for a redress of grievances."

Gag order An order by a judge restricting coverage of court proceedings.

Libel Defamation by the printed word, or a malicious, false, and defamatory statement that is printed.

Malice A desire to inflict injury upon another, in journalistic parlance, printing an item with evil intent or motive to harm.

Obscenity Printed, photographic, or other printed material intended to cause sexual excitement or lust.

Prior restraint Any attempt by the government to halt publication of a story.

Privacy The right of people to be let alone; the reporter's right to cover people involved in news events as long as they don't invade their privacy unnecessarily or carelessly.

Privileged material Material set aside as immune from prosecution under libel laws: court records, transcripts of congressional debates.

Additional Reading on Legal Problems

Barron, Jerome A. *Public Rights and the Private Press.* Ontario, Canada: Butterworth, 1981.

Denniston, Lyle. *The Reporter and the Law.* New York: Hastings House, 1980.

Gillmor, Donald M., and Jerome A. Barron. *Mass Communication Law,* 3rd ed. St. Paul: West Publishing Company, 1979.

How to Use the Federal FOI Act. Washington, DC: Reporters Committee for Freedom of the Press and the Society of Professional Journalists, 1980.

Nelson, Harold L., and Dwight L. Teeter, Jr. *Law of Mass Communications,* 4th ed. Mineola, NY: Foundation Press, 1982.

Pember, Don R. *Mass Media Law,* 4th ed. Dubuque, IA: Wm. C. Brown, 1987.

Sanford, Bruce W. *Synopsis of the Law of Libel and the Right of Privacy.* New York: World Almanac Publications, 1984.

Spencer, Dale R. *Law for the Newsman,* 5th ed. Columbia, MO: Lucas Brothers, 1980.

Appendix B
Ethical Problems and How to Avoid Them

Ethics for journalists has always been somewhat elusive and ephemeral. Although good reporters try every day to achieve ethical perfection in their work and overall conduct, no person or organization actually exists to discipline them if they fail.

Unlike medicine and law, journalism has never had a formal and binding system for dealing with those within its ranks who are unethical. People who violate ethical principles in their journalistic work are not required to appear before a grand tribunal of black-robed editors and reporters who pass judgment on their misdeeds. Lawyers can be disbarred for unethical conduct; doctors can be prevented from practicing medicine if they transgress accepted standards of behavior. In both of these professions a formal body of lawyers or doctors is empowered to take action if its investigation discovers wrongdoing.

Instead of such formal systems, journalistic ethics are governed by carefully prepared codes, one of which is reproduced at the end of this Appendix. These codes exert a great deal of moral force — presiding, in black frames, from the walls of newsrooms and broadcast stations to keep a kind of silent vigil over all that goes on in front of them.

The principles these codes espouse set high standards of ethics, but that is all they do — set them. It is up to everyone, working at all levels of the media, to see that they are followed.

Considerations of ethics begin in journalism courses in college as codes are read and discussed. Once a person starts working, a code will probably be mentioned on the first day, along with other do's and don'ts required of all employees. Ethics is a popular topic at professional journalism conferences. Panels of experts from various media and allied fields, like law, discuss real and hypothetical ethical situations and how to handle them.

In general, journalists have tried to redefine and tighten their own standards in recent years, particularly since Watergate and all the other revelations and lapses in the ethics of government, big business, the military, intelligence agencies, and other areas of national life. If they were going to call attention to the wrongdoing of others, as they had in these instances, people in media decided they had to put their own houses in order.

Because the profession consists of thousands of news organizations, large and small, the move was done piecemeal, publication by publication, broadcast station by broadcast station. In the end, even with a new stress on codes and ethical behavior, ethics remain an individual pursuit, practiced best by each person in the media every day.

Journalism has had various codes of ethics for years. No one code dominates either print or broadcast media. Some newspapers have devised their own code or follow the one first developed by the American Society of Newspaper Editors in 1923 and revised in 1978. Others use one written and adopted by the Society of Professional Journalists in 1926 and revised in 1973 and 1987. (It is reproduced later in this Appendix.)

These codes are commendable in their collective goal of achieving the ideal in journalism. How effective are they in fulfilling these lofty goals?

"The press faces no greater problem than that created by public doubt about its adherence to high principles and ideals," wrote Claude Sitton, then chairman of the ethics committee of the American Society of Newspaper Editors (ASNE) in a foreword to *Playing It Straight*, a 1983 book about ethics written by John Hulteng. Sitton goes on to note that some accusations of unethical conduct are groundless, but others are not. No one should question the need for attention to accuracy, fairness, and balance in journalism, according to Sitton. In the end, the attention to, and study of, ethics is left to individuals in journalism.

Added Charles Novitz, former president of the Society of Professional Journalists (SPJ) in a statement in that organization's 1982 ethics committee report: "As the professions go, American Journalism holds to damn high standards. Remarkably, they are not imposed. We swim in an 'ethical sea' in which self-governance is the water. Peer pressure is powerful. Legal remedies abound. The public demand for ethical journalism is ever-present. But the key is within us . . . whether we believe we have the answer or merely understand the question, only the absence of self-doubt is dangerous.''

There is another side to the matter of codes. Many reporters and editors oppose them, according to Gene Goodwin, a professor of journalism at Pennsylvania State University, who conducted interviews with a number of professionals for a book on journalistic ethics.

"The most compelling argument against journalistic codes of ethics comes from journalists who fear that judges and the courts will try to universalize them, try to apply the codes to all the media, large and small," noted Goodwin in the 1982 Society of Professional Journalists, Journalism Ethics Report. Others oppose codes because they are too general and unrealistic to be effective.

The Newspaper Guild, a nationwide union of journalists, has long been against such codes, according to Goodwin, fearing that management will use them as instruments to restrict the economic freedom and to threaten the job security of its members.

Goodwin considers codes promulgated by ASNE and SPJ as toothless, and notes that "you can drive an unethical truck" through the codes of the Society of American Travel Writers and the Outdoor Writers Association of America. He thinks that other codes are better because they are tougher and more specific; for example, the one followed by the Associated Press Sports Editors Association and the National Conference of Editorial Writers. He also compliments the strict codes at individual news organizations like the *Philadelphia Inquirer*, the *Washington Post*, NBC, CBS and ABC.

Goodwin found that the majority of daily newspapers in the United States including the *New York Times* and the *Los Angeles Times*, and most broadcast news departments, have no codes at all.

But the 1986-87 Society of Professional Journalists Ethics Report noted that actions against unethical journalists do take place. At least 48 newspaper staff members in the three years before had been fired, according to a survey of 226 editors by the American Society of Newspaper Editors ethics committee.

Plagiarism was cited as the most serious offense, followed by fabricating quotes and documentation, scalping Super Bowl tickets sent to the newspaper, fixing parking tickets through the police reporter, sharing stories with sources before publication, and taking sports bets on a newspaper's telephones.

Respondents to the 1986 SPJ National Ethics Survey strongly favored active censure of ethical violators. They also thought publishers and station managers should adhere to the same ethical standards as the journalists they employ. There was a wide difference, however, in defining the value of gifts, favors, and special treatment.

"Most respondents agreed the American public doubts the general credibility of journalists, both print and broadcast," wrote Chuck Rehberg, ethics reporter co-editor. "Strong feeling was expressed that journalism code enforcement would enhance journalism credibility."

In addition to codes, some news organizations have attempted to monitor and improve the ethical standards of their staff members by hiring ombudsmen as in-house critics with the job of investigating complaints about coverage and suggesting ways to improve it. Press councils are another way to examine lapses in coverage, with the results of their investigation made public as a means to see that such lapses do not happen again. The idea of a council—composed of journalists and non-journalists and supported by staff—never really caught on, however. The National News Council existed from 1973 to 1984 but died because many major organizations refused to accept its findings and the public seemed indifferent to its work. Several news councils now exist on the state level.

Ethical Problems

Imperfect as they are, journalistic codes of ethics at least bring potential ethical problems out in the open. Reading a code in school or the first day on the job may start the process of thinking about problems and how to avoid them.

The standards set in the codes are aimed primarily at situations in which journalists are placed in compromising and tempting positions by a number of practices that used to be widespread.

1. **Freebies.** When sources or potential sources give gifts to reporters and editors, the action may have nothing to do with influencing coverage. The appearance of the gift is the important factor, however, and it is best if reporters and editors take nothing of value. Journalists had long received free liquor and food from sources at Christmas, with nothing expected or given in return. Most news organizations have now changed all of this, however, and a few very strict codes extend the definition of "gift" to lunch or even a cup of coffee. The new structures also bring up the matter of space occupied by reporters covering local, state and federal agencies. Are reporters who cover these

agencies influenced by the official help they receive? The answer has been hard to figure out and has often meant charging news organizations for desk space or for a percentage of square footage. Sometimes, the quest for an equitable fee has proved to be more trouble than it is worth and has been abandoned.

2. **Junkets.**   When a reporter or editor goes on a trip for which all expenses are paid, such participation might be unethical. How can that reporter be objective if he or she has been "wined and dined" by the very organizations to be covered? Large corporations used to set up junkets regularly. No one doubted the enjoyment that resulted. But no measure of compromised stories has ever been tallied, and the new climate of ethics has ended the practice. Now, most reporters and editors pay for their own trips to cover legitimate stories. If an area is accessible only by private plane — like the Alaska pipeline or the Amazon jungle — each news organization will usually pay a share of the cost in order to send a reporter along. The same thing happens during presidential campaigns when the two political parties charter airplanes for the media and bill each participating news organization for a share of the total cost. Exceptions to the rule on junkets are travel writers who often cannot go on the trips they must write about without help from airlines, ocean liners, and resort hotels, and entertainment reporters from medium and small newspapers and magazines, who could not report on the fall TV season unless they accepted the all-expense-paid trips to Hollywood from the three major networks.

3. **Misuse of position.**   At times a reporter or editor is in a position to gain financially because of what he or she writes. Such cases usually involve business or financial journalists who work for national newspapers and magazines or specialized publications as noted in Chapter 12. The journalists buy stock in the company, write favorably about the company; the stock increases in value because of what is written in the important publication, and the journalist sells the stock at a profit.

4. **Memberships.**   Can a reporter or editor be fair about covering an organization if he or she belongs to it? Most media do not think so and thus prohibit staff members from belonging to all but churches. Some make this a condition of employment, although others are not that rigid. The fact remains, however, it is hard to be totally objective if a reporter or editor has "inside" information gained from membership in the organization being reported upon, and not honest reporting.

5. **Contests and awards.** In recent years, journalism has been surfeited with contests and awards of all kinds. *Editor and Publisher* lists 48 pages of such contests and prizes. The profession has honored its best practitioners for years with honors, such as the Pulitzer Prizes, the Sigma Delta Chi Distinguished Service Awards, and the Peabody Awards for television. What has happened lately to worry some reporters, editors, and broadcasters is the growth of contests and awards sponsored by professional groups and companies. The reporters who enter the competition are usually those who regularly cover the subject area of the sponsoring company or organization. If they win an award from the group, how can they remain objective in reporting about them?

   Another factor in the contest situation is the sheer number of such competitions, many of which are sponsored by journalism organizations or journalism schools as fund-raising devices or prestige-building mechanisms. In such instances, bad judges often reward bad entries. Publications enter certain issues prepared specifically to win the contest.

   No person or official organization has the authority to tell one group or another that it cannot sponsor a contest or grant an award, nor will such groups cancel them voluntarily. The only way this contest mania can be controlled is for individual news organizations to set up their own guidelines: (1) to not enter anything where the sponsor is seeking obvious commercial advantage and has its name in the title, (2) to refuse to participate in any contest with an easily discerned bias against an individual or group, (3) to decline to enter contests sponsored by interest groups, (4) to not allow the award to be exploited in public, (5) to know who the judges are and make sure they are qualified, (6) to not allow public relations people or corporate executives to be on judging panels, (7) to not enter if the fee is too high because then the group is obviously using the contest mainly as a way to raise money.

6. **Personal relationships.** When a friend or family member is involved in a story, a reporter or editor cannot be objective in covering it. In such cases, the best solution is to reveal the connection immediately and refuse the assignment because of conflict of interest.

   In a celebrated case in 1977, a reporter for the *Philadelphia Inquirer* became romantically involved with a state senator who was a key participant in the primary campaign she was covering. She accepted gifts from the senator and neglected to ask for reassignment until after the general election. The relationship was not discovered until several years later, after the reporter had been hired by the *New York Times*. When her earlier transgression was discovered, she was immediately fired by the *Times*.

7. **Objectivity.**   Bias or prejudice in news reporting is the most difficult ethical problem to overcome. Reporters and editors may be biased, almost without knowing it. The tremendous power they exert over the public must compel them to watch for instances in which they are tempted to misuse their position. It is relatively easy for reporters to "get" someone in a print or broadcast story by presenting only one side of an issue or expressing their own opinions. Often, because they are only human, reporters may get angry at sources and want to take revenge. They must resist such a course of action at all costs and give fair and balanced coverage, no matter how distasteful some sources may be as individuals.

8. **Misrepresentation of sources.**   When should a reporter disguise his or her identity to get a story? Reporters and editors differ greatly on this subject. Some will pose as someone else to uncover evil deeds, either on the telephone or by wearing a disguise. Others will never do so. It all depends on the circumstances and the ability to face oneself in the mirror in the morning. The media codes are silent on this matter, leaving it up to individuals and their news organizations. Circumstances do vary greatly enough to make a binding rule impossible.

   (Of growing concern to the media in the 1980s and the early 1990s is the tendency of law enforcement officers to pose as reporters. In 1984, for example, police officers in New Jersey pretended to be a TV crew in order to interview a group of demonstrators on the town green who were protesting a drug law. This kind of incident blurs the lines between police and media in a way that does harm to both because they have such distinctly different—and independent—roles to play.)

9. **Withholding information at official request.**   At times, police and other government officials may ask reporters to withhold information because its revelation would disrupt an investigation or harm the welfare of the nation. For example, in 1961, President John F. Kennedy requested that the *New York Times* keep advance knowledge of the Bay of Pigs invasion out of its pages in the national interest. He later said he wished he had let the paper print what it had so that he would have been forced to call off what became an unsuccessful invasion.

Former CIA director William Colby requested in the 1970s that several news organizations withhold their knowledge of the efforts to raise a sunken Soviet nuclear submarine. They complied for a time, until a columnist not bound by the agreement, broke the story. Police officials often request that reporters and editors keep quiet about negotiations to free a kidnap victim.

Such requests create ethical problems for a reporter. No reputable journalist would knowingly harm the national security or place in jeopardy a kidnap victim or a hostage. Conversely, no journalist wants to become an accomplice for officials out to squelch the truth or cover up their own mistakes. Each case must be judged on its own merit.

Ethical Case Studies

All of the Codes of Ethics and discussions about potential problems in the world, however, will not easily solve the ethical situations encountered on the job. Some defy any neat categorizations. Others constitute ethical violations prima facie. Two cases that received national attention in recent years illustrate how difficult journalistic ethics can be.

1. **Janet Cooke and the Washington Post.**   In September 1980, Janet Cooke, a reporter for the *Washington Post*, wrote a gripping story about Jimmy, an eight-year-old heroin addict, which appeared on page one of the *Post*. Her editors nominated the story for a Pulitzer Prize, the most prestigious in journalism. In April 1981, she won in the feature writing category.

Soon, however, everything about the reporter and her story began to unravel. First, her editors learned that she had falsified her academic credentials. Then she admitted that she had made "Jimmy" up. Cooke resigned and the *Post* gave back the Pulitzer.

The storm that came next damaged everyone in journalism. How had a great newspaper like the *Post*, which nearly single-handedly had revealed the Watergate conspiracy and brought down the government of President Richard Nixon, been so duped? Some observers said Cooke's editors had placed too much faith in a relatively inexperienced reporter. The editors replied that they had tried to get her to take them to "Jimmy's" home but that she had said the family had moved. She also said that "Jimmy's" drug supplier had threatened to kill her if she revealed her sources. After attempts by Washington, D.C. officials to find the boy so they could help him, the *Post* invoked the First Amendment protection of confidential sources. Even with their doubts, *Post* editors nominated their story for the Pulitzer, largely, one said, because a failure to do so would have raised even more questions about the story's authenticity, given the attention it attracted after it was printed and the fact that it was so well written.

Other critics blamed the *Post*'s internal management system of pitting reporter against reporter in sometimes savage battles, even to get stories into the newspaper, let alone be promoted up through the ranks. Cooke, these critics said, was the victim of too much ambition and a desire to beat the *Post*'s system at any cost.

But what of the once-revered Pulitzer Prizes? Would they ever again be as venerated? Other controversies over the years have never tarnished the luster of the awards quite as much as this hoax, especially in view of the way the Cooke entry was handled.

Post editors first submitted "Jimmy's World" in the general local reporting category. But jurors in that category selected instead the *Longview* (Washington) *Daily News* for its coverage of the eruption of Mount St. Helens. The Pulitzer board then moved the Cooke story to the feature category, where it eventually won. Later, jurors in both the general news and feature areas voiced their own skepticism about the Cooke story and their anger at being overruled by the seventeen-person board, which *Time* magazine press critic Thomas Griffith calls "a cozy fraternity of journalistic insiders."

In the aftermath of the controversy, the national board of the Society of Professional Journalists urged the Pulitzer Board to establish procedures that safeguard the integrity of the prizes. "The Society's grave concern is that Janet Cooke, in refusing to disclose the identity of her 'source', pretended to invoke a right that is essential to newsgathering — the right to afford confidentiality to a news source," said the Society. "Ms. Cooke's lack of professionalism should not be used by those who would seek to deny reporters this fundamental right." The statement pointed out the many instances in which low-level bureaucrats and others, fearing reprisals, tipped off reporters about misdeeds, but did so only after being promised that their identities would not be revealed. The board noted another Pulitzer Prize winning effort by the *Post*, its coverage of Watergate. "Where would our nation be today if the *Post*'s reporters had not cultivated 'Deep Throat' and other confidential sources to help uncover wrongdoing that the president and his men did not want uncovered?" concluded the statement.

That was precisely the biggest consequence of the Cooke/Post hoax. It denigrated all of journalism and made reporters and editors in all communications media have to work a bit harder in the future just to be believed at all.

Indeed, a *Newsweek* poll taken just after the hoax was revealed found a third of those questioned rejected the view that it was an isolated incident, believing reporters often make things up. More than 60 percent said they believe only "some" or "very little" of what they read in the press or see on TV.

2. **Gary Hart and The Miami Herald.**   In May 1987, the *Miami Herald* ran a Sunday story which reported that presidential candidate Gary Hart had spent the previous Friday night in his Washington townhouse with a woman other than his wife. The allegations came at the time the former senator was leading in the polls but also trying to end widespread and longstanding questions about his character. The story, quickly denied by Hart, had an immediate effect on those polls. It eventually caused him to withdraw from the race completely.

The ethical concerns arose from the manner in which *Miami Herald* reporters gathered the incriminating material on Hart. They conducted a twenty-four hour stakeout of his house during which they saw the two enter the dwelling at 11 P.M. and not leave until the next afternoon.

Should reporters adopt police surveillance techniques to gather information on the subject of stories? The *Miami Herald*'s own opinion polls showed that 63 percent of its readers found the coverage excessive. A *Newsweek* poll discovered that 64 percent of the respondents found coverage of Hart "unfair" and 52 percent thought media investigations of the private lives of candidates and public officials should be "off limits."

Editors and reporters were divided over the ethics of the reporting techniques used. Some decried them as excessive while others thought they were perfectly appropriate especially because Hart had challenged the media "to put a tail on me" in an interview several weeks before.

In the background of the entire episode was the changed nature of political reporting. For years a kind of gentlemen's agreement existed among reporters who covered public figures that certain subjects were off limits. A number of presidents — from Warren Harding to Franklin D. Roosevelt to John F. Kennedy — were widely known to be conducting extramarital affairs, but no one reported it.

Now, with the changing mores of society and enhanced status for women, there has been less tolerance by reporters and editors — and the reading and viewing public — for what *Time* magazine calls "the macho dalliances of married men." Modern political campaigns involve the slick packaging of candidates as if they were products. This tendency has heightened press interest in finding the "real" candidate and whether he/she is the same in private as in public. And, the public, for all its criticism of press behavior in cases such as the Hart episode, regularly buys millions of copies of newspapers like the *National Enquirer* or watches gossip programs on television.

In the 1992 Democratic presidential primary campaign, Governor Bill Clinton of Arkansas faced questions about his character after several news organizations revealed information charging that: 1) he avoided the draft during the Vietnam War, and 2) he had had an extramarital affair years before. The media jumped quickly on both stories and wound up being criticized for doing so.

The story of the alleged affair had originally been publicized in the *Star*, a sensational supermarket tabloid not known for its journalistic integrity. After ABC News used the story without much independent corroboration, the Clinton campaign staff accused it and other news organizations of practicing "trash journalism." Clinton successfully refuted the allegation in an appearance on "60 Minutes" on CBS and in later interviews. He did the same thing about questions of his draft status, a story that had also been played prominently on ABC News programs.

The media backed off, seemingly chastened by both incidents and exercising more care in handling similar stories for the rest of the campaign. Clinton, although dogged by questions about his character throughout the primary campaign period, went on to win nomination at his party's convention in July.

With fault on both sides, the ethical issues raised by both the Hart and Clinton cases were far from resolved. Similar incidents have happened since—and probably will again. They are what make ethics for journalists so elusive and ephemeral.

Additional Reading on Ethical Problems

Christians, Clifford, Kim Rotzoll, and Mark Fackler. *Media Ethics*. New York: Longmans, 1984.

Crawford, Nelson A. *The Ethics of Journalism*. New York: Alfred A. Knopf, 1924.

Gerald, J. Edward. *The Social Responsibility of the Press*. Minneapolis: University of Minnesota Press, 1963.

Hulteng, John. *Playing It Straight*. Chester, CT: Globe Pequot Press, 1981.

_____. *The Messenger's Motives*. Englewood Cliffs, NJ: Prentice-Hall, 1976.

Innis, Harold A. *The Bias of Communication*. Toronto: University of Toronto Press, 1951.

Liebling, A.J. *The Press*. New York: Ballantine Books, 1964.

Lippmann, Walter. *A Preface to Morals*. New York: Macmillan, 1929.

MacDougall, Curtis D. *The Press and Its Problems*. Dubuque, IA: William C. Brown Company, 1964.

Merrill, John C. *The Imperative of Freedom: A Philosophy of Journalistic Autonomy*. New York: Hastings House, 1974.

McCulloch, Frank, ed. *Drawing the Line*. St. Petersburg, FL: The Poynter Institute, 1984.

Rowse, Arthur E. *Slanted News*. Boston: Beacon Press, 1952.

The Society of Professional Journalists, Sigma Delta Chi

Code of Ethics
(Adopted 1926; revised 1973, 1974, 1987)

The SOCIETY of Professional Journalists, Sigma Delta Chi believes the duty of journalists is to serve the truth.

We BELIEVE the agencies of mass communication are carriers of public discussion and information, acting on their Constitutional mandate and freedom to learn and report the facts.

We BELIEVE in public enlightenment as the forerunner of justice, and in our Constitutional role to seek the truth as part of the public's right to know the truth.

We BELIEVE those responsibilities carry obligations that require journalists to perform with intelligence, objectivity, accuracy, and fairness.

To these ends, we declare acceptance of the standards of practice here set forth:

I. RESPONSIBILITY:

The public's right to know of events of public importance and interest is the overriding mission of the mass media. The purpose of distributing news and enlightened opinion is to serve the general welfare. Journalists who use their professional status as representatives of the public for selfish or other unworthy motives violate a high trust.

II. FREEDOM OF THE PRESS:

Freedom of the press is to be guarded as an inalienable right of people in a free society. It carries with it the freedom and the responsibility to discuss, question, and challenge actions and utterances of our government and of our public and private institutions. Journalists uphold the right to speak unpopular opinions and the privilege to agree with the majority.

III. ETHICS:

Journalists must be free of obligation to any interest other than the public's right to know the truth.

1. Gifts, favors, free travel, special treatment or privileges can compromise the integrity of journalists and their employers. Nothing of value should be accepted.

2. Secondary employment, political involvement, holding public office, and service in community organizations should be avoided if it compromises the integrity of journalists and their employers. Journalists and their employers should conduct their personal lives in a manner that protects them from conflict of interest, real or apparent. Their responsibilities to the public are paramount. That is the nature of their profession.

3. So-called news communications from private sources should not be published or broadcast without substantiation of their claims to news values.

4. Journalists will seek news that serves the public interest, despite the obstacles. They will make constant efforts to assure that the public's business is conducted in public and that public records are open to public inspection.

5. Journalists acknowledge the newsman's ethic of protecting confidential sources of information.

6. Plagiarism is dishonest and unacceptable.

IV. ACCURACY AND OBJECTIVITY:

Good faith with the public is the foundation of all worthy journalism.

1. Truth is our ultimate goal.

2. Objectivity in reporting the news is another goal that serves as the mark of an experienced professional. It is a standard of performance toward which we strive. We honor those who achieve it.

3. There is no excuse for inaccuracies or lack of thoroughness.

4. Newspaper headlines should be fully warranted by the contents of the articles they accompany. Photographs and telecasts should give an accurate picture of an event and not highlight an incident out of context.

5. Sound practice makes clear distinction between news reports and expressions of opinion. News reports should be free of opinion or bias and represent all sides of an issue.

6. Partisanship in editorial comment that knowingly departs from the truth violates the spirit of American journalism.

7. Journalists recognize their responsibility for offering informed analysis, comment, and editorial opinion on public events and issues. They accept

the obligation to present such material by individuals whose competence, experience, and judgment qualify them for it.

8. Special articles or presentations devoted to advocacy or the writer's own conclusions and interpretations should be labeled as such.

V. FAIR PLAY:

Journalists at all times will show respect for the dignity, privacy, rights, and well-being of people encountered in the course of gathering and presenting the news.

1. The news media should not communicate unofficial charges affecting reputation or moral character without giving the accused a chance to reply.

2. The news media must guard against invading a person's right to privacy.

3. The media should not pander to morbid curiosity about details of vice and crime.

4. It is the duty of news media to make prompt and complete correction of their errors.

5. Journalists should be accountable to the public for their reports and the public should be encouraged to voice its grievances against the media. Open dialogue with our readers, viewers, and listeners should be fostered.

VI. PLEDGE:

Adherence to this code is intended to preserve and strengthen the bond of mutual trust and respect between American journalists and the American people.

The Society shall—by programs of education and other means—encourage individual journalists to adhere to these tenets, and shall encourage journalistic publications and broadcasters to recognize their responsibility to frame codes of ethics in concert with their employees to serve as guidelines in furthering these goals.

Appendix C
How to Search Public Records

Public records document practically every human activity. They follow us from birth to death, from school graduation to retirement. They shadow our movements in business, politics, and crime. They capture on paper the transfer of wealth, whether it be a motor home or a 5,000-acre ranch. They remember those who pollute the air and water, those who run fire-trap hotels, those who cheat employees out of wages.

Yet, those records receive little public attention. Why? Because reporters seldom poke into government file cabinets to learn what stories documents have to tell.

Poking into such documents can help reporters in four ways.

They give detail. They allow a reporter to replace mushy generalities with specific facts. They say precisely the value of the mayor's property holdings, not "an estimated . . ."

They provide evidence. Reporters can rely on documents to back a sensitive story, to convince a nervous editor the story is truthful. They guard against libel suits.

Documents yield clues. A county commissioner's financial statement says he is a partner in a construction company. Another record will tell the reporter whether that company gets business from the county.

Most important, documents assure accuracy. The written word on a nursing home inspection report is more accurate than a source's biased statement or faulty memory.

Those benefits won't come if the reporter doesn't know where to look. This appendix bridges the gap between reporter and public records. The alphabetized listing of documents is organized by subject. A reporter will find, for example, a quick guide to records on public officials. To help you find each document, each entry tells where the record is filed.

We hope the paper trail we have mapped out here will encourage you, the reporter, to look for and produce stories that won't be found in press releases and news conferences. Too, we are sure that reporters using public records will give the public more accurate and complete stories.

Leslie L. Zaitz
Investigative reporter
The Oregonian
for The Society of Professional Journalists, Sigma Delta Chi

People

Here is a guide to public records that will help a reporter provide better accounts on people. First, we show you where to look for information on the average citizen thrust into the public spotlight. Next, we show you places to look for information about those involved in crime. Last, we give you places to learn all you can about a public official. Besides personal information, this guide allows you to check on the material possessions of any person.

The Average Person

Aircraft Registry.   Name, address of aircraft owner, aircraft N number, bill of sale, major repairs, and liens. Federal Aviation Administration, Oklahoma City, Oklahoma, (405) 686-2562.

Autopsy Report.   Medical examiner's findings of cause of death, details of condition of body, circumstances of death, and biographical information of deceased. State health division vital statistics section, county medical examiner.

Bank Records.   Records of customer checking accounts, loan accounts, and savings accounts are confidential. Such documents can be released with permission of bank customer.

Bankruptcy Petition.   Petitioner's name, address, list of assets, list of debts, and list of creditors. U.S. Bankruptcy Court, larger cities of state.

Birth Certificate.   Name, date and place of birth, mother's married and maiden name, father's name and occupation, and physician attending birth. State health division vital statistics section.

Boat Registration—State.   Name, address of boat owner, boat license number, prior owners, and type of vessel. State marine board.

Boat Registration—U.S.   Name, address of owner of vessel 16 feet or longer or with permanently mounted motor, home port, and vessel name. U.S. Coast Guard, regional office.

Child Support Payment Record.   Name, address of payer, payer's employer, amount of payment, and method of payment. State adult and family services division, or similar group.

City Directory.   Alphabetical listing of resident, spouse's name, occupation, and employer. Street index identifying occupants by name. Telephone number index identifying subscriber by name. Local library.

Civil Lawsuit File.   Name, address of plaintiffs, defendants, and description of civil dispute. Can contain affidavits, depositions, and evidence concerning dispute. Circuit court, county courthouse; U.S. District Court, larger cities.

Death Certificate.   Name, address, occupation, Social Security number of deceased, date of birth, circumstances of death, cause of death, spouse's name, disposition of body, funeral home, and cemetery where buried. State health vital statistics section.

Divorce Record.   Name, address, date of birth, Social Security number of husband and wife; previous marriages; name of children and date of birth; wife's maiden name; and court divorce decree. State health division vital statistics section.

Driver's License.   Name, address, date of birth, and physical description of license. State division of motor vehicles.

Driving Record.   Date, location of traffic conviction; date, location, circumstances of traffic accident. Record of license suspensions. State division of motor vehicles.

Income Tax Return.   Most states have a law that makes it a crime for any state Department of Revenue employee to release any information from an individual's state or federal income tax return.

Licensing Board.   Most states operate numerous boards licensing professions and trades. Licensing records generally give name, address, business affiliation, and qualifications of licensee. Boards can be identified through the state information operator.

Marriage Records.   Bride's and groom's name, age, address, occupation, Social Security number, previous marriages, parent's name, location and date of marriage, and witnesses. State health division vital statistics section, clerk's office, county courthouse.

Motor Vehicle Registration. Name, address of vehicle owner, description of vehicle, manufacturer's identification number, state license plate number, and financing institution. Registrations required for automobiles, trucks, trailers, recreational vehicles, and motorcycles. State division of motor vehicles.

Pilot's Certificate. Name, address, type of license, and date license issued. Federal Aviation Administration, Oklahoma City, Oklahoma, (405) 686-2562.

Probate Filing. Name of deceased, assets of estate, claims against estate, estate administrator, and final disposition of assets. Circuit court clerk's office, county court house.

Radio Operator's License. Name, address of licensee, type of radio license, and date license issued. Federal Communications Commission, local office; Washington, D.C. (202) 254-7674.

Residential Solar Tax Credit Application. Name, address of applicant, type of solar project, cost, and contractor.

Small Claims Suit File. Name, address of plaintiff, defendant, amount of money sought, final judgment, and source of payment of judgment. District court clerk's office, county courthouse.

Telephone Toll Records. Under federal law, a telephone company's records of long-distance calls placed by private customers is confidential.

Uniform Commercial Code Filing. Name and address of person obtaining financing, type, location of collateral, and name and address of financing institution. State secretary's office.

Voter Registration Card. Name, address, party affiliation of voter, and voter's parents' names. County elections office, county courthouse.

Welfare Recipient Records. Information about individuals receiving any type of government welfare assistance is confidential under state and federal law. State adult and family services division, or similar agency.

Criminals

Arrest Booking Slip. Arrested person's name, address, date of birth, monikers, tattoos, occupation, personal property seized, criminal charge, and bail amount. Booking officer, county jail.

Arrest Report. Name and address of arrested person, date of birth, moniker, occupation, personal property seized, circumstances of arrest, accusation, and bail. Law enforcement agency responsible for arrest.

Indictment.   Name of accused, crime charged, brief description of crime, bail, and witnesses testifying before grand jury. State circuit court clerk's office, county courthouse; clerk's office, U.S. District Court.

Personal Recognizance Release Form.   Arrested person's name, address, date of birth, occupation, employer, prior criminal convictions, names of relatives, and name of attorney of person seeking release without bail. District court clerk's office, county courthouse.

Prison Records—State.   Inmate name and age, institution of incarceration, crime charged, sentence, county of prosecution, parole date, and vocational and educational record while in prison. State corrections division.

Prison Records—U.S.   Inmate name, age, crime, past convictions, institution of incarceration, movements and furloughs, court appearances, and attorney. Federal Bureau of Prisons, Washington, D.C., (202) 724-3198.

Search Warrant.   Street address where search to be conducted, evidence to be seized, physical description of place to be searched, inventory of evidence seized, and identification of private citizen at search locations witnessing search. District court clerk's office, county courthouse; clerk's office, U.S. District Court.

Search Warrant Affidavit.   Police officer's statement of facts to justify judge issuing warrant, summary of evidence believed at search location, and use of evidence as proof of crime. District court clerk's office, county courthouse; clerk's office, U.S. District Court.

Public Officials

Campaign Committee Statement of Organization.   Name of committee, candidate supporting, party, and name and address of treasurer. State elections division; county elections division, county courthouse; city auditor, city hall.

Candidate Filing Statement.   Name and address of candidate, party affiliations, office sought. State elections division; county elections division, county courthouse; city auditor, city hall.

Contribution and Expenditure Report.   Name of candidate, office sought, name and address of treasurer; name, address, and occupation of contributors of $50 or more; detail of expenditures. State elections division; county elections division, county courthouse; city auditor, city hall.

Employer Registration—Lobbyist. Name and address of lobbyist employer, name of lobbyist, type of business of employer, and expenditures for lobbyist. State government ethics commission.

Ethics Law Complaint. Name of accused official, details of complaint, evidence from investigation, and final disposition. State government ethics commission.

Lobbyist Expenditure Report. Name and address of lobbyist, name and address of employer, money spent in calendar quarter for lobbying, name and amount over $25 spent on public official. State government ethics commission.

Lobbyist Registration Statement. Name and address of lobbyist, employer, legislators employed by lobbyists; business interests with legislators. State government ethics commission.

Political Action Committee Financial Report. Name of committee, name and address of treasurer, type of group representing, name and address of contributors of more than $50; expenditures, including contributions to candidates for public office. State government ethics commission.

Public Employee Pay Expense Records. Salary paid to public employees and reimbursement for documented expenses incurred in conduct of public business. Business office of government agency employing official.

Public Records Section Index. Name and address of state resident serving state government in elective or appointive position, date of election or appointment, and name of appointing authority. Secretary of state's public records section.

Statement of Economic Interest. Name and address of public official for appointive or elective positions at all government levels; official's source of income, property holdings, family business relationships with lobbyists. State government ethics commission.

Telephone Records. Date, time, number called on government telephone line used by public official. Business office, government agency employing official.

Voters' Pamphlet. Written statement by candidate for elective office or by supporting committee. Biographical material usually includes education, occupation, and prior service. State elections division.

Business

After attending a news conference where a South Dakota company has unveiled plans for a new shopping center, you become curious about this company. Who runs it? Who owns it? Has it done well or been in trouble? Every business is regulated by a bureaucracy somewhere, somehow. Below we list, first, some resources for researching a business. Then, we show you where to look for records on some specific businesses.

Basic Business Records

Air Contaminant Discharge Permit. Name and address of business receiving permit, type of discharge, mechanisms for purifying, conditions of permit. State department of environmental quality.

Assumed Business Name. Name and address of business, owners, and type of business. State corporation division.

Bankruptcy Petition. Name and address of business filing petition, list of assets, list of liabilities, list of creditors, affidavits, depositions, and final disposition. U.S. Bankruptcy Court, nearest large city.

Better Business Bureau File. Name of business, officers, business profile, consumer complaints, complaint investigation report. Local Better Business Bureau.

Business Energy Conservation Tax Credit. Name and address of business, description of energy system, company officers and owners, financial statement, and project costs. State department of energy.

Civil Rights Complaint. Name of accused business; details of alleged discrimination in hiring, pay, working condition, or dismissal; evidence; and disposition of complaint. State bureau of labor.

Consumer Protection Division File. Name and address of business, details of consumer complaint, business profile, complaint disposition. State consumer protection division.

Corporation Annual Report. Name of corporation, address, registered agent, stock issued, corporate president and address, and corporate secretary and address. State corporation division.

Corporation Articles of Dissolution. Name and address of corporation, date of dissolution, and name of officers authorizing dissolution. State corporation division.

Corporation Articles of Incorporation. Name and address of corporation, name and address of directors, name and address of incorporators, amount and value of stock issued, and purpose of company. State corporation division.

Corporation Filing—U.S. Name and address of corporation, significant changes in stock ownership, and significant corporation problems. U.S. Securities and Exchange Commission.

Employer Report — Labor (Form LM-10).   Name and address of business, detail of payments other than wages to union officers, union employees, detail of payments to business employees to interfere in union activities. U.S. Department of Labor.

Export Manifest.   Name and exporter, port of origin of merchandise, and description and value of merchandise. U.S. Customs Service.

Import Manifest.   Name of importer, port of origin of merchandise, shipper, description and value of merchandise, destination of merchandise, and bill of lading. U.S. Customs Service.

In-Bond Document.   Description of material shipped within U.S. but not cleared by U.S. Customs, name of foreign carrier, shipper, destination, and duty owed. U.S. Customs Service.

Industrial Health Inspection Report.   Name of company, address of plant, type of plant, health hazards identified in inspection, and corrective action ordered. State health division.

Internal Revenue Service Court Complaint.   Name and address of business taxpayer, nature of tax evasion, amount of income, and taxes owed. If case goes to trial, evidence includes business tax returns and business financial records. U.S. District court; Internal Revenue Service.

Labor Organization Annual Report (LM-2, LM-3).   Name and address of labor union, receipts, salaries of union officers, loans made to officers or businesses, record of payments, and shortages or losses of money. LM-2 for unions with receipts less than $100,000; LM-3 for unions over $100,000. U.S. Department of Labor.

Labor Organization Information Report (LM-1).   Name and address of union, union officers, type of union, anticipated union revenue, and dues assessed. U.S. Department of Labor.

Limited Partnership Agent Registration.   Name and address of partnership and name and address of partnership agent. State corporation division.

Limited Partnership Certificate.   Name and address of partnership, name of partners, investments by partners, and nature of business. State corporation division.

Nonprofit Corporation Registration.   Name and address of corporation, date of incorporation, name and address of officers, and corporation purpose. State corporation division.

Pesticide-Herbicide Registration.   Name and address of chemical manufacturer, chemical name, library of chemical labels, and chemical dealer license identifying name and address of dealer. U.S. Environmental Protection Agency.

Product Liability Insurance Claims.   Name and address of insurance company paying liability claim, name of product manufacturer, source of liability, and payment record. State insurance division.

Public Utility Commissioner Order.   Orders filed by commissioner in variety of utility cases, including orders detailing law violations by state-regulated utilities. State public utility commissioner.

Securities Enforcement File.   Name and address of accused business or securities agent, specific allegations, evidence of securities law violations, and final disposition of allegations. State corporation division securities section.

Securities Registration Statement.   Name of seller, type of security, amount offered, financial details of use and secured money, financial statement of offering business, name and address of business owners, and description of financed project. State corporation division securities section.

Small-Scale Energy Facility Loan Application.   Name and address of business, business profile, energy project description, and project financing plans. State department of energy.

Solid Waste Landfill Permit.   Name and address of business operating landfill, landfill operation details, permit conditions. State department of environmental quality.

Tariff Lien.   Name and address of carrier with claim against merchandise in international trade, location of merchandise, importer's name and address, and amount of carrier's claim. U.S. Customs Service.

Tax Appeals.   Name and address of business; name of attorney of business appealing assessment of property, income, or utility taxes; basis of appeal evidence of tax returns; tax liabilities, and court ruling. State tax court.

Wage Complaint.   Name of accused business, complainant's employment history, amount of wage owed, record of wage recovery efforts, and final disposition. State bureau of labor.

Water Contaminant Discharge Permit.   Name and address of company, address of polluting plant, details of water discharge, special conditions, permit violations. State department of environmental quality.

Specific Businesses

Adoption or Child Care License.   Name and address of business; type of business; name, address, date of birth, and Social Security number of business administrator, and details of business operation. State children's services division.

Alcohol Importer-Wholesaler Permit.   Name and address of business, type of imports, and distribution. U.S. Bureau of Alcohol, Tobacco and Firearms, Washington, D.C.

Customhouse Broker License.   Name and address of broker, business affiliation, and commodities traded. U.S. Customs Services, nearest large city.

Day Care Center Certificate.   Name and address of center, name and address of owner, names of employees, state inspection report, and type of program. State children's services division.

Employment Agency Complaint.   Name, address, and telephone number of agency, employer, and complainant; details of allegation against agency; and final disposition of complaint. State bureau of labor.

Energy Facility Site Application.   Name and address of business, names and addresses of officers, business financial statement, energy facility description, and energy production expectations. State department of energy.

Firearms Dealer.   Name and address of business; name and address of owner; hours of operation; other business conducted by dealer; type of weapons sold; names, addresses, and Social Security numbers of business owners; number of firearms sold annually; and criminal record of dealer. U.S. Bureau of Alcohol, Tobacco and Firearms, Washington, D.C.

Foster Care License.   Name and address of care center operator, name and address of owners, details of program, state inspection report, and record of payment from public agencies. State children's services division.

Hazardous Waste Treatment Facility License.   Name and address of business, address of plant, type of waste handled, state inspection reports, law violation reports, and license conditions. State department of environmental quality.

Insurance Agent's License.   Name and address of agent, type of insurance qualified to sell. State insurance division.

Insurance Agency License.   Name and address of business, name of agency operator, types of insurance authorized to sell, and insurance companies represented by agent. State insurance division.

Insurance Corporation Annual Report.   Name and address of corporation and officers; financial report detailing corporate assets and investments. State insurance division.

Investment Adviser.   Name and address of advisor, name and address of employer, employment history, and educational history. State corporation division securities section.

Medical Malpractice Report.   Name and address of insurance company, name of physician, amount of settlement, and nature of claim. State insurance division.

Motor Carrier Registration.   Name and address of operators, business name, business and operator financial resources, truck inventory, and service to be provided. State public utility commissioners.

Nursing Home Inspection Report.   Name and address of nursing home, date of inspection, name of state inspector, violations identified, corrective action ordered, and enforcement action taken. State health division.

Nursing Home License.   Name and address of nursing home, name and address of owners, name and address of administrator, number and type of patients served, and record of payments from public agencies. State health division.

Private Residential School License.   Name and address of school, name of administrator, annual budget, program description, and inspection report. State children's services division.

Private School Registration.   Name and address of school, name of administrator, description of educational program, and description of school financial resources. State department of education.

Public Contractor.   Name and address of business providing public agency service, contract, payments to contractor, name and address of company officers, business proposal for providing service, and business bid. Fiscal office of state, county, or local government agency.

Rail Crossing Complaint.   Name and address of offending railroad, detail of train blockage of public roadway, and enforcement action. State public utility commissioner.

Rail Equipment Inspection Report.   Name and address of railroad, type of equipment inspected, location of inspection, equipment defects identified and corrective action ordered. State public utility commissioner.

Rail Inspection Report.   Name and address of railroad, date of inspection, location of rail inspected, description of rail deficiency, corrective action ordered. State public utility commissioner.

Restaurant Health Inspection Report.   Name and address of restaurant, name of owner, date of inspection, health violations identified, corrective action ordered, and enforcement action taken. State health division.

Restaurant Liquor License.   Name and address of restaurant; financial statement of restaurant; type of license; names, addresses, and personal histories of restaurant owners. State liquor control commission.

Savings and Loan Institution Annual Report.   Name and address of institution, names of officers and directors, income and expenses, investments, and holdings. State corporation division, savings and loan section.

Savings and Loan Institution Registration.   Name and address of institution, branch locations, names and addresses of principal officers and directors, and financial statement. State corporation division, savings and loan section.

Securities Broker-Dealer.   Name, address, age, and Social Security number of broker-dealer; employment history; educational history; and current employer's name and address. State corporation division, securities section.

Securities Salesman Registration.   Name, address, age, and Social Security number of salesman; name and address of employer; employment history; and educational history. State corporation division, securities section.

Tavern Liquor license.   Name and address of tavern, type of license, financial statement of tavern, personal application of tavern owners, and criminal record of owners. State liquor commission.

Vocational School License.   Name and address of school; name, address, employment, and educational history of school administrator; school financial statement; description of educational program; name, address, employment, and educational history of school teachers. State department of education.

Property

Attempting to document the history of a real estate development, a land scandal, or a public official's land holdings can be a frustrating experience. In this section, we first give you a "roadmap" of documents concerning the planning, sales, and construction of real estate projects. Then, we show you where to look to discover who owns what.

Real Estate Development

Builders Registration.   Name and address of construction business, name and address of business officers, type of construction, complaints against business, complaint resolution, and enforcement action. State builders board.

Building Permit.   Name and address of owner, address of project, type of construction, contractor, and building plan. Building permits section, public works office, county or city.

Condominium Project Registration.   Name and address of developer, detailed description of condominium project, description of construction financing, details of financing plans offered to purchasers, and names and addresses of salesmen. State real estate division.

Interstate Land Sales Filing.   Name and address of business selling property interstate, details of real estate offering, names and addresses of salesmen, consumer complaints, and enforcement action. U.S. Department of Housing and Urban Development.

Planning Project Records.   Name and address of developer, detailed plans of development, local public works office review reports, and permits checklist. County planning department, city planning department.

Property Transaction Complaint File.   Name and address of complainant; name and address of accused real estate salesman, agency, or developer; details of complaint; evidence file; complaint resolution; and enforcement action. State real estate division.

Real Estate Broker's License.   Name, address, and age of broker; name and address of employer; date license issued; complaints against broker; and enforcement action taken. State real estate division.

Real Estate Salesman Application or License.   Name, address, and age of salesman; name and address of current employer; employment history; complaints against salesman; and enforcement action taken. State real estate division.

Subdivision Project Filing.   Name and address of developer, detailed plans of subdivision, construction financing details, name and addresses of salesmen, details of financing offered to purchaser, details of public services provided in subdivision, complaints against subdivision, and enforcement action taken. State real estate division.

Zone Change Petition.   Name and address of petitioner, details of request for change, local planning department review report, and effect of zone change. County planning commission or city planning commission.

Property Ownership

Assessment Record.   Legal description of property, value of land, value of improvements, true property value, assessed property value, name and address of owner of record, and property tax. County assessor's office, county courthouse.

Board of Equity Appeal File.   Name and address of property owner, legal description of property, petition for change in assessed value, evidence, and board action. County assessor's office, county courthouse.

Mortgage Contract.   Name of mortgagor, name of mortgagee, date entered, amount, legal description of property, promissory note description, and date of last payment. County clerk's office, county courthouse.

Mortgage Satisfaction.   Name of mortgagor, name of mortgagee, date contract entered, and date mortgage certified as satisfied. County recorder's office, county courthouse.

Property Address Index.   Street address, legal description, and account number of property owner. County clerk's office, county courthouse.

Property Owner Index.   Name of property owner, mailing address, account number of property owned, and legal description of property owned. County clerk's office, county courthouse.

Quitclaim Deed.   Name and address of deed grantor, name and address of grantee, legal description of property given to grantee, amount paid, and date of transaction. County clerk's office, county courthouse.

Real Estate Contract.   Name and address of seller, name and address of purchaser, legal description of property, purchase price, initial payment, amount of monthly payments, and interest rate. County clerk's office, county courthouse.

Reconveyance Deed.   Name and address of grantor, name and address of grantee, date of original trust deed, and legal description of property to be reconveyed by trust deed beneficiary. County clerk's office, county courthouse.

Tax Payment Record.   Name and address of taxpayer, amount and date taxes paid, and legal description of property producing taxes. County assessor's office, county courthouse.

Trust Deed.   Name and address of grantor, name and address of beneficiary, date of contract, legal description of property placed in trust, debt amount secured by deed, and date debt matures. County clerk's office, county courthouse.

Uniform Commercial Code Financing Statement.   Name and address of debtor, name and address of financing institution, description of property offered as collateral, and date of agreement. County clerk's office, county courthouse; state secretary of state uniform commercial code section.

Warranty Deed.   Name and address of grantor, name and address of grantee, amount paid for deed, legal description of property, and date of contract. County clerk's office, county courthouse."

Agency Index

This index lists the preceding sources by county, state, and federal agencies.

County agencies

ASSESSOR'S OFFICE

assessment record
board of equity
tax payment record

CLERK'S OFFICE

marriage certificate
mortgage contract
mortgage satisfaction
probate filing
property address index
property owner index
quitclaim deed
real estate contract
reconveyance deed
search warrant
search warrant affidavit
small claims filing
warrant deed

ELECTIONS DIVISION

campaign committee report
candidate filing
contribution report
political action committee report
voter registration

State agencies

ADULT AND FAMILY SERVICES DIVISION

child support payment
welfare recipients

CHILDREN'S SERVICES DIVISION

adoption/child care agency license
day care certificate
foster care license
private school license

CONSUMER PROTECTION DIVISION

consumer protection case file

CORPORATION DIVISION

assumed business name
corporation annual report
corporation dissolution
corporation incorporation file
investment advisor license
limited partnership certificate
limited partnership agent
  registration
nonprofit corporation
saving and loan annual report
savings and loan registration
securities broker-dealer license
securities registration
securities salesman registration

CORRECTIONS DIVISION

prisons records

EDUCATION DEPARTMENT

private school
vocational school

ELECTIONS DIVISION

campaign committee
candidate filing
contribution report
political action committee report
voters pamphlet

ENERGY DEPARTMENT

business tax credit
energy facility citing license
residential tax credit
small-scale energy project loan

ENVIRONMENTAL QUALITY DEPARTMENT

air discharge permit
hazardous waste facility license
solid waste permit
water discharge permit

ETHICS COMMISSION

employer lobbyist registration
ethics complaint file
lobbyist expenditure report
lobbyist registration statement
statement of economic interest

HEALTH DIVISION

birth certificate
death certificate
divorce record
marriage record
industrial health inspection report

Index